England's Conversion And Reformation Compared

Or, The Young Gentleman Directed In The Choice Of His Religion ; To Which Is Premised A Brief Enquiry Into The General Grounds Of The Catholick Faith ; In A Conversation Between A Young Gentleman And His Preceptor ; Divided Into Four Dialogues

Robert Manning

Alpha Editions

This edition published in 2021

ISBN : 9789354445453

Design and Setting By
Alpha Editions
www.alphaedis.com
Email - info@alphaedis.com

As per information held with us this book is in Public Domain.
This book is a reproduction of an important historical work. Alpha Editions uses the best technology to reproduce historical work in the same manner it was first published to preserve its original nature. Any marks or number seen are left intentionally to preserve its true form.

THE PREFACE.

THE following Dialogues are chiefly intended for the Benefit of *young Gentlemen*, as standing most in Need of being strongly fortified with sound Principles, and a deep Sense of Religion against the dangerous Temptations of Wordly *Interest*, *Liberty*, and *Ease*.

In order to this End, the whole Subject of the *first Dialogue* is an Enquiry into those *general Grounds* of reveal'd Religion, which young Persons, already well instructed in the first Rudiments of the Christian Doctrine, ought to be throughly acquainted with. And for this Reason I have endeavoured to bring them into as small a Compass, and render them as easy as the Matter would bear : being sensible, that young Men are no Lovers either of long or hard Lessons ; and learn with Pleasure when neither their Memories are over-charg'd, nor their Understandings put upon the Rack. But the abovesaid Enquiry is intended only as an *Introduction* to my principal Design,

which

The PREFACE.

which is to direct them in the *Choice of their Religion*, and lead them by clear Marks to that *One, Holy, Catholick, and Apostolick Church*, in which the Faith and Religion *reveal'd by God*, has been inviolably preserved throughout all Ages, and will continue to be taught in its full Purity to the World's End.

Now since no Man can either make a *rational* Choice of his Religion, or continue *rationally* in that, wherein he has been educated, unless he has solid Motives to determine him to it, (which is effectually *Choosing* his Religion, as being a deliberate Preference of one before another) I could not think of a more proper Method to direct my *young Gentleman* (who is supposed to have been brought up in the Principles of the Church of *Rome*) in this important Choice, so as to make it wholly the Result of a full Conviction of Judgment, than by *Comparing* the *Roman Catholick Religion*, which was brought into *England* by its *Conversion* from *Paganism* to *Christianity*, with the Religion now *established by Law*, which was introduced nine hundred Years after by the so much celebrated *English Reformation*. For by Comparing the one with the other, a Judgment may be form'd even by Persons of no Learning, which of the two has the *clearest Marks* of Truth on its Side, and of having had the *holy Ghost* for its principal Director. And tho' for the sake of Brevity, as well as of Perspicuity, my Comparison will, for the most Part, go no farther, than the *Roman Catholick Religion* on the one Side, and that of the *reform'd Church* of *England* on the other, it will nevertheless be equally applicable to all the other *reform'd Churches*, and they will all have their Share either in the Advantage or Disadvantage

of

of the Iſſue of this Cauſe, to what Side ſoever the Balance ſhall appear to incline.

The whole Subject therefore of the *fourth* and *laſt Dialogue*, is an *hiſtorical Compariſon* between the moſt material Circumſtances of *England*'s *Converſion* on the one Hand, and of its *Reformation* on the other. But ſince this Compariſon cannot appear in its true Light without a competent Knowledge of the Hiſtory of theſe two great *Eccleſiaſtical Revolutions*, I preſent my young Readers in the *ſecond* and *third Dialogues* with a brief but faithful Account of the moſt important Facts relating to the one as well as to the other; I mean, the *Converſion* of the *Engliſh Saxons* by the Preaching of S. *Auguſtine* and his Followers, and the ſtupendious Changes made by our *Engliſh Reformers* in the Religion brought into this Iſland by thoſe *Apoſtolical Preachers*. To which I have nevertheleſs premiſed a Relation of the *Converſion* of the *ancient Britons* four hundred Years before that of the *Saxons*; by reaſon of the frequent Mention I ſhall make of it, and the Connection it has with a material Point diſcuſſed in the 8*th Section* of the 2*d Dialogue*.

But being ſenſible, that in Compiling my ſhort Hiſtory of the *Engliſh Reformation* I was travelling in an Enemy's Country, I found myſelf obliged to take my Steps very warily, and not truſt to any but *Proteſtant Guides* to conduct me forward in my Way. Becauſe all others, tho' never ſo unexceptionable in themſelves, might be ſuſpected at leaſt of ſome Degree of Partiality, or Prepoſſeſſion in Favour of their own Cauſe.

When with this Caution I had almoſt gone through the three reforming Reigns of *Henry* VIII. *Edward* VI. and Q. *Elizabeth*, the Biſhop of *Meaux*'s *Hiſtoire des Variations*, &c. was put into my Hands, and recommended to my Perusal. It is divided into 15 Books, the 7th whereof treats wholly of the Changes in Religion in *England* under *Henry* VIII. and his Successor *Edward* VI. Those made by Q. *Elizabeth* are briefly related in his 13th Book.

I confess it was no small Satisfaction to me to find the short Account I have given of those Changes, and even my Reflections upon them, agree in every Thing that is material with that celebrated Author. But what compleated my Satisfaction, was the Declaration he makes at his Entrance upon that Subject, that *Burnet*'s own History of the *Reformation* has furnish'd him with all his choicest Materials for that Part of his Work; and that every Fact of Moment related in it, whatever Advantage may be drawn from it in Favour of the *Catholick Cause*, has that *zealous Protestant* Author for its Voucher; who, I dare say, was never guilty of a Lie in Favour of *Popery*. Whence I draw this Consequence, that my Relation of those Facts, besides it being corroborated by other *Protestant* Witnesses, has likewise a just Title to the Benefit of the Bishop of *Sarum*'s Protection, and will undoubtedly be skreen'd from all Suspicion of Falsehood by the Authority of his unexceptionable Testimony. I call it *unexceptionable*, in Reference to Facts, which bear hard upon the Honour both of the *Reformation* in general, and in particular of his great *reforming Hero*, Archbishop *Cranmer*. Unless the Reputation of his Veracity be sunk so low, that he cannot safely be believed even against himself. Which I think is too severe a Reflection upon his Memory.

I shall therefore endeavour to prevent the Prepossession, which some may be apt to have against the Truth of the Facts I shall relate, by a faithful

ful Tranflation of the abovefaid Part of the Bifhop of *Meaux*'s Hiftory, all taken, as I have faid, from *Burnet*'s own Hiftory of the *Reformation*. I intend however, for Brevity's Sake, to omit every Thing, that has not an immediate Tendency to my principal Defign. The Places, where any Thing is omitted, will be mark'd after the ufual Manner with fhort Lines. I fhall alfo fpare myfelf the Trouble of quoting the Number of the Pages fet down every where in the Margin of the Bifhop of *Meaux*'s Book. Becaufe there muft of Neceffity be a great Difference between the Number of the Pages in the *Englifh Original* of *Burnet*'s Hiftory, and the *French Tranflation* of it, which the Bifhop of *Meaux* has follow'd. In Effect, all that can be required of me, is an exact Fidelity in Delivering the true Senfe of my Author; which if any one be difpofed to doubt of, he has it in his Power to fatisfy himfelf with little or no Trouble.

The Bifhop of *Meaux* introduces his Account of the *Englifh Reformation* with obferving, that *Monfieur Burnet*, as he always ftiles him, has very much overftrained his Matter in Triumphing moft unmercifully over the *Church of Rome*, on the Score of a few groundlefs Stories (as indeed they have always appear'd to me) related by Dr. *Sanders* in his Book *de Schifmate Anglicano*: which however, whether they be true or falfe, are of fuch a trivial Nature, as not to touch in the leaft the *Heart of the Caufe*. But it feems Mr. *Burnet* either wanted fome better Topick to flourifh upon, or was of Opinion, that nothing can be writ unjudicioufly againft the *Church of Rome*, fo it be but exorbitantly fcurrilous and malicious; as will appear from the Piece quoted by the Bifhop of *Meaux*, where *Burnet* fpeaking of that Church, tells his Reader with the Gravity of an Oracle, that *a Religion grounded upon Falsehood, and raised upon Imposture, cannot maintain itself, but by the same Means, which gave Birth to it.* And again, *Sanders*'s *Book,* says he, *may be very serviceable to a Church, which hitherto has raised itself by Falsehoods and manifest Forgeries.*

Now what could have been said more outrageous, tho' it were the avow'd Practice of *Catholick* Writers to cram their Books as full with Lies and Calumnies, as the few Lines, are which I have here presented the Reader with, as a small Specimen of this Author's admirable Talent that Way? But 'tis no great Surprize, that a Person, whose poisonous Pen has blasted the Reputation of so many among the Living as well as the Dead, should have the Confidence to raise his Voice so very loud to cry out *Murder* first: or, as a modern *Protestant* Writer expresses it, *should pick out those very Crimes to charge others with, of which his own Conscience must needs tell him, he is so guilty himself.*

But what makes him so very angry at Dr. *Sanders?* I guess the Reason to be chiefly, because this Author had not the same favourable Opinion as himself of Mrs. *Anne Bolen*'s Virtue, whom he seems to regard as a Kind of Protectress in her Time of the *Protestant Cause*: And as this is with him a Merit, which covers all Defects, he strains hard to justify her Conduct upon all Occasions; but especially before she was raised to the high Dignity of being Queen Consort of *England*; whereas Dr. *Sanders,* who was perhaps too credulous in Believing common Reports, has related some Stories of her, whilst she was Maid of Honour in *France*, which reflect hard upon the Honour of her Sex. Now for my Part, I can neither think her so innocent as *Burnet* will needs make her, nor yet

yet so guilty as she is represented by Dr. *Sanders*. But whether she was a *Vestal,* or the *Hackney of France,* the *Catholick* or *Protestant* Interest is so little concerned in it, that farther than to satisfy an idle Curiosity, I would not give a Groat to be certify'd of the Truth of either. Tho' *Burnet,* that zealous Lover of Truth, is pleased to make as tragical a Business of those few trivial Stories, as if they struck at the very Vitals, or sapp'd the very Foundations of the *Protestant* Cause.

But let us now hear his *Gasconade* upon the Excellency of the *Reformation*; which he sets forth in Opposition to the Religion, he had spoken so vilely of before. *The Reformation,* says he, *is a Work of Light, which stands in no Need of the Help of Shades to heighten its Lustre, and a plain History of it is its best Justification.* These are fine Words indeed; but I fear they will be found to be meer Words without the Testimony of Facts to support them. And in Reality nothing could have been said of it more glorious and magnificent, tho' it had all the same *visible Marks* of the *divine Authority* and *Approbation* stamp'd upon it, as appear'd in the first Conversion of the World to Christianity. This is the Bishop of *Meaux*'s judicious Observation; who therefore readily accepts of his Adversary's Proposal, to put the whole Matter to the Test of a plain historical Narration. And 'tis here he takes Occasion to tell his Reader, that he stands in no Need of a *Sanders* to come to his Aid, but that *Monsf. Burnet* alone will suffice to furnish him with a Series of Facts, upon which a true and impartial Judgment may be form'd of his so much boasted *Work of Light.* I wish he may not be thought by his own Party to have intended it for a Banter. But let us now hear the Bishop of *Meaux*'s short History of it.

" The

The PREFACE.

"The first important Fact I take Notice of (says he) in *Monsieur Burnet*, asserted in his very *Preface*, and frequently confirm'd in the Body of his Book, is, that when *Henry* VIII. began the Reformation, *he seemed to intend no more than to intimidate the Court of* Rome, *and oblige the Pope to give him some Satisfaction. For in his Heart he always believed the most extravagant Opinions of the Church of* Rome. *Such as Transubstantiation, and other Corruptions relating to the Sacrifice of the Mass. So that he died in the Communion rather of the* Roman *than* Protestant *Church.* But whatever Mr. *Burnet* is pleased to say, we are not disposed to accept of the Communion, which he seems to offer us, of that Prince: and since he throws him out of his own, the immediate Consequence of this Fact is, that the first Author of the *English Reformation*, who in Reality laid the Foundation of it by the Hatred he instill'd into his Subjects against the *Pope* and the *Church of Rome*, is a Person equally rejected and anathematized by both Parties.

"But what appears most remarkable in this Prince is, that not content to believe with his Heart, and profess with his Mouth the most extravagant Corruptions of the Church of *Rome*, as Mr. *Burnet* calls them, he even gave them the Force of a *Parliamentary Law*, by Virtue of his new-acquired *spiritual Supremacy*,——— and obliged both *Thomas Cromwell* and Archbishop *Cranmer* (tho' *Lutherans* in their Hearts) as well as others, not only to subscribe to them, but see them put in Practice throughout the whole Kingdom.

"This *Thomas Cromwell* was he, whom King *Henry* in Quality of *Supreme Head of the Church*, constituted his *Vicar* or *Viceregent general*. By

"Virtue

" Virtue whereof, tho' he was but a simple *Laick*,
" and continued so to his Death, he was placed
" at the Head of the whole *prelatick Order* in all
" *Ecclesiastical Affairs*. This Dignity was never
" heard of before, either in the List of Officers
" of the Crown of *England*, or of the *Empire*, or
" of any Christian Kingdom in the World. So
" that *Henry* VIII. was the first who shew'd *Eng-*
" *land*, and the Christian World, a *temporal Lord*
" fitting at the Helm of *Ecclesiastical* Government
" in Quality of the King's *Viceregent general* in
" *Spirituals*.

" *Thomas Cranmer* Archbishop of *Canterbury* was
" *Cromwell*'s intimate Friend, and had the chief
" Management of the Design they were Project-
" ing towards a *Reformation*. This is Mr. *Burnet*'s
" great Hero. For he gives up King *Henry* as a
" Person, whose Viciousness and Cruelty were too
" publick to be conceal'd. But he was sensible,
" that to own the like Immoralities in *Cranmer*,
" whom he regards as the primary Instrument of
" the *Reformation*, would unavoidably give us a
" very bad Opinion of that Work. He is there-
" fore very profuse in his Elogiums of that Pre-
" late: and not content to admire upon all Oc-
" casions his Moderation, his Piety, and Prudence,
" he goes so far, as even to represent him as one
" equal, if not superior to St. *Athanasius*, and S.
" *Cyril*; and of so uncommon a Merit, that he
" sticks not to say, that *perhaps no Prelate of God's*
" *Church ever had so many eminent Qualities, and*
" *fewer Faults.* ——

" But to prevent our being imposed upon by
" these pompous Elogiums, let us examine the Hi-
" story of his Life from Facts related by Mr. *Bur-*
" *net* himself, his eternal Admirer; and consider
" at

"at the same Time the Spirit of the Man, to
"whom the *English Reformation* owes its Being.

"From the Year 1529 *Thomas Cranmer* had put
"himself at the Head of that Party, which fa-
"vour'd the King's Divorce from Q. *Catharine*,
"and his intended Marriage with *Anne Bolen*.
"*An.* 1530. he wrote a Book against the Vali-
"dity of his Marriage with Q. *Catharine:* and
"'tis easy to guess how acceptable this was to a
"Prince, whose predominant Passion it flatter'd.
"From that Time forward he began to be con-
"sider'd at Court as a kind of Favourite, and one
"that stood fair to succeed Cardinal *Wolsey* in
"that Rank. He was at that Time addicted to
"the *Lutheran* Doctrine; and, as Mr. *Burnet* tells
"us, look'd upon *as the most learned of those*, who
"favour'd it secretly in their Hearts. *Anne Bo-*
"*len*, says the same Author, *had likewise received*
"*some Tincture of that Doctrine.* But after that
"he represents her as one perfectly united in Re-
"ligion with those, whom he calls *Reformers*: By
"which Word we must always understand all such,
"as were secret or open Enemies to the *Mass*
"and Doctrine of the *Catholick Church*. He adds,
"that all of this Party were avow'd Abettors of
"the Divorce. 'Twas this that link'd *Cranmer* and
"his Adherents so closely to the King's Mistress.
"This laid the Foundation of his Greatness, and
"gave Birth to the *English Reformation*. The un-
"fortunate *Henry*, who suspected nothing of this
"secret Association, or the End it had in View,
"became himself insensibly a kind of Associate
"with the Enemies of that Faith, which he had
"'till then maintained with so much Honour;
"and by their underhand Contrivances, let him-
"self, without knowing what he did, become
"subser-

" subservient to the Designs they had to effect its
" utter Ruin.

" *Cranmer* was sent to *Rome* upon the Business
" of the Divorce; where he play'd the Hypocrite
" so well, that the Pope made him his *Peniten-*
" *tiary*; which shews that he was then a Priest;
" and tho' a *Lutheran* in his Heart, he made no
" Scruple to accept of that Charge. From *Rome*
" he pass'd into *Germany* to manage there his Ma-
" ster's Interest with his good Protestant Friends:
" and here it was that he married *Osiander*'s
" Sister. ——

" In the mean Time the See of *Canterbury* be-
" came vacant by the Death of Archbishop *War-*
" *ham*. *Cranmer* was nominated to it by the King,
" and accepted it. The Pope, who knew no o-
" ther Error in him than his Opinion concerning
" the Nullity of King *Henry*'s Marriage, which
" was then undecided, sent him his *Bulls*; which
" as soon as he had received, he stuck not to
" contaminate himself with *the foul Character of*
" *the Beast*, as was the usual *Protestant* Language
" in those Times.

" At his Consecration he took the usual *Oath*
" *of Obedience* to the Pope, tho' not without some
" Scruple, as Mr. *Burnet* tells us. But he had a
" pliable Conscience, and salved all by Protest-
" ing, that *he did not intend by that Oath to restrain*
" *himself from any Thing he was bound to by his Duty*
" *to God, the King, and his Country*. Which Pro-
" testation was wholly frivolous. For who of us
" all pretends to bind himself by that Oath to
" any Thing contrary to his Conscience, or the
" Duty he owes to his King and Country?——
" In short, this Oath is either an insignificant
" Form of empty Words, or it obliges the Per-
" son who takes it to own the *Spiritual Supremacy*
" of

"of the Pope. *Cranmer* therefore own'd it in
"Words, tho' he believed nothing of it. Mr.
"*Burnet* grants, that *this Expedient made Use of by*
"*Cranmer was not suitable to his Sincerity*; and to
"soften as well as he can such a criminal Dissi-
"mulation, he adds soon after, that if *Cranmer*
"did not wholly save his Integrity, yet he in-
"tended to act fairly and above board. But what
"then is Deceit or unfair Dealing? Can any
"Thing be more deceitful or unfair, than to
"swear what a Man believes nothing of, and
"come prepared with a Protestation express'd in
"equivocal Terms to elude the plain Meaning
"of an Oath he is going to take?

"But Mr. *Burnet* has been careful not to tell
"us, than *Cranmer*, who was ordain'd with all
"the Ceremonies of the *Roman Pontifical*, besides
"the Oath, which he pretended to elude, made
"several other Declarations, against which he
"did not protest. As, *to receive with Submission*
"*the Traditions of the Fathers, the Constitutions of*
"*the holy Apostolick See*; *to pay Obedience to St. Pe-*
"ter *in the Person of the Pope and his Successors ac-*
"*cording to the Canons, and to live chastly.* Which
"according to the Intention of the Church ex-
"pressly declared, when a Person is ordain'd
"*Subdeacon*, implies a Promise of living single.
"This Mr. *Burnet* has conceal'd from us. Nei-
"ther has he told us that *Cranmer* according to
"Custom, *said Mass* at his Consecration: where-
"as he ought to have likewise protested against
"this Act, and all the *Masses* he said in his own
"*Cathedral* during the Remainder of K. *Henry*'s
"Life: that is, for the Space of thirteen whole
"Years. Mr. *Burnet* has pass'd over in Silence
"all these noble Feats of his Hero. As likewise
"that when he ordain'd *Priests* (as he could not
                                             "avoid

"avoid doing in so many Years) he perform'd
"that Ceremony in the Words prescrib'd by the
"*Roman Pontifical*; in which, as neither in the
"*Mass*, K. *Henry* had not made any Alterations.
"He therefore gave them *the Power of changing*
"*by their holy Benediction the Bread and Wine into*
"*the Body and Blood of Christ, and to offer up the*
"*Sacrifice of the Mass both for the Living and the*
"*Dead*. It would have been of greater Impor-
"tance to protest against all these Things so op-
"posite to *Lutheranism*, than against the Oath of
"Obedience to the Pope. But the Mischief
"was, that King *Henry*, who relish'd well e-
"nough his Protestation against the Pope's *Su-*
"*premacy*, would not have born with it in other
"Things: and therefore *Cranmer* thought it was
"best to dissemble.

"Here therefore we have him all at once a
"*Lutheran*, a married Man, an Archbishop ac-
"cording to the *Roman Pontifical*, bound by an
"Oath of Obedience to the Pope, whose Autho-
"rity he hated in his Heart, and not only say-
"ing Mass himself, but giving to others the Po-
"wer to do it, tho' he believed nothing of it.
"Yet this Man, according to Mr. *Burnet*, was a
"Second *Athanasius*; a second *Cyril*, and one of
"the most accomplish'd Prelates the Church e-
"ver had. What Opinion must we then have
"of those two great Men? Or if S. *Basil*, S.
"*Ambrose*, S. *Augustine*, or many others, if they
"neither had more conspicuous Virtues, nor
"fewer Faults than a Person, who for many
"Years together practised Things, which in his
"Heart he judg'd to be the very Hight of
"Sacrilege and Abomination.—

"As soon as *Cranmer* was promoted to the See
"of *Canterbury*, he began to make an Interest in
"the

"the *Parliament* in Favour of the Divorce. The
"King had been privately marry'd to *Anne*
"*Bolen* in the Year 1532. and she appearing big
"with Child, it could not be conceal'd any lon-
"ger. Here then the Archbishop who was privy
"to it, began to signalize himself, and shew'd
"much Vigour in Flattering the King's Passion.
"He wrote to him with an Archiepiscopal Au-
"thority a serious Letter upon his *incestuous* Mar-
"riage with *Catharine*, which, said he, was a
"Scandal to the whole World, and declared he
"would not tolerate so great a Scandal any lon-
"ger. Here we have a Man of true Courage,
"and a second *John Baptist*. Soon after he call'd
"a Court, and cited the King and Queen before
"him. The Queen nor appearing, he pronoun-
"ced her *contumacious*, and by a definitive Sen-
"tence declared her Marriage void from the
"Beginning.—Five Days after he confirm'd the
"King's private Marriage with *Anne Bolen*; tho'
"he had been married to her some Time before
"the Nullity of his first Marriage was declared.
"But Archbishop *Cranmer* made no Scruple to
"ratify such an irregular Proceeding.

Soon after the Divorce the King was solemnly excommunicated by the Pope, and then made *Supreme Head* of the Church of *England* by the Parliament. The Bishop of *Meaux* touches but pas-singly upon these two latter Facts, and then proceeds to speak of *Henry*'s excessive Cruelty in the ten last Years of his Reign, for which he quotes several Passages in *Burnet*'s History. But the frequent and promiscuous Executions of *Protestants* as well as *Catholicks* under this sanguinary Prince being known to all Mankind, I omit them here to avoid being tedious. After that he speaks of two solemn Visitations; one made by the King's

Vicar

Vicar General Cromwell, the other by Archbishop *Cranmer*; of which he writes thus:

"*Cranmer* likewise made his Archiepiscopal Visitation; but it was by the King's *special Licence*. And then it was that Bishops began to exercise all Acts of *Episcopal Jurisdiction* by Vertue of the *Royal Mandates*. The principal End of that Visitation and other Transactions of those Times was the firm Establishment of the King's *Supremacy*, which Affair our complaisant Archbishop took most seriously to Heart; and the very first Act of Jurisdiction exercised by the Bishop of the *first See* of *England* was, to enslave the Church, together with the *Divine Right* of *Episcopacy*, to the arbitrary Will of a temporal Prince.

"These Visitations were follow'd by the Suppression of Religious Houses, the Revenues whereof were appropriated to the Crown. *Protestant* as well as *Catholick* Countries cry'd out Shame against this Sacrilegious Pillaging of Places consecrated to the Service of God. But the very *Infancy* of the *English Reformation*, besides its other Stains of *Luxury* and *Revenge*, was to be dishonoured over and above by an *Avarice* of the blackest Kind. For this was one of the most early Fruits of King *Henry*'s *Supremacy*; who seems to have made himself *Head of the Church* for no other End than to have a Title to plunder it.

"Soon after this Q. *Catharine* died: illustrious for her Piety, as Mr. *Burnet* owns.—— Her Character was indeed very different from that of *Anne Bolen*: allowing even that this unfortunate Person was innocent of the Crimes laid to her Charge before her Death. Mr. *Burnet* himself does not deny but that her Gaiety ex-

"ceeded

"ceeded sometimes the Bounds of Modesty;
"that she was indiscreet in her Liberties, and ir-
"regular in her Conduct. —— If we go to the
"Bottom of this whole Affair, we must acknow-
"ledge the Hand of God appeared visibly in it.
"She enjoy'd no longer than three Years the
"Grandeur, to which infinite Confusions and
"Troubles had raised her. A new Love became
"the Occasion of her Fall, as it had been of her
"Elevation; and the inconstant *Henry*, who had
"made a Sacrifice of Queen *Catharine* to her, soon
"after sacrificed her also to the Youth and Charms
"of *Jane Seymour*. But with this Difference, that
"*Catharine*, though she lost the King's Affection,
"preserved his Esteem to the last : whereas he
"condemned *Anne Bolen* as an infamous Woman
"to lose her Head on a Scaffold. —

"But see here another visible Mark of the
"Hand of God upon her. *Henry* always a Slave
"to the Love that possess'd him last, caused his
"Marriage with *Anne Bolen* to be declared *null* in
"Favour of *Jane Seymour*, as he had before dis-
"solved his Marriage with Q. *Catharine* in Favour
"of *Anne Bolen*; whose Daughter *Elizabeth* was
"also solemnly bastardized, as *Mary* the Daugh-
"ter of *Catharine* had been before her. So that by
"a just Judgment of God, she fell into the same
"Pit, as she had digg'd for her innocent Rival. But
"*Catharine* maintain'd to her Death the Dignity
"of her Royal Character, the Validity of her
"Marriage, and Legitimacy of her Daughter
"*Mary*; whereas *Anne* through a base Complai-
"sance own'd contrary to the real Truth, that
"when she was marry'd to King *Henry*, she was
"precontracted to the Lord *Percy* then alive : and
"so by acknowledging against her Conscience,
"that her Marriage with K. *Henry* was void, in-
"volved

"volved her Daughter *Elizabeth* in the same
"Disgrace with herself. But, that the Justice of
"God might appear more visibly in the whole
"Course of this memorable Event, *Cranmer*, that
"very *Cranmer*, I say, who had dissolved the Mar-
"riage of Qu. *Catharine*, dissolved likewise that
"of Q. *Anne*, to whom he had the greatest O-
"bligations. Thus God struck with Blindness
"all the chief Authors of the Divorce; *Henry*,
"*Anne*, and the Archbishop himself: not one
"of them escaped. But this shameful Weakness
"of *Cranmer*, and his extreme Ingratitude to *Anne*
"raised the Indignation of all good Men against
"him: and his base Complaisance in Dissolving
"Marriages at the King's Pleasure depriv'd his
"*first Sentence of Divorce* even of that small Weight
"of Authority, which his Archiepiscopal Cha-
"racter had given to it.

"Mr. *Burnet* is under some Confusion to see so
"black a Stain in the Life of his *great Reformer*,
"and endeavours to wipe it off by saying, that
"Q. *Anne* had declared to *Cranmer* her antecedent
"Marriage with the Lord *Percy*, which imply'd
"the Nullity of that with King *Henry*. So that
"he was bound in Conscience to pronounce their
"Marriage void. But who sees not that this is
"a barefaced Imposition upon the Publick? For
"it was very well known in *England*, that her
"Engagements with the Lord *Percy* never went
"beyond the bare Proposal of a Match betwixt
"them: which is so far from making any other
"Marriage void, that it does not even render it
"unlawful. Mr. *Burnet* denies none of these
"Facts, and *Cranmer*, who was privy to all that
"had pass'd, could not be ignorant of them.
"Add to this, that the Lord *Percy* had declared
"upon Oath, in the Presence of *Cranmer* and the
"Arch-

"Archbishop of *York*, that there never had been any *Contract* or even *Promise* of Marriage betwixt him and *Anne Bolen*. And to render this Oath the more solemn, he received the *Sacrament* in the Presence of the Chief of the King's Council, with this Imprecation upon himself, *that he might receive it to his Damnation, if any such Engagement had been betwixt them.*

"Now *Cranmer*, who had been a Witness of this Oath, could not but be sensible that Q. *Anne*'s Declaration to the Contrary was not a *free Act*. For when she made it [*if she made it at all.*] she was under Sentence of Condemnation, and as Mr. *Burnet* observes, not yet recover'd of the Terror, which the Judgment of Death pronounced upon her had seized her with. Add to this, that the Law had condemned her to be burnt, and the Mitigation of the Sentence depended wholly upon the King's Mercy. *Cranmer* therefore could not but reflect, that in these Circumstances she might easily be prevail'd upon to confess whatever was suggested to her, as a Means either to save her Life, or at least to obtain a Mitigation of the Sentence pronounc'd upon her: And this was a proper Conjuncture for an Archbishop to assist with his Advice an oppress'd Person; from whom a Disturbance of Mind on the one Hand, and the Hopes of having some Mercy shewn her on the other, might easily extort a Confession contrary to Truth and Conscience. — But *Cranmer* could not practise Virtues he was a Stranger to. Nay he had not Courage enough to lay before the King the Contradiction there was in the two Sentences pronounced against Q. *Anne*: One of which condemned her to Death as an *Adulteress*, and the other declared she had never

"ver been his *Wife*. *Cranmer* diffembled this
"crying Injuftice; and all he did in Favour of
"that unhappy Princefs, was to write a Letter to
"the King, in which *he wifh'd fhe were innocent*;
"and ends with a Pofticript, in which he ex-
"preffes his Sorrow, that the Crimes fhe was ac-
"cus'd of *were proved againft her, as he had been
"inform'd.* So afraid was he leaft *Henry* fhould
"fufpect, he difapproved of any Thing he did.—

"*Anno* 1539. came forth King *Henry*'s Six fa-
"mous Articles of Religion. In the *firft* whereof
"the Doctrine of *Tranfubftantiation* was eftablifh-
"ed. The *fecond* confirm'd the Lawfulnefs of
"*Lay-Communion in one Kind.* The *third* obliged
"Priefts to live unmarried. The *fourth* com-
"manded the Obfervance of *Religious Vows.* The
"*fifth* was concerning *private Maffes*: and the *fixth*
"fet forth the Neceffity of *Auricular Confeffion.*
"Thefe Articles were publifh'd by the Autho-
"rity of King and Parliament, and obftinate
"Offenders againft them were to fuffer Death,
"and others Imprifonment during the King's
"Pleafure.

"Whilft *Henry* declared himfelf in this terri-
"ble Manner againft Innovations in the ancient
"Faith, the *Vicar general* and the *Archbifhop* faw
"no other Means left to advance their *pretended
"Reformation,* than by inducing the King to mar-
"ry fome Lady, who might both protect their
"Perfons and promote their Defigns. For Queen
"*Jane* died the Year before in Childbed of *Ed-
"ward*; and *Cromwel* reflecting that Women,
"whilft they were Miftreffes of the King's Af-
"fection, had a great Afcendant over him, flat-
"ter'd himfelf, that the Princefs *Anne of Cleves*
"would be a Perfon fit for his Purpofe, and fo
"perfuaded the King to marry her. But it hap-
"pen'

" pen'd unluckily, that about the fame Time he
" fell in Love with the Lady *Catharine Howard*,
" and fo his Marriage with the Princefs *Anne*
" was fcarce accomplifh'd, but he fought to break
" it. *Crownwell* paid dear for the Advice he had
" given, and met with his Ruin, where he hoped
" to have found a Protection. It was obferved,
" that he favour'd underhand the *New-Gofpellers*
" and Enemies of the *Six Articles*, which *Henry*
" maintain'd with much Vigour. He had alfo
" dropp'd fome Words againft the King on that
" Occafion, which were reported to him. For
" which Reafons he was by the King's Orders
" attainted in Parliament, and condemned for
" *Herefy* and *High-Treafon.*———

" *Cromwel* being removed out of the Way, there
" remain'd but one Thing more to content the
" King, which was to get rid of an odious Wife,
" by Annulling his Marriage with *Anne of Cleves.*
" The Pretence indeed was very grofs. For all
" that was alledg'd to prove the Nullity of it
" was, that fhe had been precontracted to the
" Marquis of *Loraine*, whilft they were both
" *Minors*, tho' this Contract had never been
" ratified after they were of Age. 'Twas plain
" that this was infufficient to diffolve a Marriage
" fully compleated. But *Henry* had a *Cranmer*
" ready to do the Job, and fupply all the Defi-
" ciencies of folid Reafons. So he untied this
" Matrimonial Knot with the fame Dexterity, as
" he had done twice before.——Mr. *Burnet*, after
" having ftrain'd hard to palliate the Matter,
" is forced at length to own, that *Cranmer* fu-
" fpecting it was a form'd Defign to ruin him at
" Court, went along with the Current. Such was
" the Courage of this fecond *Athanafius*, fuch the
" Virtue of this fecond *Cyril.*

" As

The PREFACE.

"As soon as this unjuſt Sentence of Divorce had paſs'd the *Convocation*, in which Archbiſhop *Cranmer* preſided, and was approved by the *Parliament*; King *Henry* eſpouſed the Lady *Catharine Howard*, who, like *Anne Bolen*, was zealouſly addicted to the Reformation. But a ſtrange Fatality ſeem'd to attend the Abettors of it. Her ſcandalous Conduct ſoon brought her to the Block, and *Henry*'s Family was continually ſtain'd with Infamy and Blood.

"Soon after the Biſhops drew up a Profeſſion of Faith, which was confirm'd by the Royal Sanction.—— All the Articles controverted between us and the Reform'd Churches, excepting that of the Pope's *Supremacy* were decided in it. Yet *Cranmer* conform'd to his Fellow-Biſhops in ſubſcribing to it. For tho' Mr. *Burnet* obſerves, that ſome of the Articles paſs'd againſt his Advice, yet he join'd with the reſt in giving his Vote for them.—— The Will and Pleaſure of his Maſter was the Supreme Rule of his Faith; and inſtead of the Pope in Conjunction with the Church, the King alone was become *infallible*.——

Here the Biſhop of *Meaux* takes Occaſion to ſpeak of *Cranmer*'s extravagant Doctrine touching *Church-Government*, taken from his own Words in a Writing of his quoted by *Burnet*. Wherein he maintains, that every King as ſuch is to be conſider'd in a double Capacity, equally belonging to him by *divine Right*. To wit, as Head of the Church *in Spirituals*, and as Supreme Governor of the State *in Temporals*. That as he has a great Number of Civil Officers under him for the Government of the State, ſo has he *Biſhops*, *Curates*, *Vicars*, and *Prieſts* to ſerve under him in the Management of *Eccleſiaſtical* Affairs. That he is the

Source

Source and Fountain, whence all *spiritual* as well as *temporal Jurisdiction* flows as from its Head; and that by Consequence all *Bishops* and *Pastors* are but his *Delegates* or *Vicars*, and bound to receive from him their Powers to preach the Word, and administer the Sacraments.

This is *Cranmer*'s monstrous System of *Church-Government* in the abovesaid Writing. 'Tis true, that *Burnet*, who is here ashamed of his *Athanasius*, pretends that he afterwards retracted it by subscribing to a Book writ in Defence of the *Divine Institution* of *Episcopacy:* But the Bishop of *Meaux* observes very justly, that *Cranmer*'s Subscriptions are not to be much depended upon: since, as we have already seen, he was ready to set his Hand to any Thing to serve a present Turn. Besides that, as my Author observes, he confirm'd his Doctrine by his own Practice, and blush'd not, tho' first Bishop and Primate of *England*, to receive a special Licence from *Edward* VI. tho' but a Child, to perform his Archiepiscopal Functions in his own Diocess: He likewise taught in express Terms, as *Burnet* attests, that the Dogmatical Decisions of Councils were of no Force without the King's Approbation.

" Thus the *English Reformation* (says the Bishop
" of *Meaux*) had its Origine from the *Flatteries*
" of this Archbishop, and the Disorders of King
" *Henry*. Mr. *Burnet* takes a great deal of Pains
" to heap Examples upon Examples of *vicious*
" *Princes*, whom God has made Use of to bring
" about great Designs. And who doubts it? But
" to pass over the Instances he produces, wherein
" he mixes Truth with Falshood, and the cer-
" tain with what is uncertain; can he bring a
" single Example to prove, that A. G. intending
" to *reveal* to Men some important Truth un-
" known

The PREFACE. xxv

"known before, has chosen so wicked a Prince
"as *Henry*, and so scandalous a Bishop as *Cran-*
"*mer* to be the immediate Instruments of such a
"Mercy? If the *English Reformation* be a *divine*
"*Work*, nothing is more *divine* in it, than the
"King's *Ecclesiastical Supremacy*: Since it not only
"was the first Cause of a Separation from the
"Church of *Rome*, which, as *Protestants* generally
"maintain, is a necessary Condition, with which
"every good and solid Reformation ought to be-
"gin, but is to this Day the only Point, in which
"they never varied since the Beginning of the
"Schism. Now then it seems forsooth that God
"chose *Henry* as a proper Person to reveal this
"new Article of Faith to; yet at the same Time
"to make him an Example of his severest Judg-
"ments: Not of that Sort, by which he over-
"throws Kingdoms, and brings Monarchs to some
"tragical End; but of that other Sort, by which
"he delivers them up to their own Passions, and
"the Flatteries of those that are about them;
"and permits them to run headlong into all the
"Extravagances of a willful Blindness.

After this the Bishop of *Meaux* takes Occasion to speak of Pope *Julius*'s Dispensation, and enlarge upon the Arguments usually alledg'd to vindicate the Validity of it; which I omit, because they differ nothing in Substance from those, which the Reader will find in the Beginning of the 3d Dialogue. But what he adds concerning the Opinions of foreign Divines relating to that Matter, is curious, and deserves a Place here. It is as follows:

"I must here do this Justice to the *German*
"*Protestants*, that King *Henry* could never prevail
"upon them either to approve his second Mar-
"riage, or to condemn Pope *Julius*'s Dispensation.
"For when this Affair was proposed in a solemn
"Embassy

" Embassy sent to the confederated Protestant
" Princes in *Germany*, *Melancthon* deliver'd his
" Opinion against it. *We have differ'd*, says he,
" *in our Judgment from the* English *Embassadours:*
" *For 'tis our Opinion, that the Law, which prohibits*
" *a Brother to marry a Sister in Law, may be dis-*
" *pensed with, tho' we believe it never was abroga-*
" *ted.* L. 4. Epist. 185. And again more concisely
" thus: *The Embassadours pretend, that the Prohibi-*
" *tion of Marrying a Sister in Law is indispensable:*
" *and We on the Contrary maintain it may be dispensed*
" *with.* ibid. Epist. 183. This agreed exactly
" with what had been decided at *Rome*, and was
" the Ground of Pope *Clement*'s definitive Sen-
" tence against the *Divorce*.

" *Bucer* also was once of this Opinion, and
" grounded it upon the same Reason. Nay Mr.
" *Burnet* acquaints us, that according to this Au-
" thor, who was one of the Reformers of the
" *English* Church, *the Levitical Law could not be a*
" *moral or perpetual Law, because God himself had*
" *dispensed with it.*

" *Zuinglius* and *Calvin* with their Followers fa-
" vour'd King *Henry*; and 'tis probable the Pro-
" spect they had of Establishing their Doctrine
" in this Kingdom render'd them so complaisant.
" But the *Lutherans* gave not into it: Though
" Mr. *Burnet* makes them appear to be inconsistent
" with themselves.

" As to the Opinion of foreign Catholicks,
" Mr. *Burnet* relates, that King *Henry* bribed two
" or three Cardinals. If it were so, it is a Sign
" his Cause was none of the best; since it stood
" in Need of such infamous Means to support it.
" And as to Catholick Doctors, whose nume-
" rous Subscriptions he makes a great Boast of,
" what Wonder is it, that in so corrupt an Age,

" so

" so powerful a Prince, as King *Henry* was, should
" find many who were not proof against his Im-
" portunities and Bribes? Mr. *Burnet* pretends,
" that *Fra-Paolo*'s and Monsieur *de Thou*'s Testi-
" monies are unexceptionable. Let him then hear
" what they say: *Fra-Paolo* tells us, that *Henry*
" having consulted the Catholick Divines in *Italy*,
" *Germany*, and *France*, found some for and others
" against him. That the major Part of the *Pa-*
" *risian* Doctors were for him; and that *it was*
" *the Opinion of many, that they had been prevail'd*
" *upon rather by the King's Money, than by his Rea-*
" *sons*. Monsieur *de Thou* says likewise, that *Hen-*
" *ry* labour'd to draw over to his Side foreign Di-
" vines, particularly those of *Paris*; and that it
" was noised about, that his Money had pre-
" vail'd with these to subscribe to the Divorce.

" I will not here positively determine, whether
" the *Conclusion* of the Faculty of *Paris* produc'd
" by Mr. *Burnet* be a forg'd Piece or not; others
" will do it for me. I will only say there are
" Reasons to suspect it. *First*, because the Stile
" is very different from what that Faculty is wont
" to use. And 2*dly*. because it is, according to
" Mr. *Burnet*, dated *July* 2. *An*. 1530. at the *Ma-*
" *thurins*. Whereas some Years before that, the
" Assemblies of the Faculty were usually held at
" the *Sorbon*.

" In the Notes of that famous Lawyer *Charles*
" *du Molin* Mention is made of a Deliberation of
" the Doctors of *Paris* in Favour of King *Henry*,
" *June* 1. 1530. But he says their Meeting was
" at the *Sorbon*. Besides that he lays very little
" Stress upon the Result of that Deliberation,
" wherein the King had a small Majority of Voices
" for him: *Which no Man*, says he, *ought to be*
" *much surprized at, by Reason of the* English *An-*
" *gels*

"gels of Gold, which were diſtributed about to ſecure
"thoſe Voices. And he declares farther, *that he
"was aſſured of the Truth of this Fact by the Teſtimo-
"nies of the Preſidents* du Freſne *and* Paliot. ———
"He concludes in the whole, that the true and
"genuine Senſe of the *Sorbon,* that is to ſay, that
"which they had not been bribed into with Mo-
"ney, was againſt the Divorce. But over and
"above it is certain, that in the Time of the
"Deliberation, *Francis* I. who was then a Well-
"wiſher to K. *Henry*'s Cauſe, charged Monſieur
"*Liſet,* the *firſt Preſident* of the Parliament of
"*Paris,* to make an Intereſt in the *Sorbon* for
"him; as appears from the Original Letters kept
"to this Day in the King's Library; wherein he
"gives an Account of the Diligence he had uſed.
"——— Now 'tis plain, that ſuch unfair Ways as
"theſe of Conſulting the Opinions of Divines, to
"wit, by *Intrigues, Briberies,* and the Authority
"of two powerful Kings to over-awe their Deli-
"berations, were much more proper to raiſe than
"lay Scruples in K. *Henry*'s Mind. Neither were
"the Methods uſed in other Univerſities leſs un-
"fair. Mr. *Burnet* himſelf ſpeaks of a Letter
"writ by the King's Agent at *Rome*; wherein he
"tells him, that if he had but Money enough,
"he would engage all the Divines in *Italy* to ſub-
"ſcribe to the Divorce. ———

[It ſeems then he had tried the Power of Money, and we may preſume that many of the Divines of *Padua* and *Bolognia* had been convinced of
the Juſtice of King *Henry*'s Cauſe, by this compendious Way of Reaſoning.]

"But Pope *Clement* had proceeded upon more
"ſolid Grounds in his Deciſion of the Point in
"Queſtion. It appear'd evident that the *Levitical*
"Prohibition had not the Force of a natural and
"indiſpenſa-

The PREFACE.

"indispensable Law; since God himself had set
"the Example, that it might be dispensed with.
"Now Pope *Julius*'s Dispensation being grounded
"upon this Reason, had such a probable Foun-
"dation, that the Generality of *German Prote-
"stants* themselves judg'd it to be good and va-
"lid. And tho' there might be a Diversity of O-
"pinions about it, 'twas sufficient that it appear-
"ed not manifestly contrary to the Law of God,
"which all are bound to observe. It was there-
"fore one of those Cases, in which we are to
"have Recourse to the prudential Judgment and
"Discretion of Superiours, whereon they, who
"use no double Dealing, may depend with an
"Entire Repose of Conscience. Besides there was
"the strongest Presumption possible, that had it
"not been for *Henry*'s violent Passion, he never
"would have troubled the Church with the shame-
"ful Proposal of a Divorce, after a Marriage so
"lemnly contracted, and continued for the Space
"of 20 Years, without the least Scruple of Con-
"science on either Side. Here lay the real Stress
"of the Cause. And, whether Pope *Clement* was
"or was not mistaken in his Politicks, or whether
"he did or did not carry them to greater lengths
"than he ought, the Equitableness of his Deci-
"sion in the Bottom will bear Testimony to all
"future Ages, that the Church is incapable of
"Flattering the Passions of Princes, or approv-
"ing their scandalous Proceedings.

After this the Bishop of *Meaux* enlarges upon some controverted Points, which I omit as being foreign to my Purpose. Then he gives the following short Account of King *Henry*'s Death.

"It is reported that this unfortunate Prince,
"some time before his Death, had a Remorse of
"the criminal Excesses, he had committed, and
"sent

" sent for some Bishops to ask their Advice con-
" cerning the proper Means to settle his Con-
" science. I will not aver it as a certain Truth.
" But they who are always for Discovering in
" scandalous Sinners, and above all in Kings, such
" sharp Remorses, as appear'd in *Antiochus*, do
" not consider all the secret Ways of God, nor re-
" flect upon the stupid Insensibility, or false
" Peace, which he suffers his greatest Enemies
" to fall into. But let that be as you will, tho'
" King *Henry* had applied himself to his Bishops
" for Advice, what could be expected from Per-
" sons who had enslaved the Church, and be-
" trayed her Faith? Whatever Shew *Henry* should
" have made in that Occasion of Desiring sincere-
" ly their Advice, he could not restore them to
" the Liberty, his Tyranny had robb'd them of.
" For they would always have dreaded a Relapse
" into one of those Fits of Inconstancy, which that
" Prince was subject to. And in Reality he who
" had refused to hear the Truth from the Mouth
" of the holy Bishop of *Rochester* and Sir *Thomas*
" *More*, both whom he put to Death for speak-
" ing it, deserved not to hear it any more.

" In this Condition he died: and 'tis no Won-
" der, that Things grew still worse after his
" Death. For no Part of a Building can stand
" long, when its Foundations are spoil'd. *Ed-*
" *ward* VI. King *Henry*'s only Son succeeded him
" according to Law: and being not quite ten
" Years old, the Kingdom according to his Fa-
" ther's Settlement was to have been govern'd
" by the Lords of the Council. But *Edward*
" *Seymour*, the King's Uncle by the Mother's
" Side, assumed the chief Authority with the
" Title of *Lord Protector*. This Person was a
" *Zuinglian* in his Heart, and *Cranmer* his Confi-
" dent,

"dent: who then diffembled his Religion no
"longer, but openly gave Vent to all the Poifon,
"which 'till then had lain conceal'd in his Heart,
"againft the *Catholick Church*.

"To prepare the Way for their intended Re-
"formation in the King's Name, he was imme-
"diately declared, as his Father had been before
"him, *Supreme Head* in *Spirituals* as well as in
"*Temporals* of the Church of *England*. For from
"the Time that *Henry* took upon him the *Spiri-
"tual Supremacy*, it became a Maxim, *that the King
"was Pope in* England. But greater Preroga-
"tives were beftow'd upon this *new Pope*, than
"the Popes of *Rome* had ever claim'd. For the
"Bifhops were obliged to receive *new Commiffions*
"from K. *Edward* revocable at Pleafure, as *Hen-
"ry* had before declar'd: and it was thought ne-
"ceffary for the Advancement of the Reformation
"*to fubject the Prelatick Order to the Yoke of an ar-
"bitrary Power*. The Archbifhop of *Canterbury*
"and Primate of *England* led the Way, and was
"the firft that bent his Neck under this fhame-
"Yoke: tho' fome fmall Mitigation was conde-
"fcended to not long after, and the Bifhops were
"bound to take it as a Favour, *that the King
"vouchfafed to beftow Bifhopricks for Life*. But Care
"was taken, as in *Henry*'s Reign, to fpecify ve-
"ry plainly in the Tenor of their Commiffions,
"according to *Cranmer*'s Syftem, that all *Epifcopal*
"as well as fecular Power in the Realm flow'd
"from the King as from its *Source*; that the Exer-
"cife of their *Epifcopal Jurifdiction* was *precarious*,
"and *revocable at the King's Pleafure*, by whom it
"was communicated to them. In a Word, it
"was the King *that gave them their Faculties to
"ordain and depofe Priefts; to ufe the Power of the
"Keys againft fcandalous Perfons, and to perform all
"the

" the Duties of their Pastoral Charge.———Commis-
" sions for the Consecrating of Bishops were also
" issued out by the King, and directed to whom
" he pleased. So that according to this new-
" model'd Hierarchy, as Bishops were not con-
" secrated but by the King's Authority, so they
" could not ordain, but as commission'd and de-
" legated by him. Nay the very Form of Con-
" secrating Bishops or Priests was regulated by the
" Parliament. Which also took upon itself to pre-
" scribe the Form of *publick Prayers*, and the Manner
" of *Administring* the *Sacraments*.—All which En-
" croachments upon the *Hierarchy* were grounded
" upon the new Article of Faith the *Parliament*
" had coin'd, to wit, that all *Jurisdiction, Ecclesi-*
" *astical as well as Secular flow'd from the Royal Au-*
" *thority as from its Source and Fountain.*

" 'Tis to no Purpose here to lament the mi-
" serable State of the Church of *England* brought
" under Servitude, and shamefully degraded by
" her own Ministers. An impartial View of the
" Facts suffices alone to shew the Enormity of
" their Proceedings. But not long after the King
" declared, *he intended a general Visitation, and for-*
" *bad all the Bishops to exercise any Ecclesiastical Ju-*
" *risdiction as long as that Visitation should last.* There
" was also an Injunction put forth by the King,
" whereby he commanded himself to be pray'd
" for in publick Service *as Supreme Head of the*
" *Church of* England : *and the Transgressors against*
" *it were liable to the Penalties of Suspension, Depo-*
" *sition, and Excommunication.* Thus the whole pa-
" storal Authority together with the Power of the
" *Keys* was openly invaded by the King ; and the
" most sacred Trust of the *Sanctuary* wrested out
" of the Hands of the *Priestly Order.*

" I shall

"I shall here stop a Moment to take a View
"of the whole Ground-work of the *English* Re-
"formation; that *Work of Light, the plain History
"whereof is its best Justification*, according to Mr.
"*Burnet*. And indeed no Nation glories more
"than *England* in its having been reform'd, as it
"pretends, by the most legal Assemblies, and
"with the utmost Order and Regard to the *Ca-
"nons*. But to give some Colour to this Boast,
"it ought to be supported by this Principle, that
"the *Clergy* had at least the principal Part in the
"Management of this *Ecclesiastical Revolution*:
"Whereas on the Contrary from the Time of
"*Henry*'s Assuming the *Supremacy*, the Clergy
"had no Authority to intermeddle in Matters of
"Religion, unless they had his Orders for it.
"And the only Remonstrance they made against
"this Hardship put upon them was, *that it was
"an Encroachment upon their Privilege*. As if med-
"ling with Matters of Religion were but a *bare
"Privilege*, and not an *Essential Prerogative* of the
"*Ecclesiastical Order*.

"But was their Condition any Thing better un-
"der K. *Edward*? When, as Mr. *Burnet* pretends,
"the Reformation was establish'd upon a more so-
"lid Bottom. Nothing less. For the *Convocation* of
"the Clergy only begg'd of the *Parliament*, that
"no Statute might pass concerning Religion with-
"out their Advice.—But it could not be obtain'd.
"— Soon after the King's *Privy Council* resolv'd
"to send *Visitors* into all Parts of the Kingdom,
"furnish'd with *Ecclesiastical Constitutions* and *Ar-
"ticles of Faith*, —— and they were not ashamed
"to require of the Bishops an express Declara-
"tion, that they would teach such Doctrines, as
"should f om Time to Time be establish'd and
"explain'd by the *King* and *Clergy*. But 'tis manifest,

"nifest the *Clergy* was only mention'd for Form-
"sake, and every Thing was done by the King's
"Authority. —— They went still farther. For
"there came forth a Mandate forbidding all
"Preaching without Licence either from the
"King, or his Visitors, or the Archbishop, or the
"Diocesan. —— But the Year following the Bi-
"shops had their Powers of Giving Licences to
"preach revok'd, and it was limited to the King
"and Archbishop only. —— At last they car-
"ry'd Things so far, that having given the Peo-
"ple to understand, that the King had set Per-
"sons at Work to take away all Subjects of Con-
"troversy, *a general Prohibition was publish'd of*
"*Preaching in the Interim in any Assemblies whatso-*
"*ever*. Here then we see all Preaching suspend-
"ed throughout the Kingdom; the Bishops si-
"lenced by the King's Orders, and the whole
"Nation left in Suspence, not knowing what
"Faith would come forth with the *Royal Stamp*
"upon it. An Admonition was tack'd to it ex-
"horting all Persons *to receive with Submission the*
"*Orders, that should in a short Time be sent down to*
"*them*. Thus was the *English Reformation* esta-
"blished: *that Work of Light, the plain History*
"*whereof*, says Mr. *Burnet, is its best Justification*.

"These Preparations being made, the *English*
"Reformation was set on Foot by the Duke of
"*Sommerset* and *Cranmer* in the King's Name, and
"began with pulling down by the *Regal Authori-*
"*ty* of the *Son*, what the *Regal Authority* of the
"*Father* had set up before. For the *six famous*
"*Articles* which *Henry* VIII. had established with
"the whole Authority both of his *spiritual* and
"*temporal Supremacy*, were forthwith abolish'd; and
"in spite of all the Precautions he had taken even
"in his last Will to preserve those precious Re-
"mains

The PREFACE.

" mains of the *Catholick Faith*, and perhaps with a
" Defign to have it re-eftablifhed in due Time,
" the *Zuinglian* Doctrine fo much detefted by that
" Prince got the upper Hand.

After this, the Bifhop of *Meaux* fpeaks of the Coming over of *Peter Martyr* and *Martin Bucer*, two Apoftate Monks, to affift in the Work of the Reformation. He alfo fpeaks of the Difputes that were betwixt them concerning the *Prefence* of *Chrift's Body and Blood* in the *Sacrament*: of the Changes made in the *Liturgy*; of what ancient *Ceremonies* and *Cuftoms* were kept, and what rejected: and many other Things, which I omit, as having no Relation to my principal Defign. But the Reader muft not forget, that all the above-mention'd Facts, how aftonifhing foever, are taken from *Burnet*'s own *Hiftory of the Reformation*; who notwithftanding glories in the rapid Succefs it met with, as a kind of *Miracle* But let us hear the Bifhop of *Meaux*'s Anfwer to this Boaft.

" Mr. *Burnet*, fays he, has the Boldnefs to re-
" gard the fudden Progrefs of the *Reformation* as
" a *vifible Miracle*, and Teftimony of the *Divine*
" Affiftance. But with what Face can a Man
" talk fo, who has himfelf difcover'd the true
" Reafons of that unhappy Succefs? In the firft
" Place a Prince blinded with an inordinate Paf-
" fion, and condemn'd by the Pope, fets Perfons
" at Work to exaggerate certain particular Facts,
" fome odious Exactions, and Abufes condemn'd
" by the Church herfelf. The Minifters of the
" Altar, by Reafon of the Ignorance of fome and
" Scandals of others, are every where declaim'd
" againft from the Pulpits, and reprefented un-
" der the moft contemptible Characters even up-
" on the Stage: Of the Indignity whereof Mr.
" *Burnet* himfelf is fenfible. And under the Au-
" thority

" thority of an *Infant-King* and a *Protector* poi-
" fon'd with *Zuinglianism* thefe Satyrs and In-
" vectives were carried to a greater Hight;
" and the ignorant Populace being thus work'd
" up into a Hatred and Contempt of their Spi-
" ritual Guides, fwallow'd down greedily any
" new Doctrines."

[To fay nothing of the Violence that was ufed to drag both *Clergy* and *Laity* to a Compliance againft their Confcience, the *grand Secret* to which the fpeedy Progrefs of the Reformation was chiefly Owing, confifted in making every Thing fmooth and eafy both as to *Faith* and *Practice*. Of which my Author fpeaks thus.]

" In the Myftery of the *H. Eucharift* the Senfes
" were flatter'd and deliver'd from their Subjection
" to *the Obedience of Faith*. Priefts were difcharg'd
" from their *Celibacy*, Monks from their *folemn*
" *Vows*, and all in General from the Yoke of *Con-*
" *feffion*. Which tho' a wholefome Prefervative
" againft Vice, is a Burden to Nature. A more
" commodious Morality was therefore preach'd
" up, which as Mr. *Burnet* fays, *mark'd out a plain*
" *and eafy Way to Heaven*. Now fuch good-na-
" tured Injunctions could not but meet with an
" eafy Compliance. So that of 16000 *Ecclefi-*
" *afticks*, 12000, if Mr. *Burnet* may be believed,
" renounced their *Celibacy* in the fhort Reign of
" *Edward* VI and all thefe rotten Members of
" the Church of *Rome* became *good Proteftants*, by
" becoming unfaithful to their Vows.

" 'Twas thus the *Clergy* was gain'd. As to
" the *Laity*, the Revenues and Riches of the
" Church laid open to Rapine was become their
" Bait. The Plate belonging to Churches fill'd
" the King's Coffers. The Shrine of St. *Thomas*
" *of Canterbury* with the ineftimable Prefents,

" that

The PREFACE.

" that had been made to it from all Parts, pro-
" duced immense Sums for the Royal Exche-
" quer; and this was enough to attaint that
" *holy Martyr*: He was condemn'd to be pillaged,
" and the Riches of his Tomb was his greatest
" Crime. In a Word, they judg'd it more Expe-
" dient to plunder the Church's Patrimony, than
" apply it to the Use intended by the Founders.
" And is it then a Wonder, that both the *Gran-*
" *dees*, the *Clergy* and *People* were so easily gain'd
" over to the Reformation? Is it not rather a vi-
" sible Miracle, that there remain'd a Sparkle in
" *Israel*, and that other Countries did not follow
" the Example of *England*, *Denmark*, *Sweden* and
" *Germany*, which were all reform'd by the same
" Methods?

" But amidst all these Reformations there was
" one which made no Progress, to wit, the *Re-*
" *formation of Manners*. I have already taken
" Notice of the Decay of Piety, which follow'd
" *Luther*'s Reformation in *Germany*. And, we
" need but read Mr. *Burnet*'s History to be con-
" vinced that the *English Reformation* produced
" the very same Effects. *Henry* the 8th was the
" first, who undertook that Work. And we have
" seen the Extravagances he fell into, as soon as
" he commenc'd *Reformer*. The ambitious Duke
" of *Sommerset*, who push'd on the Reformation,
" which *Henry* had begun, tho' he was but a
" Subject, put himself upon the Level with So-
" veraigns, and took the Title of *Duke of Som-*
" *merset by the Grace of God*. This Person a-
" midst the general Confusion *England* was in
" about Matters of Religion, and the City of
" *London* over and above with a raging Plague,
" had his Thoughts chiefly intent upon Building
" a magnificent *Palace* for himself. And what
" added

" added to it the Aggravation of *Sacrilege* was,
' that he raised this vast Structure upon the Ru-
" ins, and with the Materials of *three Episcopal*
" *Palaces* and a *Parish-Church*, and the Revenues
" extorted from several Bishops and Chapters;
" none daring to oppose his Will. 'Tis true, he
" begg'd them of the King: But his Abusing in
" this Manner the Authority of a *Minor*, and
" Accustoming his Pupil to such sacrilegious Do-
" nations, are Circumstances which aggravated
" his Crime still more.

" I pass over his other Misdeeds, for which he
" was condemn'd by the Parliament, first, to be
" depriv'd of the Authority he had usurp'd over
" the Council, and then to lose his Head. Neither
" will I examine the Reasons he had to condemn
" the *Admiral* his Brother to the Block. But
" was it not shameful to subject a Person of that
" Rank, and his own Brother, to the unjust Law
" of being condemned upon the bare Allegations
" of Witnesses without being allow'd to make a-
" ny Defence? Yet by Virtue of this Law the
" *Admiral* besides many more were attainted
" without being heard, and the *Protector* pre-
" vailed upon the King to send down his Orders
" to the *Commons* to proceed against him with-
" out suffering him to speak for himself. And
" thus it was he train'd up his Pupil to Justice.

" Mr. *Burnet* takes here a great deal of Pains
" to excuse his *Cranmer* for signing the Death of
" this unhappy Person, and meddling in a *Cause*
" *of Blood* contrary to the *Canons*.——But he
" declines coming to the main Point: For if
" *Cranmer* was to be excused, it ought not to
" have been barely for a Violation of the *Canons*,
" which indeed as Archbishop he was bound a-
" bove all others to have had a tender Regard

" for

" for, but for having violated the *Law of Nature*
" facred even amongst *Pagans*, of not condemn-
" ing a Person without hearing his Defence. But
" *Cranmer* in spite of this Law condemned the
" *Admiral*, and signed the *Dead Warrant* for his
" Execution. Ought not so eminent a *Reformer*
" as he was, to have stood up against such a bar-
" barous Practice? O no; it was more suitable
" to his Character to pull down Altars, beat
" down Images, not sparing those of *Jesus Christ*
" himself, and abolish the *Sacrifice* of the *Mass*
" which had been offer'd up by so many Saints,
" from the Time that *Christianity* had been esta-
" blish'd amongst the *English*.

" To make an End of *Cranmer*'s Character, at
" the Death of King *Edward* he set his Hand to
" his last Will, in which this young Prince out
" of Hatred to his Sister *Mary*, who was a *Ro-
" man Catholick*, changed the Order of Succession.
" Mr. *Burnet* will have it, that the Archbishop
" set his Hand to it with great Reluctance, and
" thinks it a sufficient Excuse for this *great Re-
" former*, that he committed Crimes with some
" Scruple. However, the Council, of which he
" was Head, gave all Orders necessary to arm
" the People against Queen *Mary*, and maintain
" the Title of the Lady *Jane Gray*. Preachers
" were employ'd for the same Purpose, and *Rid-
" ley* Bishop of *London* had Orders to beat the
" *Drum Ecclesiastick* in Favour of her. But when
" her Affairs were become desperate, *Cranmer*
" with the rest of his Associates acknowledg'd
" his Crime, and threw himself upon the Queen's
" Mercy. ——

After this the Bishop of *Meaux* touches pas-
singly upon Queen *Mary*'s Reign, *Cranmer*'s Imprisonment and Condemnation, his double Abjuration

juration of *Lutheranism*, whilst in Prison, and his Retractation of it at the Stake, &c. and concludes with a Parallel between him and S. *Thomas of Canterbury*.

"It is not to be wonder'd, says he, that during the Life of an Archbishop of *Cranmer*'s Character, there was no Regard for the Doctrine of his holy Predecessors, S. *Dunstan*, St. *Lanfrank*, S. *Anselm* and such others, whose admirable Virtues, and particularly that of Continency, were an Honour to the Church. Neither do I wonder that in his Time, S. *Thomas of Canterbury*'s Name, whose Life was a Condemnation of *Thomas Cranmer*, was struck out of the Calendar of Saints. S. *Thomas of Canterbury* opposed the unjust Attempts of Kings; but *Thomas Cranmer* prostituted his Conscience, and was a Slave to their Passions. The one under Banishment, the Confiscation of his Goods, and the most cruel Persecution of his Friends as well as of himself, purchased the glorious Liberty of speaking the Truth with a generous Contempt of all the Conveniences of Life, and of Life itself. The other to please his Prince, spent above thirteen Years of his Life under a shameful Dissimulation, and continual outward Conformity to a Religion, which he condemned in his Heart. The one maintained with his Blood the very smallest Rights and Immunities of the Church, and defended the very Outworks of the Holy City, by not only standing up for those Prerogatives, which had cost the sacred Blood of *Jesus Christ*, but those also which the pious Liberality of Princes had bestow'd upon her. But the other gave up every Thing belonging to her: her most sacred Trust, her Doctrine, her Worship, her Sacraments,

"ments, her Power of the Keys, her Discipline, her Faith. All was brought under the Yoke, and the whole Hierarchy enslaved to the Crown.

"Lastly, the one having been a Man of Courage and exemplary Piety in the whole Course of his Life, was still more remarkably so in his last Moments: whereas the other always pusillanimous and fearful, never betray'd more Weakness than at the Approaches of Death; and at the Age of Threescore and Two sacrificed his Religion and Conscience to the miserable Remnants of a short Life. In Effect, he has left an odious Name behind him, and his own Party cannot cover the Stains of his Life, but with artificial and studied Glosses, to which plain Facts give the Lie. But the Memory of S. *Thomas* of *Canterbury* will be venerable in all Ages, and his Virtues, which *England* and *France* have honoured with a kind of Emulation, will never be forgot. Nay the more doubtful the Cause of that holy Martyr appear'd to the politick World, the more the divine Power declared itself in Favour of him by the remarkable Chastisements of *Henry* the 2d. his Persecutor; the exemplary Penance that Prince perform'd to appease God's Wrath, and such illustrious Miracles wrought at his Tomb, as drew to it the Kings of *France* as well as *England*. Miracles, I say, so frequent, and so unanimously attested by Historians of those Times, that to question the Truth of them is to turn all History into Scepticism.

I omit the rest. For the Pieces I have here translated will suffice to answer the End I propose to myself in this *Preface*, which is to convince the Reader, that the historical Account he will find

find in my *Third Dialogue* is entirely free from Mifrepresentation or Exaggeration: Whether we confider the Facts I have related, or the Reflections I have made upon them; or finally the Characters I have given of the chief Authors of the Changes made in the Religion of our Ancestors during the Reigns of *Henry* VIII. and his Succeffor *Edward* VI.

As to Qu. *Elizabeth*'s Reformation, my Author gives a very fhort Relation of it in his 10th Book. Where after having fet forth the extreme Abfurdity of Conftituting a Woman *Supreme Head* of the Church of *England* in Spirituals, his chief Bufinefs is to fhew the Variations of this laft *Royal Reformer* from her reforming Predeceffor, in the feveral Corrections and Alterations made by her in her Brother *Edward*'s Reformation.

But fince I have been under a Kind of Neceffity of relating feveral ungrateful Truths of, and making fome harfh Reflections upon this Princefs, which will not be well relifh'd by thofe, who have been brought up with the higheft Ideas of her eminent Virtues and religious Zeal, unlefs their Palates be prepar'd and feafon'd againft the Prepoffeffions of their Education; I fhall here for the Sake of thefe (if my Book fhould happen to fall into any of their Hands) tranfcribe her Character, as it is drawn by the impartial and unfufpected Hand of a profefs'd Member of the Church of *England as eftablifhed by Law*. The Perfon I mean is the ingenious Author of the *Short View of the* Englifh *Hiftory*, who writes thus of Queen *Elizabeth*.

" This Princefs reverfed all her Sifter had done
" in Favour of the *Roman Catholick Religion*, which
" fhe abolifh'd and reftored the reform'd.———
" The firft Step was to order, that the Service
" of

The PREFACE.   xliii

" of the Church should be read in the Vulgar
" Tongue. After which she abolish'd the *Supre-*
" *macy*, and assumed that Title to herself. Which
" at first seem'd a Jest to the rest of the World,
" by Reason of the Incapacity of her Sex for the
" ministerial Functions.

Here the Author touches briefly upon the Reasons that moved Queen *Elizabeth* to reject the several Matches proposed to her: and then proceeds to a Relation, how the Troubles of *Scotland* were fomented by her.

" The first Occasion of Drawing her Sword
" were the Troubles of *Scotland*, in which Occa-
" sion the Measures she took did not so much
" redound to her Interest and Advantage, as they
" were destructive to her *Honour* and *Conscience*.
" For how far one Prince may assist the *Rebels*
" of another in Time of actual War, I leave to
" *Civilians* and *Casuists* to decide. But to raise
" and encourage Sedition among the Subjects of
" another Prince, with whom there is outward-
" ly a good Understanding, is certainly a Viola-
" tion of the Laws of Nations, and all that is sa-
" cred between Man and Man. The Tumults in
" *Scotland* about Religion, *so scandalous to the Re-*
" *formation*, gave an Opportunity to Queen *Eli-*
" *zabeth* to foment a Faction against the Queen
" of *Scots*; of whose Title to the Crown of *En-*
" *gland* she was so jealous. For if the Marriage
" between her Father and *Anne Bolen* was not
" lawful, *Mary* of *Scotland* had undoubtedly a
" certain Right, to which she inopportunely laid
" Claim upon her Marriage with *Francis* the 2d.
" by Quartering the Arms of *England:* But tho'
" this imprudent Conduct in the Queen of *Scots*
" might justly irritate and disgust *Elizabeth*, yet
" she had Reason afterward to be satisfy'd, when
" upon

"upon a Treaty betwen them the *Scotish* Queen
"renounced all Claim and Pretence to the Crown
"of *England* during the Life of Queen *Elizabeth*.
"This was a greater Confirmation of her Title
"than if it had never been disputed before; tho' at
"the same Time she refused to ratify the Trea-
"ty of *Edinburgh*, in which there were some
"Clauses relating to the Subjects of *Scotland*,
"in which *Elizabeth* without any just Reason
"would intermeddle.

"The Queen of *Scots* upon this Refusal was
"deny'd Leave to pass through *England* [after
"the Death of her Husband *Francis* the 2d.] to
"her own Kingdom. But what was more un-
"generous than this Denial, a Fleet was sent to
"intercept her in her Passage by Sea. But not-
"withstanding all the Vigilance of the *English*,
"in a great Fog she went by their Fleet undef-
"cry'd, and arriv'd safely in *Scotland*, where we
"cannot choose but pity this poor Princess, who
"was now obliged to live among such lamentable
"Creatures as the *Scottish Fanaticks*, after having
"been bred in the politest Court of the Universe.
"She had not been long at Home, when the Am-
"bition of her Bastard Brother the Earl of *Mur-*
"*ray*, on whom she herself had conferr'd that
"Title, began by his Artifices to lay the Foun-
"dations of all those Evils, which involved this
"poor Princess in great Troubles the rest of her
"Life, and at last terminated in her final De-
"struction. *All which Misfortunes were immediately*
"*owing to the unjust Politicks of Queen* Elizabeth,
"*who always underhand, and sometimes publickly a-*
"*betted the Rebellion of* Mary's *Subjects, even when*
"*she most pretended to be her Friend and to support*
"*her Cause, until she had reduced this unfortunate*
                                            "*Queen*

The PREFACE.

" Queen to a Necessity of Demanding that Protection,
" which she had not the Generosity to give her.

" For the Queen of *Scots*, after a Treatment
" in her own Country, which filled the rest of
" Mankind with Horror, thought she could fly
" no where so properly for Refuge as to her Si-
" ster of *England*, whom *Honour*, *Conscience*, *Good*
" *Nature*, and *Nearness of Blood* obliged to protect
" her. But the unhappy Queen was mistaken;
" she had only now escaped from her own barba-
" rous Subjects to fall into *more cruel and inhospitable*
" *Hands*. The ill Usage of this Princess in both
" Kingdoms must give the rest of the World
" a strange Idea of our Barbarity; it being im-
" possible such Beauty and Majesty in Distress
" could want Protection in any Country, where
" the Men were susceptible of Love, Honour or
" Pity.

" *Mary* was no sooner arrived in *England*, but
" she sent a Letter to *Elizabeth*, in which she gave
" her an Account of her Circumstances, and
" begg'd her Protection, desiring at the same
" Time to be admitted to her Presence, that
" she might have an Opportunity to clear her-
" self from the slanderous Aspersions, with which
" her Enemies had loaded her: Of these the
" chief were *Knox* and *Buchanan*; the first of
" whom was a turbulent Preacher and mutinous
" Enthusiast; the other would have been the
" greatest Writer among the Moderns, if his Sin-
" cerity, the most necessary Quality in an Hi-
" storian, had been equal to his Genius and Ca-
" pacity. But notwithstanding he had so much
" endeavour'd to blacken the Character of his
" Mistress by the most impudent Falsehoods, that
" Disingenuity and Malice could invent, when
" he came to die, which is a Time if ever, one

" may

"may venture to believe even a *Scottish Fanatick*,
"he recanted all that he had said derogatory to
"the Honour of that injured Queen.

"This Request, tho' so reasonable, *Elizabeth*
"thought fit to deny : but the true Reason was
"the Envy we bore to the Beauty of *Mary*, to
"whom she was unwilling to be a Foil by being
"seen at the same Time : The Desire of being
"admired, as it is the most common Passion
"in the Fair Sex, so it was the most deeply
"rooted in *Elizabeth*, which Vanity was sup-
"ported by the Insincerity of her Looking-
"Glasses. But notwithstanding the good Opi-
"nion *Elizabeth* had of herself, the Queen of
"*Scots* was too uncontestable a Rival for such
"a Dispute ; being as much above her in the
"Empire of Beauty, as below her in that of For-
"tune. To these Charms of her Person, and
"the natural Vivacity of her Wit, she had ad-
"ded the Ornament of Letters, and a great
"Knowledge in Books and foreign Languages,
"being Mistress not only of the Living but the
"Dead ; with all other Qualifications not only un-
"common to her Sex, but even admired in Men,
"who make those Accomplishments their only
"Business. These distinguishing Charms were
"none of the least Causes of *Mary*'s Misfortunes
"by making ill Blood in the Heart of *Elizabeth*
"towards her. — By this we may see how liable
"we are to be mistaken, when we judge of
"Causes and Effects by the outward Appear-
"ance of Things : whereas could we dive into
"the secret Recesses of Man's Mind, we should
"find some of our most hidden and ridiculous
"Passions give Birth to the most important E-
"vents, and govern the World.

"The

The PREFACE. xlvii

"The Queen of *Scots* unable to get Admit-
"tance, now plainly saw what she must expect
"at the Hands of a *cunning and jealous Woman,*
"who *had given her civil Invitations, and so many*
"*Promises of Protection, only to draw her within her*
"*Power.* But tho' the World was generally so
"abandon'd at this Time, there were some few
"of the *English* who had Compassion for distres-
"sed Innocence: among the Nobility the chief
"were the Duke of *Norfolk,* one of the most con-
"siderable Subjects of *Europe* at this Time, the
"Earl of *Sussex,* and *Leicester* himself, who', *tho'*
"*one of the worst of Men, pretended at least to be*
"*ashamed of this infamous Conduct.* But the Ge-
"nerosity of the Duke had the more fatal Con-
"sequences on the Life and Fortune of that wor-
"thy Nobleman, who imposed on by the Craft
"and Cunning of *Leicester,* was drawn into a
"Design of Marriage with the Queen of *Scots: Murray*
"himself had first proposed this Match
"to the Duke, with a Design to finish the Ruin
"of the Queen his Mistress with *Elizabeth,* whose
"jealous Nature he knew would entertain the
"greatest Apprehension of such an Alliance. This
"Amour was carry'd on by secret Intrigues, and
"several Love-Letters to Queen *Mary,* all which
"were constantly intercepted, and came to the
"Hands of Queen *Elizabeth.*

"Tho' the Duke might be hurried by his
"Passions of Love and Ambition to pursue this
"Match with some Warmth, however he never
"design'd to accomplish that Affair without the
"Queen's Knowledge, and Leave first obtain'd:
"In order to which he desir'd *Leicester* to procure
"her Consent, which he promised to do, tho'
"he never design'd to serve the Duke; for he
"daily deceived him, by pretending a Want of
"Oppor-

xlviii   *The* PREFACE.

"Opportunity: upon which the Duke of *Nor-*
"*folk* resolved to speak himself, but was pre-
"vented by the fresh Assurances that *Leicester* gave
"him of Performing his Promises immediately.
"But *Leicester*, instead of managing this Affair
"with Sincerity, when he saw a proper Jun-
"cture of ill Circumstances for the Duke, finish'd
"his Ruin. For observing the Queen grown
"daily more jealous of the Duke's designed Mar-
"riage, which was no Secret to her, and at the
"same Time alarm'd with the Noise of a Re-
"bellion in the *North*, he thought this the most
"proper Time to make his villainous Designs
"succeed, when the Queen's Fears thus high-
"ten'd made her the more susceptible of any
"Impressions. To this Purpose the perfidious
"*Leicester* counterfeits himself sick, and pre-
"tends to be in the last Danger. Upon which
"the Queen, who had always a great Affection
"for him, came to make him a Visit; when
"being alone together, *Leicester* after several
"Grimaces and counterfeited Sighs, on Pretence
"of Discharging his Conscience, sets forth the
"dangerous Consequences of this Amour be-
"tween the Duke of *Norfolk* and the Queen of
"*Scots*; not letting *Elizabeth* know that he had
"been commissioned by the Duke to ask her
"Consent, but made as if this Discovery had
"meerly proceeded from a Sense of her Danger,
"and his own Compunction and Penitence.

"This Trick had its design'd Success. *Eliza-*
"*beth* with all the Fear and Jealousy of her Sex,
"swallows the Bait, and sends the Duke to the
"Tower, soon after which he was condemned
"and executed.

"This Example of Perfidy will give the World
"a Character of *Leicester*, who had all the Am-
                                          "bition

"bition and ill Principles of his Father *Northum-*
"*berland:* for he broke the Neck of his Wife
"down Stairs to make Room in his Bed, when
"he should have the Happiness to accomplish
"his Designs on Queen *Elizabeth*; the Hopes of
"which had made him obstruct the Match under-
"hand, which *Elizabeth* had proposed between
"the Queen of *Scots* and himself; who preferr'd
"the happy Grandeur of his own plain Mistress
"to the unfortunate Beauty of the most charm-
"ing Woman then alive. But *Leicester* was not
"alone in this Court, *which had the most wicked*
"*Ministry that ever was known in any Reign.*

"After this Queen *Elizabeth* began to exercise
"great Severity on the *English Roman Catholicks,*
"to which she was instigated by *Leicester, Walsin-*
"*gham,* and others; *who having already tasted the*
"*Sweetness of Confiscations, design'd to make that Par-*
"*ty desperate by ill Usage, in Hopes they would*
"*rebel, and forfeit their Estates.* But when Truth
"enough could not be found against them, *Wal-*
"*singham* by *counterfeit Letters,* and *Confessions ex-*
"*torted by the Pains and Terrors of the Rack,* tumul-
"tuated the People with chimerical Dangers on-
"ly to prepare them for the intended Murder
"of the Queen of *Scotland*; in whose Behalf the
"Remonstrances from the several Courts of *Eu-*
"*rope,* join'd to the Condescensions of this poor
"Princess, who offer'd to sign a *Chart blanche,*
"and ratify whatever should be demanded, were
"all to no Purpose. Nor was there indeed any
"just Ground to hope for her Liberty, after the
"Measures that Q. *Elizabeth* had lately taken by
"which she convinced the World of her ill In-
"tentions to *Mary,* by suppressing the small Rem-
"nant of a Party, who adhered to her in *Scot-*
"*land:* for she assisted *Morton* with Men and
"Cannon

The PREFACE.

"Cannon in the Reduction of *Edinburgh Castle*, "which was defended by some gallant Men, "who in so general a Corruption retain'd a Sense "of their Honour and Duty. These brave Men "compell'd to surrender were sacrificed to the "Revenge of *Morton*, who was made Regent by the "Interest and Power of *Elizabeth*; notwithstand- "ing the whole World knew how great a Hand "that Nobleman had in the Assassination of the "late King: nor was she less concern'd to save his "Life, when by the divine Justice he was after- "wards brought to condign Punishment for that "horrid Murder, which he own'd at his Death: "The forward Appearance of Qu. *Elizabeth* in "Behalf of a Man condemn'd for so flagitious a "Crime, gave her Enemies an Occasion to af- "firm, that she was not unacquainted with the "Design of that Murder: But however she made "herself a Party, and contracted a Share of the "Guilt in supporting the known Assassines to "the very last: But we shall have the less Rea- "son by and by to wonder at any Thing she did "to *Darnley*, when we see what an Outrage will "be committed on the Person of his unfortunate "Widow, whose Catastrophe now approach'd.

"The Emissaries and Creatures of *Walsingham*, "who was the most deeply dipp'd in the Blood "of this Princess, had inveigled several Catho- "licks and others into a Design of Rescuing the "Queen of *Scots* by Force of Arms: For this *Ba- "bington* and others were executed. The People "frighten'd and alarm'd with this Conspiracy, "they thought it a proper Time to bring on the "Tragedy, which they had been so long Prepa- "ring: At first they were at a Loss on what Sta- "tute to indict her: that of the 25th of *Edward* "the IIId. not laying hold of her Case, they re-

"solved

The PREFACE.

" folved to proceed on a Statute made in this
" Reign fome time before for this very Purpofe.
" But the Queen of *Scots* afferting her Soverainty
" and Independance, refufed to acknowledge the
" Authority of any earthly Court, 'till threat-
" ned to be condemned for Contumacy, after
" having in vain requefted to be heard before
" the Queen in Parliament, fhe fubmitted to her
" Trial; at which Time fhe confefs'd, *that thro'*
" *Defpair of her Liberty, fhe had endeavoured to make*
" *her Efcape; in which fhe thought herfelf juftified by*
" *the Laws of Nature and Self-prefervation. But as*
" *to any Defign againft the Perfon or Authority of the*
" *Queen, with the moft folemn Affeverations fhe de-*
" *clared her Innocence.* Neverthelefs the barbarous
" Delegates proceeded to the infamous Sentence,
" and that the whole Nation might fhare the
" Guilt, it was contrived afterward, that the Par-
" liament fhould folicit the Queen of *Scot's* Death,
" which *Elizabeth* was to refufe feveral Times;
" 'till at laft fhe fhould feem to comply, as if
" tired with the repeated Remonftrances of her
" People. The Houfe of Lords particularly di-
" ftinguifh'd themfelves in this Affair, by an
" Addrefs againft the Queen of *Scots*, worded in
" a very *ridiculous Cant*, fetting forth the Judg-
" ments of God on *Saul* for fparing the Life of
" *Agag*, and on *Ahab* for *Benhadad*. Thus were
" the Scriptures perverted to deftroy an innocent
" Woman. This odd Petition, much fitter for
" Tub-Preachers than Cavaliers and Men of Ho-
" nour, muft give us a ftrange Idea of the No-
" bility at this Time.

" Now follow'd the fecond Act of *Hypocrify* in
" Queen *Elizabeth*, through a Shame to juftify
" what fhe had fo little Confcience as to com-
" mand. The Queen of *Scots* muft be executed
" without

The PREFACE.

"without her Knowledge: But the Person must
"be very ignorant of the World, who could be
"imposed on by such a Shift. Every Body, who is
"acquainted with the Government and Constitu-
"tion of *England*, knows that the Privy Council,
"and the Ministers of the Law, durst not proceed
"in an Affair of that Nature, especially in so
"unprecedented a Case, without the Authority
"of the Sovereign Power. But supposing a Pos-
"sibility of that extraordinary Conduct in the
"Privy Council, it is unconceivable that no Body
"in the mean while should acquaint the Queen
"with what was transacted, who had Time e-
"nough to have countermanded the Order for
"the Execution, if she had inclined to Mercy.
"However *Davison* the Secretary (to blind the
"World) was sentenced in the Star-chamber to
"pay ten thousand Pounds Fine, and to suffer
"Imprisonment during the Queen's Pleasure:
"But underhand the Fine was remitted, and he
"privately rewarded; tho' at his Trial he made
"it appear in his own Defence, notwithstanding
"he was as tender as he could be of the Queen's
"Honour, that he had acted nothing in this Af-
"fair, but for what he had plain Insinuations of
"her Pleasure, tho' not positive and direct Com-
"mands. So that the whole Juggle is plain by
"*Davison*'s own Vindication, who was brought
"into the Office meerly to serve this Turn.

"It is reported that *Leicester*, who tho' he had
"no more Conscience than the rest, was a Man
"of better Sense, came to the Queen, and con-
"jured her not to commit *so infamous an Action*,
"which would strike at herself, and affront the
"common Majesty of crown'd Heads. Upon
"which the Queen ask'd him, *what she should do
"in this Case?* Madam, (reply'd *Leicester*) send
"an

The PREFACE.

" *an Apothecary and not a Hangman. If she must die,*
" *let it be done with Decency.* Prudence would cer-
" tainly have rather follow'd this Advice: for
" if she had Authority to put her Death, the
" Manner, as to the conscientious Part, was a
" Thing indifferent. This would have prevented
" the ill Consequences of so dangerous a Prece-
" dent; which as *England* only could give, so
" the horrid Example could be follow'd in no
" other Country beyond the Bounds of that un-
" fortunate Island. For when it was debated
" among the Regicides, what they should do
" with the Person of this Queen's Grandson,
" *Charles* the *First, Harry Martin* proposed to
" serve him, as they had his *Scottish* Grandmo-
" ther before.

" The Manner of this Queen's Death, her
" Resignation to the Will of God, her Greatness
" of Spirit, which seem'd supported by some
" other Power, than the common Assistance of
" natural Courage, have recommended her Name
" to the Veneration of future Ages, and *cover'd*
" *the Authors of this barbarous Cruelty with indelible*
" *Infamy and Reproach.* The Persons, who were
" commission'd to see the Execution perform'd,
" were the Earls of *Shrewsbury, Kent, Derby,* and
" *Cumberland;* one of whom had so divested him-
" self of common Humanity, as to toss up his
" Cap, and huzza at the Cutting off the most
" charming Head that ever wore a Crown. But
" this was not the only Circumstance of Barba-
" rity shewn to this Princess, they carried their
" Cruelty to such a Degree, as to deny her the
" Assistance of her ghostly Father in her last A-
" gony; a Favour not refus'd by christian Chari-
" to the most common Malefactor. But they

" resolved

" resolved to be all of a Piece, and shew no more
" Mercy to her Soul than to her Body.

" Such was the deplorable Fate of *Mary*, So-
" veraign Queen of *Scotland*, and Dowager of
" *France*, in a Country, *whither she was invited by*
" *the most solemn Assurances of Protection, Honour,*
" *and Safety:* all which were violated, first by an
" Imprisonment of 19 Years, and afterwards by
" an infamous Death. This unparallel'd Action
" justly fill'd with Horror and Resentment all
" the other Princes in *Europe*, who had in vain
" solicited her Cause.

Here we have the Character of a *crafty jealous Woman*, *perfidious* in her Nature, *cruel* in her Temper, versed in the Art of *Hypocrisy*, and govern'd by Ministers of the corruptest Morals in the most weighty Concerns both of *Church* and *State*. Good God! What a Character is this of a *capital Reformer*, the *Foundress of a Church*, and one chosen by God to restore Religion to its ancient Purity! But I leave the World now to judge, whether *Burnet* was not under a kind of *Dilirium*, and without Thought or Reflection, when he made this ridiculous Boast; to wit, that *a plain History of the Reformation is its best Justification?* For the obvious and natural Meaning of this is, that all the *most considerable Facts* relating to it, the *Authors* and *Instruments* of it, the *Motives* upon which it was begun and carried on, and the *Methods* by which it was establish'd, were such, as redound manifestly to the Honour and Credit of it, and may suffice to convince an unbiass'd Judgment, that the *Holy Ghost* was the principal *Author, Manager*, and *Director* of it. Whereas on the contrary, the very Facts related by *Burnet* himself, tho' never so artfully disguised and varnish'd over by that un-

faithful

faithful Writer, are in themselves so scandalous, as suffice alone to cast the blackest Stains upon any *religious Cause*. And what is most remarkable, we have not found one Person of Note concern'd in the Promoting of his so much boasted *Work of Light*, whose Character would not at any Time be reckon'd a *Scandal* even to a Cause of far less Moment, than that of *Reforming* the *Faith* and *Discipline* of a whole *national Church*, on which the Salvation or Damnation of Millions of Souls must unavoidably depend. So that I dare boldly assert, that the very Reverse of *Burnet*'s Boast approaches much nearer to Truth; to wit, that *a plain History of the Reformation is its best Confutation*. I flatter myself it will appear so to all such, as shall read my two last Dialogues with an unprejudic'd Mind.

THE FIRST DIALOGUE.

CONTAINING,

The general Grounds of the CATHOLICK FAITH.

SECT. I.

The Obligation of Submitting *our private Judgment do's not exclude* Examination.

GENTLEMAN.  Find Sir, I am like to be a Confiderable Lofer in this World by the Religion, I have been educated in. It behoves me therefore not to fit down content with a Superficial Knowlege of it, but to fearch diligently into the very Bottom of the Caufe: That I may not fall juftly under the Reproach of Suffering like a Fool, for I know not what.

PRECEPTOR. What you fay, Sir, is perfectly confonant to Reafon. Nay, St. *Peter* exhorts all Chriftians, *to be always ready to give an Anfwer to every Man that asketh us an Account of the Hope*

that

Dial. 1. §. 1. *Submitting do's not that is in us.* 1. Pet. 3. v. 15. And can any Man give an *Account of the Hope* (or *Faith*) that is in him, without a due Examination of the *Grounds* or *Motives* that induce him to it? No surely. And therefore, nothing ought to hinder you from examining throughly the Grounds of your Religion. Nay I exhort you to examine them over, and over again, till you have a full Conviction of Conscience, that it is not *Education*, but the prevailing Force of Truth, that determins you in the Choice of it.

G. I own, Sir, I am charm'd to hear you say so. But I have some Difficulty to reconcile this with what you have often repeated to me, to wit, that we are bound *to captivate our Understanding unto the Obedience of Faith*, and pay an *entire Submission* to the Decisions of the *Catholick Church*. Now I cannot well conceive how *Submitting* and *Examining* can be join'd together: Which therefore I desire you to explain to me, that I may be furnish'd with a satisfactory Answer to those, who are continually reproaching us, that *we are kept in the Dark* by our politick Guides, and bid *to shut our Eyes against the Light of Reason*, least it should discover to us the *Follies* and *Errors* of our Religion.

P. This, Sir, is not the only Thing *Protestants* wrong us in. Nor do I wonder at it. For Misrepresentation is the easiest Way of confuting, and has always been found to be of exquisite Use in maintaining a bad Cause. But let that pass, to come directly to the Point we have before us. You say, you cannot well conceive how *submitting* and *examining* can be join'd together. Yet nothing will appear more easy, supposing only some general Principles agreed to without Contradiction by *Protestants* as well as by *Catholicks*.

1.

1. That there is such a Thing as a *reveal'd Religion*, which no Acuteness of Wit, or Strength of human Reason could ever have discover'd; nor can comprehend now it is discover'd to us.

2. That whatever God *reveals*, is most *infallibly true*; tho' it be never so seemingly contrary to human Reason.

3. That there is a wide Difference between a Thing being *above* Reason, and being *against* it.

4. That *Truth has always Reason on it's Side*.

From the two first of these Principles, which are unquestionable, it follows, that *Captivating our Understanding*, or *Submitting* our private Judgment to all such *reveal'd Truths*, as are above our Reason, is an *indispensable Duty*. And from the two latter it follows, that this Submission is perfectly *reasonable*: and if it be reasonable, it must be grounded upon *solid Motives*; and these Motives cannot affect us, or have an Influence upon our Faith, unless they be known and *examined*.

First then as to the Obligation of *Submitting*, it is manifest that amongst the *reveal'd Truths* of Christian Religion there are Mysteries so sublime, as to be above all human Understanding. Such as the *B. Trinity*, the *Incarnation and Death of the Son of God*, the *Propagation of Original Sin*, &c. and in Reference to these and such others, *Reason* can have no other Part to act than that of an *entire Submission*, whenever the *Revelation* of them is declared to us by that Authority, which *Christ* has appointed to be our *Guide*. For surely whoever gives his interiour Assent to any Thing above his Understanding, is properly said to *submit* his Judgment to it: And this is all the Submission we require of the Members of our Church; which if it be not reasonable, meerly because the Mysteries, they

they submit or assent to, are above the Reach of their Understanding, we must even join with *Atheists* and *Deists*, and renounce all *reveal'd Religion*.

G. Sir, all this notwithstanding *Protestants* insult over us, and say our Faith is wholly *implicit*. That according to the Doctrine of our Leaders we never see better than when we shut our Eyes, and act the most reasonably, when we suffer our Reason to be hoodwinked. In a word, that when our *Romish* Guides are put to a *Nonplus*, and have nothing to say for themselves, their last Shift is to have Recourse to the Doctrine of *Submission*; which, as they say, is but in Effect a softer Term for *blind Obedience*, and a meer Cloak to cover any Absurdity, they have a Mind to impose upon the Credulity of the People.

P. It seems then that St. *Paul* was a rank Impostor, when he wrote thus to the *Hebrews*. *Obey them that have the Rule over you, and submit yourselves: For they watch over your Souls, as being to give an Account.* Heb. 13. v. 17. Nay all this Buffoonery will reach the Person of Christ himself, who has declared that *he who will not hear the Church,* (that is, *submit* to her Decisions) *shall be reputed as a Heathen and a Publican.* Math. 18. v. 17. However I should not wonder to hear an *Atheist* or *Deist*, who makes a Mockery of *Revelation*, discourse in this manner: But it sounds very absurdly in the Mouth of a *Protestant*, who makes Profession of Believing a *reveal'd Religion*. For is it not a manifest Contradiction to own that amongst the *reveal'd Truths* of Christianity there are many above the Reach of human Understanding, and by Consequence *above Reason*, tho' not *against it* (for if they were *against Reason*, they could

could not be *Truths*) to own, I fay, all this, and at the fame Time ridicule an humble Submiffion to fuch Truths? Is not this fapping the very Foundations of *Faith*, and Encouraging every Body to fet up the proud Idol of his own *private Judgment* againft the *Revelation of God*, and believe no farther than his poor narrow Capacity can comprehend.

G. What you have faid, Sir, convinces me fully, that whoever believes, that is, gives his interiour Affent to any thing he neither do's nor can comprehend, is properly faid to *submit his Judgment*: Nor do I fee how it can be exprefs'd in Terms more intelligible and fignificant. Since therefore *Proteftants* themfelves profefs the Belief of many incomprehenfible Myfteries, they *Submit* their Judgments juft as we do, and act incoherently in ridiculing in us, what they are obliged to practife themfelves. However tho' I am now convinced that the *Submiffion* you fpeak of is abfolutely neceffary in Reference to all fuch Truths, as are above our Underftanding, I am not yet fatisfied as to the Bufinefs of *Examination*. Nay, the more I am convinced of the Neceffity and Reafonablenefs of *Submitting*, the more I am at a lofs to find any Room left for *Examination*. For to what Purpofe is it to *examine*, when I am convinced it is my Duty to *Submit*.

P. Sir, if it be a *Duty*, it muft be *reafonable*; For we can never act *againft Reafon* in Doing our *Duty*: And if it be *reafonable*, there muft be *folid Grounds* or *Motives* for the Doing of it: That is to fay, fuch *Reafons*, *Grounds*, or *Motives*, as exclude all rational Doubts, and ought to be yielded to by any Man, that pretends to act rationally.

G. That's very certain.

P. Since therefore no Man can be convinced by *Reasons* or *Motives*, unless he knows their Weight, and this cannot be known without a *diligent Examination*, the Consequence is, that every one according to the Measure of his Capacity ought to *examine* them with all the Seriousness and Application, that is possible; To the End that by this diligent Examination he may render himself a competent Judge of the *Reasonableness* of his *Submission*. Whence it follows plainly that *Examination* is so far from being inconsistent with *Submission*, that even the principal End of it is no other, than a full Conviction that our *Submission* is not a rash and inconsiderate Act, but grounded upon *solid Motives*.

Let us exemplify in the Mystery of the *B. Trinity*, which of all the Mysteries of Christian Religion is the most unsearchable, and the most seemingly contrary to human Reason. For who is there that dares presume to fathom the Depth of it, or form to himself any Idea, but what falls infinitely short of it? Here then we must either renounce *Christianity*, or *submit* to the Belief of what is wholly incomprehensible to us: And to render this Act of Submission *reasonable*, what have we else to do but to *examine* the solidity of the Motives upon which it is grounded. Suppose then any one should ask you, why you believe this dark Mystery, since it is wholly incomprehensible to you? What Answer would you give him?

G. My Answer would be, that I believe it because *God has reveal'd it*; and 'tis impossible he should reveal a Falshood.

P. Very right, Sir. For the *Revelation* and *infinite Veracity* of God is the proper and essential Motive of every Act of *Divine Faith*: Because as

human

human Faith relies upon human Authority; fo *divine Faith* has nothing lefs than *divine Authority* to vouch for it. But fuppofe he fhould prefs you farther, and ask how you are affured, *that God has reveal'd it* ?

G. Sir, you have often told me, that we have the *greateſt Authority* upon Earth to affure us of it: To wit, the *Catholick* or *univerfal Church* founded by Chriſt himfelf, and appointed by him to be our *Guide* in all fpiritual Matters.

P. 'Tis very true, I have fo: And I told you nothing but what I was myfelf convinced of by a long and ferious Examination of the full Weight of that Authority; which to Saint *Auſtin* appear'd fo great and fo well eſtabliſh'd, that he made no Difficulty to declare, that nothing but *the moſt infolent Madnefs* could hinder any Man from fubmitting to it's Decifions; and *that he would not believe the Gofpels themfelves, unlefs the Authority of the Church compell'd him to it*. Cont. Epiſt. Fund. C 4. meaning doubtlefs, that he would not believe their having been written by *divine Infpiration* upon any other Authority, than that of the *Catholick Church*.

G. But what then is properly the *Subject* of our *Examination*? I conceive it is not the *Truth* or *Nature* of the Myſteries themfelves, which furpafs all human Underſtanding. For who can examine the Truth of a Thing he cannot underſtand?

P. That's impoſſible. And therefore we do not pretend to Search into the *Nature* of the Myſteries themfelves; becaufe they are infinitely above the Reach of our Underſtanding, and no natural Principles can lead us to any Idea of them. Nor do we examine whether a *reveal'd Myſtery be true*

true or *false*; for if it be *reveal'd*, it is impiety to question the Truth of it; because God's infinite Veracity is as essential to him as his very Being. But the proper Subject of our Examination is, whether we have sufficient Motives to believe, that such or such a Point of Doctrine has been effectually *reveal'd by God*. That is to say, whether the Proofs or Inducements (commonly call'd the *Motives of Credibility*) are of sufficient Weight to convince a rational Man, that the *Church's Authority* declaring the *Revelation* of that Doctrine, may be securely depended upon in the important Concern of our Soul's Salvation? For without this our Belief, that such or such a Point of Doctrine is *reveal'd by God*, would not be a reasonable Act, but rash and inconsiderate: As it is inconsiderate in any Man to believe a Thing without sufficient rational Motives to induce him to it. And will any one after this have the Confidence to reproach us, that we oblige our People to proceed *blindly*, and forbid them to *examine* the *Grounds* of their *Faith*? Nothing surely but a prejudiced Heart can prompt them to imagine any such Thing.

SECT. 2.

Faith *is not against* Reason.

G. PRay Sir, will you do me the Favour to explain yourself by some particular Example.
P. With all my Heart; and I cannot do it better than by making the Application of what I have said, to the Proceedings of the first Christians converted by the Apostles. The Fact is this. Twelve poor illiterate Men, in whom there appear'd

pear'd nothing to recommend them to the Eyes of the World, prefented themfelves on a fudden in the open ftreets of *Jerufalem*; and the People being gather'd about them, St. *Peter* in the Name of all the reft began to preach to them a Doctrine, which moft certainly was furprizing in the higheft Degree: To wit, that the Perfon call'd *Jefus* of *Nazareth*, whom but a few Weeks before they had feen publickly executed as an infamous Malefactor, was the *true Son of God*: That he had rifen from the Dead, fat at the right Hand of his Father in Heaven, and that in a Word, he was the very *Meffias* foretold by *Mofes* and the *Prophets*. This was the Subftance of his Sermon; and we all know the Effect it had. Three thoufand *Jews* and *Gentiles* were immediately converted by it, and embraced the *Chriftian Faith*.

Now 'tis plain the Doctrine here deliver'd by St. *Peter*, contain'd Myfteries which were wonderful and furprizing to human Reafon. Yet they firmly believed it; And I prefume no *Proteftant* at leaft will fay they acted *irrationally* in fo Doing. It muft therefore be granted, that they had folid Motives or Inducements to determine them to it. *Firft*, in all likelihood the numberlefs and ftupendious Miracles, which Chrift himfelf had wrought, and which many of them had feen, others at leaft had heard of, difpofed them very much to it. But 2*dly*, they had an uncontestable Miracle before their Eyes in the Perfon of St. *Peter* and his Fellow-Apoftles. For tho' they knew them to have been ignorant Fifhermen by Trade, that had never ftudied the Law, yet all on a fudden they heard them quote and explain the Scriptures with the fame Facility, as if they had made it the Study of their whole Lives:

Whence

Whence they judg'd, that their Knowledge was not acquired by ordinary human Means, but infused from above. They likewise observed their miraculous *Gift of Tongues*. For tho' there were Persons present of many different Nations, as the *Acts* inform us, *they all heard them speak in their own Tongues. Acts* 2. v. 8. and since this could not be ascribed to any natural Cause, they justly concluded (God enlightning their Understanding, and touching their Hearts with his holy Grace) that they were *inspired Men*, and that, by Consequence they might safely depend upon the Truth of their Doctrine, to which God himself bore Witness by such *Miracles*, as could not be contested with any colour of Reason. These were the *Motives* or *Inducements*, which render'd their Faith perfectly *rational*, tho' the Mysteries they believed were infinitely *above their Reason*.

G. But what Consequence do you draw from thence?

P. I infer from it, that if these Motives were a sufficient and solid Ground of a *rational Submission* to the *Church*'s *Faith* even in her very Infancy, when the *Prophecies* concerning her future *Encrease, Magnificence*, and *Splendor* were not yet verified as they are now, those we have at present to convince us of the *Reasonableness* of our Relying upon her Authority, are much more forcible, when *Millions* of *Martyrs* have seal'd her Faith with the last Drop of their Blood; when she has peopled both Earth and Heaven with Multitudes of holy *Confessors* and *Virgins*, whose stupendious Lives and Miracles proclaim the Purity of her Doctrine; When *Kings* and *Nations* have flock'd to her from the remotest Parts of the World, and the greatest Monarchs upon Earth have submitted to her Laws.

When

When finally she has now already had a *visible Being* for near upon Seventeen Hundred Years, in spite of all the Persecutions raised against her by the *Powers of Darkness*, and can shew *in her own Communion* an uninterrupted Succession of *Bishops* and *Pastors* from the *Apostles*, down to this very Time.

G. These *Motives of Credibility*, as you call them, are strong indeed; and must either suffice to render the Church's Testimony *credible*, or there is no Testimony upon Earth to be securely depended upon.

P. Whoever examines them seriously will most certainly find them so. And since they contain nothing but historical Facts, which may easily be examined, the Case fairly and clearly Stated between *Protestants* and the *Church of Rome* may be decided by this one Principle, to wit, *that it is an indispensable Duty, and by Consequence most highly rational, to believe a Thing, tho' never so seemingly contrary to Reason, when we have a* MORAL CERTAINTY *that God has reveal'd it.*

G. I think the Principle is self-evident, and will not bear a Dispute. Because a *moral Certainty* of any Fact excludes all reasonable Doubt of it: And if I have no Reason to doubt but that God has *reveal'd* such or such a Thing, I must be an *Atheist* or *Madman* not to believe it. For my Refusing to believe it in that Case is nothing less, than Rejecting or setting at nought the *Testimony of God himself*, whereof I am supposed to have a *moral Certainty*.

P. Yet, as I told you just now, there is not a controversial Point between *Protestants* and us, but is fully decided against them by this one general Principle.

G. I

G. I desire you Sir, to make this plain to me.

P. I prove it thus. Whatever Fact has the Testimony of the *greatest Authority upon Earth* to vouch for the Truth of it, has on it's side an Evidence amounting to such a Degree of Certainty as is wholly inconsistent with a reasonable Fear or suspicion of Falsehood. And this is what we call *a moral Certainty*: Which tho' it relies entirely upon *human Authority*, that is, *the Testimony of Men*, consider'd barely as such, and is therefore far inferiour to the *infallible Certainty* of *Divine Faith*; yet it is a Certainty of such a Nature, that a Man of sound Judgement cannot but yield to it; and none but Persons prejudiced to a Degree of Folly or Madness can resist the Force of it. For if it were rational to refuse our Assent to a Fact thus attested, it would likewise be rational to deny all historical Facts whatsoever related since the Death of the *sacred Penmen*: since for the Truth of all such Facts we neither have nor can have any more than a *moral Certainty* to depend upon.

G. Thus far is clear; and if you can shew that the *Revelation* of all the Points of *Christian Doctrine* held by us and deny'd by *Protestants*, is attested by an Authority equal to that, upon which all Men of Sense believe the most uncontested historical Facts, it will follow that *Catholicks* act most rationally in believing them, and *Protestants* act contrary to common Sense and Reason in their Disbelief of them: And so all Controversies may be decided against them by the abovesaid Principle, to wit, *that it is an indispensable Duty, and by Consequence most highly rational to believe a Thing, tho' never so seemingly contrary to Reason, when we have a* MORAL CERTAINTY *that God has reveal'd it.*

P. Well

P. Well then Sir, the *Authority* I speak of is not only equal to that, upon which all Men of Sense believe the most uncontested historical Facts, but far superiour to it. It is the *Authority* of the *whole Catholick Church* in all Ages since the first Preaching of the Gospel down to this Time: which *Authority* is uncontestably the greatest upon Earth.

Now this Church founded by *Christ* himself to be our *Guide* to Heaven; this Church so venerable for her *Antiquity* and the lineal Descent of her *Bishops* and *Pastors* in the same Communion from the *Apostles*, so eminent for her *Learning*, so respectable for the many *crown'd Heads* and *Nations* subdued by her, not by Violence or Force of *Arms*, but by the *Lustre* of her *Miracles* and *Holiness* of her *Doctrine*; finally, so illustrious for the Millions of holy *Martyrs*, and other eminent Saints all nursed in her Bosom, this Church, I say, attests and has always attested the following Historical Facts, to wit, that the *twelve Apostles* (the first Planters of her Faith) were all *inspired Men*; that whatsoever they taught relating to the *Christian Doctrine*, either by *Word of Mouth* or by Writing, were Truths *reveal'd by God*, and dictated by the *Holy Ghost*; that they committed these heavenly Truths either in *Writing* or by *Word of Mouth*, as a *sacred Trust* to their Successors the *Bishops* and *Pastors* ordain'd by them; that these were likewise commission'd to deliver them to those, who were to succeed them in the sacred Ministry; and that by these and their Successors after them they have thus been handed down to us for *reveal'd Truths*, from Bishop to Bishop, from Pastor to Pastor, from Father to Son, and from Generation to Generation throughout all Ages, to this very Time, in the very same Manner as the *Apostles Creed* has been.

These,

These, I say, are Facts, which have the Testimony of the *Church of Christ* in all Ages, that is, of the most *credible* and *illustrious Body* or Society of Men upon Earth to vouch for the Truth of them; and are therefore even more authentick and better warranted than the most memorable Facts of prophane History, which however were never doubted of by any reasonable Man.

Hence I infer 1*st*. that she have the *greatest moral Certainty possible*, that all the Articles of *Christian Doctrine* now taught by the *Catholick Church* are the very same, as were at first *deliver'd to the Saints* for *Divine* and *Reveal'd Truths*.

I infer 2*dly*, that all such Points of Doctrine, as are maintain'd by *Protestants* in Opposition to the *Catholick Church* (tho' consider'd barely as she is the *Church of Christ*, that is, a *creditable* and *illustrious Society*) have the plainest Mark of Falsehood stamp'd upon them: To wit, their having the whole Weight of the *greatest Authority* upon Earth, and by Consequence the greatest *moral Evidence* against them.

I infer 3*dly*, that all doctrinal Points deliver'd to us for *reveal'd Truths* by the *Catholick Church*, stand upon the same Bottom, that is, have all the same Degree of *Certainty*: Whether we consider them with Relation to the *Divine* or to *human Authority*, by which they are asserted. Whence

I infer 4*thly*, that we have the same *Certainty* of the *Revelation* of Chrifts *real Presence*, for Example, in the *B. Sacrament*; of the Doctrine of *Transubstantiation, Purgatory, Invocation of Saints, Honouring their Reliques* &c. as we have of the *divine Inspiration of Scriptures*: because we have the same *Testimony* or *Authority* to rely upon for the Truth of both. Nor can we reasonably reject the one without rejecting the other; and then we may bid adieu to all *Reveal'd Religion*. Sup-

Suppose I should ask a *Protestant*, how he comes to be assured that all the *Canonical Books* of *Scripture* were written by *divine Inspiration*, and contain *the pure Word of God*? For the *Inspiration* of them is neither evident to any Man's Senses, nor can it be drawn as a necessary Consequence from any Principle of pure Reason: What other tolerable Motive or rational Inducement could he alledge for his Belief of this capital Point, than the *Testimony* or *Authority* of the *Church of Christ* in all Ages asserting it to be an unquestionable Truth? But if this Suffice's to convince his Judgement of the *Inspiration* of *Scriptures*, and to oblige him to venture his Soul's Salvation upon his Belief of it, why will not the same *Testimony* and *Authority* oblige him likewise to believe the *Revelation* of the other Articles just now mention'd by me? For either the *Church* appointed by *Christ* to be our *Guide* may be securely relied upon or not. If not, a *Protestants* Belief of the *Inspiration of Scriptures* is rash and inconsiderate. But if it may be securely relied upon, he acts incoherently in not Believing the other Articles declared by her to be *reveal'd Truths*.

G. I confess, I do not see by what Slight or Artifice *Protestants* can escape from the two Horns of this *Dilemma*. For whether they say *yes* or *no*, it gives their Church a mortal Blow.

P. I will only add one Thing more, to wit, that since all are bound under Pain of eternal Damnation to believe the Faith *reveal'd to*, and preach'd by the *Apostles* (*he who believeth not, shall be condemn'd.* Mark. 16. v. 16) it is incredible that God should lay this Obligation upon us, and at the same Time leave those, who are to be saved by their *Faith in Christ*, without sufficient Means to know, what Truths

Truths he has *reveal'd*, what not. Now if the *Testimony* of the *Church of Christ* be not a sufficient Means to convey securely down to us all *reveal'd Truths*, I desire a *Protestant* to mark out to us some other better and surer Guide appointed by God in order to that End. But if he cannot do this, as most certainly he cannot, yet at the same Time refuses to join with us in submitting to all the Decisions of the *Catholick Church*, he must either renounce all *reveal'd Religion*, or profess one without having any solid or rational Motives to induce him to it.

If he says, *the Scriptures divinely inspired* suffice alone to teach him all *reveal'd Truths*, the only Answer I shall give him at present is, that this eludes the Difficulty, but do's not clear it. For it remains still unanswered, how a *Protestant* without Relying upon the *Church's Testimony* or *Authority*, can have a rational Motive to assure him of the *divine Inspiration of Scriptures?* And if he be obliged to depend upon her Testimony in this capital Point, how can he reasonably refuse to pay the same Submission to her in other Articles as positively declared by her to be *reveal'd Truths*, as the *divine Inspiration of Scriptures?* For surely all the *Motives of Credibility* are as strong on her side in her Testimony of the one as of the other.

SECT. 3.

Faith *depends in a different Manner on the* Testimony *of God, and on the* Testimony *of Men.*

G. SIR, Tho' I am fully convinced that *Protestants* act incoherently in Depending upon the *Church's Testimony* in some Things and rejecting it in others, because her Authority has the same
Weight

Weight in all her Decisions, yet since her Testimony is but the *Testimony of Men*, on which no more than a *human Faith* and *moral Certainty* can be built, I cannot yet conceive how we attain that *divine Faith*, which can never be without an *infallible Certainty*.

P. Sir, the *Faith* you speak of is *a supernatural Gift of God, form'd in us by the Holy Ghost*. Eph. 2. v. 8. But this excludes not the Use of such *natural* and *human Means*, as God demands of us to dispose our Souls for this *heavenly Blessing*. So that altho' *divine Faith* be wholly *Supernatural* in itself, yet in as much as it is likewise *rational* (for otherwise it would not be a *Virtue*) it presupposes and depends upon a natural and acquired Knowledge of the *Proofs* and *Motives*, which by the Help of God's holy Grace dispose us to it.

Hence it is that every Assent of *divine Faith* may be consider'd either as it is *infallibly certain*, or as it is *reasonable*; and in Regard of these two inseparable Properties, it depends upon a twofold Testimony, *viz.* the Testimony of *God*, and the Testimony of the *Church of Christ*, consider'd barely as it is a *creditable* and *illustrious* Body or Society of Men. An assent of Faith, consider'd as *infallibly certain*, relies wholly and solely upon the *Revelation* or *Testimony of God*: For to believe a Thing upon any other Motive than *because God has reveal'd* it, is not *divine* but *human Faith*. But because this *divine Testimony* or *Revelation* is not self-evident, therefore to render our Belief of it *rational*, it is necessary to depend upon the *Church's Testimony* to inform us, what those Truths are, which were *reveal'd to the Apostles*, and by them committed as a *sacred Trust* to their Successors, in Order to be handed down to us for *reveal'd Truths* from Age to Age.

For this Reason St. *Paul* says that *Faith is by Hearing*. Rom. 10. v. 17. to wit, by Hearing the Voice of the *Church* appointed by God to be our *Guide*. For unless we hear the Voice of the *Church* speaking to us by the Mouths of her *Bishops* and *Pastors*, how shall we know what are *reveal'd Truths*, and what not? And if we know not what Truths are *reveal'd*, we cannot make the *Testimony* or *Revelation of God* the Motive of our Belief of them. Whence it follows, that tho' our Faith relies wholly and solely upon the *Divine Testimony* as it's *proper* and *essential Motive*, it relies also upon the *Testimony of Men* as on a *Condition* necessary for the secure Conveyance of it to us.

The *Voice* of the *Church* is as an *Echo* between the *Word of God* and us. What God has *spoken* (that is, *reveal'd*) is most *infallibly true* ; and we believe it for no other Reason, but because he who is Truth itself, has *spoken it*. But unless the *Church* perform'd the Part of a *faithful Echo*, how should we know that God has *spoken* ? Or how would *Faith be by Hearing*, as the Apostle tells us, unless *God's holy Word*, which he *spoke* or *reveal'd* to the Apostles, were made *audible* to us by their Successors in all Ages ? We therefore believe the *reveal'd Mysteries* of Faith, meerly *because God has reveal'd them* : And we believe the *Church*, as the most *credible* and *illustrious Witness*, that God has effectually *reveal'd* them.

G. But, Sir, you have always told me that the *Church of Christ* is *infallible*. And why then do you insist so much upon her *Authority*, meerly as she is an *illustrious Society* of Men ? For surely her Testimony carries much more Weight, if we consider her as absolutely *infallible*. Nay a Man must be stark mad not to submit to an *infallible Guide*.

P. Sir, the Reason why I have hitherto consider'd her barely as an *illustrious* and *creditable Society*, that is, without any Regard to the *Divine Promise*

Promise of *Infallibility* made to her, is, *first*, Because her Testimony, barely as such, suffices alone to render our Belief of the *Revelation*, even of the darkest and sublimest Mysteries, perfectly *rational*, which is the Point I just now undertook to prove. But 2*dly*, to avoid the just Reproach of supposing what I ought first to prove. For the *Church's Infallibility* is itself a *reveal'd Truth*; and if I should prove the *Reasonableness* of my Belief of it from the Church's Testimony consider'd as *infallible*, my Argument would run thus; *'tis reasonable to believe that the Church's Infallibility is a reveal'd Truth, because the infallible Church declares it to be so*; which is the same absurd Way of Arguing, as if I should say, *it is reasonable to believe a Thing is so, because it is so.* But since the *Church's Testimony*, tho' consider'd barely as the *Testimony of Men*, has the same Weight and Authority in Declaring to us the *Divine Revelation* of her own *Infallibility*, as it has in Declaring all other *reveal'd Truths*; I act as *rationally* in suffering myself to be directed by her Judgment in this Point as in any other: That is, in Believing the *Divine Revelation* of her own *Infallibility*, with the same Firmness and Security, as I do for Example, the *divine Inspiration of Scriptures*: Because I have the same rational Motives or Inducements to convince me, that the one is as credibly and truly convey'd to me as the other.

Now then to come to your Question, *how we attain that Divine Faith, which is attended with an infallible Certainty?* I answer, that the Church's Authority, tho' consider'd barely as an *illustrious Society*, being once clearly establish'd by those rational Proofs, which we call *the Motives of Credibility*, her Testimony is a legal and sufficient Evidence to build a *moral* Certainty upon, that God has effectually *reveal'd* those Doctrinal Points, which she proposes to her Children as Articles of *saving Faith*, and *Terms of Communion*. Now when the *Divine Revelation* of any doctrinal Point is so credibly manifested to us, as to leave no Room for any reasonable Doubt of the Truth of it: That is, when we have a *moral Certainty* that God has *reveal'd* it, we are then bound to believe it upon his *Testimony* or *Revelation*, as is manifest to common Sense: And our Assent to it upon this Motive being form'd in our Souls by God's Grace enlightening our Understanding and Touching our Hearts, is what we call *Divine Faith*; because it's immediate and only Motive is wholly *Divine*: tho' the Conveyance and Application of it to us depends remotely upon the human Means I have just now mention'd. And so it is that our *Faith* is both *divine* and *rational*. It is *Divine* in being built upon the *Testimony of God* as on its only proper Motive; and it is *rational* in relying upon the *Church's Authority* for the conveying of the divine Testimony truly and credibly to us.

Hence it is, that the *divine Inspiration* of *Scriptures*, for Example, being thus credibly convey'd to us as an Article of *reveal'd Faith* by the Church's Testimony, we regard those sacred Oracles in all their Parts, whether *historical* or *dogmatical*, not as the Writings or Doctrine of *Men*, but as the *pure Word of God*: So that whatever we believe upon their Testimony, we believe upon the Testimony of God himself, and as having the *divine Veracity* to vouch for the Truth of it.

Now amongst many other sacred Truths clearly deliver'd in holy Writ, that of the *Church's Infallibility* may justly claim an eminent Place; tho' *Protestants* use their utmost Efforts to ridicule what they cannot solidly confute.

SECT.

SECT. 4.

The Church of Christ *consider'd as* infallible.

G. BUT if the *Church's Infallibility* be so clearly taught in holy Writ, as you say it is, how comes it that the whole Body of *Protestants*, amongst whom there are numberless Persons eminent for Wit and Learning, should see nothing of this Doctrine in those sacred Writings? For whatever is clear in itself, is obvious to be seen by every Body, at least by Persons of sound Judgment.

P. Sir, If this Reason were conclusive, the World would be much happier than we have hitherto found it to be. For all *wilful Blindness* and *Obstinacy* would be banish'd out of it: Whereas we find the contrary almost by daily Experience even in the most ordinary Occurrences of human Life; and it is a good Saying of Mr. *Lesley* in his Treatise of *private Judgment*, to wit, *That it is in vain to offer to shew a Man any Thing, till you have first persuaded him to open his Eyes.* Because none are so blind as they who will not see, and none so deaf as they who will not hear. If a Man be resolved to shut his Eyes at Noonday, the brightest Objects and the Sun itself will become invisible to him: And so will the clearest Truths to one blinded against them with *Interest* or any prevailing Passion.

G. I own, Sir, that tho' I am but young, I have observed a great Deal of this in several Persons I have been conversant with: Who, tho' otherwise esteem'd Men of sound Judgment, seem'd to be utter Strangers even to common Sense, when the Discourse chanced to fall upon Subjects, wherein either their *Interest*, or some *Party-cause* was concern'd.

cern'd. But can we say that this is the Case of *Protestants* in Reference to the Subject in Question?

P. Sir, It is their Case in the highest Degree: Because the main *Strength*, *Interest*, and *Reputation* of their Cause depends upon their Running down the Church's *Infallibility*. For if they allow'd her to be *infallible* in her Decisions of *Faith*, the immediate Consequence would be, that they must likewise allow her to be *irreformable* in her *Faith*. And what would then become of the *pretended Reformation*? 'Tis manifest the Authors and Abettors of it would be regarded as Persons fitter to be begg'd than reason'd with. And so it is no wonder that all the *reformed Churches*, tho' disagreeing among themselves in many other doctrinal Points, join unanimously in Opposing the Church's Title to *Infallibility*. Because their ALL is at Stake in this Controversy: And if it be clearly decided against them by the Unerring Testimony of *Scriptures*, the whole Structure of the *pretended Reformation* must fall to the Ground of Course, or like the Tower of *Babel* stand only as a Monument of the Extravagance and Folly of the Architects, that built it.

G. I plainly see, that if the Church's Title to *Infallibility* were so clearly made out, as to force her Adversaries to an Acknowledgment of it, the *Reformation* would be not only a defenseless, but an impudent Cause, and the Reforming Trade would starve for Want of Business to employ it: Which indeed renders it very suspicious, that their unanimous Opposition to it is not wholly the Effect of a *disinterested Zeal*, but favour's very much of that of the *Ephesian Silver-Smiths* who rais'd a furious Tumult against St. *Paul*, for Fear of Losing the chief Profit of their Trade, if the

Worship

Worship of their Goddess *Diana* should by his Preaching have been brought into Contempt. *Acts.* 19. v. 23. 24. &c.

P. Your Observation is very just, and you will be more fully convinced of it, when I have brought you acquainted, as I shall do hereafter, with some remarkable Circumstances relating to those astonishing Changes in Religion, which were gloss'd over with the specious Name of a *thorough Godly Reformation.* I will only tell you at present, that the fiery zeal of the chief Managers of this pretended Godly Work, would in all Probability soon have been cool'd, had they not found *Reforming* in those Days of *Sacrilegious Spoil* and *Rapine* a much more beneficial Trade than that of the *Ephesian Silver-Smiths,* who work'd only for Bread, which they were afraid would be taken out of their Mouths, if St. *Paul* had been suffer'd to continue his Preaching amongst them. But our reforming Gentlemen had nothing less in view than the Wallowing in Wealth and Pleasures, by the *Plunder* of their *Mother-Church*; And the glittering prospect of enriching themselves, with the *costly Plate* and *Jewels,* besides the *goodly Mannors,* wherewith the religious Generosity of her pious Ancestors had endow'd her, glared so in their Eyes, and dazled their Sight in such a Manner, that tho' they had themselves acknowledg'd and respected her for several Years, as the *beautiful Spouse* of *Jesus Christ,* without *Spot* or *Wrinkle* in her *Faith,* they could at that Time see no Remains in her of her former Beauty. The venerable *Antiquity* of her *Doctrine,* her *Catholicity,* the Lustre of her *Miracles,* the Stateliness and Solemnity of her *Heirarchy* derived from the *Apostles* themselves, the *Celibacy* of her *Clergy,* and the austere Lives of her *religious Orders,* and the *Majesty* of her *publick Service*

Service (all which had in former Ages render'd her the Admiration of Mankind, and with their powerful Attractives drawn Multitudes of *Infidels* into her Fold) had then lost all their Charms in the Eyes of her own rebellious Children, who made them the Subject of their prophane Lampoons and Satyrs, as they intended to make her *sacred Ornaments* and *Vessels* the Instruments of their Luxury and Riots.

But her Title to *Infallibility*, the most valuable of all the *Prerogatives* bestow'd upon her by her *heavenly Spouse*, was their greatest Grievance. And it was indeed a Grievance not to be tolerated: For unless this *Stone of Offence* and *Rock of Scandal*, had first been removed, there would have been no Room even for the weakest Foundation to build the Reformation upon. No Impeachment of *Idolatry* and *Superstition* could have been forged, no Bill of *damnable Errors* brought against her: And without *Errors* there could be no *Reformation*, and without a *Reformation* there was no Hopes of *Plunder*; which was too sweet a Morsel to be slighted for the insipid Advantage of a little Truth. And so it was resolved, *Nemine Contradicente*, by all the Apostles of the Reformation, that there should be no such Thing as an *infallible Church* upon Earth; in spite of all that *Papists* should produce for it either from the unanimous Testimony of the *ancient Fathers*, or from the *constant Faith* of former Ages, or from the clearest and strongest Texts of *holy Scriptures*.

As for the *Fathers*, they easily got rid of them by saying they were all *Parties*, and avow'd Abettors of *Popery*. *To what Purpose* (said the courageous *Martin Luther*) *should any Man rely on the ancient Fathers, whose Authority was revered for so many Ages? For were not they too all blind?* L. d. Serv. Arb. Tom. 2.

2. Fol. 408. 2. And again, *neither do I concern myself what Ambrose, Austin, the Councils or Practice of Ages say. I know their Opinions so well, that I have declared against them.* Cont. Regem Ang. Tom. 2. Fol. 347. 1. *I care not a Rush if a thousand Austins, or a thousand Cyprians stood against me.* Fol. 344. This was plain Dealing without Hypocrisy or Dissimulation.

As to the Faith of *former Ages*, besides that both *Luther* and *Calvin* confess'd without Hesitation, that they had separated themselves from the Communion of all the preexisting Churches in the World, the *Book of Homilies*, highly valued by the *Church of England*, declares positively, *that both Laity and Clergy, learned and unlearned, all Ages Sects and Degrees of Men, Women, and Children of whole Christendom, have been at once drown'd in abominable Idolatry; and that for the Space of* EIGHT HUNDRED YEARS AND MORE. Which, tho' in very abusive Language, is a full Acknowledgement of a Fact, which do's no Honour to the *Reformation*; to wit, that not one of the *reform'd Churches*, had a *visible Being* in the World for *eight hundred Years and more*: And so the Faith of *former Ages*, stigmatized indeed with the injurious Title of *abominable Idolatry*, was fairly given up to the *Church of Rome*, and acknowledg'd to have been wholly on the *Popish Side*.

But as to the Texts of *holy Scriptures*, which *Protestants* own to be *divinely inspired*, and by Consequence out of the Reach of a *Godly Reformation*, here indeed they were put to very hard Shifts. For the Texts are clear and Strong, and must be tortured in the most unmerciful Manner, or read backwards to discover any Thing in them but the Church's *perpetual Infallibility* settled upon the most solid Foundations.

G.

G. Pray Sir, do me the Favour to let me hear those Texts.

P. The first is Christ's positive Promise to *build his Church upon a Rock, and that the Gates of Hell shall not prevail against it.* Math.16.v.18. For if the *Word of God* may be securely depended upon, nothing surely can be clearer or stronger than this Promise: Since it is manifest, that if the *Church of Christ* were ever really guilty of the damnable Errors, *Protestants* have charged her with, *the Gates of Hell* would have effectually *prevail'd against her*, and her divine Founder proved false to his Word.

G. That's Blasphemy with a Witness. But will not *Protestants* say, it is not the *true Church of Christ*, but the *corrupt Church of* Rome, they accuse of *damnable Errors*; and that these are as different as *Light* and *Darkness*?

P. Sir, the Dispute is precisely concerning the Church *founded* by *Christ*, which they maintain to be not only *fallible*, but that it has effectually faln into the *damnable Errors* of *Popish Idolatry* and *Superstition*. 'Tis therefore in vain to pretend to elude the Force of the abovesaid Text by saying, that it is not *the true Church of Christ*, but the *Corrupt Church of Rome*, they accuse of *dammable Errors*; and there is an unanswerable *Dilemma* against them. For *Christ* either had a *true Church* upon Earth before the *Reformation*, or he had not. If not, then his Church was utterly destroy'd, and by Consequence *the Gates of Hell prevail'd against it*, contrary to his Promise. But if he had a *true Church* upon Earth, the *Church of Rome* was most certainly that Church, since according to the large Concession made in the *Book of Homilies*, it was in Possession of *whole Christendom* for many Ages before the *Reformation*: And if that Church was

in

in all that Space of Time guilty of *abominable Idolatry*, as is pretended, then the *true Church of Christ* was guilty of it: And so what Part soever of the Dilemma *Protestants* choose, they charge Christ with a Breach of Promise, in suffering the *Gates of Hell to prevail against his Church*. But to resume the Thread of my Discourse, which you have interrupted,

2*dly*, Christ's Promise to his Apostles of *abiding with them always, even unto the end of the World*. Math. 28.v.20. establishes the Church's *perpetual Infallibility* as fully and clearly as the other. For it cannot be pretended, that this Promise regarded the Persons of the Apostles alone, who were not to live *to the End of the World*, but comprehended equally all their Successors in the *Apostolick Ministry*, as long as the World shall last. So that the Force of it cannot be eluded by the precarious Interpretation of those, who presume to limit it to the three or four first Ages, during which, say they, the Gospel was preach'd in it's full Purity, that is, without any Mixture of those *Idolatrous* and *Superstitious* Practices, which crept afterwards insensibly into the Church. For can any Man be so exorbitantly blind as not to see that this is a flat Contradiction to the express Words of the Text? Since our Saviour said not, *lo I am with you for such or such a Term of Years*: But he said, *lo I am with you* ALWAYS, EVEN UNTO THE END OF THE WORLD. If therefore Christ has kept his Word, which no Man can deny without Blasphemy, one of these two Things must be granted, to wit, that either he promised to remain with *Idolaters* in Order to be their *Guide* and *Teacher* even *unto the End of the World* (and this is most highly absurd) or that his Church, by being in all Ages under the promised Direction and Assistance of her heavenly Guide,

Guide, has always continued untainted in her Faith, and will continue so to the World's End.

3dly, The Church's Charter of *perpetual Infallibility* is confirm'd to her by our Saviour's Promise of sending the *Holy Ghost* not only to the *Apostles,* but to all their Successors. *I will pray my Father, and he will give you another Comforter, that he may abide with you* FOR EVER, *the Spirit of Truth.* Joh. 14. v. 16. 17. But to what End was he *to* abide with them for ever? Let us hear Christ himself answer the Question. *When the Spirit of Truth come's, he will guide you into all Truth.* Joh. 16. v. 13. And again. *The Holy Ghost, whom the Father will send in my Name, will teach you all Things, and bring all Things to your Remembrance, which I have said unto you.* Joh. 14. v: 26.

G. Really, Sir, I am astonish'd, that Persons, who pretend to believe, that the Scriptures are *divinely inspired,* and contain the *pure Word of God*; nay and profess to make them the *only Rule* of their *Faith* (as you have often told me) can read these repeated Promises express'd in Terms so strong and clear, so obvious and easy, that even the most ordinary Capacities cannot well mistake their Meaning without Studying to deceive themselves, yet at the same Time have the Confidence to oppose the Doctrine, thus plainly asserted by them, with the same Positiveness and Obstinacy, as if they had the *Alcoran* instead of the *Word of God* before them.

P. Sir, you have all the Reason in the World to be astonish'd at it, and I verily believe, that if a Friend should leave to any *Protestant* a considerable Legacy, or settle an Estate upon him and his Heirs *for ever,* in Terms as strong and clear, as our blessed Saviour has by *his last Will* and *Testa-*
ment

ment bequeath'd to his Church the *divine Legacy* of his *perpetual Direction* and *Assistance*, he would be clear-sighted enough to understand the true meaning of it; and there would be no need of any persuasive Arguments or Reasons to convince him of the Justice of his Title. But, alas, to a Person, whose Heart is insincere and biass'd by an Interest irreconcilable with the *Gospel*, to such a one, I say, the *Word of God* is as *Seed* that falls upon a *barren Ground*, and remains without Fruit. The very clearest Light is Darkness to him, and he can extract Falshood out of Truth itself, when it chimes not with his Interest.

G. 'Tis very certain, that whoever has his Heart strongly set upon any worldly Interest, sees every Thing through false Glasses. For it lessens or magnifies Things, and makes them appear beautiful or deform'd, right or wrong, true or false just as they flatter or thwart that Interest: And we may almost with as much Hopes of Success undertake to calm a Storm, or silence a Hurricane with Demonstrations, as make a Man yield to Reason against an Interest, that lies near his Heart. Nay, I have known Persons as sharp-sighted in their temporal Concerns as the cunningest Sophisters upon Earth, yet at the same Time as dull and blind as Beetles in all Matters relating to the Concerns of the other World. So true it is, that Interest both opens and shuts Men's Eyes, according as the Objects, that present themselves, are agreeable or disagreeable to it.

However that be, since the Doctrine of the *Church's Infallibility* is a Point of such great Importance, how comes it that it has not a Place allotted to it in the *Apostles Creed?*

SECT

SECT. 5.

The Church's perpetual Indefectibility *and* Infallibility, *proved from the* 9th. *Article of the* Creed.

P. YOU may as well ask, why the *Sacraments*, the *divine Inspiration* of *Scriptures*, and many other Articles of great Importance have no place in it? But are they therefore not to be believed? God forbid they should not. The Reason therefore of both is, because that Profession of Faith, which is call'd the *Apostles Creed*, never was intended to express all Doctrinal Points, but only the principal and most distinguishing Mysteries of Christian Religion. As for the rest, they are all contain'd in general under the *Article* concerning the *Church*: Because Believing the *Church* implies Believing her whole Doctrine.

G. But pray, Sir, was this *Creed* composed by the *Apostles* themselves?

P. Several of the ancient Fathers were of Opinion it was. As St. *Leo*, St. *Austin*, St. *Jerom*, &c. quoted by Mr. *Nicol* in his Exposition of the *Creed*. But whether it be so or no, the *Authority* and *Antiquity* of it, were never questioned by any: Nor was it ever doubted, but that the 12 Articles, whereof it is composed, contain nothing but *reveal'd Truths*, and were deliver'd for such to the first Christians by the Apostles themselves.

Now then let us consider what this *Creed* says, concerning the *Church of Christ*. The 9th Article is worded thus. *I believe the holy Catholick Church, the Communion of Saints.* To which are added in the *Nicene Creed* the two Titles of *One* and *Apostolical*: And the 8th. of the 39 Articles of Religion

from the Creed.

on declares, *that both these Creeds ought throug[hly] be received and believed, because they may be pr[oved by the] most certain Warrant of holy Scriptures.* In effect the *Nicene Creed* is nothing but the *Apostles Creed* somewhat enlarged upon.

But I desire you to take Notice, that according to this 8th. *Article of Religion*, neither of the two abovesaid *Creeds* can ever be false. 1st. Because they may be both *proved by most certain Warrant of holy Scriptures*; and 2dly, because we are bound *throughly to receive and believe them.* Now surely no *Falshood* can be proved *by most certain Warrant of holy Scriptures*; nor can the contradictory to that, which is so proved, be the necessary Object of a *Christian's Faith.* But before I make my own Remarks upon the *Creed* itself, I will repeat to you the Words of a learned *Protestant* Bishop, Dr. *Pearson*, Bishop of *Chester* in his *Exposition of the Creed* quoted by the Author of *the Rule of Faith.* 2d. Part. Pref. p. vii. &c. His Words, as far as are relating to my Subject, are these.

" When I say, *I believe the holy Catholick Church,*
" I mean (says he) that there is a Church, which
" is *Holy*, and which is *Catholick*. p. 335. Edit. 4.
" It is not only an Acknowledgement of a Church
" which *shall be*, but also of that *which is*. p. 341.
" That which was, when the *Creed* began, and was
" to continue till the *Creed* shall End, is proposed
" to our Belief in every Age *as Being:* And thus
" ever since the Church was constituted, the
" Church itself *as Being* was the Object of the
" Faith of the *Church Believing.* The Existence
" therefore of the *Church of Christ* (as that Church
" is before understood by us p. 336. that is, as a
" *visible* and *known Society*) is the Continuation of
" it in an *actual Being* from the first Collection of
" it in the Time of the Apostles unto the Con-
" summation

"summation of all Things. A Collection *unin-*
"*terruptedly continued* in an *actual Existence* of be-
"lieving Persons and Congregations in all Ages
"unto the End of the World. p. 342.

"Now this indeed is a proper Object of Faith,
"because it is grounded *only upon the Promise of*
"*God.* There can be no other Assurance of the
"Perpetuity of this Church, but what we have
"from him that built it. The Church is not of
"such a Nature, as would necessarily once begun,
"preserve itself for ever. Many thousand Per-
"sons have faln totally from the Faith profess'd,
"and so apostatiz'd from the Church. Many
"particular Churches have been wholly lost, many
"Candlesticks have been removed. p. 342. But
"tho' the Providence of God do's suffer many par-
"ticular Churches to perish, yet *the Promise of*
"*the same God will never permit that all of them at*
"*once shall perish.* When *Christ* spoke first parti-
"cularly to St. *Peter,* he seal'd his Speech with a
"powerful Promise of Perpetuity, saying: *thou*
"*art* Peter, *and upon this Rock I will build my Church,*
"*and the Gates of Hell shall not prevail against it.*
"When he spoke generally to all the rest of the
"Apostles, *go teach all Nations baptizing them* &c.
"Math. 28. 19. he added a Promise to the same
"Effect, *and lo I am with you always even unto the*
"*End of the World*. The first of these Promi-
"ses assures us of the *Continuance* of the Church,
"because it is *built upon a Rock*—— the latter of
"these Promises gives not only an Assurance of
"the Continuance of the Church, but also the
"Cause of that Continuance, which is the *Pre-*
"*sence of Christ.* p. 342. Wherefore being Christ
"do's promise his *Presence* unto the Church even
"*to the End of the Word,* he do's thereby assure
"us of the Existence of the Church until that
"Time,

"Time, of which his Presence is the Cause. In-
"deed this is *the City of the Lord of Hosts, the City
"of our God: God will establish it for ever*, as the
"great Prophet of the Church has said. *Psal.* 48.
"v. 8. p. 342. Upon the Certainty of this Truth
"*the Existence of the Church has been propounded as an
"Object of our Faith in every Age of Christianity*, and
"so it shall be still unto the End of the World. p.
"343."

I omit a great deal relating to the Church's Unity; that is, her being in *one Communion*, out of which he proves Salvation to be impossible from many Texts of Scripture. But he concludes his Discourse in the following Manner.

"Whoever then professes to believe *the holy
"Catholick Church*, is understood to declare thus
"much. I am fully persuaded and make a free
"Confession of this as of *a necessary and infallible
"Truth*, that Christ by the Preaching of the Apo-
"stles did gather unto himself a Church con-
"sisting of Thousands of believing Persons, and
"numerous Congregations, *to which he daily added
"such as should be saved, and will successively and
"daily add unto the same, to the End of the World.*
"So that by Virtue of his all-sufficient Promise,
"I am assured that *there was, has been hitherto,
"now is*, and *hereafter will be*, as long as the Sun
"and Moon endure, *a Church of Christ* ONE AND
"THE SAME. This Church I believe in General,
"holy in Respect of the *Author, End, Institution*,
"and *Administration* of it. Particularly in the
"Members here I acknowledge it *really holy*, and
"in the same hereafter *perfectly holy*. I look up-
"on this Church not like that of the *Jews*, limi-
"ted to one People, confined to one Nation, but
"by the Appointment and Command of Christ,
"and by the Efficacy of his assisting Power to be

"dis-

"disseminated through all Nations, to be extended
"to all Places, to be propagated to all Ages, *to
"contain in it all Truths necessary to be known, to exact
"absolute Obedience from all Men, to the Commands
"of Christ*, and to furnish us with all Graces ne-
"cessary to make our Persons acceptable, and our
"Actions well-pleasing in the Sight of God.
"And thus *I believe the holy Catholick Church*."

'Tis thus this learned Writer has deliver'd the true and genuine Meaning of the 9th Article of the *Creed*.

G. It really appears to me, that if the *Church of Rome* had given this *Protestant Bishop* a Fee to plead her Cause, he could not have done it more effectually: And it puts me in Mind of this celebrated Maxim, *magna est Veritas & prevalet*. The Force of Truth is great, and Triumphs over Falshood, even *by the Judgment of it's Enemies*.

P. I shall content myself with inferring only one Consequence from his Words: *viz*. That the *Indefectibility* of the *true Church of Christ* is an Article of Faith invincibly proved from the *Apostles Creed*; which whoever pronounces, *makes an Acknowledgement* (says the Bishop) *not only of a Church which* HAS BEEN *or of a Church which* SHALL BE, *but also of that Church* WHICH IS. And again, *I am assured* (says he) *that there was, has been hitherto, now is, and hereafter will be as long as the Sun and Moon endure*, A CHURCH OF CHRIST ONE AND THE SAME. Which in effect is the same as to say, that when we say the *Creed*, we profess it to be an *Article of Faith*, that *the true Church of Christ is indefectible*: That it has subsisted in all past Ages since it's first Establishment, and will subsist in all succeeding Ages to the End of the World.

Christ therefore according to the *Creed* has always had, and always will have a *true* and *orthodox Church*

upon

from the Creed.

upon Earth. But what are the essential and unchangeable Attributes or Proprieties of this Church according to the same *Creed*? They consist in her being *One*, *Holy*, *Apostolical*, and *the Communion of Saints*. Now this is an unanswerable Proof both of her *Indefectibility* and *Infallibility*. For if she should——

G. Hold Sir, before you proceed, pray let me know the Difference between the Church's *Indefectibility* and *Infallibility*.

P. Sir, by the former is meant, that she never will perish, or fail, or be destroy'd entirely: And by the latter, that she will always be an *unerring Guide* in her Decisions of Faith: and by both together, that she is an *unerring Guide* always *in Being*, always *subsisting*, always *visible*. For if the Church of Christ should ever become *invisible*, or be entirely destitute of *true Bishops* and *Pastors*; that is, if the Succession of her Bishops and Pastors descending from the Apostles should fail entirely, then as a Family without an Heir is said to be extinct, so the *true Church of Christ*, which was built by him *upon the Foundation of the Apostles*, and subsists by the spiritual Generation of her *Bishops* and *Pastors*, would properly be said to perish and lose her Being: And the impossibility of this, as being inconsistent with the *Promises of God*, is called her *Indefectibility*.

In like Manner, if she should teach Doctrines opposite to *the Faith once deliver'd to the Saints*, that is, to the Faith *reveal'd* to the *Apostles*, and by them deposited as a *sacred Trust* with their Successors; If she should impose *abominable Errors* (such as *Idolatry* and *Superstitions*) upon the Faithful, and demanded of them *Terms of Communion*, which are inconsistent with Salvation, she would most certainly

tainly cease to be an *unerring Guide:* The Impossibility whereof, as being likewise inconsistent with the positive and repeated Promises of God, is what we call her *Infallibility*: Which in Reality means no more, than that the *Divine Providence* will in Spite of *the Gates of Hell*, or *Powers of Darkness*, most *infallibly* bring to pass, what he has most mercifully promised. And for the Certainty of this we have the Testimony of the *Creed* itself; as I was just now going to prove, when you interrupted me.

G. I remember you told me, that the essential and inseparable Attributes or Proprieties of the *true Church*, according to the *Creed*, consist in her being *One*, *Holy*, *Apostolical*, and the *Communion of Saints*.

P. Very right Sir; and this, as I likewise told you, is an unanswerable Proof both of her *Indefectibility* and *Infallibility*. For if she should either *fail entirely*, or cease to be either *One*, or *Holy*, or *Apostolical*, or *the Communion of Saints*, the 9th. Article of the *Creed* would then be false, and whoever should at that Time say it, would utter a downright *Lie* in making a Profession of the *Christian Faith*. But since it is manifest Blasphemy to say that the *Creed* (which *may be proved by most certain Warrant of holy Scriptures*) can ever be false; or that a Person can be guilty of *Lying* in Professing the Christian Doctrine taught by the *Apostles*, it follows that the above-said 9th Article of the *Creed* contains a demonstrative Proof, that the *Church of Christ* has always been, and will always be an *unerring Guide*, that is, *infallible* in her Decisions of Faith, and that by Consequence, she never was guilty of the *abominable Errors* laid to her Charge by her rebellious Children.

That

That the *Creed* in the suppofed Cafe would be *falfe*, is manifeft to common Senfe. Becaufe if the Church really fell into thofe *damnable Errors*, how can it be faid, that fhe was then either *One*, or *Holy*, or *Apoftolical*, or *the Communion of Saints*? This implies a manifeft Contradiction. For in the firft Place, fhe would then moft certainly have forfeited her *Unity*, by Falling from her *former Faith*. For can a Church, that Changes her Faith, be properly call'd *one* and the *fame*? On the Contrary inftead of Continuing what fhe was by her *divine Eftablifhment*, (viz.) the *true* and only *orthodox Church of Chrift*, fhe would have become an *heretical Communion*, and the very *Synagogue of Satan*: Nay a Source of *Divifions*, and Author of *Schifm*; in as much as her own Children would then have been bound to feparate themfelves from her. Nor could fhe then be *holy*, unlefs Idolatry or other *grofs Errors* be a *holy Doctrine* : nor *Apoftolical* ; becaufe the *Apoftles* never taught *Idolatry*, nor any *damnable Errors* : Nor finally, *the Communion of Saints* ; becaufe they cannot be *Saints*, who communicate with an *Idolatrous Church*.

G. Sir, if I have a true Underftanding of your meaning, the Subftance of what you have faid may be fumm'd up in this fhort *Syllogifm*. If the *Church*, which in the *Creed* we profefs to be One, Holy, Apoftolical, &c. fhould ever fall into any Errors deftructive to the *faving Faith at firft deliver'd to the Saints*, then the *Creed* would be *falfe* : But the *Creed* can never be *falfe*, therefore fhe can never fall into any fuch Errors : And is by Confequence *infallible* in all her Decifions of Faith.

P. You have taken my Meaning very exactly : And I dare prefume to fay the Argument is conclufive againft all fuch, as pretend to believe the *Creed*. I fhall only add the Teftimony of St. *Paul*,

Dial. 1. §. 5. *The Church prov'd infallible* who relying with an entire Confidence upon the Promises of God, made no Difficulty to pronounce the *Church of Christ* to be *the Piller and Support of the Truth.* 1. Tim. 3. 15. Now I presume these Words of St. *Paul* have always been, and will always be true. But how can they be true, if the Church establish'd by *Christ* ever proposes *false Doctrines* for *reveal'd Truths*? Or requires Things inconsistent with Salvation for *Conditions of Communion*? Can she always be *the Pillar and Support of the Truth*, unless she be always an *unerring Guide* in Matters of *Faith*? And if she be such a Guide, I shall ask one Question more, how can her *Faith* be *reform'd*?

G. I see no other Answer to be made to this Question but boldly Asserting, that St. *Paul's Epistles*, nay and the *Gospels* as well as the *Creed*, all which give Evidence for the Doctrine of *Infallibility*, stand full as much in need of a *thorough Godly Reformation* as the *Church of Rome* itself. However I have a small Difficulty to propose, viz. How a Body or Society of Men can be *infallible*, when all the Members that compose it are *fallible*, as most certainly all Men are.

P. You may as well ask, how can the *Nation* assembled in *Parliament* make Laws, when there is not a single Man in the whole Nation can make a Law? This however is the wise Objection of several *Protestant* Writers, and the short Answer to it is, that God bestows his Favours *on whom*, and in *what Manner* he pleases. Now the *Church's Infallibility* do's not depend upon any extraordinary *inward Lights* or *Inspirations* of particular Persons, but is grounded wholly upon the *gratuitous Promises of God*. And cannot he bestow this Privilege upon the *whole Body* of the Church, with granting it to each, or even to any one particular Member

of

from the Creed.

of it? Cannot he permit this or that *Bishop* or *Pastor* in particular to apostatize from the Faith, without permitting the whole *Episcopal Order* and *Hierarchy* to be involved in the same Apostacy? The Contrary is manifest from numberless Facts. For (as Bp. *Pearson*, has very judiciously observed) *tho' the Providence of God has suffer'd even whole particular Churches to perish, yet the Promises of the same God will never permit, that they all perish at once.* So that altho' many dead Branches have already been cut off, and more will perhaps be cut off hereafter, the *Body* of the *Church* will always continue alive and Growing: Because *Christ* has promised *to abide with her always even to the End of the World.* And so she will always continue to be *the Pillar and Support of the Truth*; the Divine Providence disposing all Things so for her perpetual Preservation, that in Spite of the natural Infirmities or *Fallibility* of her *Bishops* and *Pastors*, God's Promises will infallibly be made good, and he will never suffer his Church to impose on her Children any Doctrines for *reveal'd Truths* or *Terms of Communion*, but what were at first deliver'd for such by the *Apostles* themselves, and have since been handed down from them by their Successors in the *Apostolick Ministry*.

SECT. 6.
The Rule of Faith.

THIS leads me to the Examination of another material Point relating to the *general Grounds* of *Catholick Religion*, to wit, the *Rule* by which the *Catholick Church*, which is our Guide, directs itself in all it's *Decisions of Faith*: That is, by which it judgeth, *what Doctrines have been reveal'd* veal'd to the *Apostles, what not.* This we call the *Rule of Faith*: And the Question concerning it is, whether the *written Word of God alone* be such a *full* and *compleat Rule*, that all Points of *reveal'd Faith*, are plainly express'd in it. *Protestants* generally hold it is. But the *Church of Rome* has constantly maintain'd, that *Apostolical Tradition* is a necessary Part of this Rule, and that without it we should be wholly in the Dark, in Reference to many important Articles, both of the *Christian Faith* and *Worship*: As has of late been fully demonstrated in a Book entituled *the Rule of Faith*; printed An. 1721. the Author whereof has handled this Subject so amply as well as solidly, that nothing can be added to it. So that I need but make Choice of a few Arguments out of many, he has furnish'd his Reader with, to convince you of the Weakness of the *Protestant Cause* on the one Hand, and of the Strength of the *Catholick Doctrine* on the other.

G. Before you proceed, pray let me ask, whether *the Word of God alone* be not *the whole Rule of Faith*? For if it be, it seems to follow, that *Scriptures*, which are undoubtedly *the Word of God*, are alone a *full* and *compleat Rule* of Christian Faith.

P. Sir, as to your Question I answer, that *the Word of God* is most certainly the *whole Rule of Faith*: But the Consequence you draw from it is not conclusive; Because it supposes that the Scriptures alone contain *the whole reveal'd Word of God*, and that the *sacred Penmen* have set down in *Writing* every Thing they taught by *Word of Mouth*: Which Supposition is wholly groundless. On the Contrary it has always been the Doctrine of the Catholick Church, that there is an *unwritten* as well as *written Word of God*, and that these are of
equal

equal Authority, and make up together *one Rule of Faith*.

G. But are then the *Traditions of Men of equal Authority* with the *express Word of God*?

P. No Sir, Nothing but the *Word of God itself*, can be of equal Authority with *the Word of God*: And therefore the *unwritten Word of God* deliver'd to us by the *Tongues of Men*, cannot but be of equal Authority with the *written Word of God* deliver'd to us by the *Pens of Men*. For I presume the Apostles were equally Men, whether they *spoke* or *wrote*: But since they were equally *inspired Men*, it was equally the *reveal'd Word of God*, whether they deliver'd it by *Word of Mouth* or in *Writing*. Nay it is plain Fact, *first*, that *Christ* himself laid the Foundation of the Church by *Preaching* only: 2*dly*, That he never laid any Command on the Apostles to *write*, but only to *preach* the Gospel to all Nations; and 3*dly*, that in Effect they preach'd for several Years before they wrote any of the *Canonical Books* of *Scripture*: And tho' they had never written at all, but deliver'd the whole Christian Doctrine only by *Word of Mouth* to those, who succeeded them in their Apostolical Charge, we should have been obliged to receive it as *the Word of God*, and therefore with the same Respect, as we now do the *holy Scripture*.

Whence it follows *first*, that the *unwritten Word of God* was the *whole Rule of Faith* to the primitive Christians, before the *Scriptures* could possibly be a Part of it; and it might have continued so for ever, if Providence had pleased to order it so. It follows 2*dly*, that *Scriptures* are so far from being the *whole necessary Rule* of the *Christian Faith*, that they are not (absolutely speaking) even a *necessary Part* of that *Rule*: As the above-said Author has fully proved. *Postcript.* p. 14. 15. &c.

G. But

G. But could all *necessary Points* of *reveal'd Faith* have been safely convey'd to us, tho' the *new Testament* had never been writ?

P. There can be no Doubt of it. As for Instance, could not the *Creed* have been remember'd in all Ages, tho' the four *Evangelists* had never committed any Thing to Writing?

G. Ay but all *necessary* Points of Religion are not express'd in the *Creed*.

P. 'Tis true they are not. But they may be all reduced to so small a Compass, that they might have been transmitted to the most distant Times and Places with the same safety as the *Creed* itself, by *Tradition* only: And the *faithful* might have preserved them in their Minds and Hearts, tho' they had never had those farther Lights, which the *new Testament* now furnishes them with.

However, as Providence has order'd Things, the *holy Scriptures* are without all Dispute, a most inestimable Treasure, and an *infallible Rule of Faith* when rightly understood. But that they are not the *whole Rule of Faith*, and that *unwritten Apostolical Traditions* have always been at least a *necessary Part* of this Rule, may be clearly made out.

First, From the *Scripture* itself. For besides that it no where declares, that all the particular Points of the Christian Doctrine, which the Apostles taught by *Word of Mouth*, are express'd in their *canonical Writings*, it over and above recommends *Apostolical Traditions* in the most express and positive Terms. *Now I praise you Brethren* (says S. Paul. 1. Cor. 11. 2.) *because you remember me in all Things, and keep the Traditions, as I have deliver'd them to you.* And again 2. Thes. 2. 15. *Therefore Brethren, stand fast, and hold the Traditions, which you have been taught, whether by* WORD *or by our Epistle.* And
soon

of Faith. 43

foon after 2. *Thef.* 3. 6. he fays, *now we command you Brethren in the Name of our Lord* Jefus Chrift, *to withdraw yourfelves from every Brother, that walks diforderly, and not after the Tradition, which he received of us.* Upon which a *Proteftant* Author of a Book entituled *Tradition neceffary* makes the following Reflection p. 32. 33. *Here* fays he, *we fee plain Mention of St.* Paul's *Traditions, confequently of Apoftolical Traditions deliver'd by Word of Mouth as well as by Epiftles or in Writing; and a Condemnation of thofe, who do not equally obferve both.*

I heartily wifh the Author may not fall under that Condemnation. This however is certain, that the Apoftles were extremely vigilant in giving full Inftructions to thofe they ordain'd, that they might alfo be able to inftruct others. Thefe Inftructions are the *facred depofitum,* of which St. *Paul* fays to *Timothy, keep that which is committed to thy Truft.* 1. Tim. 6. 20. And again, *hold faft the Form of found Words, which thou haft* HEARD *of me: that good Truft, which was committed to thee, keep by the holy Ghoft, who dwelleth in us.* 2. Tim. 1. 13. 14. and more fully; *The Things, which thou haft* HEARD *from me before many Witneffes, the fame commit thou to faithful Men, who may be able to teach others alfo.* 2. Tim. 2. 2.

" Thus it is evident from Scriptures themfelves
" (fays the abovemention'd *Proteftant* Writer p.
" 78.) that the whole of Chriftianity, was at firft
" deliver'd to the Bifhops fucceeding the Apoftles
" by *oral Tradition;* and they were alfo comman-
" ded to keep it, and deliver it to their Succeffors
" in the fame Manner. Nor is it any where
" found in Scripture by St. *Paul* or any other of
" the Apoftles, *that they would either jointly or fepa-*
" *rately write down all that they had taught as neceffary*
" *to Salvation*; or that they would make fuch a com-
" pleat Canon of them, that nothing fhould be
necef-

necessary to Salvation, but what should be found "in those Writings."

The same is proved from the constant Doctrine of the *ancient Fathers*, who are faithful Witnesses of the Doctrine of the Church in their Times. St. *Chrysostom* in his 3d. Sermon upon 2 *Thes.* 2. when he comes to the 15th Verse, just now quoted, discourses thus upon it. *Hence*, says he, *it is plain, that the Apostles did not deliver all things in Writing; but many Things without it: And these ought to be believed as much as those. Let us then give Credit to the Tradition of the Church. It is Tradition, seek no farther.*

St. *Basil* upon the same Text of St. *Paul.* 2. *Thes.* 2.v.15. discourses thus. *Of Doctrines held by the Church, we have some in holy Scriptures, others in an unwritten Apostolical Tradition; and both have an equal Force in Reference to Piety. Nor will any one contradict this, who has any Knowledge of Church-matters. For if unwritten Customs be laid aside as Things of no great Authority, we shall secretly give the Gospel a mortal Stab, or rather shall reduce it to an empty Sound.*

This is a full Confutation of those, who pretend that no Ceremonies are to be practised in the *publick Worship* or Administration of the *Sacraments*, but what are clearly mark'd out in *Scripture*: And this they call bringing Religion back to it's *ancient Purity*: Tho' in Effect it is robbing it of all it's outward Ornaments, and stripping it as naked as an Infant newly born.

St *Epiphanus* Hær. 61. tells us in positive Terms: *that Tradition also is necessary. For all Things*, says he, *cannot be had from Scripture. And therefore the Apostles left us some Things in Writing, and others by Tradition.* He presses the same Hær. 75. § 8 particularly in the Case of *Praying for the Dead*: For which *of Faith.* 45

which there is no positive Direction to Christians in the *new Testament*.

Tertullian do's the same in Reference to the *Ceremonies* of *Baptism*, of the *Eucharist*, the frequent Use of *the Sign of the Cross*, *anniversary Oblations* for the *Dead* and in *Honour of the Martyrs*. L. de corona. C. 3. *Of these*, says he, *and otherlike Customs, if you look for a Command of Scripture, you will find none : But it will be told you, that they are authorized by Tradition, confirm'd by Custom, and observed by Faith.*

Lastly, St. *Irenæus* a Father of the Second Age, sends us expresly to the *Church*, and to *unwritten Traditions* for the true Sense of *Scriptures* " Truth,
" says he, is not to be sought for from others,
" which you may have easily from the *Church*,
" with which the Apostles have fully deposited *all*
" *Truth*, to the End that whoever desires it, may
" from her receive the living Waters. For she
" is *the Door of Life*, but all the rest are *Thieves* and
" *Robbers*. We must therefore avoid them; we
" must diligently pursue what belongs to the
" Church, and *learn from her the Tradition of Faith*.
" For if the Dispute were of any little Matter,
" should we not consult the most ancient Churches,
" and derive our Evidence from thence? And what
" if the Apostles had left us no Scriptures, *must*
" *we not follow the Rule of Tradition entrusted with*
" *them, to whom they left their Sees*? As many bar-
" barous Nations *without any Books of Scripture*, yet
" believing in Christ have Salvation written in
" their Hearts by the *holy Ghost*, and carefully
" preserve *the old Traditions*. L. 3. C. 4."

G. Sir, you have here produced the clear Testimony both of *Scriptures* and of the *ancient Fathers* for *Apostolical Traditions*. And what more can be desired by one, who is sincerely disposed to ac-
know-

knowledge the Truth, when it is made plain to him? But can you give me any particular Instances of necessary Duties, or Articles of Christian Faith, allow'd for such by *Protestants* themselves, which cannot be proved from *Scriptures*, and are grounded wholly upon *Apostolical Traditions*?

P. I could produce a considerable Number: But to avoid being tedious, I shall make Choice only of *three*, allow'd of, as you desire, by *Protestants* themselves. 1. The Observance of the *Christian Sabbath* against *Jews* and *Sabbatarians*. 2. The Validity of *Infant Baptism* against *Anabaptists*. and 3*dly*, The Validity of *Baptism* administer'd by *Hereticks* against the *Donatists*. In which three Points there is no Difference between the *reform'd Churches* and us. I shall touch briefly upon each.

First then, There is no Text in *Scripture* commanding the *Sunday*, that is, the first Day of the Week to be kept *holy*; as there is most certainly one, which appoints the *Saturday* or last Day of the Week for the *Sabbath*, or *Day of Rest*. Exod. 20. v. 8. And yet the keeping of *Sunday* exclusively of the *Saturday*, is a Duty indispensably obliging all Christians, *Protestants* there ore as well as *Roman Catholicks* are under a Necessity of having Recourse to *Apostolical Tradition* to justify this remarkable Change in setting aside the *Saturday*, and substituting the *Sunday* instead of it. For nothing else can possibly be alledg'd to authorize either the Obligation, or even the Lawfulness of this Practice.

2*dly*, *Protestants* hold, as we do, the Validity of *Infant-Baptism*. Yet it is not authorized by any one plain Text of *Scripture*, nor have we any Thing for it but the Authority of *Apostolical Tradition*; tho' it be a Point of such Importance, that the Salvation of Millions of Souls depends upon it. The Custom, says St. *Austin*, *which our Mother the Church has of Baptizing Infants is not to be slighted,*
nor

nor thought superfluous in any Manner: Nor ought it to be believed, WERE IT NOT AN APOSTOLICAL TRADITION. L. 10. de Gen. ad Lit. C. 23. he therefore was convinced, that there was no *Scriptural Text* for it: For if there had been any, there would have been an Obligation of Believing it upon the Testimony of *Scriptures*.

3*dly*, The Validity of Baptism administer'd by *Hereticks* is likewise own'd by *Protestants*. It was the Subject of the Dispute between St. *Cyprian* and Pope *Stephen*, and afterwards between the *Donatists* and the *Catholick Church*. But St. *Augustin*, who drew his learned Pen in Defence of the *Catholick Cause* against those Hereticks, own'd frankly that it could not be decided by *plain Scripture*; but that after the Death of St. *Cyprian*, the Church had interposed her Authority in the *Council of Arles*, and determined the Matter by the *Infallible Rule* of *Apostolical Tradition*. St. *Augustin's* Words are remarkable. *Of this*, says he, *the Apostles have left us no Direction in Writing. But the Custom, which was objected against St.* Cyprian MUST BE BELIEVED TO HAVE BEGUN BY TRADITION FROM THEM. *As there are many Things, which are held by the whole Church, and are therefore rightly believed to have been order'd by the Apostles*, ALTHO' THEY BE NOT FOUND IN SCRIPTURE. l. 5. *de bapt. contra Don. c.* 23.

How different is the Doctrine of this learned Champion of the Church from that of the 6th. *Protestant Article of Religion?* By which it is declared *that holy Scripture containeth all things necessary to Salvation: So that whatever is not read therein, nor may be prov'd thereby, is not to be required of any Man, that it should be believed as an Article of Faith, or be thought requisite or necessary to Salvation.*

G. What! Is that the Doctrine of the 6*th*. *Protestant Article of Religion!* If it be, I am sure the *Church of England* is incoherent with herself.

For

For do's she not *require of any Man* to believe the indispensable Obligation of Observing the *Christian Sabbath*? And where is that *read in Scripture*, or how can it be *proved thereby*? Again, do's she not require of all *true Protestants* to believe the Validity of *Infant-baptism*, and that this Sacrament is validly administer'd by *Hereticks*? Or do's she require of them to believe both the one and the other, without judging the Belief of them *necessary to Salvation*? That would be strange indeed. It follows therefore that she requires *the Belief* of some *Articles of Faith*, as necessary to Salvation, which *cannot be read in Scripture*, nor *proved thereby*: unless she has perhaps made some new Discovery of *Scriptural Texts,* which poor St. *Augustin* knew nothing of.

P. That might be probable, if *Scriptures*, like the *golden Mines* of *Peru*, had lain hid under Ground in former Ages. But that a Person so deeply read in those sacred Writings, as St. *Austin* was, who studied them Day and Night, in Order to employ them against the Enemies of Truth, should be ignorant of such Texts, if there were any, is altogether improbable.

But there is another remarkable Incoherency in the same 6th. *Article*: For it go's on thus. *By holy Scriptures we understand those Canonical Books of the old and new Testament, of whose Authority was never any Doubt in the* Church. Now I presume the Belief of the *Canonical Books* both of the *Old* and *New Testament* is required by the *Church of England,* as an Article of Faith *necessary to Salvation*: Unless she will allow Salvation to Persons, who deny any Part of *the Word of God*, when it is declared to them, that it is *the Word of God*, by sufficient Authority. And yet the above-said Article refers us to the Judgment of the *Church,* and not to *Scriptures themselves* (which indeed would be absurd)

of Faith.

furd) to learn what Books are *Canonical*: *those of whose Authority there never was any Doubt in the Church*: And what is this but making *Tradition* the *only Rule* of Distinguishing betwixt *inspired* and *uninspired Writings*? That is, the *only Rule* of a very important Article of *Christian Faith.*

I say nothing of the gross Mistake implied in these last Words of the abovesaid Article; to wit, *of whose Authority was never any Doubt in the Church.* For both the Book of *Esther* in the *Old Testament,* and several Parts of the *New Testament,* allow'd of by the *Church of England* for *Canonical,* were doubted of by Eminent Men in the Church even till the End of the 4th. Century: About which Time the *Canon* both of the *Old* and *New Testament* was after the most diligent Examination settled upon the same Footing, as it has been since by the *Council of Trent.*

SECT. 7.
Of Scriptures *and* Church-Authority.

G. BUT how comes it, that the *reform'd Churches* appear to be so zealous for the *Scriptures,* and at the same Time have so little Regard to *Church-Authority*? Since without that Authority we should not even be sure of the *Scriptures* themselves.

P. 'Tis very hard to give a Reason for the Proceedings of Men, when they are once engaged in an unreasonable Cause: For they usually approve or reject, cry up or run down Things, not by a steady Principle of Reason, but as they appear favourable or unfavourable to the Interest they have espoused. I shall Instance in the very Points you have now mention'd. The *reform'd Churches,* as you

50 Dial. 1. §. 7. *Of* Scriptures *and*
you obferve, affect a wonderful Zeal for *Scriptures*, and pretend to make them the *whole Rule* of their *Faith*. And would not any one now imagine to find them the moft zealous People in the World for every Thing, the *Scriptures* recommend ?

G. I fhould really think fo.

P. But, Sir, it is not a *Proteftant* Virtue to fpeak or act coherently in religious Matters. You have already had fome Specimens of their true Zeal for *Scriptures*, in rejecting the Doctrines of *Infallibility* and *oral Tradition*, tho' eftablifh'd by fuch clear and ftrong *Scriptural Texts*, as fully convinced the ancient Fathers of the Truth of thofe two important Points. I fhall now give you another Specimen of it in their Oppofition to *Church Authority*, tho' it has likewife the plaineft Teftimonies of Scriptures to recommend it. For *firft*, it is plain from *Scripture*, that the Church has her Eftablifhment from *Chrift* himfelf. *Upon this Rock I will build my Church*: fays *Chrift*, Math. 16. v. 16. He therefore was the *Builder* or *Founder* of it: which alone gives her an Authority fuperiour to all Societies upon Earth.

2*dly*, She has her Commiffion of *Teaching* immediately from the fame divine Perfon. *All Power in Heaven and on Earth* (fays he) *is given unto me*. This is the Preamble: and it gives the greateft *Weight* and *Authority* poffible, to the Commiffion deliver'd in the following Words. *Go ye therefore and teach all Nations*, Math. 28. v. 18. 19. But leaft it fhould be imagined that the Commiffion he then gave, was to expire with the Apoftles, he immediately added, *and lo I am with you always even unto the End of the World.* v. 20. which cannot be underftood otherwife than of the Succeffors of the Apoftles in all Ages. This then again makes the *Church's Authority*, in determining Matters relating

lating to the *Christian Doctrine*, the greatest upon Earth; because he has promised to *abide*, that is, to continue *Teaching with her even unto the End of the World.* Hence he has pronounced this terrible Sentence, against any Man that refuses to submit to her Decisions, to wit, *that he shall be reputed as a Heathen and a Publican.* Math. 18. v. 17. that is as one in a damnable State. Nay our B. Saviour appears to be so jealous of the *Authority* of his future Church, in the Persons of his Ministers, that he seems to make no Difference between their Authority and his own. *As my Father sent me, so do I send you.* Joh. 20. v. 21. And again, *he that hears you hears me, and he that despises you despises me.* Luke 10. 16.

St. *Paul,* the faithful Apostle of Christ, and Interpreter of his Doctrines, takes all Occasions to establish the *Church's Authority* in the Persons of her Ministers appointed by Christ to be our *Guides* in *Spirituals.* When he was upon his Voyage to *Jerusalem,* he assembled the Clergy of *Ephesus,* and spoke thus to them. *Take heed therefore unto yourselves, and to all the Flock, over which the holy Ghost has made you Overseers, to feed* (or *govern*) *the Church of God which he has purchased with his Blood.* Act. 20. v. 28. Now *Feeding* and *being fed, Governing and being govern'd* have a reciprocal Relation: And the same divine Authority, which gives the Power of *Governing* to the *Pastors* of the *Church,* requires Submission and Obedience of their Flock. Upon this Principle St. *Paul* in his Epistle to the *Hebrews,* instructs them in the important Lesson of Submission to their *Spiritual Guides. Obey them,* says he, *that have the Rule over you, and submit yourselves.* Heb. 13. v. 17. and speaking of the same *Guides,* he commands the *Hebrews* to *follow their Faith.* v. 7.

The same Apostle in his Epistle to the *Ephesians* tells us, that *Christ* besides *Apostles* and *Evangelists*, has given to his Church *Pastors* and *Teachers, for the Perfecting of the Saints, for the Work of the Ministry, for the building up of the Body of Christ, till we all meet in the Unity of Faith —— that we be no more Children wavering, and carried to and fro, with every Blast of Doctrine in the Uncertainties of Men, and their Crafty Contrivances to deceive.* Eph. 4. v. 11. 12. 13. 14. Here then we are taught *first*, that the *Pastors* of the Church are appointed by God to be our *Guides* in *Faith*, and that he has establish'd this Method for the *Uniting* all Men in one and the same Belief; to the End *that we be not like Children wavering and carried to and fro with every Blast of Doctrine.* We are taught 2*dly*, that these Guides shall continue in the *Church* of *Christ*, without Ceasing, *till we all come to the Unity of Faith* : That is, to the End of the World; And that by Consequence in all Controversies of Religion, it belongs to these *Guides* to fix the wavering Judgments of the People, against all the Uncertainties of Men, and the wicked Arts of *Impostors* and *Seducers*.

Thus it is manifest, that the *Authority* of the *Church* in her *Pastors* is establish'd by the clearest and strongest Texts of *Scripture*. And what Judgment must we then make of the Sincerity of the *first Reformers*, who whil'st they pretended to make *Scriptures* their *only Rule*, acted openly against that very Rule by Rejecting the *Authority*, it so expressly recommends ? Truly we cannot rationally form any other Judgment, than that all their Shew of Zeal for *Scriptures* and the *Word of God*, which was the universal cry in the Beginning of the *Reformation*, was no more than a meer theatrical Farce to amuze the ignorant Populace, and a Cloak to cover their premeditated Design of sub-
verting

verting the whole Frame of *Church-Government,* which Chrift had eftablifh'd; of bringing the *Guides* of *God's Appointment* into Contempt, and Dreffing up the Idols of their own Imaginations with the fpecious Gloffes of *Scriptural Texts* wrefted from the Senfe intended by the *Holy Ghoft.*

G. But are not the *firft Reformers* and their *Followers* as pofitively condemn'd by *their own Rule,* I mean, the *Scriptures,* as by the *Authority* of the *Catholick Church?* And why then have they fo great a Spleen againft the one, and fhew fo great a Refpect for the other?

P. The Reafon in fhort is, becaufe the *Church* is fomewhat harder to be managed than the *Scriptures.* You fhall hear what Anfwer the Author of *the Rule of Faith* gives to it p. 178. 179. "Eve-
" ry one *(says he)* fees, that he can give what
" Senfe he pleafes to a *Writing,* which is obfcure
" in feveral Points relating to Confcience and Re-
" ligion. So that an *infallible Rule (as Scriptures*
" *doubtlefs are, when rightly underftood)* without an
" *infallible Interpreter,* puts little or no Reftraint
" upon many unwarrantable Paffions, Prejudices,
" and Opinions, of which a great Part of Man-
" kind is generally too fond. But an *infallible In-*
" *terpreter (meaning the Church)* is not fo tame. He
" will not fuffer his Sentence to be wrefted againft
" his Meaning. If they mifconftrue his Words,
" he will ftill fpeak plainer, and confute their
" Doubts."

Here then lies the whole Secret. The *dead Letter* of *Scriptures* cannot fpeak for itfelf; and tho' it be never fo much put to the Torture, it cannot complain, nor make any farther Difcoveries, nor give us any farther Lights, than the *Sacred Penmen,* thought fit to communicate to us in their Writings. But the *Church* is a *living Judge* always in

Being:

Being: So that if her Decrees be call'd in Question, she can exert her Power, and stand up in Defence of them. If her Words be misinterpreted, She is a *living Interpreter*, and can do herself Justice by explaining her own true Meaning. Tis therefore obvious to common Sense, why the Leaders of the *Reformation* hated the *Church*, and appeal'd from her *Authority* to the *dead Letter* of the *Scripture*. They hated the *Church*, as Criminals hate the *Judge*, by whom they are sure to be condemned; and their appealing to *Scriptures* was in effect appealing to their own *private Judgment*, where they were as safe as they could wish. For what Criminal would fear to appear before a Tribunal, where himself sits as *Judge* and *Interpreter* of the *Law*, by which he is to be tried? And indeed the World soon saw the Fruit of their politick Zeal for *Scriptures*. For in a very short Time it stock'd Christendom with as many Religions, as there were anciently *Deities* amongst the *Heathens*. The *written Word of God* being wrested out of the Hands of it's only lawful *Interpreter* the *Catholick Church*, and seized on by these usurping Intruders, was so dexterously managed by them, that like the *Pagan Oracles* of Old, it was made to speak just what they pleased; and there was nothing so impious or absurd, which was not found *plain* in *Scripture*, when it suited with their *Prejudices* or *Passions* to find it so.

Thus *Martin Luther*, *Carolstadius*, *Oecolampadius*, *Bucer*, and other *apostate Priests* and *Monks*, found it plain in *Scripture*, that *solemn Vows* of Chastity made to God were not binding. Thus the same *Martin Luther* found it no less plain in *Scripture*, that *Free-will is but an empty Name.* Tom. 2. Fol. 3. 2. Thus *Calvin* likewise found it plain in *Scripture* that *God is the Author of Sin.* That all *the Children of the Faithful, whether baptized or unbaptized, are in the Number of the*

the Elect; and that *a Person once justified can never lose the Grace of Adoption, tho' he should fall into the most enormous Crimes. Hist. des Variat.* L. 9. p. 351. 352. &c. which last abominable Doctrine is expresly defined in the *Synod of Dort. Hist. des Variat.* L.14. p. 41. 42. And yet this true *Protestant Synod*, to which the *Church of England* as well as other *reform'd Churches*, sent their *Representatives*, and to the Decrees whereof they all subscribed, pretended to decide every Thing by *the plain Word of God*. Such impious Errors do's God permit Men to fall into, when they cast off the *Authority*, he has appointed to be their *Guide*, and set up their own *private Judgments* to be the *Interpreters* of his *Sacred Word*.

Thus again by the same Delusion justly permitted by God, three of the *Head Patriarchs* of the *Reformation*, to wit, *Luther, Calvin,* and *Zuinglius*, ran into the three disagreeing Systems relating to the *Sacrament* of the *holy Eucharist*; and all three pretended to have the *sacred Text* most evidently on their Side; nay and continue in the some contradictory Preventions to this Day. "To a *Zuin-*
"*glian* (*says the Author of the* Rule of Faith p. 26.
" 27.) it is wonderfully plain from *Scripture*, that
" there is nothing received in the *Sacrament* but
" *Bread and Wine*. To a *Calvinist* it is infinitely
" plainer, that *Zuinglius* is mistaken, and that the
" *true Body* and *Blood* of Christ are actually pre-
" sent, not indeed to the *Sacrament*, but to the
" *worthy Receiver*. But *Luther* tells us, that his
" Brother Reformers are a *Couple of Asses*; *that they*
" *have learnt their Doctrine from the Devil*; and that
" *we must either charge a Lie upon the holy Ghost, or*
" *confess that the sacred Body and Blood of Christ, are*
" *truly and really present to the Sacrament itself,*
" *as well as to the Receiver.* Serm. de Sacr. An.
" 1527."

Thus finally the *Scriptures*, as managed by the *reform'd Churches*, are to this very Day plain and positive for *Lutheranism* in *Germany*, for *Calvinism* at *Geneva*, for *Zuinglianism* in *Switzerland*, for *Wyclifism* and *Hussitism* in *Bohemia*; and in the Dominions of *Great Britain*, not only *parliamentary Protestantism*, but *Presbyterianism*, *Anabaptism*, *Quakerism*, and *Socinianism*, besides numberless other Fanaticisms of less Note, have all *plain Scriptures* on their Side.

I conclude in the whole, that *Scriptures alone* are so far from being a *full* and *complete Rule of Christian Faith*, that they even are no Rule at all, at least in any doubtful or disputed Case, unless they be interpreted by *that Authority*, which *Christ* has establish'd upon Earth to be our *Guide*, and to which he has promised his perpetual Assistance. For if they be left to the arbitrary and precarious Interpretation of every Man's private Judgment, instead of being a Means to unite Men in the same Faith, they must unavoidably be the very Apple of Discord, and a Source of endless Disputes: As is manifest not only from the few Instances I have produced, but from the whole History of the *Reformation* from End to End; which will be an everlasting unanswerable Proof, that *Scriptures* read without the Submission and Deference, which is due to the *Guides* appointed by Providence to lead us into the true meaning of them, have been the Cause of all the Disputes, that have divided whole Christendom these two hundred last Years, but never put an End to any. For how can that be a proper Means to end Disputes, which in all Controversies, that are to be decided by *Scriptures*, is itself the principal Subject of the Dispute? All indeed agree that there are *such* and *such Words* in *Scripture*; but since it is the *Sense* and not the

Sound of *Words*, which is *the Rule of Faith*, and the whole Quarrel is about the *Sense*, 'tis impossible the contending Parties should come to an Agreement, unless they sacrifice their own *private Judgments*, and submit to a *Tribunal*, from which there is no Appeal.

G. 'Tis indeed but obvious to common Sense, that the Thing, which is itself the Subject of the Quarrel, cannot by itself alone End it. So that unless it be referr'd to the Decision of a Judge duly qualified, the Dispute will last till Doom's Day.

P. Suppose there were a Nation, that should give full Liberty to every one to interpret it's Laws by his own private Judgment, would it be possible in that Case either to condemn any Criminal, or put an End to any Law-Suit? Nay would not Anarchy and Confusion be the unavoidable Consequence of it? The Matter will not bear a Dispute. And therefore there is not a civilized Nation in the World, but has a *supreme Tribunal* establish'd, from which there is no Appeal. Now this *supreme Tribunal* in Matters relating to *Faith* and *Worship* is the *Catholick Church*, which St. *Paul* calls the *Pillar and Support of the Truth.* 1. Tim. 3. v. 15. whose Decisions our Blessed Saviour commands us to submit to under Pain of being regarded by him as *Heathens* and *Publicans.* Math. 18. v. 17. and with the *Pastors* whereof he has promised *to abide for ever*; in Order to encourage us to rely upon their Judgment with an entire Repose of Mind.

SECT.

SECT. 8.

A Recapitulation of the foregoing Sections.

BUT I have now done with the *general Grounds* of the *Catholick Faith*, which I have laid before you as briefly as the Matter would permit. However, if it will not tire you Patience, before we break up this Conference, I will sum up in short the chief Heads of what I have said with some Reflections upon it, that you may have a clear sight of them at once, and for your farther Satisfaction examine them more fully at your Leisure.

 P. Sir, I shall listen to you not with Patience but Pleasure.

 P. This I am sure of, that they will stand the Test of the strictest Examination; and the more they are consider'd, the more they will convince you, that the *Church*, in which alone the *Catholick Faith* is taught, is built upon the strongest Foundations.

 Christ himself is both it's *Founder* and it's *chief Corner-stone*: It's *Law-giver, Supreme invisible Head,* and *perpetual Protector*. He laid the first Foundations of it by personally Preaching *the Word of Life* for three whole Years. When he was at the Eve of his Departure out of this World, he comforted his Apostles with a Promise of sending down to them the *Holy Ghost*, who *should guide them into all Truth*. Joh. 16. v. 13. and *bring all Things to their Remembrance, whatever he had said unto them.* Joh. 14. v. 26. Some Time after his *Resurrection* he committed the Charge of his *whole Flock* in a special Manner to St. *Peter*. Joh. 21. v. 15. &c. and by that establish'd the Form of Government, which

was

was ever after to be inviolably obferved in his Church. A little before his *Afcenfion* into Heaven, he gave his Apoftles their Commiffion to *go and teach all Nations*, which he accompanied with a Promife of *Abiding with them to the End of the World*. Math. 28. v. 20.

The 10th Day after his *Afcenfion*, the *promifed Spirit of Truth* defcended vifibly on the *Apoftles*, who thereupon began immediately the Exercife of their Apoftolical Miniftry, and that with fuch an aftonifhing Succefs, that in a very fmall Time a numerous Church was form'd at *Jerufalem*, and a few Years after the Gofpel was preach'd to the remoteft Parts of the World; as is attefted by St. *Paul* in his Epiftle to the *Romans*, C 1. v. 8. which was written but fifteen Years after St. *Peter*'s coming to *Rome*. Now it cannot furely be doubted, but that this ftupendious Succefs was much more Owing to the *Hand of God*, than to any Concurrence of natural Caufes. As, for Example, it was not humanly poffible, that *three thoufand Men*, fhould by hearing a plain and fhort Difcourfe utter'd by an *obfcure Perfon*, be in a Moment prevail'd upon to embrace a Religion unheard of before, and the moft feemingly contrary to Reafon; unlefs a Supernatural Power had come in to his Affiftance, and given a Strength to his Words above all the Force, that human Eloquence was ever capable of: yet the Fact is recorded by one, who had it from thofe, that were Eye-witneffes of it. Neither was it morally fpeaking poffible, that a World drown'd in *Senfuality* and *Idolatrous Superftitions*, fhould be perfuaded to renounce both the one and the other by the Preaching of a few Men deftitute of all worldly Advantages, unlefs *Almighty God* had efpoufed the Religion they
preach'd

preach'd as his own Cause, and given a powerful Blessing to their Apostolical Labours: So that it is manifest, that the Doctrine they taught came from Heaven, and had the divine Approbation stamp'd upon it in the clearest Characters.

As the Number of the Faithful encreased, the Apostles took Care to provide them with a proportionable Supply of *Pastors*, who being likewise vested with a Power of Ordaining others, might by a kind of *Spiritual Generation* preserve the Succession of the *Prelatick* and *Priestly Order*; by which alone the *Church of Christ* was to be govern'd in all Ages. But the perpetuating of the *Priesthood* of *Christ* was not their only Concern: That of Perpetuating his *sacred Doctrine* was of no less Importance. They therefore spared no Pains to instruct throughly those, they had ordain'd, in all the *holy Mysteries* of *Christian Religion*, and carefully deposited with them all the *Sacred Truths*, which God had *reveal'd* unto them; that they might thereby be enabled to communicate them to their Successors, and they again transmit them to theirs; in Order to have them securely convey'd down from Pastor to Pastor, in all succeeding Ages.

In this Manner were the Foundations of the *Church of Christ* fully perfected, and the superstructure itself considerably advanced by the *Apostles* themselves. And since they follow'd faithfully in all Things the Directions of their *heavenly Master*, 'tis plain that whether we consider it's Origine, it's Establishment and Constitution, or the Sacredness of it's Laws and Doctrine, every Thing in it is wholly *Divine*, and savours nothing of *human Invention*.

This

This Church has ever since it's Establishment, been the *Nursery* of innumerable eminent Saints of both Sexes, and of all Ages and Conditions; the *Sanctuary* of repenting Sinners, the *School* of Learning, and the *faithful Depository* of all the *sacred Mysteries* of saving Faith.

This Church has by the Lustre of her *Miracles*, the *exemplary Holiness* of her Children, the *Decency* and *Majesty* of her *publick Worship*, and the *Purity* of her *Morals*, subdued the greatest Monarchs upon Earth, and extended her Conquests even beyond the farthest Bounds of the *Roman Empire*.

Finally, this Church has now already had a *visible Being* for the space of almost seventeen hundred Years; and can shew *in her own Communion*, an uninterrupted Succession of *Bishops* and *Pastors* from the *Apostles*, down to this very Time; in spite of all the *Powers of Darkness*, that have from Time to Time combined together to destroy it. Nay for the first three hundred Years she stood her Ground not only against the unwearied Malice of the *Jews*, but against the whole Power of the *Pagan Emperors* of *Rome*: And the large Effusion of Christian Blood during the ten general Persecutions, instead of weakening *Christianity*, only gave it a greater Lustre in the glorious Triumphs of it's *Martyrs*, whose invincible Courage and Constancy, amidst the most cruel Torments, not only drew upon them the Admiration of *Heathens* themselves, but converted many Thousands of them to the *Faith of Christ*. So that the powerful Hand of God appear'd visibly in Turning the very Means intended for the utter Ruin of the *Church*, into an Occasion of it's greater Encrease.

Now all these Considerations put together prove invincibly that the *Church of Christ*, tho' consider'd barely as such, that is, without any Regard to the *repeated Promises* of *Infallibility* made to her, is the most *illustrious Body*, or *Society of Men* upon Earth: And that her *Testimony* in *religious Matters* has a *Weight* and *Authority* which cannot be equal'd by any other, that is purely *human*. For what is properly the *Testimony* of the *Church of Christ*? 'Tis the *Testimony* of a *standing visible Body*, or *Society of Men*, whereof *Christ* himself is the *Supreme invisible Head*, and which he has entrusted with all the *sacred Mysteries* of saving Faith. It is the *Testimony of Millions* in every Age since it's Establishment; who therefore could not possibly combine together to deceive one another even in any Matter of Importance, much less to cheat one another into a *Religion* directly opposite to all the Inclinations of Nature, which promised indeed inestimable Rewards in the Life to come, but proposed nothing but *Crosses*, *Self-denials*, and *Persecutions* in this World. It is the *Testimony* not of a *Rabble* considerable only for it's Numbers, but of the *Wisest*, the *Greatest*, the *most Learned*, and *Best* of Men in all Ages, and in all Nations of the Universe. A *Testimony* confirm'd by Thousands of uncontestable *Miracles*, and seal'd with the Blood of many thousand illustrious *Martyrs*. Finally a *Testimony*, which was not extorted by *Violence* or *Force of Arms*, but which all came into by a *free* and *voluntary Consent*, and upon a full Conviction of Conscience, that the Doctrine preach'd to them was the *Word of eternal Life*.

It being therefore manifest, that the *Testimony* of the *Church of Christ*, tho' consider'd barely as an *illustrious Society*, has in all Religious Matters a
Weight

Weight and *Authority*, which cannot be equal'd by any other, that is purely *human*, it follows, that it gives us the *greatest moral Evidence* or *Certainty*, we can possibly have of the Truth of any *doctrinal Point* attested by her; and that, by Consequence, our Belief even of the darkest and sublimest Mysteries, declared by her to be *reveal'd Truths*, is perfectly *rational:* Because nothing can be more *rational*, than to believe a Thing, of the Truth whereof we have the *greatest moral Evidence* or Certainty possible. Nay if this be not rational, we might rationally doubt even of the best attested historical Facts, and believe nothing, but what we are sure we see with our own Eyes: Which is most highly absurd.

Now 'tis upon the *Authority* of this Testimony of the *Church of Christ*, that we receive *Scriptures* and *Apostolical Traditions* as the *written* and *unwritten Word of God:* Which therefore we regard as an *infallible* and *compleat Rule* of Christian Faith: So that whatever we believe upon their *Authority*, whether jointly or separately, we believe upon the *Testimony* of God himself; which alone is the *proper* and *essential Motive* of that *divine Faith*, by Means whereof we have not barely a *moral*, but *an infallible Certainty* of the Truth of every Thing, we believe upon *that Testimony*.

Hence it is (as I have before observed to you) that our Faith is both *Divine* and *rational*. It is *Divine* in being built upon the *Testimony of God* as it's only *proper* and *essential Motive*; and it is *rational* in relying upon the *Church's Authority*, for the Conveyance of the *divine Testimony* truly and credibly to us. For how should we know, what Truths God has effectually *reveal'd*, what not, but from the Testimony of *that Church*, which the *Apostles* themselves entrusted with all the Sacred Mysteries

reveal'd

reveal'd to them? And so, altho' our *Faith*, which *comes by Hearing*, depends indeed upon the *Testimony of Men* as a *necessary Condition* for the secure Conveyance of those Mysteries to us, that Testimony is no Part of the *essential Motive* of our Belief of them; which relies wholly and solely upon the *Word of God*, whether *written* or *unwriten*. In a Word, the Church informs us what Truths God has *reveal'd*, and we believe them purely *because he has reveal'd them*.

'Tis upon this solid Foundation, that our Belief of the Church's *Infallibility* is grounded, to wit, the *infallible Promises of God* recorded in *holy Writ*: By which we are assured, that *The Spirit of Truth shall abide with his Church for ever*, and *lead her into all Truth*: And that therefore *the Gates of Hell shall never prevail against her*. This renders the *Church of Christ* not only a *safe* but *infallible Guide* in all Matters appertaining to Salvation. This renders her incapable of misleading us into Errors destructive to the *saving Faith once deliver'd to the Saints*: That is, to the Faith *reveal'd* to the Apostles, and by them deposited as a *sacred Trust* with their Successors. This finally renders her incapable either of demanding of her Children any *Terms of Communion*, which are displeasing to God, or of imposing on them any Doctrines for *reveal'd Truths*, but what were at first deliver'd for such by the *Apostles* themselves either in *Writing*, or by *Word of Mouth*; as has been fully shew'd.

Thus has the divine Goodness provided both an *infallible Rule*, to wit, his own *sacred Word*, and an *infallible Guide*, to wit, his *holy Church* for the Security of the *Catholick Faith*. An *infallible Rule*, to be the Measure and Standard of *reveal'd Truth*; and an *infallible Guide*, to explain the true meaning of it. And must not they then be very fond
of

of going astray, who pretending to follow the *Rule*, destroy it in Effect, by abandoning the *Guide*, whom God has appointed to be the *infallible Interpreter* of it? Nay, tho' Christ had made no Promise to his Church of a *perpetual Infallibility*, nothing but a Presumption to a Degree of Madness, could prompt a Man to oppose his *private Judgment* to the *solemn Decisions* of such an *illustrious Body* or Society of Men, as the *Church of Christ* would nevertheless have been. But not to acquiesce to her definitive Sentence, after all the *divine Promises* made to her of a *perpetual Protection* and *Assistance*, is not only the Hight of Madness, but of Impiety, and a barefaced Contempt of God himself.

G. Sir, you have given me a full and clear Idea of the *Authority* of the *Church of Christ*, whether consider'd as an *illustrious Society*, or as she is *the Pillar and Support of the Truth* by Virtue of the Promises of a *perpetual Infallibility* made to her. You have likewise fully convinced me, that *Scriptures*, tho' *infallible* in themselves, cannot be a *Rule of Faith* in any obscure or controverted Point, unless *this Church* be our *Guide*, and *Interpreter* of the true meaning of them. But since there are a great Number of Churches, all differing from one another, and all pretending to be the *true Church of Christ*, how is this Church to be found? Or by what distinguishing Marks must I know her?

P. A full Answer to this Question, will require more Time than we have at Present. So let us leave it to some other Meeting.

G. With all my Heart: For I desire to be throughly satisfied in it.

The End of the first Dialogue.

THE
Second DIALOGUE.

CONTAINING,

A brief historical Account of the Conversion of the Britons *and* Saxons; *with* Proofs *of their Agreement in* Faith, *and some Remarks upon Circumstances relating to the Conversion of the* Saxons.

SECT. I.

The Importance of Enquiring into the Marks *of the* true Church of Christ, *in which alone Salvation is proved to be possible.*

G. BEING already fully convinced (as I told you at our last Meeting) that I am bound to take the *Church of Christ* for my *Guide*, in all Matters, wherein Religion is concern'd, I desire now to be inform'd, by what Means this Church may be securely found amidst the great Number of Churches, which tho' all differing from one another, pretend all to be the *true Church of Christ*. For unless this Point be made clear to me, I may as easily

be

be mistaken in the Choice of my Religion, as Travellers in an unknown Country often are in the Choice of their Road, when there is no Mark set up to direct them. But pray, Sir, is not every particular *Christian Church* a Part of the *true Church of Christ*?

P. Sir, every *particular Christian Church*, in what Part soever of the World it be, if it be united in *Communion* with the *Catholick Church*, is a Part of the *true Church of Christ*: But if it be separated by *Heresy* or *Schism* from the *Communion* of the *Catholick Church*, it is no Part of the *true Church of Christ*.

G. You make then a large Difference between *Catholick* and *Christian*.

P. I do so. For tho' all *Catholicks* are *Christians*, all *Christians* are not *Catholicks*: Because there are *Heretical* and *Schismatical*, as well as *Catholick Christians*. And the *Creed* do's not say, *I believe the Christian*, but *I believe the holy Catholic Church*.

But as to the Thing, you are in search of, and desire to be satisfied in, it leads us directly to the Examination of a Point of the greatest Importance; to wit, how the *true Church of Christ* may be found? And by what *distinguishing Marks* you may know her, in Order to make a right Choice of the Religion you are to live and die in? This, Sir, is an Enquiry truly becoming a *Christian*, what State or Condition soever the divine Providence has placed him in. Many take a great Deal of Pains to fill their Heads with vain Curiosities and Speculations, which are of no Consequence, whether they be true or false. Others make it their whole Study to improve their Fortune in this World, and let the other take it's Chance, as if it were a Trifle beneath their Concern. But, alas, what will it avail a Man to be at his Ease during the short Course of this Life, to be advanced to Honours, or wallow in Riches, if after all he loses his Soul?

Now every Man's eternal Happiness or Misery has so close a Connection with the Choice he makes of his Religion, that as on the one Hand, he puts himself most certainly into the true Way to Salvation, if he makes a right Choice: So on the other it is no less certain, that he enters into the high Road to Perdition, if either *Sloth*, *Indifference*, or *Interest* prevails upon him to make a wrong one. He may indeed have *Wealth* and *Grandeur*, he may have *Liberty* and *Ease*, and in a Word he may have every Thing but *Salvation* out of the *true Church of Christ*.

St. *Augustin* is positive in this Matter. For writing to *Donatus* Epist. 204. he addresses himself to him, in the following Words. *Being out of the Pale of the Church thou wouldst not escape Damnation, tho' thou shouldst be burnt alive for Confessing the Name of Christ*. And he is seconded by St. *Fulgentius*, saying, *neither Baptism nor liberal Alms, nor Death itself can avail a Man any Thing in Order to Salvation, if he do's not hold the Unity of the Catholick Church*. C. 39. ad *Petrum Damianum*. And both these Fathers have but copied after their Predecessor St. *Cyprian*, who in his Treatise of *the Unity of the Church* declares, that *whoever, leaving the Church, cleaves to an Adulteress, is cut off from having any share in the Promises made to the Church*. And again, *If it was possible for any to escape that were not in the Ark of* Noah, *it will likewise be possible for Him to escape, who is not in the Church*. And this was the constant and uniform Doctrine of the ancient Fathers, when they wrote against the *Hereticks* and *Schismaticks* of their Times.

G. It seems then that these ancient Fathers differ'd very much in their Judgment from many of
our

our *modern Proteſtants*, who value themſelves highly for their *extenſive Charity* in allowing a Poſſibility of Salvation to all *Chriſtians*, whatever *Church* or *Communion* they are of, ſo they lead but moral Lives, and wrong no Body.

P. Nay ſome (as Mr. *Leſly* by Name) extends this their pretended Charity even to *Heathens* and *Mahometans*; who, according to that Author, may be ſaved by an *uncovenanted Mercy*. But St. *Paul*, from whom the ancient Fathers ſuck'd their Doctrine, was an utter Stranger to it. For he lays his Curſe even upon an *Angel* from Heaven, *if he ſhould preach any other Goſpel*, or Faith, *than that which he himſelf had preach'd*. Gal. 1. v. 8.

The ſame Apoſtle tells us, that as we are call'd to *one Hope*, *one Lord*, and *one Baptiſm*, ſo to One Faith, Eph. 4. v. 4. and he aſſures us likewiſe, that *without Faith it is impoſſible to pleaſe God*. Heb. 11. v. 6. Now theſe two Texts join'd together make up a demonſtrative Proof that there is but *one Church* or *Communion*, in which Salvation is poſſible. For if there be but *one Faith* (and who can doubt it?) It follows, that amongſt the many Churches, which all teach *different Faiths*, there can be but *one*, which teaches the *Faith*, St. *Paul* ſpeaks of, which is undoubtedly the *true one*. And ſince the *true Faith* can only be found in the *true Church of Chriſt*, and we are aſſured by the ſame Apoſtle, that *without this Faith it is impoſſible to pleaſe God*, the Conſequence is, that unleſs we be Members of this Church, we cannot be pleaſing to him. And can Salvation be poſſible to thoſe, who live and die in a State, wherein they are *diſpleaſing to God*?

But I cannot here forbear reciting, the excellent Words of Dr. *Pearſon* upon this Subject. " We " read, ſays he, that at the firſt *the Lord added* " *to the Church daily ſuch as ſhould be ſaved*. Act. 2 v. 47.

The Importance of enquiring

"v. 47. and what was then daily done, has been done since continually. CHRIST NEVER APPOINTED TWO WAYS TO HEAVEN; NOR DID HE BUILD A CHURCH TO SAVE SOME, AND MAKE ANOTHER INSTITUTION FOR OTHER MEN'S SALVATION. *There is no other Name under Heaven given among Men, whereby we must be saved, but the Name of Jesus.* Act. 4. 12. AND THAT NAME IS NO OTHERWISE GIVEN UNDER HEAVEN THAN IN THE CHURCH. As none were saved from the Deluge, but such as were in the *Ark of Noah* framed for their Reception by the Hand of God: As none of the *first-born* of *Egypt* lived but such as were within those Habitations, whose Door-posts were sprinkled with Blood by the Appointment of God for their Preservation: As none of the Inhabitants of *Jerico* could escape the Fire and Sword, but such as were within the House of *Rahab*, for whose Protection a Covenant was made, *so none shall ever escape the eternal Wrath of God, who belong not to the Church of God.* p. 349. 350."

All this is perfectly conformable to the Sense of *Scriptures* and *Apostolical Tradition*.

G. Surely this learned *Protestant Bishop* had a full Conviction of Conscience, that he was a Member of the *true Church of Christ*, when he wrote this Piece. For 'tis plain on the one Hand, that he was no *Latitudinarian* by Principle, like the Gentleman you mention'd just now: And we cannot reasonably suppose on the other, that being fully convinced in his Judgment of the *Impossibility* of *Salvation* out of the true *Church of Christ*, he would under this Conviction continue a Member of the *Church of England*, unless he judg'd at the same Time, that the *Church of England* was a Part of the *true Church of Christ*.

P. Sir,

P. Sir, as to the real Conviction of his Confcience, we muſt leave that to the *great Searcher of Hearts.* But this we are ſure of, that an *erroneous Conſcience* may eaſily be form'd, when it is under the Direction of any wordly *Intereſt* or *Paſſion* prevailing in the Soul. We are likewiſe very ſure, that the powerful Charms of *Liberty* and *Eaſe*, have lull'd the Conſciences of many Thouſands ſo faſt aſleep, that they never awaked till Death open'd their Eyes, and put it out of their Power to deceive themſelves any longer. Nor do we want Examples of thoſe, whoſe *Hearts* reſiſt, when their *Judgments* are ſubdued ; as the humble St. *Auguſtin* accuſes himſelf in his *Confeſſions* : Where he frankly owns, that his Will rebell'd ſeveral Years after his Underſtanding was fully convinced of the Truth of the *Catholick Religion.* And who will be a Voucher for the *learned Proteſtant Biſhop* we ſpeak of, that he was above this Weakneſs ? The honourable Character of a *Biſhop*, is not exchanged without great Reluctance for an obſcure Station, attended with Reproach and Contempt : And the Revenues annex'd to it are a moſt powerful Perſuaſive againſt *Popery*, on this Side of the Seas, where the *Biſhop's Lady* with her dear Children taſte the ſweets of the eaſy income of her *Spiritual Lord*, and employs her beſt Rhetorick to convince his Lordſhip, that *State* and *Plenty* are much prettier and convenienter Things than *Evangelical Poverty.* Which alone ſuffices to to ſtifle the beſt Thoughts, and render the beſt Diſpoſitions towards a Change ineffectual.

But let that be as it will, you plainly See of what Importance it is not to make a falſe Step in the Choice of our Religion ; Becauſe there is but *one*, wherein our eternal Welfare can be ſecured ; as there was but *one Ark* to ſave any Man from periſhing in the Flood. Whoever neglected to enter into it was loft; And whoever neglects to enter into the *true Church*, will perish eternally: As has been fully proved.

It behoves us therefore, as we tender the eternal Welfare of our Souls, to examine with the utmost Diligence and Impartiality, where this *one Church* is to be found. That is, by *what Marks* we may clearly know her, and distinguish her from all others; to the End, *first*, that they who see those Marks in the Church, whereof they are already Members, may be fully assured that they are in the *right Way*, and may enjoy this Blessing, bestow'd upon them by the special Providence of God, not only with a due Sense of Gratitude, but also with an entire Security and Repose of Mind: And 2*dly*, that they who find none of these Marks in the Church, into which they have been misled either by *wilful Neglect*, or by the Misfortunes of *Education*, may be convinced that they are in a *wrong Way*; and upon this Conviction endeavour to find out that *one true Church*, in which those Marks are manifestly apparent.

SECT. 2.

Neither Education *nor* Interest *are to be consulted in the Choice of our Religion.*

G. I Perceive then, that a Person's having been educated in this or that Religion, is not a solid Motive for his continuing in it.

P. Nothing is more certain than that it is not. Because whoever acts upon a solid Motive acts prudently: And so if Education were a solid Motive for any Man's continuing in this or that Religion, the greatest Part of the World, as *Pagans, Jews, Mahometans, Socinians, Quakers,* and in a Word all *Hereticks,* and *Schifmaticks* brought up in their respective

spective Ways, would act prudently in continuing their whole Lives in a State of eternal Damnation. For all these have *Education* to plead for them, and may say, *I have received my Religion from my Parents, who ventured their Souls upon that Bottom. Therefore I ought to sit down satisfied with it, and not be running about in Search of I know not what.* But this is as irrational, as if any one should argue thus: *I have got the Leprosy or King's Evil of my Parents: Therefore I ought to rest content with it, and not give myself the trouble of seeking after Remedies for my Cure.*

G. But is it not rational to say, *I have been brought up in the true Faith; Therefore I ought to persevere in it?*

P. It cannot be doubted, but that whoever has been brought up in the *true Faith*, is bound to persevere in it. But then he ought to have some better Motive than that of *Education* to convince him, that the Faith he has been brought up in is the *true one*. For if he has little or nothing more to say for his Religion, than that he has been educated in it; this is so weak a Foundation to build upon, that the very first violent Storm of Persecution may suffice to make him stagger in his Faith, and incline him to believe, that his Education has been his Misfortune rather than a Blessing; and that the best Religion is that, in which there is some Prospect of Gain, and no Danger of losing: Because good Sense alone will tell him, that Education is of itself no Argument either for or against the Truth: And if at the same Time, he be ignorant of the *true* and *solid Grounds* of his Religion, he will be strongly tempted to choose that, in which his temporal Interest will be best secur'd.

G. Yet

G. Yet all this notwithstanding we find by Experience, that the Generality of Mankind, take up their Religion just according to their Education: And it is very probable, that if you and I had been brought up *Socinians* or *Quakers*, we might have been as zealous in that Way, as the most zealous amongst them.

P. That's very certain. And therefore we have Reason to bless God for not having permitted us to be of that Number. For since *Christ* has positively pronounced, that *he who believeth not, shall be condemn'd*, Mark 16. v. 16. we may easily guess, what Fate would have attended both you and me, in Case we had been brought up *Socinians* or *Quakers*, and continued so to the End of our Lives. For I do not find that Christ made any Exception in Favour of the Case of *Education*: Which therefore will not excuse any of those, who being come to the perfect Use of Reason, and render'd capable of Examining the true Grounds of *reveal'd Religion*, choose to go on blindfold in their Errors, rather than give themselves the Trouble of a diligent Enquiry into the Truth.

G. However there are many, who appear very solicitous and sincere in their Search after the Truth, and profess a Readiness to embrace it, if they were convinced of their being in a wrong Way; Yet for all that never make a Discovery of the *hidden Treasure*, they seek after.

P. But is their Desire to find the Truth as hearty and sincere, as what we usually observe in those, who are in search of some valuable *worldly Treasure?* Have they no Interest at Heart, inconsistent with that of embracing the Truth? Are they ready to imitate the couragious Virtue of *Tobie*, who when all flock'd to the *golden Calves* set up by *Jeroboam*, separated himself from the *Communion* of his Fellow-low-Citizens, and went up alone to the *Temple at Jerusalem* to make his Offerings there to God, according to the Law of *Moses*? Tob. 1. v. 5. 6. where these Marks of a true Zeal appear, it cannot be question'd but the Heart is sincere. But as long as Persons, tho' dissatisfied in their Minds, go on in their accustomed Conformity to the *Religion a la mode*, and are afraid either to read proper Books, or apply themselves to proper Persons for their full Instruction, we may say of them without the least Danger of rash Judgment, that the *golden Calves* of *Liberty* and *Interest*, have the prevailing Power over their Hearts, notwithstanding the shew they make from Time to Time, of some Inclinations towards the Truth, which they are but too apt to mistake for *sincere Desires*; And so flatter themselves into a Persuasion, that if they be in a *wrong Way*, it is their Misfortune, but not their Fault, because they know no better: Whereas if they call'd their own Hearts to an impartial Account, they would find that the *Love of Ease*, the *Solicitudes of this Life*, the Fear of incurring the *Censure* or *Displeasure* of Friends, or falling under the Lash of *persecuting Laws*, are the real Obstacles to their finding and embracing the Truth. For it has been found unquestionably true both from the Nature of the Thing and from long Experience, that whoever has any *Interest* nearer to his Heart, than that of *Saving his Soul*, will upon all Occasions, when either the one or the other must be sacrificed, strike in with that Religion, whether *right* or *wrong*, which suits best with his temporal Interest.

G. I find at least that *Interest* and *Truth*, are not utterly irreconcilable, but that a Man may consult his *temporal Interest*, without Betraying his Conscience.

P. It

P. It would be a Madneſs to diſpute it: For otherwiſe a Man would be damn'd for Profeſſing the *true Religion* in a Country, where it has the *Law* on it's Side. What therefore I aſſert is this; that no Man ought to conform to, or choſe any Religion, meerly becauſe *it has the Law on it's Side.* That is to ſay, that neither *Intereſt* nor *Education,* but barely the *Force of Truth,* ought to be conſulted by him as a Motive to determine him in the Choice of the Religion, he intends to live and die in: That therefore he muſt not conſider, whether the Church he is, or intends to be a Member of, be the *prevailing Church* of the Country where he lives, or has been born: Nor whether it be moſt favourable to his *Liberty* and *Eaſe:* Nor finallly, whether it be the Church, in which he is moſt like to make his *Fortune*; But his whole Examination ought to be of this one ſingle Point, whether it has all the *neceſſary* and *eſſential Marks* of the *true Church of Chriſt,* in which alone Salvation is to be found, as has been fully proved.

G. I muſt own, Sir, this is as ſure and eaſy a Method to direct us to the *true Church,* as a Pillar ſet up on Purpoſe to ſhew the Road to any Place, is to direct Travellers to find their Way to it. I therefore deſire you to let me know, what thoſe *Marks* are.

P. I preſume Sir, you ſtand in no need to be convinced, that the Way you are in is preferable to that of *Jews, Turks, Pagans, Deiſts, Socinians, Quakers,* and ſuch others, who cannot even ſtile themſelves *Chriſtians*.

G. No Sir, the Point I deſire to be ſatisfied in, lies in a much narrower Compaſs, and only regards the *Church of* Rome, on the one Hand, and the *Church of* England, on the other. For ſince all the *reform'd Churches* ground their Separation,

from

Interest are to be consulted &c.   77

from the *Church of* Rome, upon the same specious Pretence, to wit, the supposed *gross Errors* and *unwarrantable Practices* of that Church; If you can fully convince me, that all the Marks of the *true Church of Christ* belong so wholly and solely to the *Church of* Rome, that they cannot with any Appearance of Truth, be appropriated to the *Church of England*, nor by Consequence to any other of the *reform'd Churches*, as being all upon the same Bottom, I shall then venture to maintain boldly, that it is not my having been brought up a *Roman Catholick*, but the clear Evidence and invincible Force of Truth, that keeps me stedfast in the *Roman Catholick Church*. The Reason is clear, because a Man must be either destitute of common Sence, or void of all Concern for his Soul's Salvation, if he do's not choose preferably to any other Communion that Church, which alone has *all the Marks* of it's being the *true Church of Christ* on it's Side. For where is *true Faith* to be found but in the *true Church*? And how is the *true Church* to be found but by the *Marks*, which distinguish her from all other Churches?

P. What you say, Sir, is unanswerable. Nay if *true Faith* is not to be found in the *true Church of Christ*, we must give the Lie *first* to St. *Paul*, who calls it *the Pillar and Support of the Truth*. 1. Tim. 3. v. 15. 2*dly*, to the *Creed*, which declares the *Church of Christ* to be *holy*, and the *Communion of Saints*. And 3*dly*, to *Jesus Christ* himself, who has solemnly promised that *the Gates of Hell shall not prevail against it*. Math. 16, v. 18. That *the Spirit of Truth shall guide it into all Truth*. Joh. 16. v. 13: And that *he will be with it always even unto the End of the World*. Math. 28. v. 20.

This then is the Church we are bound to seek after, to wit, the *true Church of Christ*. And since
there

there is no other Way poſſible to ſucceed in this Enquiry, than by a diligent Examination of the *neceſſary* and *eſſential Marks*, by which this Church may be diſtinguiſh'd from all others, the whole Iſſue of the Controverſy between us and *Proteſtants* relating to this Subject, depends upon the Deciſion of this one Queſtion, to wit, *on what Side theſe Marks appear*? That is, whether on the *Roman Catholick* or *Proteſtant* Side? If any of the *reform'd Churches* (as for example the *reform'd Church of England*, which according to your Propoſal, I ſhall ſingle out for Brevity's Sake, and to avoid Confuſion) if, I ſay, the *reform'd Church of England*, can effectually prove, that ſhe has on her Side the *neceſſary* and *eſſential Marks* of that *Apoſtolical Church*, which *Chriſt* eſtabliſh'd upon Earth, and to which he made the *Promiſes* of a *perpetual Aſſiſtance*, I will then own her to be a part of the *true Church of Chriſt*. But if on the contrary I make it appear manifeſtly, that they belong entirely to the *Church in Communion with the See of Rome*, excluſively of all the *reform'd Churches*; Then the *Church of England* muſt own, that ſhe is engaged in a defenſeleſs Cauſe, and can have no Title to the *Promiſes*, till ſhe returns to her old *Mother-Church*, whereof ſhe was a Part for the Space of no leſs than *nine hundred Years*.

'Tis this I ſhall now endeavour to make out. But becauſe the clearing of this Matter has a great Connection with the Hiſtory, both of the firſt *Eſtabliſhment* of *Chriſtianity* in this Iſland on the one Hand, and of the *pretended Engliſh Reformation* on the other; It will be neceſſary to bring you throughly acquainted with the moſt material *Facts* and *Circumſtances*, relating to the one as well as to the other. And indeed there needs nothing more than a plain and impartial View of them

to

to render you capable of forming a solid Judgment, *first*, whether the *Conversion* or *Reformation of England* was properly *the Work of God*; For he could not be the Author of both. And 2*dly*, Whether the *essential external Marks* of the *true Church of Christ*, to wit, her *perpetual Visibility*, her *uninterrupted Succession* of *Bishops* and *Pastors* in *the same Communion* from the *Apostles* down to this Time, and her *Catholicity* or *Universality* both of *Time* and *Place*, are applicable to the *reform'd Church of England*, or to the Churches *in Communion* with the *See of Rome*. That is, whether they be on the *Protestant* or *Roman Catholick* Side.

G. You know, Sir, I have always been a Lover of History. And therefore, since the historical Account you have promised me, will be so conducible to my forming a true Judgment of the two important Points mention'd by you, I shall listen to you with the greatest Attention.

SECT. 3.

Of the first entrance of Christianity *into* Britain: *It's Progress and Establishment there, in the Reign of King* Lucius.

P. ALL Ecclesiastical Historians mention two *general Conversions* of this Island. The *first* under Pope *Eleutherius*, towards the end of the second Century, and the other under Pope *Gregory the Great*, about the end of the sixth, or Beginning of the seventh; Tho' there were several particular Conversions of a much earlier Date. For it cannot be question'd, but that several Persons professing the *Christian Faith* came over into *Britain*, not only in the *Apostolick Age*, but even soon after the first Preaching of the Gospel, which

by

The first general or publick by the indefatigable Zeal of the Apostles, was in the Space of a very few Years, carried into all the chief Parts of the known World. *Rom.* 1. v. 8. as I have already told you.

Our blessed Saviour was pleased to suffer Death, in the 18th Year of *Tiberius*, who succeeded *Augustus* in the Government of the *Roman Empire*. *Tiberius* lived but 5 Years after, and his Successor *Caligula* reign'd but 4 Years in all, and was succeeded by *Claudius*; In the second Year of whose Reign, that is eleven Years after the *Ascension* of *Christ*, St. *Peter* came to *Rome*, and there fix'd his Episcopal Seat according to *Eusebius*, who writes thus of him. " *Peter* the Apostle of the Country " of *Galilee*, the *first chief Bishop* of Christians, " after he had founded the Church of *Antioch*, " went to *Rome*; and having there preach'd the " Gospel, remain'd Bishop of that City for 25 " Years together. *Eus: in Chron. An. Christi* 44."

The very next Year after St. *Peter's* coming to *Rome*, the War between the *Britons* and *Romans*, broke out into such a violent Flame, that the Emperor *Claudius* resolved to go over in Person into *Britain*, as he did effectually. And 'tis very probable that several Christians accompanied him in that Expedition; Because the Gospel had then been preach'd for full 12 Years, and great Numbers converted to the Faith of Christ. So that we may date the first Entrance of *Christianity* into this Island from that Time: Tho' the Number of the Faithful in it was but small, and made an inconsiderable Figure in the Eyes of the World. But this War continuing for the Space of 40 Years together, that is, to the 4th Year of *Domitian*, when the whole Country was subdued, and reduced into the Form of a *Roman Province*, it appears very reasonable to conjecture, that during these

long

Wars, as the Number of Christians encreased daily at *Rome*, by the continual Preaching of St. *Peter*, and his immediate Successors, as likewise of his Fellow-Apostle St. *Paul*, who was there with him for several Years; So it encreased amongst the *Britons* in Proportion by the frequent Intercourse of Persons going to, and coming from *Rome*, occasion'd by those Wars.

The Reason is plain, because *Rome* being then the *Metropolis* of the whole Empire, and the most beautiful and magnificent City in the World, 'tis probable that many *Britons* went thither partly for Pleasure, or to satisfy their Curiosity, and partly to avoid being personally involved in the Calamities of a bloody War: Or at least to keep at a Distance, from the melancholy Sight of the utter Ruin and Desolation of their Native Country. Besides that there were then at *Rome* several *Britons* kept there as Hostages, and great Numbers of Prisoners were also sent thither: As amongst others King *Caractacus*, who together with many of the Nobility was, as *Tacitus* relates, sent Prisoner to *Rome*, in the eleventh Year of *Claudius*, by *Ostorius*, the then *Roman* General, or Governour in *Britain*.

Now 'tis not improbable, that many of these *Britons* residing for several Years at *Rome* (where the Gospel was very much propagated towards the latter End of *Claudius*'s Reign, as appears from St. *Paul*'s Epistle to the *Romans*, address'd about that Time to the converted *Jews* and *Gentils* of that populous City) 'tis not improbable, I say, that many of these *Britons* were of the happy Number of the *converted Gentils*, and when they return'd back to their own Country, as they believed the Christian Doctrine themselves, so they became the

82 Dial. 2. §. 3. *The first general or publick*
providential Instruments of the Conversion of
others.

Add to this that many grave Authors, whose Testimony is not to be despised, assert positively, that at the same Time when all *Jews* were by an Edict of the Emperor *Claudius* banish'd from *Rome*, St. *Peter* amongst others, being a Native of *Galilee*, retired for some Time in Obedience to the Emperor's Edict, and took that occasion to pass over to this Island, where, according to these Authors, he became the first *Ecclesiastical Planter* of the *Christian Faith*. It is likewise credibly asserted, that *Aristobulus* an eminent *Roman* Convert mention'd by St. *Paul* Rom. 16. v. 10. was sent over into *Britain* by St. *Peter*, whose Disciple he was: As also that St. *Joseph of Arimathea* was directed thither by the same Apostle; or as others say, by St. *Philip*, with about 12 other Christians, and obtain'd there a Place in the Island call'd *Avallonia*, where *Glastenbury* was afterwards built, and where they spent the Remainder of their Days in continual Retirement and Prayer, and other penitential Exercises, *in Order to train themselves up to the Bearing of the Cross*, as *Cambden* expresses it.

But let this be as it will, For I lay no Stress, nor build any Argument upon these Facts, 'tis manifest, that the Seeds of Christianity were sown very early in this Island; Tho' as in other Countries, they were not ripen'd into a publick and total Conversion till many Years after. Nay *Rome* itself continued to be the great *Metropolis* of *heathen Idolatry* as well as of the Empire, and the declared Enemy to Christianity for near upon 300 Years after the first Preaching of the Apostles; tho' both St. *Peter* and St. *Paul* had for some Years labour'd for it's Conversion with an unwearied Patience

tience and Zeal; tho' it had been honour'd for those three Centuries by a Succession of Bishops, all eminent Saints and Martyrs, and tho' it was the very Fountain, whence all the Streams of the living Waters of the Gospel flow'd into allmost all the *Western* Parts of the World. So true it is, that the Works of *Grace* have their gradual Progress like those of *Nature*; and the *Christian Rome* was almost as long a Building, as the *Heathen Rome*, before it came to it's Hight and Splendor.

G. I conceive then that in the first Century, or *Apostolick* Age, there was not in *Britain* a Christian Church, regularly form'd under the Government of *Bishops* and *Subalternate Pastors*. Nor any publick or solemn Exercise of *Catholick Religion*, as there is now in all Countries, where the *Catholick Faith* is profess'd.

P. Very right, Sir: that Blessing was reserved for the latter end of the following Century, when *Lucius* King of the *Britons*, was himself converted to the Faith of Christ.

This *Lucius* was the Son of *Coilus* King of *Britain*, in the Reign of *Trajan*, and his Successor *Adrian* Emperors of *Rome*, to whom tho' the *British* Kings were become tributary by the Conquest of their Country, yet were they permitted to exercise regal Power in their Dominions. King *Coilus*, altho' there be not sufficient Grounds to assert positively, that he became himself a Christian, as some say, yet it is recorded by very authentick Historians, that being moved partly by the Relation he had of the stupendious Miracles, wrought every where by those, who had received the Faith, and their invincible Courage in suffering the most cruel Torments in Defence of it; and partly by the exemplary Lives of the Christian Preachers and Converts in his own Dominions, of which he was an Eye-witness, he was not only very much inclined to it himself, but even favour'd the Conversion of all such amongst his Subjects, as were desirous to embrace the Faith of Christ. So that it cannot with any Reason be question'd, but that he instill'd the same favourable Dispositions to Christianity into his Son *Lucius*; which by God's Grace he retain'd after his Accession to the Crown; and so gave all Encouragement possible to Evangelical Preachers, both foreign and domestick, to propagate the Gospel in his Dominions.

The chief amongst these was one *Timothy* the younger Son of *Pudens* a *Roman* Senator, and *Claudia* both mention'd by St. *Paul* 2 Tim. 4. v. 21. and converted by St. *Peter* at his first coming to *Rome*, where he had his usual Residence in their House, as likewise many of his holy Successors after him: Which together with their boundless Charity, and Hospitality to all distress'd Christians, drew so great a Blessing upon them, that both they and their four Children, *Novatus*, *Timothy*, *Pudentiana* and *Praxedes*, became all eminent Saints.

S. *Timothy* after having been fully instructed in all the principles of Christian Religion by such excellent Masters as were constantly harbour'd in his Father's House, was ordain'd Priest, and sent into *Britain*, where he preach'd for several Years, with so much Zeal and Fruit, that he converted great Numbers, not only of the common People, but of the Nobility also; and by disputing publickly with the *Heathen Priests* call'd *Druids*, brought several of them over to the Faith of Christ; Which some Years after facilitated very much the total Conversion of *Britain*. For many of these being Men of Learning, like the *Athenian Philosophers* brought up in *Heathen Schools*, were afterwards ordain'd *Bishops* or *Priests*, and became excellent Labourers in Christ's Vineyard.

But that which gave the finishing Stroke to this great Work, was the publick Conversion of the King himself. He had been well disposed even before his coming to the Crown, as I have already observed: And many Things concurr'd afterwards to cultivate this Disposition in him: As on the one Hand the inhuman and scandalous Practices of the *Druids*, who for their Insolence, Barbarity, and Lewdness were then become both odious and contemptible to the Generality of Mankind: And on the other the innocent and edifying Behaviour of Christians, the Purity of their Doctrine, and the prodigious Encrease of their Numbers in all Parts of the Empire, notwithstanding the repeated Sanguinary Edicts publish'd against them, and usually executed with the utmost Rigour. Add to this the persuasive Discourses of St. *Timothy* and other Apostolical Preachers, which convinced King *Lucius* so fully of the Cheat and Vanity of *heathen Idols*, and the solid Truth of the Christian Faith, that he resolved seriously, and promised to embrace it openly; tho' he did not judge it seasonable till some Years after to put this good Purpose effectually in Execution.

There were two main Obstacles, which tho' he was a Convert in his heart, kept him back for some Time from declaring himself in a publick Manner. *First*, the Opposition he was afraid of from his own People, which might occasion a general Disturbance or Revolution in his Kingdom; As Changes in Religion usually do. And 2*dly*, his Fear of incurring the Displeasure of the *Roman* Emperors, of whom he had a great Dependance in the

Dial. 2. §. 3. *The first general or publick*
Exercise of his regal Power. The *first*, was gradually removed by the Conversion of many of the Nobility, as likewise of several amongst the *Druids*; both which had great Influence upon the common People, and ripen'd them for an entire Change of Worship. The *Second* was some Time after through the merciful Disposition of Providence, removed by the Emperor himself then reigning; I mean, *Marcus Aurelius Antoninus*; who after the miraculous Deliverance of his Army from imminent Destruction by the Prayers of the Christians that served in it, became from a violent Persecutor their powerful Protector, and put forth an Edict, with positive Orders to have it sent into all the Provinces of the Empire, forbidding all his Subjects under pain of being burnt alive to prosecute any Christian on the Score of Religion.

As soon as this Edict was publish'd in *Britain*, King *Lucius*, having then both the Emperor and the general Inclinations of the People favourable to him, hesitated no longer to declare himself, and confess with his Mouth what he believed in his Heart. He therefore sent an Embassy to *Rome*, desiring St. *Eleutherius*, who then sat in St. *Peter's Chair*, to furnish him with Persons proper to accomplish the Work already so happily begun. I shall relate the Fact in the Words of *Hollingshead* a Protestant Historian.

"King *Lucius*, says he, sent unto *Eleutherius*
"Bishop of *Rome*, two learned Men of the *British* Nation, *Elvan* and *Wedwin*, requiring him to
"send some such Ministers, as might instruct him
"and his People in the true Faith more plenti-
"fully, and baptize them according to the Rules
"of Christian Religion. Hereupon were sent by
"the said *Eleutherius* two godly learned Men, the
"one

" one named *Fugatius*, and the other *Damianus*.
" Holins. *Hist. of England.* L. 4. C. 19."

Thefe two holy and learned Bifhops St. *Fugatius* and *Damianus*, who came over about the Year of *Chrift* 178 with full Powers from the *Apoftolick See*, being favour'd by a great part both of the Nobility and common People, and powerfully fupported by the regal Authority, exercifed all Apoftolical and Epifcopal Functions in this Land, preach'd and baptized, ordain'd Bifhops and Priefts, caufed the *heathen Idols* to be pull'd down every where, converted their prophane Temples into *Chriftian Churches*; and in a Word, God giving a plentiful Blefling to their pious Labours, in a few Years Time, that is, before the End of the Second Century, abolifh'd *Paganifm*, and brought at leaft that Part of the *Britifh Nation*, which was fubject to K. *Lucius* over to the *Chriftian Faith*.

G. But how long did it continue fo?

P. All agree that (allowing only for fome Errors of the *Pelagiam Herefy*, from which it was foon after purged by the preaching of St. *Germanus* and *Lupus* two *French* Bifhops) the Chriftian Faith was maintain'd in it till the *Saxon Conqueft*, when the *ancient Britons* being driven out of their own Country by thofe, whom they had unadvifedly call'd in to affift them againft the *Scots*, were forced to fly for Shelter into the mountainous Country of *Wales*, and other neighbouring Places; And frefh fwarms of *Saxons Idolators* pouring in continually into the Provinces they had abandon'd, tho' they themfelves perfevered, as I have already faid, in the Profeffion of the Faith they had received, almoft all that Part of *Great Britain*, which we now call *England*, became once more a Prey to *Paganifm*, and continued fo, till the latter End of the fixth Century; when by the Difpofitions of

Pro-

§. 4. *The second general* Providence, *which reaches strongly from End to End, and disposes all Things sweetly,* King *Ethelbert* together with his Kingdom of *Kent*, embraced the Gospel, preach'd to them by Persons sent thither for that End by the *Apostolick See*: And their Example was soon after follow'd by the other six Kingdoms of the *Heptarchy*, into which *England* was then divided by it's *Pagan* Conquerors the *Saxons*. And this is the *Second general Conversion* of *England*, for which it stands indebted next to God, to the Piety and Zeal of the *Bishop of Rome*. In Recompence whereof his *holy See* has since been distinguish'd here by the honourable Title of the *Whore of Babylon*, and his sacred Person by that of *Antichrist*.

SECT. 4.
Of the Conversion of the English Saxons *from* Paganism *to* Christianity.

G. BUT since that Part of *Great Britain*, which is now call'd *England*, (to distinguish it, as I suppose from *Scotland* and *Wales*) was by that general Inundation of the *Saxons*, once more almost entirely drown'd in *Paganism*, as you have told me, I must beg the Favour of you to inform me of the most material Particularities relating to it's *Second general Conversion*. As, who were the principal Undertakers of that difficult Task; and by what Means it was effected.

P. Sir, I will endeavour to make my Relation of it, as succinct as is possible. Pope *Gregory* the first of that Name, and most deservedly sirnamed *the Great*, in Regard of his great Abilities, his Holiness, his Learning, and unbounded Zeal for the Conversion of Souls, * as he happen'd one Day,
when

---
* Johan. Diacon. *vit. Greg.* L. 1. C. 21.

when he was yet a private Prieſt at *Rome*, to walk through the Market, where Slaves were expoſed to Sale, obſerved amongſt them ſome very beautiful Youths, both for the Fineneſs of their Complexion, and comelineſs of their Perſons: And having aſk'd the Merchant they belong'd to, what Country they were of? He was anſwer'd, they came from *Britain*, and that this Country was full of ſuch comely Perſons. Then he aſk'd whether theſe Iſlanders were *Chriſtians* or *Heathens?* And being told they were *Heathens*, he fetch'd a deep Sigh and ſaid, *It was a lamentable Conſideration, that the Prince of Darkneſs ſhould be Maſter of ſo much Beauty, and have ſo many graceful Perſons in his Poſſeſſion, and that ſo fine an Outſide ſhould have nothing of God's Grace to adorn it within.*

But not content with meer good Wiſhes or barren Deſires of their Converſion, he ſolicited Pope *Benedict* to ſend ſome able Miniſters, to preach the Goſpel to them. The Propoſal was not at all diſreliſh'd by the Pope, but the Difficulty was to find proper Perſons, that would undertake ſo hard a Task; and ſeveral having excuſed themſelves partly on Pretence of their own Diſabilities, and partly in Regard of the Savageneſs of the People they ſhould have to deal with, the Barbarity of their Language and Manners, and in a Word the Uncertainty of the Event, St. *Gregory* freely offer'd himſelf, and upon having his Requeſt granted, was already advanced two or three Days Journey from *Rome*, when the Pope was forced to recal him, to quiet the Commotions of the People loudly murmuring to be deprived of ſo excellent a Perſon,

Thus things remain'd till about 7 Years after, when *Benedict* and his Succeſſor *Pelagius* being Dead,

St. *Gregory*

Gregory was promoted to the *Chair of St. Peter*: And then it was that he resolved to execute that by the Ministry of others, which he had not been permitted by the Providence of God to perform in his own Person. It was in the 4th Year of his Pontificate, he began to put this Christian Design in Execution, and the principal Instrument he made choice of for so great a Work, was one *Augustin* a Monk of his own Monastery at *Rome*, whom he knew to be a Person of so extraordinary Merits, and with whom he associated several other Monks of the same Monastery. These in Obedience to his Command immediately set forward on their Journey to *Britain*; The particularities whereof I shall recite from *Bede's* Ecclesiastical History as *english'd* last Year by the worthy Mr. *Stevens*.

" Pope *Gregory* (says this venerable Author)
" being moved by divine Inspiration sent the Ser-
" vant of God *Augustin* and with him several other
" Monks fearing the Lord to preach the Word of
" God to the *English* Nation. They having in
" Obedience to the Pope's Commands undertaken
" that Work, and gone Part of their Way, being
" seiz'd with a slothful Fear, began to think of
" returning home rather than to proceed to a bar-
" barous, fierce and unbelieving Nation, to whose
" very Language they were Strangers: And this
" they unanimously agreed was the safest Course.
" In short, they sent back *Augustin*, (whom he
" (*the Pope*) had appointed to be consecrated Bi-
" shop, in Case they were received by the *English*)
" that he might by humble Entreaty obtain of the
" holy *Gregory*, that they should not be compell'd
" to undertake so dangerous, so toilsome and so un-
" certain a Journey."

Conversion of England.

The Pope finding his *Miſſioners* thus diſpirited, ſent *Auguſtin* back to them with a Letter to encourage them to proceed in their Journey, as alſo with another Letter to *Etherius* Archbiſhop of *Arles* to deſire him to give his Miſſioners a friendly Reception, and furniſh them with what Conveniences he could for their Journey. Both theſe Letters are to be ſeen in *Bede's Eccles. Hiſt.* L. 1. C. 23. 24. The ſame Author proceeds thus C 25.

"*Auguſtin* being ſtrengthen'd by the Confirma-
"tion of the bleſſed Father *Gregory*, return'd to
"the Work of the Word of God with the Ser-
"vants of Chriſt and arrived in *Britain*. *Ethel-*
"*bert* was at that Time the moſt potent King of
"*Kent*, who had extended his Dominions as far
"as the great River *Humber*, by which the *Sou-*
"*thern Saxons* are divided from the *Northern*.
"On the *Eaſt* Side of *Kent* is the Iſle of *Thanet*.
"——In this Iſland landed the Servant of our
"Lord *Auguſtin* and his Companions, being as is
"reported near 40 Men. They had by Order of the
"bleſſed Pope *Gregory* taken Interpreters of the Na-
"tion of *Franks* [whoſe Language differ'd but lit-
"tle from that of the *Saxons*.] By theſe *Auguſtin*
"ſending to *Ethelbert*, ſignified to him, *that he was*
"*come from* Rome, *and brought a joyful Meſſage, which*
"*moſt undoubtedly aſſured all, that took the Advan-*
"*tage of it, of everlaſting Joys in Heaven, and a*
"*Kingdom that would never End with the living and*
"*true God.* The King having heard this, order'd
"them to ſtay in the Iſland where they had lan-
"ded, and that they ſhould be furniſh'd with all
"Neceſſaries, till he ſhould conſider what to do
"with them. For he had heard before of the
"*Chriſtian Religion*, as having a *Chriſtian Wife* of
"the Royal Family of *France* call'd *Berta*; whom
"he had received from her Parents upon Conditi-
"on,

"on, that she should be permitted to practise her
"Religion with the Bishop *Luidhard* given her to
"preserve her Faith.

"Some Days after, the King came into the I-
"sland, and sitting in the open Air, order'd *Au-*
"*gustin* and his Companions to be brought into
"his Presence: For he had taken Precaution, that
"they should not come to him in any House, ac-
"cording to the ancient Superstition, least if they
"had any magical Spells, they might at their co-
"ming impose upon, and get the better of him. But
"they came arm'd with *divine Virtue*, not with
"diabolical Charms, bearing a *silver Cross* for
"their *Banner*, and the *Image* of *our Lord and Sa-*
"*viour* painted on a Board; and singing the *Li-*
"*tany* offer'd up their Prayers to the Lord for their
"own and the eternal Salvation of those to
"whom they were come.

"Having pursuant to the King's Commands,
"after sitting down, preach'd to him and all his
"Attendants there present the Word of Life, he
"answer'd thus. *Your Words and Promises are very*
"*taking, but in Regard that they are new and uncertain,*
"*I cannot approve of them so as to forsake that which I*
"*have so long follow'd with the whole English Nation.*
"*But because you are come from far into my Kingdom,*
"*and, as I conceive, are desirous to impart to us those*
"*Things, which you believe to be true, and most be-*
"*neficial, we will not molest you, but rather give you*
"*favourable Entertainment, and take Care to supply*
"*you with necessary Sustenance; nor do we forbid you*
"*by Preaching to gain as many as you can to your Reli-*
"*gion.* Accordingly he gave them a dwelling
"Place in the City of *Canterbury*, which was the
"*Metropolis* of all his Dominions: And pursuant
"to his Promise, besides allowing them their Diet
"permitted them to preach. It is reported, that
"as they drew near to the City, after their Man-
"ner

"ner with the *holy Crofs* and the *Image* of the
"great King our Lord *Jesus Christ*, they in Con-
"sort sung this *Litany* or Prayer. *We beseech thee,*
"*O Lord, in thy Mercy; That thy Anger and Wrath*
"*be turn'd away from this City and this thy holy*
"*House because we have Sinned,* Allelujah."

Thus the *holy Crofs* took once more Possession of the Place, from whence it had been banish'd ever since the *Saxon Conquest*; and there it continued for above 900 Years; that is, till the Reign of *Edward* vi. when to the everlasting Shame of *Christianity* it was treated as an Image of some infamous Traitor to the State, and pull'd down every where in this Island by the blessed Reformation.

G. It appears to me very surprizing, that a *heathen Prince*, should at the very first sight of Persons of a different Religion, who even profess'd themselves Enemies to his, should entertain them with so much Courtesy.

P. Sir, you have already heard from venerable *Bede*, that King *Ethelbert* had by a special Providence of God been married for some Years to a Christian Princess of *France*, who had the Practice of her Religion secured to her by Articles of Marriage, and had for that End brought over with her the holy Bishop *Luidhard*, or *Lethardus*; Besides several Christian Servants, whose moral Lives far different from that of *Heathens*, had doubtless very much recommended the Religion they profess'd, and inspired the King with a favourable Opinion of it. Which having in a great Measure removed the usual Prejudices of Education, occasion'd without all Dispute the favourable Reception, which St. *Augustin* and his Companions met with.

But

But to proceed in my Account of these holy Missioners, whom I left in their Mansion at Canterbury, let us now hear what *Bede* has transmitted to Posterity concerning their Way of living there. This holy and learned Writer flourish'd here in *England* in the very next Age after the entire Conversion of it. That is, when all Transactions of any Moment relating to it, were as fresh in the Minds of all Men of Literature, as the History of the happy Restoration of King *Charles* the 2d is now still fresh in the Minds of Persons of any Reading.

This Author therefore tells us L. 1. C. 26. that " As soon as they enter'd into the Dwelling place
" assign'd them, they began to imitate the Course
" of Life practised by the primitive Church. That
" is, apply'd themselves to frequent *Prayer*, *Watching*, and *Fasting*; preach'd the *Word of Life* to
" as many as they could; despising all worldly
" Things as not belonging them, receiving
" only what was necessary for Food from those they
" taught, living themselves in all Respects conformably to what they prescribed to others,
" and being always disposed to suffer any Adversity, and even to die for the Truth they preach'd.
" In short, some believed and were baptized admiring the Simplicity of their innocent Course
" of Life, and the Sweetness of their heavenly
" Doctrine.

The same Author go's on thus in the same Chapter: " There was, *says he*, on the East-side
" near the City a Chappel dedicated to the Honour of St. *Martin*, whil'st the *Romans* were still
" in the Island, wherein the Queen, who, as has
" been said, was a Christian, used to pray. In
" this they first began to meet, to sing, to SAY
" MASS, to preach and to baptize, till the King
" being

"being converted to the Faith, they had leave
"granted them more freely to preach, and build
"or repair Churches in all Places. But when he
"among the rest being taken with the unspotted
"Lives of these holy Men, and their most agree-
"able Promises, which they proved to be most
"certain by *working of many Miracles*, believed and
"was baptized, greater Numbers began daily to
"flock to hear the Word, and forsaking their
"Heathen Rites to associate themselves by
"Faith to the Unity of the *Church of Christ*.
"Whose Faith and Conversion the King so far
"encouraged, as not to compell any to embrace
"*Christianity*, but only to shew more Affection
"to the Believers, as to his Fellow-citizens in
"the heavenly Kingdom. For he had learned
"from his Instructors and Leaders to Salvation,
"*that the Service of Christ ought to be voluntary, not
"by Compulsion*. Nor was it long before he gave
"his Teachers a settled Place in his *Metropolis* of
"*Canterbury* with the necessary Possessions in seve-
"ral Sorts."

After this St. *Augustin* cross'd the Seas into *France*, travell'd to *Arles*, and pursuant to St. *Gregory*'s Order's was consecrated *Metropolitan* of the *English* Nation by *Etherius* Archbishop of that City, So that all the Bishops of *Britain*, were by Pope *Gregory* put under St. *Augustin*'s Jurisdiction.

St. *Augustin* being thus qualified return'd back to *Britain*, where by the King's Conversion he found the Number of the Faithful encreased to such a Degree, that this saying of Christ, *the Harvest is plentiful, but the Labourers are few*, Math. 9. v. 37. was literally verified, and he found it necessary to apply himself to the *Apostolick See* for a new Supply of Missioners. He therefore deputed to St. *Gregory*, two very holy Persons, the one named *Lau-*

rence,

96 Dial. 2. §. 4.   *The second general*
rence, who afterwards fucceeded him in the Archbifhoprick of *Canterbury,* the other *Peter,* who was made *Abbot* by him of the firft Convent of *Monks* founded by King *Ethelbert* in the fame City. Thefe two after fome Stay at *Rome,* return'd back accompanied by an Addition of twelve able Miffioners all Monks, and chofen by St. *Gregory* himfelf ; who (as *Bede* relates L. 1. C. 29) *Sent over with them all Things neceffary for the Worfhip of God and Service of the Church,* viz. *Sacred Veffels,* and *Veftments for Altars;* alfo *Ornaments for Churches,* and *Veftments for Priefts and Clerks,* as likewife Relicks *of the holy Apoftles and Martyrs*; *Befides many Books.*

Among thefe new Miffioners was St. *Melitus,* to whom, whil'ft he was upon his Journey to *Britain,* St. *Gregory* wrote, that whereas he had before given his Advice to King *Ethelbert,* that the Idol-temples fhould be demolifh'd, he had upon Recollection alter'd his Mind, and fo gave the following Directions, viz. that the Temples themfelves ought not to be deftroy'd. *But* (fays he) *let the Idols that are in them be deftroy'd* ; *Let* Holy Water *be made and fprinkled in the faid Temples, let Altars be erected, and* Relicks *be depofited in them.* Meaning, as he explains himfelf a little after, the *Relicks* of thofe *Saints,* in whofe Honour the Churches were to be dedicated to God. L. 1. C. 30.

The new Miffioners being thus provided with Things neceffary for their Fuuctions arrived fafe in *England* An. 601. and putting themfelves under the Conduct of their holy Archbifhop, labour'd in Chrift's Vineyard with that happy Succefs, that the whole Kingdom of *Kent* was foon after converted, and became a beautiful Part of *Chrift's Myftical Body,* the *holy Catholick Church.*

SECT.

SECT. 5.

A Relation of St. Auguſtin's *Conference with the* Britiſh Biſhops.

G. BUT, Sir, I cannot well conceive, what need there was of ſending as far as *Rome*, for a new ſupply of Miſſioners, ſince it appears to me, that they might have been got much nearer home from the *ancient Britons*; amongſt whom there were doubtleſs ſeveral *Biſhops*, and great Numbers of the *inferiour Clergy*.

P. That's very true. But moſt Hiſtorians obſerve, that they bore ſuch a mortal Hatred to the *Saxons* for having driven them out of their Native Country, that they could not be prevail'd upon to afford any Aſſiſtance towards their Converſion. Add to this, that (as it is atteſted by *Gildas*) they were faln into ſo great a Decay of Piety, and Corruption of Manners, that the Generality of the *Clergy* as well as *Laity* had in a Manner loſt all Senſe of Religion; and the Zeal for God's Glory and the Converſion of Souls, was utterly extinguiſh'd in their Hearts. So that inſtead of coming to St. *Auguſtin*'s Aid, and going Hand in Hand with him, they were as Spies upon his Actions, jealous of his Authority, and envious of the great Reputation he had got among the People. Nay *Bede* L. 2. C. 20. relates that one *Caedwal* King of the *Britons*, tho' he bore the Name of, and profeſs'd himſelf a *Chriſtian*, rebell'd againſt *Edwin* King of the *Northumbers* who but ſix Years before had been converted, and received into the Church by St. *Paulinus*, and was a moſt religious Prince. That the ſame *Caedwal* join'd with the *Pagan Penda* King of the *Mer-*

H *cians*

tians, againſt the *Chriſtian Northumbers*, and was more barbarous and cruel than *Penda* himſelf: "For that he neither ſpared the female Sex, nor "the innocent Age of Children, but with ſavage "Cruelty put them to tormenting Deaths, reſol- "ving to cut off the Race of the *Engliſh* within "the Borders of *Britain*, without having any "Regard to the *Chriſtian Religion*, which had "newly taken Root among them. And the ſame "Author adds, that even to his Time it was the "Cuſtom of the *Britons* not to have any Regard to "the *Faith* and *Religion* of the *Engliſh*, nor to cor- "reſpond any more with them than with *Pagans*."

Such was their Hatred to the *Saxons*; which however did not hinder our holy Apoſtle from Uſing his utmoſt Endeavours to bring them to a more Chriſtian Diſpoſition; and in Order to it, being ſupported by the Intereſt of King *Ethelbert*, he prevailed upon the *Britiſh Biſhops* and *Doctors* to come to a publick Conference with him.

Cambden in his Account of *Worceſterſhire* gives the following brief Relation of this Aſſembly. "About this Territory, ſays he, there is a Place, "but the Poſition of it is uncertain, call'd *Au-* "*guſtin's Ake*, or *Oak*, at which *Auguſtin* the *Apo-* "*ſtle of England*, and the *Britiſh Biſhops* met: "And after many hot Diſputes about *celebrating* "*Eaſter*, Preaching the Word of God to the *Sax-* "*ons*, and Adminiſtring *Baptiſm* after the *Roman* "*Rite*, they parted from one another with diſ- "agreeing Minds."

This is *Cambden*'s ſhort Account of this Conference, and is very exact as far it goes. But ſince the learned Mr. *Collier* in his *Eccleſiaſtical Hiſtory of Great Britain*, has been pleaſed to draw ſome Conſequences from the Subject and particular Circumſtances of it, which appear to me

not

not to be so solid and conclusive, as might be expected from a Person of his Capacity, I shall recite to you the whole Relation of it Word for Word from *Bede*, who writes thus. L. 2. C. 2.

"In the mean Time *Augustin*, with the Assistance of King *Ethelbert*, drew together to confer with the Bishops and Doctors of the next Province of the *Britons*, at a Place, which is to this Day call'd *Augustin's Ac*: That is, *Augustin's Oak*; on the Borders of *Wiccii* [*Worcestershire*] and the *West-Saxons*: And began by brotherly Admonitions to persuade them, to preserve Catholick Unity with him, and undertake the common Labour of Preaching the Gospel to the *Gentils*. For they did not keep *Easter* at the proper Time—besides they did several other Things, which were against the Unity of the Church. They after a long Disputation not complying with the Entreaties, Exhortations, or Rebukes of *Augustin* and his Companions, but preferring their Traditions before all the Churches in the World, which in Christ agree among themselves, the holy Father *Augustin* put an End to this troublesome and tedious Contention by saying, *Let us beg of God, who causes those who are of one Mind to live in his Father's House, that he will vouchsafe by his heavenly Tokens to declare to us, which Tradition is to be follow'd, and by what Means we are to hasten to the Entrance of his Kingdom. Let some infirm Person be brought, and let the Faith and Practice of those, by whose Prayers he shall be heal'd, be look'd upon as acceptable to God, and to be follow'd by all.*

"The adverse Party unwillingly consenting, a blind Man of the *English* Race was brought, who having been presented to the Priests of the *Britons*, and finding no Benefit or Cure by

"their Ministry, at length *Augustin* compell'd by
"real Necessity bent his Knees to the Father of
"our Lord *Jesus Christ*, praying that his lost Sight
"might be restored to the blind Man, and that
"by the corporeal Enlightning of one Person, the
"brightness of spiritual Grace might shine in the
"Hearts of many. Immediately the blind Man
"received his Sight, and *Augustin* was by all de-
"clared the Preacher of Sovereign Light. The
"*Britons* then confess'd they were sensible that
"the true Way of Righteousness, was that which
"*Augustin* taught; but that they could not depart
"from their ancient Customs without the Con-
"sent and Leave of their People. They there-
"fore desired that a second Synod might be ap-
"pointed, at which more of their Number would
"be present.

"This being decreed, there came (as is asser-
"ted) seven Bishops of the *Britons*, and many
"most learned Men; particularly from their no-
"ble Monastery, which in the *English* Tongue is
"call'd *Bancornaburg*, over which the Abbot *Di-*
"*nooth* is said to have presided at that Time.
"They that were to go to the aforesaid Council,
"repair'd first to a certain holy and discreet Man,
"who was wont to lead an Eremitical Life a-
"mongst them, advising with him, whether they
"ought at the Preaching of *Augustin* to forsake
"their Traditions. He answer'd, *If he is a Man*
"*of God follow him.* But *how shall we know that,*
"said they. He replied; *our Lord saith,* take my
"Yoke upon you, and learn of me, for I am
"meek and lowly in Heart. *If therefore that*
"*Augustin is meek and lowly of Heart, it is to be be-*
"*lieved, that he has taken upon him the Yoke of Christ,*
"*and offers the same to you to take upon you.* But if
"*he be stern and haughty, it appears that he is not of*
"God,

" God, *nor are we to regard his Words.* They infisted
" again. *And how shall we discern even this? Do you con-*
" *trive,* said the Anchoret, *That he first arrive with*
" *his Company at the Place where the Synod is to be held,*
" *and if at your Approach he shall rise up to you, hear*
" *him submissively, being assured that he is the Ser-*
" *vant of* Christ; *but if he shall despise you and not rise*
" *up to you, whereas you are more in Number, let him*
" *also be despised by you.*

" They did as he directed: and it happen'd that
" when they came, *Augustin* was sitting on a Chair;
" which they observing were in a Passion, and
" charging him with Pride endeavour'd to contra-
" dict all he said. He said to them, *you act in*
" *many Particulars contrary to our Custom, or rather to*
" *the Custom of the universal Church. And yet, if*
" *you will comply with me in these* three Points, *viz.*
" *to keep Easter at the due Time, to administer Bap-*
" *tism, by which we are again born to God, according*
" *to the Custom of the holy* Roman *and* Apostolick
" *Church, and jointly with us to preach the Word of*
" *God to the* English *Nation, we will readily tolerate*
" *all other Things you do, tho' contrary to our Customs.*
" They answer'd they would do none of those
" Things, nor receive him as their *Archbishop.*
" Alledging among themselves, *That if he would*
" *not now rise up to us, how much more will he con-*
" *temn us as of no Worth, if we shall begin to be under*
" *his Subjection.* To whom the Man of God *Au-*
" *gustin* is said to have foretold in a threatning
" Manner; *that in Case they would not join in Unity*
" *with their Brethren, they should be warr'd upon by*
" *their Enemies: And if they would not preach the*
" *Way of Life to the* English *Nation, they should by*
" *their Hands undergo the Vengeance of God.* All
" which through the Dispensation of the Divine
" Judgment fell out exactly as he had foretold."

SECT.

SECT. 6.
St. Auguſtin *vindicated.*

THIS is holy *Bede*'s Relation of the two unſucceſsful Conferences, St. *Auguſtin* had with the *Britiſh Biſhops*: In the firſt whereof he proved his *Miſſion*, and the *Truth* of his Doctrine, by that unconteſted and celebrated *Miracle* of Reſtoring in a Moment by his Prayers a blind Man to the perfect Uſe of his Sight. Which tho' it was attended with the publick Acclamations of all the Spectators, and even drew an Acknowledgment from his *Britiſh* Adverſaries, *that it was the true Way of Righteouſneſs, which Auguſtin taught,* yet could not overcome the Prepoſſeſſion and Obſtinacy, they labour'd under. So that altho' their Judgments were convinced, their obdurate and exulcerated Hearts continued to rebel againſt the Truth.

G. However they demanded a ſecond and more numerous Meeting, which ſhew'd at leaſt that they were not wholly averſe from joining with St. *Auguſtin.*

P. Pardon me Sir; it only ſhew'd, that they were under a very great Confuſion at the unexpected Sight of a Miracle, which could neither be denied, nor diſcredited by any Artifice; yet was a flat Condemnation of their Noncompliance. In a Word, it ſhew'd that tho' they had nothing to ſay for themſelves, they were reſolved not to yield, but only ſought to gain Time, as Men under great Perplexities are wont to do: Becauſe they might in the interim concert Meaſures together, and ſome Expedient to retrieve their loſt Credit might poſſibly occur to their Minds. But I muſt needs ſay, they were put to very hard Shifts, when they

they could pitch upon no better Expedient than that of confulting a poor ignorant *Ermite,* who in all Likelihood was as fit to be a *Secretary of State,* as to refolve judiciously their Queftion, *whether* Auguftin's *Doctrine or their own Traditions were to be follow'd?* For that was the important Queftion put to him.

G. But Sir, you do not reflect, that *Bede* calls him a *holy and difcreet Man.*

P. As to his *Holinefs* and *Difcretion* in his own private Conduct, I have nothing to fay. But I dare boldly affirm, he was neither a *Prophet* nor *Conjurer*: And he fufficiently fhew'd the Narrownefs of his Capacity in the wretched Advice he gave to his Confultors. For was it even agreeable to common Senfe, that the final Determination of *three important Points,* befides the Reputation of a venerable Archbifhop over and above, fhould be hazarded upon the bare Cafuality of a Perfon's *Sitting* or *Standing*? Was that Ground enough either for a *Rupture* or *Union* of the two Churches, without entring any further into the Bottom or Merits of the Caufe?

G. But Sir, the *Ermite* was a very *fpiritual Man,* and judg'd according to the Rules of the Gofpel, that if *Auguftin* was *proud* and *haughty, he could not be of God*; *nor was his Preaching then to be regarded.* And what better Mark could he give the *Britifh Bifhops* to judge by, whether he was *humble* or *proud,* than his Rifing or not Rifing to them?

P. Sir, the Ermite was in the right in faying, that if *Auguftin* was *proud,* he could not be of God. But as to your Queftion, *what better Mark he could give to* the Britifh Bifhops *to judge by, whether he was proud or humble?* I anfwer directly, that his *Zeal* for the Converfion of Souls, his *Difinterestednefs,* the *Aufterity* of his Life, his earneft In-

vitation

vitation of the *Britons* to be Partakers with him in the Glory of gaining Souls to Chrift; and laftly his *Miracles* were much better and furer Marks of his folid Virtue, which cannot be without *Humility*, than the outward Obfervance of a trivial Ceremony: For a Man may be very *proud*, tho' very *ceremonious*, and very humble without being fo: So that I think it was no great Mark of the Ermite's *Spirituality* to direct his Confultors to pafs a preremptory Judgment upon a Man's *inward Difpofition* to the Prejudice of his Reputation from an *ambiguous outward Mark*; but to pronounce in fuch an uncharitable Manner upon a Perfon of St. *Auguftin*'s Character, that is, upon an *Archbifhop*, venerable for his extraordinary Piety and Zeal, and even Working *Miracles*, was wholly inexcufable.

G. But perhaps the *Ermite* knew nothing of St. *Auguftin*'s true Character, or his having work'd any Miracles.

P. Either he did or did not. If he did, it is impoffible to excufe him from a grievous Sin in the Advice he gave. If not, the *Britifh Bifhops* acted a very unfair Part in concealing from him thofe Circumftances, the knowledge whereof was abfolutely neceffary to inform him of the true State of the Queftion; as the Concealment of them occafion'd in all Likelihood his being trapan'd into that ridiculous Piece of Cafuiftry, which they made foon after the Rule of their Conduct.

But of what Nature foever the Ermite's Overfight was in giving the abovefaid Advice; I am fure the *Britifh Bifhops* were highly blameable in following it preferably to the avow'd Conviction of their Judgments, *that it was the true Way of Righteoufnefs which* Auguftin *taught*. For what need was there after that even to advife with any Body, *whether they ought to follow his Doctrine, or adhere to their own Traditions?* Had they any Colour of Reafon to doubt either of the *Holinefs of his Life*, or of the *Truth of his Doctrine*, after God had attefted both the one and the other by the Miracle they had been Eye-witneffes of? Or is there fuch a *Chimera* to be imagin'd, as a *proud Saint*? Or is God wont to work Miracles by the Miniftry of a proud and haughty Perfon? Now it can fcarce be queftion'd but thefe or fuch like Reflections occurr'd to their Minds; and if they had not been ftrangely prepoffefs'd, it would have been obvious to conclude from them, that it was their Duty to fubmit to Saint *Auguftin* without any farther Enquiry: Or if they would needs out of Curiofity hear, what the good *Ermite* had to fay to them, the *holy* and *miraculous Auguftin*, whether found *Sitting* or *Standing* ought moft certainly to have been follow'd; at leaft in the *three Articles*, he infifted vpon: The *firft* whereof could fcarce be rejected without the Guilt of *Schifm* after the Decree of the *Council of Nicea*. The fecond was neceffary to prevent fcandalizing the *new Converts* by their Difagreement in adminiftring the *Sacrament of Baptifm*. And the *third* would have been highly conducing to God's Honour and the Converfion of Souls.

G. However it was fomewhat odd, that St. *Auguftin* fhould not rife up at the Approach of the *British Bifhops*.

P. Let it be as odd as you pleafe; It was moft certainly a very rafh Judgment in them to attribute it peremptorily to *Pride*; and fhew'd they were difpofed rather to pick a new Quarrel, than lay afide their former Animofities. But for my Part I do not fee any Thing fo very odd in it, at

leaft as the Fact is related by *Bede*, who is the original Recorder of this hiftorical Paffage. *It happen'd*, fays he, *that when they came*, Auguftin *was fitting in a Chair. Which they obferving were in a Paffion, and charging him with Pride, endeavour'd to contradict all he faid.* What! did they expect that St. *Auguftin*, wearied perhaps with walking to the Place of Conference, fhould not have the Liberty to reft himfelf, but wait for them in a ftanding Pofture! For I obferve that *Bede* do's not fay, that St. *Auguftin* continued *Sitting*, when he faw them near enough to falute them, but he only fays, *that when they came he was fitting*; which Expreffion admits of a Latitude of a greater or leffer Diftance: And it is very poffible that St. *Auguftin*, whofe Mind was doubtlefs fill'd with a great many weighty Objects, and perhaps in a deep Contemplation, might through an innocent Inadvertency not obferve their Coming towards him in the very Moment, that they, who came as Spies upon him, faw him *Sitting*. Nay the *Britifh Bifhops* had not Temper enough to give him a few Moments for Reflection, but feeing him (perhaps at fome Diftance, for the Congrefs was in the open Field under an Oak) *fitting in a Chair*, fell immediately into a violent Paffion; and the firft Compliments they made him was to charge him with *Pride* and *Haughtinefs*: Tho' the modeft Anfwer he made them, and his fhewing no Refentment of their harfh Language, might, I think, have fufficed to give them a better Opinion of him, if they had been capable of it. However let us fuppofe, that St. *Auguftin*, who had been brought up in a Monaftery, was not the politeft Man in the World, I hope at leaft that every Degree of Impolitenefs is not an infallible Mark of *Pride*, nor fuffices to *unfaint* a Man: Which is a
very

vindicated. 107

very material Point in this Question; becauſe it is impoſſible for a *proud Man* to be a *Saint*.

But laſtly let us ſuppoſe that St. *Auguſtin* (who doubtleſs thought himſelf their *Metropolitan* and *Primate*) was of Opinion, that it became him to maintain the Dignity of his Character and the *Apoſtolick See*, to which he was indebted for it, by that diſtinguiſhing Mark of his *Superiority*, to wit, his Receiving the *Britiſh* Prelates *ſitting* : Suppoſe, I ſay, that this was *Auguſtin's* Opinion (for I will not preſume either to approve or condemn it) it is manifeſt that in this Suppoſition his not riſing up to them was not an Effect of *Pride*, but at the very worſt an *Error of Judgment*. Whence I conclude in the whole, that the Mark given by the *Ermite* to judge by, whether *Auguſtin* was a *proud* or *humble* Man, was in itſelf very equivocal, and ought not to have been laid hold of by the *Britiſh* Prelates, who had much ſolider Grounds to form a Judgment upon of his intrinſick Merit.

G. But Sir, what makes you ſo ſolicitous to vindicate the Honour of this *great Saint?* Have any ancient Hiſtorians ſpoken ill of him?

P. No Sir; his Memory was venerable in all Antiquity both at Home and Abroad till the *reforming Age*; when a violent Hatred to the Religion he had planted embolden'd ſome ſhameleſs Writers to draw their Pen againſt him, and aſperſe both his *Miniſtry* and *Perſon*. " This *Auguſtin*
" (ſays *Holinſhead* in Deſcript. Brit. C. 27. Col. 1.)
" after his Arrival converted the *Saxons* indeed
" from *Paganiſm*. But, as the Proverb ſays,
" bringing them out of *God's Bleſſing* into the
" warm Sun, he imbued them with no leſs hurtful
" Superſtitions, than thoſe they were infected
" with before. For beſides the *bare Name of*
" *Chriſt*

"*Chrift* and external Contempt of priftinate Idolatry, he taught them nothing at all; but rather made an Exchange from grofs to fubtle Treachery, from open to *Secret Idolatry*, and from the Name of *Pagans* to the *bare Title of Chriftianity.*"

G. This is outrageous indeed. For, according to this Author, the *Heathen Paganifm* profefs'd by the *Saxons* before their Converfion, was comparatively at leaft *God's Bleffing*; and the *Chriftianity* taught by St. *Auguftin* was but a *meer empty Name.* So that all our *Englifh Anceftors* for 900 Years together were no *Chriftians*; and it will be very hard to fhew, by what Means either *Catholicks* or *Proteftants*, are become *Chriftians* fince; Or that there is fuch a Thing as a *true Chriftian* in the World.

P. Have a little Patience: I have a brace more of *Proteftant Hiftorians*, not at all inferiour to *Holingfhead* either for Exactnefs in Truth, or Nicety of good Manners; I mean, honeft *John Bale*, and his Name-fake *John Fox*.

G. Pray what Sort of a Man was the honeft *John Bale*, you fpeak off?

P. You fhall have his Character drawn in Miniature by his own Pen. *When I was a Boy of* 12 *Years old* (fays he *Cent.* 5. *fol.* 245.) *I was thrown into the Hellifh Dungeon* [barathrum] *of Carmelite Friars in Norwich*. I prefume he was put there to learn his *Catechifm*, or the Rudiments of the *latin* Tongue. For no one was ever admitted to be a *Religious Man at* 12 Years old.

G. But how did he get out of that terrible Dungeon?

P. You fhall hear. *The Word of God appearing* (fays he) *I faw my own deform'd State.* To wit, his being both a *Friar* and a *Prieft. I immediately fcraped out the curfed Character of the horrible Beaft*; and
took

took to myself a most faithful Wife named Dorothy, *not from any Man, nor by the Help of any Man* (pray mark the Prophaneness of his Words) *but by the special Gift and Word of Christ.*

Here you have an eminent *Convert* and *Champion* of the *Reformation,* throwing off his *religious Habit,* renouncing his *sacred Priesthood,* which he calls *the cursed Character of the horrible Beast,* and breaking through all the *solemn Vows* he had made to God: And all this (I am ashamed to repeat it) *by the special Gift and Word of Christ.* But you shall be acquainted with more of this sort of Converts hereafter.

This worthy Gentleman therefore comes in as an Evidence against St. *Augustin,* who indeed was never disposed to *scrape out the cursed Character of the horrible Beast,* nor to take a faithful *Dorothy* to his Bed. And 'tis perhaps one Reason of the Spleen *John Bale* bore him. For he tells us, that *Augustin* the *Roman* was sent by *Gregory the first* to convert the *English Saxons* to the *Papistical Faith.* And again, that K. *Ethelbert* at length received *Popery* with all it's *Superstitions;* yet so, that every one should receive *this new Worship of Gods* freely and without Compulsion. So that St. *Augustin* is here made a Teacher and Worshipper of many Gods.

G. I am glad at least to find him bear Witness that St. *Augustin* was a *Papist,* and taught *Popery.* For it makes that Religion above 900 Years older than his own: And how black soever the Colours are, in which he has represented it, I would rather choose to have my Portion in the other World with *Augustin,* than with *John Bale,* and his *most faithful* Dorothy.

P. But pray hear out the rest. For he tells us farther, *that* Augustin *made himself Archbishop by Violence,*

Violence. *That he was more Solicitous to get Tiths and Oblations for Masses than to preach the Gospel, and that he was the Cause of the Slaughter of* 1200 *Monks.* But here the poor Fellow overshot himself most grievously: Not reflecting, that holy *Bede*, who knew St. *Augustin*'s Character much better than he could possibly do, gives him flatly the Lie in every Part of his Story; especially as to the Slaughter of the 1200 Monks, which happen'd above a Year after St. *Augustin*'s Death, and was order'd by a *Pagan* King of the *Northumbers*, with whom St. *Augustin* never had the least Communication.

The third *Protestant* Historian, that appears as an Evidence both against St. *Gregory*, and our holy Apostle, is *John Fox*: in whose Writings Father *Parsons*, who had examined them throughly, declares, that to speak modestly there were at least ten thousand notorious Lies, either expresly asserted or insinuated. This vile Author, (whose Pen throws no Scandal but on those, whom he commends; in so much that to call a Man one of *Fox's Saints*, is proverbially become the same as to call him a *great Rogue*) writes thus of St. *Gregory*. *About this Time departed* Gregory *Bishop of Rome: Of whom it is said, that of the Number of all the first Bishops before him in the primitive Church, he was the* BASEST. *And of all that came after him he was the* BEST.

G. *Basest* and *best* chime very prettily. But pray who is it that *said this* of Pope *Gregory*.

P. Do you ask who said it? Why, *John Fox* himself: And 'tis the only shift I can find to save him from a Lie. For surely none but himself was ever so impertinent as to accuse that eminent Saint of *Baseness*. Much less to say, he was the *basest* of all the first Bishops before him in the primitive Church: Which Comparison reflects at

least

leaſt a leſs Degree of *Baſeneſs* even on St. *Peter* himſelf and all his holy Succeſſors; who for 300 Years together were all *eminent Saints*, and almoſt all *Martyrs*.

G. However *John Fox* has made St. *Gregory* ſome Amends by ſaying, that of all who came after him he was the *beſt*.

P. That Complement was not intended to ſet off Pope *Gregory*, but to make *Monſters* of all his Succeſſors. But ſee now in what beautiful Colours he has painted St. *Auguſtin, ſitting* at the Approach of the *Britiſh* Biſhops. *Much leſs*, ſays he, *would his Phariſaical Solemnity have girded himſelf, as Chriſt did, and waſh his Brethren's Feet after their Journey. Seeing his Lordſhip was ſo high, or rather ſo heavy, or rather ſo proud, that he could not find in his Heart to give them a little moving of his Body.* Was there ever any Thing more impertinent or ſcurrilous?

G. I hope at leaſt that Mr. *Collier*, whom you mention'd a while ago, do's not join with theſe Libellers in Traducing our holy Apoſtle.

P. No Sir, he is very far from it. On the contrary he gives a very honourable Character of him, as becomes a Chriſtian Writer. As to St. *Auguſtin's* being found *ſitting* by the *Britiſh* Biſhops, he neither condemns nor juſtifies it directly, but only anſwers *Baronius*'s Way of Vindicating it: which, to deal ſincerely, I reliſh as little as Mr. *Collier* himſelf; and I heartily wiſh we agreed in all other Things as much as in this.

But, to come now to an end of my hiſtorical Account of this ſecond publick Converſion, the Conference being thus ended, as you ſee, without Succeſs, St. *Auguſtin* return'd to his Flock, comforted at leaſt with the Conſciouſneſs of his own ſincere Intentions, tho' fruſtrated by the Perverſeneſs

112   Dial. 2. §. 6.   *St.* Auguftin

nefs of thofe he had to deal with. But he found the *Kentiſh Saxons* in a much more Chriſtian Diſpoſition.

G. You have already told me, that K. *Ethelbert* being converted and baptized, the whole Kingdom of *Kent* foon after following his Example, received the *Faith of Chriſt.* But were the other fix Kingdoms of the *Heptarchy* alfo favour'd with the fame Bleſſing?

P. Yes Sir, they all came into the Fold one after another. I will give you a brief Account of their Converſion as near as I can according to the Order of Time. The *Eaſt Saxons* were converted the firſt after the People of *Kent* by the preaching of St. *Melitus* firſt Biſhop of *London.* After them the *Eaſt-Angles* principally by the preaching of their firſt Biſhop *Felix.* The Kingdom of the *Northumbers* was converted An. 625. by the preaching of St. *Paulinus* the firſt Archbiſhop of *York.* That of the *Weſt-Saxons* by the preaching of St. *Berinus,* and that of the *Mercians* or Mid-land Counties, the largeſt of all the feven about the fame Time under King *Peda,* who was baptized by Biſhop *Finian* during the Life and againſt the Will of his Father *Penda*; being perfwaded to it by *Oſwin* King of the *Northumbers,* who gave him his Daughter in Marriage upon Condition that he would embrace the *Faith of Chriſt.* And thus fix Kingdoms of the *Heptarchy,* were converted within about 40 Years more or lefs after St. *Auguſtin*'s coming into *England.* But the 7th. to wit, that of the *South Saxons* did not receive the Gofpel till about 20 Years after under K. *Ethelwold,* chiefly by the preaching of St. *Wilfrid* their firſt Biſhop.

G. I prefume then that St. *Auguſtin* did not live to fee the Converſion of the whole *Engliſh* Nation.

P. No

vindicated.

P. No Sir, he died in the Year 608; and was buried firſt near the Church of St. *Peter* and St. *Paul* in *Canterbury*; Becauſe it was not then quite finiſhed. But as ſoon as it was finiſh'd and conſecrated, his Body was brought into the Church, and decently buried in the *Northern* Porch, with an honourable Inſcription upon it. I ſhall conclude with Mr. *Colliers*'s Character of him.

"To ſpeak a Word or two of him, ſays he, by
"Way of Character; he was a very graceful
"Perſon, lived ſuitably to the Buſineſs of a Miſ-
"ſioner, and practiſed great Auſterities. And if
"he fell into any Inequalities of Temper; If
"he was too warm in his Expoſtulations, or
"ſtrain'd his Privilege too far upon the *Britons*,
"it ought to be charged upon the ſcore of human
"Infirmities, and cover'd with his greater Merit.
"This is certain, he engaged in a glorious Un-
"dertaking, broke through Danger and Diſcou-
"ragement, and was bleſs'd with wonderful Suc-
"ceſs. He converted the Kingdom of *Kent* by
"the Strength of his own Conduct and *Miracles*;
"and that of the *Eaſt-Saxons* by his Agent and
"Coadjutor *Mellitus*. The ſpreading of Chriſtia-
"nity thus far among the *Saxons* was a great Step
"towards the Converſion of the reſt. Let his
"Memory therefore be mention'd with Honour;
"and let us praiſe Almighty God for making him
"ſo powerful an Inſtrument in the Happineſs of
"this Iſland. L. 2. p. 78."

Thus, Sir, I have given you as compendious a Relation as was poſſible of this celebrated Converſion of our Country; begun about the End of the 6th Century, and perfected not long after the middle of the next.

G. Sir, I have hearken'd to you both with Attention and Pleaſure, and laid up in my Memory all

114 Dial. 2. §. 7. *Roman Catholicks profess*

the principal Heads of your Relation. But is it not somewhat surprizing that Mr. *Collier* should not only own, that St. *Augustin* converted the Kingdom of *Kent* by the Force of *Miracles*, but even regard the Religion, to which it was converted by him, as *the Happiness of this Island*? For did God ever concur by *Supernatural Signs* and *Wonders*, to the setting up of a *false Religion*? Or can a *false Religion* be the *Happiness* of any Nation? 'Tis therefore manifest that Mr. *Collier* is convinced in his Heart, that St. *Augustin* and his Followers preach'd the *true Faith* in this Island.

SECT. 7.

Roman Catholicks *profess to this Day the Faith, which St.* Augustin *preach'd*.

P. THE Consequence, which you draw from his Words is incontestable: and I shall only draw one Consequence more; *viz.* That the Faith and Religion profess'd at this Time by the *English Roman Catholicks*, cannot but be the true one, if it be the same as was taught by St. *Augustin*: Because it is impossible that the same Christian Faith shall be *true* in one Age, and *false* in another.

G. But do's Mr. *Collier* allow, that the Faith and Religion profess'd at this Time by the *English Roman Catholicks* is the same as was taught by St. *Augustin*?

P. No Sir, he strains hard to shew the Contrary. But he has not only all *Catholick* Historians, but a whole Cloud of *Protestant* Witnesses against him: Amongst which, tho' some indeed express themselves somewhat more politely than *Holinshead*

head, *Bale*, and *Fox*, yet they all agree in Substance, that *Augustin* and his Fellow-Missioners brought *Popery* into *England*; and the *Book of Homilies*, recommended by the 37th *Article* of Mr. *Collier*'s Church, declares positively that before the Reformation *whole Christendom was drown'd in abominable Idolatry*, and that for the space of EIGHT HUNDRED YEARS AND MORE. Which in true *Protestant* Language brings *Popery* not only in *Great Britain*, but in *whole Christendom*, up to the very Time of *England*'s Conversion.

But let us hear his Reasons against it. He writes thus L. 2. p. 65. " *Baronius* in transcribing
" this Passage of *Bede* [*relating to St.* Augustin's
" *having a silver-Cross together with the Picture of our*
" *Saviour for a Banner carried before him*] falls into
" some tragical Reflections upon the Condition
" of the modern Church of *England*. He repre-
" sents the Case, as if the *English* in this Time
" had in a Manner apostatized from *Christianity*,
" and turn'd *Monsters* in Belief. But with due
" Respect to the Cardinal's Memory, his Decla-
" mation runs strangely upon Misapplication."

Under Mr. *Collier*'s Favour, I cannot believe, *Baronius* thought the *English Church* had apostatized from *Christianity*. Tho' I don't question, but he thought she had apostatized from *Catholicity*; which sufficed to make him lament her Condition without any *Misapplication*: Because the Thing he lamented was, that they, who had been zealous *Catholicks* for many Ages, were then faln into *Heresy* and *Schism* by their Separation from their *Mother-Church*. And if Mr. *Collier* will needs dignify such as these with the Name of *Monsters*, he is free to do as he pleases. He go's on thus to prove that *Baronius*'s Lamentation runs upon *Misapplication*.

I 2 " For

"For, says he, THE TERMS OF COMMUNION STAND BY NO MEANS UPON THE SAME FOOT THEY DID IN GREGORY THE GREAT'S TIME. ib.

This is Mr. *Collier*'s Position: Which without any straining or Misconstruction implies no less, than that he has no Exception against such Articles of our Faith, as were *Terms of Communion* in Pope *Gregory*'s Time. But then he must be content to go to *Mass* with us: Nay he is bound to do it; because the Belief of the *Mass* was unquestionably a *Term of Communion* in the Time of *Gregory the Great*. The Thing is notoriously known, and Mr. *Collier* cannot have the Confidence to deny it. So I shall go no farther in Quest for a Proof than the Fact already quoted by *Bede* viz. that St. *Augustin* and his Fellow-Missioners after their coming to *Canterbury* began first to *meet, sing*, and SAY MASS in an old Neighbouring Chappel dedicated to the Honour of St. *Martin*. I observe indeed that Mr. *Collier* in his Relation of this historical Passage instead of SAY MASS (which are a true and verbal Translation of *Bede*'s Words, whom he quotes in the Margin) has render'd it thus: *And perform'd all the solemn Offices of Religion*. p. 67. He knows best himself what Reason he had to do so. But I think it was not fair to wrap up a Fact of Moment thus clearly specified, in such general and ambiguous Terms, as might signify the *Protestant Office* as well as the *Mass*.

Holy *Bede* has likewise told us, that Pope *Gregory* took Care to send over into *England* all Things necessary for the Service of the Church, as *sacred Vessels, Ornaments for Altars, Vestments for Priests, Reliques of the holy Apostles and Martyrs* &c. and gave Directions how the *Heathen Temples* should be converted into *Christian Churches*; to wit, by sprinkling

ling them with *holy Water*, by erecting *Altars*, and placing in them the *Reliques* of the Saints, in whose Honour they were to be consecrated.

Now all this is as plain *Popery* as ever was practised: And if Mr. *Collier* will but stand to the *Terms of Communion*, as they were in Pope *Gregory*'s Time, and profess himself as true a *Papist* as that great Prelate and St. *Augustin* were, I will answer for him, that there will not be a *truer Papist* than himself in *Great Britain*. The Thing is manifest as to the abovesaid Articles relating to the *Sacrifice of the Mass*, the Use of *holy Water*, the religious Honour paid to *Images* and *Pictures*, and the Respect and Veneration paid not only to the Saints themselves by Dedicating Churches in Honour of them, but even to their *Reliques*. Besides that nothing is more certain than St. *Gregory*'s Belief of a *Purgatory*, or *middle State of Souls*: And that this Doctrine was preach'd by St. *Augustin* and his immediate Successors, is apparent from the many early pious Foundations made in all Parts of this Kingdom for the maintenance of Priests to pray and offer up the holy *Sacrifice* of the *Mass* for the Souls of their respective Founders. And it is to be observed, that *Aerius* and *Vigilantius* were condemn'd by the Church as *Hereticks*, in the 4th. Age, about 200 Years before St. *Gregory*; the one for Opposing the Doctrine of *Purgatory*, and the other for holding that all Prayers made to Saints deceased were fruitless and in Vain, that no Honour was to be paid them, and that to give any Respect to their *Reliques* was downright *Idolatry*.

'Tis therefore plain, that these three Articles concerning *Purgatory*, *Invoking the Saints*, and paying a *religious Respect* to their *Reliques*, were *Terms of Communion* in St. *Gregory*'s Time, since the Tenets contrary to them had been condemn'd as Heresies

118 Dial. 2. §. 7. *Roman Catholicks profess*
long before; And therefore Mr. *Collier* muft own, that at the Beginning of the Reformation the *Roman Catholicks* of *Great Britain* had been in quiet Poffeffion of thefe and the other abovefaid Articles for above 900 Years; and that by Confequence, *the Terms of Communion are upon the fame Foot now as they were in Pope* Gregory's *Time*, refpectively to all thofe Articles.

G. But what then are the Articles, which Mr. *Collier* excepts againft?

P. You fhall have them in his own Words. For having laid down this general Pofition, that *the Terms of Communion ftand by no Means upon the fame Foot, they did in* Gregory's *Time*; he go's on thus.

"To give an Inftance or two from the Matter
"before us; *Baronius* here takes Notice, that *Au-*
"*guftin* the *Englifh Apoftle* was a *Monk*; and that
"the reft of the Miffioners were of the fame
"Order. That they appear'd at their Audience,
"and made their Entrance into *Canterbury* with
"the *Crofs*, and the *Picture* of our Saviour car-
"ried before them, and then complains that thefe
"Things were all forgotten, and laid afide by the
"*modern Englifh*.

"To fpeak to this Charge by Parts, it may be
"replied in the firft Place as to the *Monaftick Life*,
"the Church of *England* has not declared againft
"it in any of her *Articles*. Befides the Cardi-
"nal may remember, that the Diffolution of Ab-
"beys here was an Act of the *State* and not of
"the *Church*; that it was *Prior* to the *Reformation*,
"and carried on by the *Prince* and *Parliament*
"of the *Roman Communion* in all Points excepting
"the *Supremacy*.

But with Mr. *Collier*'s good Leave, tho' *human Politicks* enter'd as a principal Motive in the Diffolution of *Abbeys*, yet it was more properly an Act
of

to this Day the Faith &c.　119

of the *Church* than of the *State*. Becaufe *Vifiting, Reforming,* and *diffolving religious Houfes,* is moſt certainly an Exerciſe of *Ecclefiaſtical Jurifdiction*. Befides that the Diſſolution of them was commanded by K. *Henry* not as *temporal* Sovereign in his Dominions, but as *Supreme Head* of the *Church of England* in *Spirituals*; and executed by *Thomas Cromwel* not as acting in a *Lay Capacity*, but as the King's *Vicar general in all Ecclefiaſtical Affairs*. Neither was the Diſſolution of Abbeys wholly *prior* to the Reformation, as Mr. *Collier* is pleaſed to tell us. Unlefs he means that it was *prior* to the Reformation in the Reign of *Edward* vi. and Queen *Elizabeth*. But was not the difcarding of the Pope, and Veſting the *Spiritual Supremacy* in the *Crown* a part of the *Reformation?* I think it was the very capital Branch of it in all the three reforming Reigns; and in the Reign of *Henry* viii. made the firſt Separation of the *Church of England* from the *Church of Rome*. Now the Diſſolution of Abbeys, was not *prior* to this part of the Reformation, but the firſt Fruit of it, and by Confequence, pofteriour to it.

But, ſays Mr. *Collier, it was carried on by the Prince and Parliament of the Roman Communion in all Points excepting the Supremacy*. But this Exception fpoils all. For no Man was ever acknowledged to be a Member of the *Church of Rome*, who denied the Pope's *Supremacy*. And ſo it is plain, that the *Prince* and *Parliament*, whatever Communion they were of, were not in the Communion of the *Roman Catholick Church*, when having feparated themfelves from the *Supreme Head* of it, they join'd together in the Plunder and Diſſolution of religious Houfes. Mr. *Collier* continues thus.

" Secondly, As to the *Crofs* and our Saviour's
" *Picture,* the Church of *England* has a great Re-
" gard

120 Dial. 2. §. 7. *Roman Catholicks profess*

"gard to both of them [*Witness, Queen* Eliza-
"beth's *not leaving a publick Cross or Crucifix standing*
"*in the whole Kingdom*] and makes use of the first
"in the solemn Administration of Baptism. 'Tis
"true we dare not carry our Respects to the
"Lengths of the *Church of Rome.* And if we
"examine this Passage in *Bede,* tho' we find St.
"*Augustin* and his Company carry the *Cross* and
"our Saviour's *Picture* in their Procession, yet
"there is not the least Intimation that they *wor-*
"*ship'd* them. Nay it is plain, that *Image-Worship*
"was none of the Doctrine of *Rome* in that Age.
"For *Gregory the Great* determines flatly against
"it. 'Tis in his Letter to *Serinus* Bishop of *Mar-*
"*seilles.*"

G. I am glad at least to hear Mr. *Collier* declare, that the *Church of England* has a great Regard to the *Cross* and *Picture* of our Saviour. For the smaller the Breach is, the more easily it is made up. However the nakedness of *Protestant Churches* seems to speak another Language. For I have seen indeed the Pictures of *Moses* and *Aaron* in some of them: But never found a *Crucifix* or *Picture* of our Saviour in any. Nor have I ever seen a *Protestant* bless himself with the *Sign of the Cross,* but have seen those laugh'd at, who by Inadvertency have done it in *Protestant* Company.

P. Sir, it was the Practice of Christians above fourteen hundred Years ago to bless themselves upon all Occasions with the *Sign of the Cross*: Witness *Tertullian,* who writes thus L. *de corona Militis,* C. 3. *At every Step and Motion, at our coming in and going out, when we put on our Clothes or Shoes; when we wash, sit down to Table, light Candles, go to Bed, sit down, or whatever Employment we are about, we make the Sign of the Cross on our Foreheads.* This was the ancient Practice. But it is regarded as an

un-

unfashionable Thing, or superstitious Custom in the *reform'd Churches.*

 G. I find indeed that *Papists* alone keep up the old Mode. But what do's Mr. *Collier* mean by his saying, *that Protestants dare not carry their Respects to the Lengths of the Church of* Rome? *And that there is not the least Insinuation in* Bede, *that St.* Augustin *and his Company worship'd the Cross and Picture of our Saviour?*

 P. Truly Sir, I know not what he means. But this I am sure of, that if he means to insinuate, that we pay an *Idolatrous Worship* to *Images* and *Pictures*, he wrongs us most grievously, and I fear his own Conscience into the Bargain. For a Man of his Learning cannot be ignorant, what our true and real Doctrine is in Reference to the Matter before us. It is thus deliver'd in Pope *Pius's Profession of Faith* from the very Words of the Council of *Trent.* Sess. 25. *I most firmly hold that the Images or Pictures of Christ, of the blessed Mother of God always a Virgin, and of other Saints ought to be kept and reserved, and that a due Honour and Veneration ought to be given them.* This and no more is the true Standard of our Faith in Reference to the Point in Question. And as it is thus stated, it has been a *Term of Communion* ever since the *Manichees* began to shew themselves profess'd Enemies of holy Pictures, that is, some Ages before Saint *Gregory*'s Time. So that whatever Mr. *Collier* out of his Abundance of Charity towards us is pleased to add to this, is all his own: For we utterly disclaim it and protest against it. And if this will not suffice to clear us from the Imputation of paying an *Idolatrous Worship* to *Images* and *Pictures*, I know not what can possibly do it. I dare therefore confidently assure Mr. *Collier*, that he may with the same Safety of Conscience carry his Respects for

those

122 Dial. 2. §. 7. *Roman Catholicks profess* those pious Objects, *to the Lengths of the Church of Rome*, as he *kisses* the *Bible*, or *bows* to the *Communion Table*, or to the *venerable Name of Jesus*: Or finally, as he keeps *holy days* in Honour of *Saints* departed: All which are undoubtedly *religious Respects*, as being paid upon a *Religious Motive*, and ultimately refer'd to God himself. And of this Nature was the religious Devotion, which St. *Augustin* and his Company paid to the *Cross* and *Picture* of our Saviour, when it was carried as a *Banner* before them.

'Tis very true indeed, that *there is not the least Intimation* in *Bede, that they worship'd it*. And God forbid there should be any such Intimation; if by the Word *Worship* (the ambiguous Signification whereof, is of wouderful Use to *Protestants* in this Controversy) If, I say, Mr. *Collier* is pleased to mean the same, as paying *divine Honours* to it. This indeed is not intimated by *Bede*. But the Relation of the very Fact before us is more than a bare Intimation, that they paid a *religious Devotion* to it; this being wholly inseparable from their carrying it in a *Religious Procession* as a *Banner* before them. For I presume Mr. *Collier* will not deny, that when in our solemn Processions abroad, we have the *Cross* and the *Reliques* and *Pictures* of Saints carried before us, we intend to pay a *religious Honour* to 'em by so doing. And so did without all Dispute St. *Augustin* and his Company, who by their Example introduced that Form of Devotion into this Island.

But Suppose they had prostrated themselves before the *Cross* or *Picture* of Christ, or *bow'd* down to it, or *kiss'd* it, as we yearly do in a solemn Manner upon *Good Friday*, to testify our Gratitude to Christ for having died on the Cross for us: If Mr. *Collier* will needs call this *Worshipping*,

then

then he is a *Worshipper* of the *Communion Table,* when he bows down to it, and of the *Bible* when he *kisses* it, and of the *Sacramental Bread* and *Wine,* when he *kneels down* out of Respect before it; and so *he carries his Respects* for holy Things of the same *created* Nature as a *Cross* or *Picture, to all the Lengths of the Church of* Rome; and our paying a *due Honour* and *Veneration* to such Things, let him call it by what Name he pleases, is a *Term of Communion* he cannot reasonably Scruple at.

G. But Mr. *Collier* farther tells us, that *Image-Worship* was so far from being the Doctrine of *Rome* in Pope *Gregory*'s Time, *that he determines flatly against it in his Letter to* Serinus *Bishop of* Marseilles.

P. Sir, Pope *Gregory* writes nothing in that Letter, but what every *Roman Catholick* in the World will subscribe to. It appears from it, that the People at *Merseilles* had effectually carried their Devotion to the Pictures hung up in their Churches, even to a *criminal Excess,* as St. *Gregory* calls it. Which, by the by, is at least an unanswerable Proof, that *holy Images* and *Pictures* were not only kept in Churches, but a religious Honour was paid to them long before that Time. For People do not usually come to *Excesses* all on a sudden, but pass gradually and by Steps from the moderate Use of Things to an Abuse of them, when that happens to be the Case. However the Bishop of the Place being made sensible of these Abuses, commanded the *Church-pictures to be broken and thrown away.* Whereupon St. *Gregory* wrote to him, and commended indeed his Zeal in endeavouring to reform the *Excesses,* the People had run into, but blamed the Methods he had taken in Order to it. And in another Letter to the same Bishop quoted by Mr. *Collier,* after having expres'd

his

124 Dial. 2. §. 7. Roman Catholicks profess his Dislike of the Bishop's *Breaking the Pictures*, he writes thus. " In short, says he, let no Statuary or Painter be discouraged in their Profession;
" but take all imaginable Care that nothing made
" by them may be honour'd to Adoration. Thus
" by this Temper the Understandings of the un-
" learned may be instructed, and their Affections
" warm'd at the Sight of Church-Pictures, and
" our Worship at the same Time be all of it
" *refer'd to God*, and *directed to the holy Trinity*."

Now it is plain from these Words of St. *Gregory*, that the People of *Marseilles* were fal'n into such *criminal Excesses*, as to give that *Honour* and *Adoration* to *Pictures*, which is due only to *God* and the *blessed Trinity*. And Mr. *Collier* has the Charity to apply this to us, and represent the *Church of Rome* as guilty of the same *criminal Excesses*, which Pope *Gregory* condemn'd in the People of *Marseilles*. For otherwise it is Nonsense in him to say, that Pope *Gregory* has in the abovesaid Letters *determined the Matter flatly against us*. I heartily pray God to forgive him and his Brethren the Injustice they continually do us in their Misrepresentations of our Doctrine.

M. *Collers*'s second Instance to prove, That *the Terms of Communion are not upon the same Foot now, as they were in Saint* Gregory'*s Time*, is, *Because that Pope*, says he p. 66. *Did not carry the Supremacy up to the Pretensions since insisted on by the Court of* Rome.

I answer *first* that the Question is not concerning the *Court of Rome*, but the *Faith* of the *Church* in Communion with the *See of Rome*: Which are two very different Things. For I hope that by the Grace of God, I shall always live and die a true Member of the *Church of Rome*, tho' I never did,

did, nor ever was ambitious to belong to the *Court of Rome.*

I answer 2*dly*, that if Mr. *Collier* speaks of *Pretensions*, for Example, to *Infallibility*, or the *depoſing Power*, they neither are now, nor ever were *Terms of Communion*. And ſo it is wholly wide from the Purpoſe, whether St. *Gregory* did or did not carry the *Supremacy* up to thoſe Pretenſions. Or if Mr. *Collier* only hints at real or ſuppoſed *Encroachments* of the Pope upon the Privileges of particular Churches, I don't find it was ever look'd upon as a *Breach of Communion* to oppoſe him in ſuch Caſes.

But that St. *Gregory* maintain'd the *divine Right* of his *Supremacy* over the *whole Church* as vigorouſly as any Pope ever did, is manifeſt from his own Words. For *(L.* 11. *Epiſt.* 56. *vet. edit.)* he writes thus concerning a Biſhop who pretended to be exempted from the Juriſdiction of his *Metropolitan*. *If it be pretended*, ſays he, *that the Biſhop has neither a Metropolitan nor Patriarch, I anſwer then that his Cauſe is to be heard and decided by the See Apoſtolick*, WHICH IS THE HEAD OF ALL CHURCHES. This ſurely is plain and deciſive. Again, he writes thus to the Biſhop of *Syracuſa* L. 9. Epiſt. 59. *As to what they write of the Church of* Conſtantinople; *who doubts but that it is ſubject to the See Apoſtolick?* Now Conſtantinople was not ſubject to the Biſhop of *Rome*, either as it's *Metropolitan* or *Patriarch*. Since therefore St. *Gregory* thought it ſubject to him, he muſt neceſſarily believe, that his *See* had a *Spiritual Supremacy* over the whole Church. And the Belief of this, with Mr. *Collier*'s good Leave, was a *Term of Communion* in Pope *Gregory*'s Time, as well as it is now.

G. What you have ſaid amounts to an unanſwerable Proof, that the Belief of the Pope's *Supremacy*,

126 Dial. 2. §. 7. *Roman Catholicks profess*
as it is a *Term of Communion*, stands upon the same
Foot now, as it did in Pope *Gregory*'s Time. But
I should be glad to hear what Proof Mr. *Collier* has
alledg'd against it.

P. After having said, that St. *Gregory* did not
*carry the Supremacy up to the Pretensions since insisted on
by the Court of Rome*, he go's on thus. " This we
" may fairly collect from his Complaint against
" *John* Bishop of *Constantinople* for taking the Title
" of *universal Bishop* upon him. This in his Letter
" to *Constantia* the Empress he inveighs against as
" great *Pride* and *Presumption* in his Brother and
" Fellow-Bishop *John*. He declares against this
" haughty Title as a Contradiction to the Tenor
" of the Gospel, an Infraction of the Canons, and
" an Injury to the whole Catholick Church."

Thus Mr. *Collier*: And the Fact is unquestionable; to wit, that St. *Gregory* in several Letters,
complains bitterly of *John*'s taking upon him the
haughty Title of *Universal Patriarch*; which he
even calls a *Luciferian Pride:* And he was so far
from Assuming it to himself, that he only stiled
himself in his Letters, *the Servant of the Servants of
God*. But I am somewhat surprized to find Mr.
Collier step out of his Way, and interrupt the
Course of his History to pick up an Argument,
that has long since been worn thread-bare by a
hundred Repetitions of it, and as many Answers
to it. I shall therefore be very brief in mine,
which is grounded upon Monf. *Du Pin*'s short Relation of this Matter. Cent. 6. p. 67. where he
tells us, that John *of* Capadocia, *sirnamed the* Faster
was sharply reprehended by St. Gregory *for taking upon him the Title of* universal Patriarch: *Because this
Pope look'd upon this Title as a Mark of Ambition:
Tho' in the Sense of the Greeks it was innocent, and
signified nothing less than what St.* Gregory *thought.*

How-

However as that Saint underſtood it, the Title was unjuſtifiable on ſeveral Accounts. *Firſt*, becauſe it ſeem'd to import a Juriſdiction over the whole Church, which did not belong to the Biſhop of *Conſtantinople*, nor was indeed challenged by him. And 2*dly*, becauſe it ſeem'd to import that he was the *only Biſhop* in the World; or at leaſt, that all other Biſhops were but his *Deputies* and *Vicars*; a Dignity belonging to *Chriſt* alone. St. *Gregory* at leaſt underſtood it ſo, as appears from his own Writings, and particularly from his Words to the Empreſs *Conſtantia*, to whom he complains thus. *'Tis a lamentable Thing,* ſays he, *to be forced to bear, that my Brother and Fellow-Biſhop* John *deſpiſing all others, endeavours to be call'd the* ONLY BISHOP. L. 5. Ep: 20.

Hence it is plain, that Mr. *Collier*'s Argument to prove his Point is wholly inconcluſive. For it runs thus: *Pope* Gregory *rejected the Title of univerſal Biſhop, ergo, he did not carry the Supremacy up to the Pretenſions ſince inſiſted on by the Popes.* This I ſay, is inconcluſive; Becauſe no Pope in any Age ever took upon him the Title of *univerſal Biſhop* in the Senſe that it was inveigh'd againſt and rejected by St. *Gregory*. For if any Pope had ever declared himſelf to be the *Univerſal Biſhop* in ſuch a Manner, as to regard all other Biſhops as no better than his *Deputies* or *Vicars*, I am of Opinion he would have ſoon heard of it, and found by Experience, that he had reckon'd without his Hoſt. But if by the Title of *univerſal Biſhop* no more be meant, than a *Superintendency* over the *univerſal Church of Chriſt* belonging by *divine Right* to the Succeſſors of Saint *Peter*, this Title never was rejected, but always vigorouſly maintain'd by St. *Gregory*, as is evident from the Paſſages I have quoted from him. Whence I conclude that the *Supremacy*, conſider'd as *a Term of Communion*, ſtands *upon the ſame Foot*

128 Dial. 2. §.8. *The same Faith was preach'd* now, as it did in Pope *Gregory*'s Time: And so I shall always insist upon it as an incontestable Truth, that *Roman Catholicks* not only continue now in the Religion, which was profess'd by the *whole English Nation* in the 16 Century before the Apostacy of *Hen.* viii. but likewise profess to this Day the *Faith*, which St. *Augustin* preach'd. Because it is impossible to prove from any authentick History, that there happen'd any Change in the *publick Faith* of the *English Church* from its *Conversion* under the *Saxon* Kings till the *pretended Reformation*. In all which Space of Time our *Forefathers* (says a *Protestant* Writer) *were all* Papists *with a Vengeance:* Unless *sometimes a few* Lollards *started up, who were far liker the Disciples of* Fox *and* Naylor, *than Members of the true protestant Religion*.

G. But, Sir, what will it avail us to bring our Religion as high as the End of the 6th *Century*, unless we can also find it in the *primitive Ages*? I therefore desire to be satisfied in this Point, to wit, whether the Faith preach'd to the *Saxons* by St. *Augustin* was the same as had been preach'd to the *Britons* 400 Years before by *Fugatius* and *Damianus*.

SECT. 8.

The same Faith *was preach'd to the* Saxons, *as had been preach'd four hundred Years before to the* Britons.

P. SIR, the Answer to your Question will oblige me to clear a Point of no small Importance. For since I have now proved that the Religion profess'd to this Day by the *English Roman Catholicks* is the very same as St. *Augustin* preach'd to the *Saxons*; if it be made clear that the Faith preach'd preach'd by that holy Bishop to the *Saxons*, was the same as had been preach'd to the *Britons* 400 Years before by St. *Fugatius* and *Damianus*; two undeniable Consequences will follow, *viz. first*, that the Faith now profess'd by *Roman Catholicks* was the Faith of the *Second Century*; that is, the *ancient* and *primitive Faith*. And 2*dly*, that the Doctrine of the *reform'd Churches* is an *Innovation of that Faith* in all dogmatical Points, wherein it differs from the *Church of Rome*.

G. I plainly see these Consequences will follow, if it can be proved, that the *Britons* and *Saxons* received the same Faith at their Conversion.

P. *First* then, I prove it from this undeniable Fact, to wit, that the *Britons* as well as *Saxons* were converted by *Missioners* sent from *Rome*: The former by St. *Fugatius* and *Damianus* sent into *Britain* by Pope *Eleutherius*; and the latter by St. *Augustin*, and *his Company*, sent thither by Pope *Gregory the Great*.

G. But what's that to the Purpose? For cannot a Country at different Times receive different Religions from the same Place, if that Place changes it's Faith.

P. Yes, Sir, it may. But then it must be proved from unquestionable historical Facts, that *Rome* changed it's Faith in the Interval of Time between the Conversion of the *Britons* and that of the *Saxons*. For otherwise a Man must be void of all Modesty to assert it, and of Sense to believe it.

Let us suppose a Man should pretend to maintain, that the *Primacy* of the *See of Canterbury* is an *Innovation* introduced into the *English Church* five or six Ages after the Conversion of the *Saxons*; Suppose, I say, any one should pretend to maintain this, would he not be look'd upon as an er-

Dial. 2. §. 8. *The same Faith was preach'd* rant Trifler, unless he produced undeniable historical Facts to support his Assertion? And why so ? Because such an *Innovation*, join'd with the Circumstances, that must have attended it, could not, morally speaking, have escaped being recorded in some authentick History of the Time in which it happen'd. And if no such History can be produced, this universal Silence amounts to a moral Demonstration, that there never was any such Innovation ; and is a full Confutation of any Man, that should have the Confidence to impose it for a Truth, upon the Credulity of ignorant People.

In like manner therefore it suffices not barely to say, as *John Fox* do's, that the *Faith of Rome* was not the same in Pope *Gregory*'s Time, as it was in the Time of Pope *Eleutherius* ; But whoever will pretend to make good this bold Assertion, must produce plain and undeniable historical Facts to prove, that there was a *Change of Faith* in *Rome*, between the *Second* and *sixth Century* ; and to render this credible, he must descend to Particularities, and specify the most remarkable Circumstances of it ; as in what *Age*, and under what *Popes* and *Emperors* it happen'd ; who were chief *Promoters* or *Opposers* of it ; what *Disturbances* it caused ; what Books were writ *for* or *against* it, and what Synods were call'd to *approve* or *condemn* it. For these are the constant and natural Effects of Changes in Religion ; and if any such Changes had really been at *Rome* in the Interval of Time between the *Pontificates* of Pope *Eleutherius* and Pope *Gregory*, it is as incredible as the most palpable of Fictions, that they should not appear upon Record attended with all the material Circumstances belonging to them in every History writ in or about the Time, which produced those Changes.

Nay

Nay the bold Afferters of thefe pretended Innovations muft likewife inform us very particularly, who was the *firft Pope*, that laid claim to the *Supremacy*: Who it was that introduced the *Invocation of Saints*, the *Veneration* of their *Relicks*, the honouring of *pious Images* and *Pictures*, and Praying for the *Souls departed*. But above all they muft let us know, who was the firft Pope that *faid Mafs*. For if this was an *Innovation*, it was one of fuch an extraordinary Nature, that no Hiftorian could poffibly be ignorant either of it's Beginning, Progrefs, or full Eftablifhment in the *Church of Rome*.

However we are very fure, that St. *Gregory* was a *Maffing Pope*, and claim'd the *Supremacy* over the *whole Church*. And we are no lefs fure (as has been fully fhew'd) that the *Church of Rome* was in his Time in a full and quiet Poffeffion of all the other abovefaid *popifh* Articles. If therefore all thefe were *Innovations* brought in betwixt the *Second* and *fixth* Century; if there was no *Mafs* faid at *Rome* in the Days of *Eleutherius*; If that Pope was not acknowledg'd *Supreme Head* of the Church, if in his Time there was no *Invocation of Saints*, no Honour paid to their *Reliques*, no *Praying for the Dead*: In a Word, if *Proteftancy* was the Religion of *Rome* in thofe Days (for that muft have been the State of Religion in *Rome* before the fuppofed Change) I muft make bold to demand a particular Account taken from good Records and authentick Hiftory, how *Proteftancy* (as it is now call'd) came to be entirely banifh'd the City, and *Popery* fet up in it's Place before the End of the *Sixth Century*? For if no good Records or authentick Hiftoryan be produced to prove this

132 Dial. 2. §. 8. *The same Faith was preach'd* wonderful *Metamorphosis* of Religion in the most famous City of the World, no rational Man can possibly believe It: Because there is no Example of a Business of that Importance transacted upon so noble a Theater as the City of *Rome*, without being mention'd, nay particularized in every Circumstance by some Historian of Note.

G. I must needs own, it looks more like a *Romance* or *poetical Fiction* than a real Truth, that such a Revolution in the publick Faith and Religion of the *Metropolis* of the World should happen without being transmitted to Posterity even in all the Histories of the Time, in which it happen'd.

P. However this is not all. For it is an undeniable Truth, that *whole Christendom* was in Communion with Pope *Eleutherius* in the End of the *second Century*, and with Pope *Gregory* in the End of the *Sixth*: Excepting some scatter'd Remains of *Heresies* condemn'd in the four first *General Councils*. Whence it follows, that the pretended Change of Religion was not only in the City of *Rome*, but throughout *whole Christendom* both in the *East* and *West*: For no Pope ever communicated with a Nation that openly profess'd a different Religion from his own. So that we must suppose, that the *universal Church* in Communion with Pope *Eleutherius* being *stanch Protestants* in the *Second Century*, were all turn'd *rank Papists* before the End of the *Sixth*. 'Tis this chimerical Supposition they are bound to maintain, who assert that the *Faith of Rome* was not the same in Pope *Gregory*'s Time, as it was in the early Days of *Eleutherius*, to whose Zeal the *Britons* ow'd their Conversion.

But

But this wonderful Change of *whole Christendom* from the Religion now call'd *Protestancy*, to that which is now nicknamed *Popery*, is either recorded in some ancient History, or it is not. If not; By what Means have the bold Assertors of it come fairly and honestly to the Knowledge of it? For I should be apt to suspect they had dealt in the *black Art*, and conjured up some Spirit to inform them of what had pass'd in Reference to the pretended Innovations during the four Ages between Pope *Eleutherius* and *Gregory the Great*. But if it be recorded in any ancient History, (as it must undoubtedly be, if it happen'd at all) I desire to know when, and by what Methods this stupendious Revolution in the *universal Church* was brought to pass? As, whether it was done *clandestinly* or *openly*; Whether by *Violence* or *Fraud*? Whether *whole Christendom* was bribed or bullied into this strange *Apostacy* from its *ancient Religion*? Whether it was compass'd all at once or by Degrees, and whether it met with any Opposition or not? When these few Questions are clearly answer'd, I shall have double the Number ready for any one, that is disposed to undertake that Task.

G. I fear indeed there will not be many Pretenders to it. For I perceive there lie Objections in Ambuscade, to what side soever the Answerer shall turn himself.

P. I believe indeed he will meet with some Rubs in his Way. But I will now briefly shew the utter Improbability of any such Change in the Faith of *Rome* from the Silence of the four first *general Councils*; which are all received as true and Orthodox Councils by the *Church of England*, and were all four held in the Interval of Time between Pope *Eleutherius* and *Gregory the Great*: The *first* An. 325. And the last of the four An. 451. which

The same Faith was preach'd was about 250 Years after the Conversion of the *Britons*, and but a 150 Years before the Conversion of the *Saxons*.

Now if the pretended Changes in the *ancient Faith of Rome*, happen'd at any Time between the *Pontificate* of Pope *Eleutherius*, and the *fourth general Council*, it is altogether incredible, that not one of those August and Orthodox Assemblies should take any Notice of such *Monstrous Innovations*, as they must be supposed to have been. On the contrary it cannot be question'd, but they would have exerted themselves as vigorously against those pernicious Novelties and Errors, as they did against the new-broach'd Heresies of the *Arians, Macedonians, Nestorians, Eutychians,* and other Hereticks of those Times. Since therefore it is plain Fact, that not one of those four Councils impeach'd the *Church of Rome* of any Error or Novelty in Faith, it is a demonstrative Proof, that no Pope or Popes, between Pope *Eleutherius* and the *fourth general Council* had made any Innovations in the ancient Faith of the Church.

G. But was there any other *general Council* held before Pope *Gregory*?

P. Yes, Sir, the *fifth*, or *second* of *Constantinople* was held a hundred and two Years after the *fourth*; That is about the Middle of the Age, in which St. *Gregory* was chosen Pope. And this, tho' held as the *first* of that Name, in the very *Metropolis* of the *East*, which always regarded the *See* of *Rome* with a kind of jealous Eye, had as little to object against that *See* on the Score of *Errors* and *Novelties* in Faith, as any of the four former Councils: All which put together proves demonstratively that the *Church of Rome* was not then guilty of any: And it follows from it, by an undeniable Consequence, that there had been no

Innova-

Innovations made in the Faith of that Church from the Time of Pope *Eleutherius*, who sent Miffioners to inftruct the *Britons*, to that of Pope *Gregory*, who sent St. *Auguftin* to convert the *Saxons*. Whence it follows again, that the Faith preach'd by St. *Auguftin* to the *Saxons* was the fame as had been preach'd 400 Years before to the *Britons*, by St. *Fugatius* and *Damianus*: Which is precifely the Point I have undertaken to prove. Becaufe this brings the *Roman Catholick Faith* up to the very *primitive Ages*, and at the fame Time fhews, that all the *Proteftant Articles of Religion*, as far as they are contrary to that Faith, are truly *Novelties* introduced into *England* by the pretended Reformation.

But I fhall now pafs to a fecond Proof of the Point we have before us, grounded upon *Bede*'s Relation of the Conference between St. *Auguftin* and the *Britifh Bifhops*: By which we are inform'd, that he only required of them a Conformity in *three Things*, viz. 1. In keeping *Eafter* at it's due Time. 2*dly*, In adminiftring *Baptifm* according to the Manner ufed in the *Church of Rome*, and 3*dly*, in Preaching with him the Word of God to the *Saxons*. Upon which he promifed to *tolerate* many other Practices, not fpecified by holy *Bede*, tho' differing from the *Cuftoms* of the Church of *Rome*.

Hence it appears evident to me, that the *Britons* were not of the *Proteftant Religion* in any of thofe doctrinal Points, which are now controverted between us and the *reform'd Churches*; but that on the contrary they agreed with St. *Auguftin* in all thofe Points. Becaufe nothing can be more improbable than that he fhould importune them, as he did, to be Fellow-Labourers with him in Preaching to the *Saxons*, if their Faith and Religion

had

136 Dial. 2. §. 8. *The same Faith was preach'd*
had differ'd from his in in any of those important Articles; which now make the irreconcileable Breach between the *reform'd Churches* and the Church of *Rome*; since he even required an entire Uniformity both in the Celebration of *Easter*, and the Manner of administring the Sacrament of *Baptism*. And he had Reason to insist upon the one as well as the other. Because a difference in either might have been a Source of Divisions in our *Infant-Church*, scandalized the *new Converts*, and, by Consequence, obstructed the Progress of the *Gospel*. But if he had found, that besides their Disagreement in these two Articles (which in the Bottom were but Points of *Discipline*) they differ'd from the Church of *Rome*, as *Protestants* now do, in Matters of *reveal'd Faith* and *Doctrine*, I think it more probable, that he would have endeavour'd to convert the *Britons*, than importuned them to join with him in preaching to the *Saxons*. For was it ever known in the Christian World that a *Catholick Bishop* invited *Protestant Ministers* to preach to his Flock? This would be very extraordinary indeed. And yet the Case would be exactly parallel, if it were true, that when St. *Augustin* invited the *British Bishops* to labour jointly with him in the Conversion of the *Saxons*, their *Faith* and *Religion* was the same, as is now profess'd by our modern *Protestants*.

G. However we are informed by holy *Bede* of St. *Augustin*'s telling the *British Bishops*, that *they acted in many Particulars contrary to the Customs of the Church of Rome*. And who can tell what those *many Particulars* were? Or whether some of them at least were not the same as are now maintain'd against us by the *reform'd* Churches?

P. Whatever they were, for holy *Bede* has not specified them, I can say with an entire Assurance, that they had no Relation to the *doctrinal Points*, which

which are now maintain'd againſt us by the *reform'd* Churches. Becauſe St. *Auguſtin* declared, that if they would but comply with the three Conditions he propoſed, he would *tolerate* all other Differences. Now ſince he judged that they might lawfully be *tolerated* for the Sake of Peace, 'tis manifeſt he did not look upon them as *Errors* in *Faith*: Becauſe Errors deſtructive of the *Faith once deliver'd to the Saints*, cannot be tolerated upon any Pretence whatſoever.

As for Example, if St. *Auguſtin* had found the *Britiſh Biſhops* rejecting, as *Proteſtants* do, the *Maſs*, ridiculing the Doctrine of *Purgatory*, or running down as an *Idolatrous Worſhip* the *Honour*, which he and his Company paid to *Saints*, their *Images*, and *Reliques*, would there have been any Room for a *Toleration?* Has the *Church of Rome* ever communicated with a Nation, that openly condemn'd theſe Things, or any one Article of her Faith? No, there is not an Example of it. And therefore ſince St. *Auguſtin* (who brought from *Rome*, and preach'd to the *Saxons* all the *Papiſtical* Doctrines we now profeſs) was content to communicate with the *Britons*, and tolerate all their Practices, tho' diſagreeing from the Cuſtoms of his own Church, provided they would but comply with the few Things he demanded of them, he was moſt certainly convinced, that they agreed with him in all thoſe Articles of Religion, which have ſince been rejected by the *reform'd Churches*, and that the Practices he intended to tolerate, regarded only ſuch Points of *Diſcipline*, as are indifferent in themſelves, and wherein moſt *national Churches*, tho' of the ſame *Faith* and *Communion*, are wont to differ more or leſs from one another.

This I take to be a full Proof, that the *ancient Britons* were no *Proteſtants*; and that the Faith they had

138 Dial. 2. §. 9. *The same Faith was preach'd* had received from *Rome* under Pope *Eleutherius*, was the same, as St. *Augustin* preach'd four hundred Years after to the *Saxons*.

SECT. 9.
The same Subject continued.

'TIS however my Misfortune here to have Mr. *Collier* once more my Adversary in the Article of the *Pope's Supremacy*; which he pretends to have been disown'd by the *Britons*. But I must here distinguish between Mr. *Collier* as an *Historian*, and as a *Disputant*. As he is a *Disputant*, I will endeavour to give Satisfactory Answers to his Arguments. But as he is an *Historian*, I think he has not acted with the Sincerity he ought in Relating the Articles insisted on by St. *Augustin*, otherwise than they are set down in *Bede*. For he tells his Reader p. 76. *that the Articles insisted on were, that they* [*the British Bishops*] *should keep* Easter, *and administer Baptism according to the Usages of the Roman Church,* AND OWN THE POPE'S AUTHORITY.

Now there is not a Word of this last Article in *Bede*. For the *third* according to this Author was, *that the British Bishops should join with St. Augustin in preaching to the Saxons*. And the Pope is not so much as mention'd in any of the three Articles. Neither do I find that *Geoffrey of Monmouth*, an ancient Historian, in his Relation of the Conference between St. *Augustin* and the *British Bishops*, makes any mention of their *Disowning the Pope's Supremacy*. He speaks indeed of *Dinoth* the Abbot of *Bangor* as a Prolocutor of the Assembly on the *British* Side; and tells us, that the Answer he gave to St. *Augustin's* Proposals was, *that the Britons ow'd no Subjection to him, as having an Archbishop*

bishop of their own: Nor would they give themselves the Trouble to preach to their Enemies. That the Saxons had taken their Country from them, for which they hated them extremely, and cared not what Religion they were of: Nor would they communicate with them any more than with Dogs. L. 11. C. 7.

This was the Substance of *Dinoth*'s Answer according to *Geoffrey* of *Monmouth*; in which there is not the least Insinuation, that St. *Augustin* had insisted on *their owning the Pope's Supremacy*: But the most that can be gather'd from it is, that in the Conference he had made some Mention of his being their *Archbishop* and *Superiour*. And even that is not a necessary Consequence. Because the hot *Dinoth* speaking from the Abundance of his gall'd Heart, might sally forth into that warm Expression *of Owing no Subjection* to St. *Augustin*, on Purpose to affront him, tho' he had not claim'd any *Jurisdiction* over them in Quality of their *Archbishop*, in express Terms. Because we may easily suppose they had been inform'd of it, before their second Meeting.

G. But what Drift had Mr. *Collier* in inserting that Article concerning the *Pope*; since there is no Mention of it in *Bede*, who is the most ancient Recorder of that celebrated Conference?

P. It cannot be question'd, but he intended it as an *Innuendo*, that the *British Bishops* did not own any Subjection to the *See of Rome*. 'Tis true, he has produced a *Welsh Manuscript* to make this suspected Article pass for current. But it appears somewhat singular, that after having follow'd *Bede*'s History Step by Step in every Thing relating to St. *Augustin*, he should on a sudden give his *venerable Guide* the slip in so critical a Passage, to take up with a *Manuscript*, which has neither *Date* nor *Name* set to it to recommend it, as he observes him-

140 Dial. 2. §. 9. *The same Faith was preach'd*

self, and is of a doubtful Authority, as appears from the Arguments he has alledg'd *for* and *against* it. For the Testimony of *Bede* is surely of greater Weight, than an *anonymous Manuscript*, which may be a spurious Piece for ought we know.

G. But, Sir, I remember that St. *Augustin* had no sooner proposed to the *British Bishops* the three Conditions he required of them, but they answer'd him peremptorily, that *they would do none of those Things, nor receive him as their Archbishop*. And the same is confirm'd by *Geoffrey of Monmouth*, as you told me this very Moment. Now this seems to imply their Disowning the *Pope's Authority*, who had constituted St. *Augustin* their Archbishop, and given him Jurisdiction over them.

P. This is the Ground of Mr. *Colliers*'s Argument, when he turns *Disputant* upon the Point. And least it should lose any Grains of it's Weight, I shall deliver it to you in his own Words.

"But farther, *says he*, the Certainty of the *Bri-*
"*tish* Churches rejecting the *Pope's Authority*, and
"*Augustin* the Monk's *Jurisdiction* do's not de-
"pend on the Credit of this *Welsh Manuscript*.
"For this Point is sufficiently clear'd from *Bede*'s
"own Words; where the *British Clergy* declare
"against *Augustin* for their *Archbishop*. Whereas
"had they own'd the *Pope's Authority*, they ought
"to have submitted to *Augustin*, who acted by
"the Pope's Commission, and had his Orders to
"be their superiour. Now 'twas not possible for
"them at such a Distance from *Rome*, to express
"their Disowning the *papal Authority* more ef-
"fectually than by rejecting him, whom his Ho-
"liness had sent to be Archbishop over them.
"p. 76."

Thus

Thus Mr. *Collier*. But his Argument will not hold Water. For tho' it be true indeed that the *Britons* refused to receive Saint *Augustin* for their *Archbishop*, it do's not follow from it, that therefore they disown'd the *Pope's Supremacy*, which I presume is the Point Mr. *Collier* drives at. For otherwise he says nothing to the Purpose.

G. Sir, Mr. *Collier* says, that *had the* British *Bishops own'd the Pope's Authority, they ought to have submitted to* Augustin, *who acted by the Pope's Commission, and had his Orders to be their Superiour.* And I confess he seems to me to have Reason on his Side.

G. Sir, if they had own'd, that the Pope's Authority extended to the placing one as an *ordinary Superiour* over their own Archbishop, they ought in Consequence to have submitted to St. *Augustin*. But there was no incoherence in their acknowledging Pope *Gregory Supreme Head* of the universal Church, and their refusing to pay Obedience to a Person sent by him in Quality of an ordinary Superiour over themselves and their Archbishop. Because they might think that the Pope had carried his Pretensions too high in Degrading, as it were, their own *Archbishop*, and subjecting both him and them to a *foreign Jurisdiction*. And I really believe, that, tho' there be not a Catholick Nation upon Earth, but what acknowledges the *divine Right* of the Pope's *Supremacy*, yet if he should take upon him to send over a foreign *Archbishop* with a Commission to exercise *an ordinary Jurisdiction* over the Archbishop of *Prague, Toledo*, or *Paris*, for Example, he would be as vigorously opposed now, as St. *Augustin* was by the *British Clergy*, and in all Likelihood be sent back with the same Answer as that Prelate was, to wit, *That they would not receive him as their Archbishop.*

But,

142 Dial. 2. §. 9. *The same Faith was preach'd*

But would any Man interpret this as a Disowning of the *Pope's Supremacy*? No surely; For all that could be legally infer'd from it, would be, that it was their Judgment, that the Pope had exceeded the just Limits of his Authority: There being a large Difference between Disowning a Person's just Authority, and declaring against the real or supposed Excesses committed by him in the Exercise of it. And therefore Mr. *Collier* argues but weakly in Adding, *that it was impossible for the British Clergy to express their Disowning the papal Authority more effectually than by rejecting him, whom his Holiness had sent to be Archbishop over them.* For they might have express'd it much more effectually by telling St. *Augustin*, that the Pope, who had sent him, had no Authority at all to exercise any Jurisdiction over their Church, much less to obtrude a foreign Archbishop upon them. This would have been an obvious and natural Answer, had they disown'd the *Pope's Supremacy*. But they did not so much as mention him in their Answer: And their Refusing to receive St. *Augustin* for their Archbishop implied no more, than that they were convinced in their Judgment, that the Pope had exceeded the just Bounds of his Authority, in placing him over them, and resolved to maintain the Liberties and Privileges, which their Church had possess'd by a long Prescription.

I only add, that there are innumerable Instances in *Ecclesiastical* History of particular Churches maintaining their Privileges against the *See of Rome*; and that, without Derogating any more from the *Divine Right* of the *Pope's Supremacy*, than a Subject is supposed to derogate from the *just Prerogative* of the *Crown*, when he go's to Law with his Sovereign; or a Son to disown the Authority, his Father has by Nature over him, when he refuses to obey a Command, that appears unreasonable to him.   G.

G. But who then was in the Wrong? St *Gregory* or the *British Bishops*?

P. Perhaps neither the one nor the other: As it often happens in Disputes about Privileges, and Law Suits, wherein both Parties for the most Part think they have Reason on their Side. As to St. *Gregory*, Mr. *Collier* himself has made his Apology in very strong and pathetick Terms p. 79. where he concludes his honourable Character of that Pope in the following Manner.

To conclude, says he, *if the rest of his Successors had kept close to his Doctrine, govern'd themselves by his Plan, and moved within the Compass of his Pretensions, 'tis probable the Church might have continued in it's primitive good Correspondence, and the Divisions of Christendom might have been prevented.* It appears then to be Mr. *Colliers's* Judgment, that St. *Gregory* did not carry his Pretensions to any Excess, when he constituted St. *Augustin* Superiour over the *British Bishops*. And as to the *Doctrine* taught by that Saint, I appeal to Mr. *Collier's* own Conscience, whether *Roman Catholicks* or *Protestants* keep closer to it.

However to say something in Justification of St. *Gregory's* Proceedings in Reference to the *British Bishops*, it may be alledged, that the *British Clergy* were at that Time, as *Gildas* laments, faln into very great and scandalous Irregularities, which their Bishops either connived at, or neglected to correct. Now St *Gregory*, who had the pastoral Care of all Churches incumbent on him, might easily think he did not act beyond the just Limits of the Authority, God had bestow'd upon him, in Employing proper Means to reclaim that ancient Part of his Flock, which was thus gone astray: And the placing a Superiour of an unspotted Character over them, with full Powers to reform the

Abuses,

Dial. 2. §. 9. *The same Faith was preach'd*
Abuses, he should find amongst them, was the Expedient he judg'd proper for that charitable Design, tho' the Opposition it met with from the *British Bishops*, render'd it ineffectual.

But as to what regards those Prelates, whether they had or had not Reason on their Side in refusing receive St. *Augustin* as their *Archbishop* (for I will not presume to decide the Matter) they were most certainly to blame in not complying with the *three Atticles* he insisted on: Which were both reasonable in themselves, and might have been accepted of without any Prejudice to the disputed Privileges of their Church. Nay I cannot tell how to excuse them from the Guilt of *Schism* in continuing obstinately in their particular Way of keeping *Easter*, even after it had been solemnly decreed against by the great Council of *Nicea*. And what aggravated their Singularity in this Practice was, that their pretended Tradition for it could not be traced any higher on this Side of the *British* Seas, than the Abbot *Columba*. As may be seen in *Bede* L. 2. C. 19. and L. 3. C. 25. and this *Columba* was born and died in the very Age, that St. *Augustin* converted the Kingdom of *Kent*. But let that be as it will, 'tis manifest that their refusing to acknowledge Saint *Augustin* for their Archbishop is no Proof of their Disowning the *Pope's Supremacy*. And so the Arguments I have made Choice of to establish the principal Point before us, to wit, that the *Britons* had received the same Faith, which St. *Augustin* preach'd to the *Saxons*, continue in their full Force.

However I prove it 3*dly*, thus. If the *Britons* had been persuaded that they and St. *Augustin* differ'd in their System of Faith and Religion, as *Protestants*, and *Roman Catholicks* do now; It is but rational to think, that when he importuned them

to

to join with him in preaching to the *Saxons*, they would have told him in plain Terms, that it was in vain to make any such Proposal to them; because they being in many weighty Points of a different Persuasion from him and his Company, could not possibly resolve to preach Doctrines contrary to their own Judgment, and to what they had received from their Forefathers. That for their Parts the *Mass* was to them an Abomination; That the Popes had usurp'd a *Supremacy*, which belong'd not to them by *divine Right*; That his praying to the *Saints*, and honouring their *Images* and *Reliques* was downright *Idolatry*, and his *Purgatory* a meer Fable; and that therefore they could not in Conscience communicate with him, nor regard him otherwise than as a *Heretick*, and Promoter of false Doctrines. This, I say, would have been a much more rational and obvious Answer, if especially they had been *Protestants* in the Articles I have mention'd (as *John Fox* pretends) than the frivolous and unchristian Reason alledg'd by them according to *Geoffrey of Monmouth*, to wit, that they would not preach the Gospel to their Enemies, who had driven them out of their Country.

I prove it 4*thly*, because there is not an Example of a *Protestant Saint* in the *Roman Calendar*; or that the *Church of Rome* ever canonized a Person, that differ'd from her in any one Article of Faith defined by her as such. Now she acknowledges a great Number of those for Saints, who preach'd in *Britain*, or govern'd the *British Church* long before the coming of St. *Augustin*. As St. *Fastidius* Archbishop of *London* in the Beginning of the fifth Century. St. *Ninian*, who was of the Blood Royal, studied his Divinity at *Rome*, converted the *Picts*, and died, An. 432. St. *Palladius*, who was sent

146 Dial. 2. §. 9. *The same Faith was preach'd* sent into *Britain* by Pope *Celestin* in the very Year that St. *Ninian* died. And lastly (to omit many others for Brevity Sake) St. *Dubritius* Archbishop of *Caerleon*, and his Successor St. *David*. The former of which, says *Geoffrey of Monmouth*, *being Primate of* Britain, *and Legate of the See Apostolick, was so famous for his religious Holiness, that he cured any Man by the Force of his Prayers.* Hist. Brit. L. 9. C. 12. he died An. 522. And of St. *David* (who translated the Archiepiscopal See to the Town call'd to this Day by his Name, and lived to a very great Age) *John Bale* writes, *that he was put into the Catalogue of Papistical Gods by Pope* Calixtus *the second*.

These eminent Persons therefore, and many more of the ancient *British* Church were all *Papistical Saints*, and have always been acknowledg'd for such by the *Church of Rome*; which never put any *Protestant*, or any Man of a different Faith from her own into the Catalogue of *Papistical Gods*, as honest *John Bale* is pleased to call them. And this I take to be an unanswerable Proof that the *ancient Britons* (excepting those, who were for a Time infected with the *Pelagian* Heresy) agreed in all doctrinal Points with the *See of Rome*; for otherwise we should not have heard of so many *Calendar-Saints* among them. And 'tis remarkable, that there is not the least mention in *Bede*, that when St. *German* and St. *Lupus* came into *Britain* (which was about the Year 440) to purge it from the *Pelagian Heresy*, they found any other Errors in Faith, that wanted a *Reformation*. Whence it follows, that they found the Faith of the *Britons* conformable to their own in all other Respects. And we may easily know, what Religion these two Apostolical Men were of from a few Instances related by the abovesaid venerable Historian.

For,

For, (besides that they are honour'd as *Saints*, and have their festival Days allotted them by the *Church of Rome*; which is a Demonstration that they were not *Protestants* either in Doctrine or Practice,) holy *Bede* tells us, that a blind Girl being presented to St. *German* by her Parents, *he made a short Prayer, and being full of the holy Ghost invok'd the Trinity, and taking into his Hands a Box of Reliques, which hung about his Neck, he apply'd it to the Girl's Eyes, which were immediately deliver'd from Darkness, and fill'd with the Light of Truth.* L. 1. C. 18. After this the two holy Bishops went to the Tomb of St. *Alban* to pay their Devotions to that holy Martyr. Where after having pray'd a considerable Time, St. *German* commanded the Tomb to be open'd, and deposited therein some of the Reliques of the Apostles and other Martyrs, which he had brought with him out of *France*, and in exchange thereof carried away some of the Earth, which had been sprinkled with the Martyr's Blood. *ibid.*

How rank do's every Part of this Relation favour of *Modern Popery*? For I am very sure no Bishop of *Protestant* Principles would have carried a *Box of Reliques* about his Neck; Nor have had Faith enough to believe, that the Touch of them would restore Sight to the Blind. Nor would he have made a Pilgrimage to St. *Alban*'s Tomb; much less carried away with him as a valuable Treasure a Part of the Earth, on which the Martyr's Blood had been shed. 'Tis plain then that this eminent Prelate was a stanch *Roman Catholick*. And since at that Time (which was above a 150 Years before St. *Augustin*'s coming) he found no Errors to be reform'd in the *British Church*, but those of the *Pelagian Heresy*, we may reasonably conclude their Faith was the same as his, and even their Practice in the keeping of *Easter*. For otherwife he would most certainly have taken Notice of its Singularity, and reform'd it according to the Decree of the Council of *Nicea*, and the Practice of the universal Church. And so the Religion establish'd amongst them was the very same *Popery* which St. *German* profess'd, and St. *Augustin* preached above 150 Years after to the *Saxons*.

To conclude, I argue thus from the Premises I have establish'd. The *English Roman Catholicks* profess the same Faith now, as was preach'd by St. *Augustin* above *eleven hundred* Years ago. But the Faith taught by St. *Augustin* was in all Points, wherein *Protestants* and *Catholicks* differ, the very same that St. *Fugatius* and *Damianus* had preach'd to the *Britons* four hundred Years before; therefore in all contested Points the *English Roman Catholicks* profess the same Faith now, as was preach'd by those two holy Bishops in the very *second Age* of *Christianity*. That is, in one of those two primitive Ages, in which according to the common Way of speaking among *Protestants* the Gospel was preach'd in its *full Purity*. If this Argument be not conclusive, I desire to know where the Defect of it lies. But if it be conclusive, as I conceive it is, the *Reform'd Churches* are in a defenseless Condition; as being convicted of Teaching in every Article, wherein they differ from the Church of *Rome*, a Doctrine directly contrary to that of the *primitive Church*.

SECT. 10.

Some Observations upon the Conversion *of* England *under Pope* Gregory.

G. SIR, I have kept Pace with you from Argument to Argument, with the best of

my

Attention, and laid them up as well as I could in my Memory. But I am still at a Loss to know what Connection the historical Circumstances of *England*'s Conversion have with the *external Marks* of the true Church, by which she is distinguish'd from all others.

P. Sir, you will see it in due Time. But I must beg leave to premise some Observations upon the short History I have entertained you with. For these will serve as Lights to direct you to the Point you are in Search of.

First then, I observe that the Persons employ'd in the Conversion of this Island had their Commission given them by the undoubted Successor of St. *Peter*, and St. *Peter* had his immediately from *Christ*. So that the Legality of their *Mission* and *Ministry* was as unquestionable, as the *Commission* of a *civil* or *military Officer*, Which he receives from the Hand of the *prime Minister* vested with that Power by the Supreme Magistrate. This is so essential an Article, that they, who cannot derive their *Ecclesiastical Mission* and *Ministry* originally from *Christ* himself and his blessed *Apostles*, by a continued Succession of *Bishops* descending from them in the *same Communion*, are stigmatized by our blessed Saviour with the infamous Character of *Thieves and Robbers, who enter not by the Door, but climb up another Way.* Joh. 10. v. 1.

2*dly*, St. *Augustin* and his Companions brought into *England* the Religion of the *Place* from whence they came, and of the *holy Bishop*, by whom they were sent: And the Profession of this Religion alone was supported by publick Authority in all Parts of this Kingdom for the Space of little less than 900 Years, counting from the Conversion of the whole *Heptarchy*. Whence it follows that if Pope *Gregory* was orthodox in his Faith, St. *Au-*

150 Dial. 2. §. 10. *Some Observations upon the* *gustin* and his Fellow-Missioners were so too: And if St. *Augustin* and his Fellow-Missioners were orthodox in their Faith, the *Saxons* converted by them were so likewise. And hence it follows, again, that they, who continued for 900 Years in the Profession of that very Faith and Religion, to which the *Saxons* were converted, it follows, I say, that they have the same Assurance of the Truth and Purity of their Faith as St. *Gregory* himself had: And all *Roman Catholicks*, who to this Day profess no other Religion than that of their Ancestors, have the same Security for the Truth of theirs.

Now I may safely say, he must be a bold Man, who dare accuse of Errors in Faith so great a Man, both for his eminent Learning and Holiness of Life, as St. *Gregory* has always been esteem'd; and whom the unanimous Consent of Antiquity has ever regarded as one of the most illustrious *Saints* and *Pillars* of God's Church: In so much that the *Greeks* as well as *Latins* solemnize his annual Feast, and never mention him in their Writings but with the profoundest Respect, and Veneration for his Memory. So that whoever makes a Difficulty in Matters of Faith and Religion to venture his Soul (as all *Roman Catholicks* do) upon the same Bottom with St. *Gregory*, has I fear some Interest in View much dearer to him, than that of Arriving safe in the Harbour of eternal Salvation.

Pray tell me, Sir, suppose you were to die this Moment, in whose Company, would you now chose to venture your Soul? With St. *Gregory* who transplanted to this Island the Faith, of which he was himself convinced, or in the Company of those *reforming Gentlemen*, who fell from that Faith, and set up a new System of Religion upon the Ruines of it?

G. I

G. I think indeed the Choice will not admit of much Deliberation. For, if *true Faith* be necessary to Salvation, as you have proved it to be, I really believe the Company of those Gentlemen, who apostatized from the Faith taught by St. *Gregory* and his faithful Disciple St. *Augustin* is not much to be coveted in the other World.

P. 3*dly, England* being converted was at the same Time incorporated with the *great Body* of the *Catholick* or *universal Church*. That is to say, it became not a *separate Communion* standing by itself like the upstart Churches of the *Lutherans* and *Calvinists*, who by their pretended Reformation divided themselves from all the pre-existing Christian Churches in the World, but it enter'd on the contrary into the common *Sheepfold*, and united itself by *Faith* and *Communion* to the whole visible Body of the *Catholick Church* upon Earth. So that it's *Faith*, tho' newly communicated to it, was not new in itself, but perfectly *Catholick* and *Apostolick*. *Catholick* both in Regard of *Time* and *Place*, and *Apostolick*, by having been received from the undoubted Successors of the Apostles.

4*thly*, Tho' the several petty Kingdoms of the *Saxons*, as likewise the Kingdoms of *Scotland* and *Ireland* were converted by different Missioners, and at different Times, they all received the *same Faith* in every Point, wherein there is any Disagreement between the *reform'd* Churches, and the Church of *Rome*. I shall shew hereafter the Force and Consequences of this Observation; wherein that *Unity of Faith*, which is an essential Attribute of the *true Church of Christ*, is concern'd.

5*thly*. The Truth of St. *Augustin*'s Doctrine was attested by *undoubted Miracles* In Reference to which

152 Dial. 2. §. 10. *Some Observations upon the*
which I muſt obſerve, that ſince the Belief of *reveal'd Truths* is a rational Act, tho' the Truths themſelves ſurpaſs all human Underſtanding, therefore the Providence of God has taken Care to furniſh Men with ſuch ſolid and rational Motives to ground their Belief of ſupernatural Truths upon, that they who refuſe to yield to ſuch Motives act contrary to the Dictates of Reaſon and common Senſe. Now one of theſe, and I may ſay the ſtrongeſt of them, is the Teſtimony of *vndoubted Miracles*: Becauſe they are the Teſtimony of God, by whoſe inviſible Hand they are wrought, and God, who is eſſentially Truth, cannot bear Witneſs to any Falſhood.

For this Reaſon the Son of God himſelf not only condeſcended to prove the Truth of his Doctrine by *Miracles*, but declared moreover, that *if he had not done the Works which no Man ever did, they* [the *Jews*] *would have had no Sin.* Joh. 15. v. 24 And why ſo? Becauſe God will have Men act like Men, that is, *rationally*. And thoſe among the *Jews*, who believed effectually in him, would not have acted rationally, if they had believed the *Incomprehenſible Truths* he taught, upon his bare Word; That is, without any Motive to recommend to them the *divine Authority* of it.

For the ſame Reaſon Chriſt impower'd his Apoſtles to work as great Miracles as himſelf had done, according to his Promiſe *John.* 14. v. 12. For theſe were to be their *Credentials* upon Sight whereof both *Jews* and *Heathens* might form a rational Judgment that the *new* and *incomprehenſible* Doctrines they taught, were not the Inventions of any Man, but Truths *reveal'd* by God, who vouchſafed to ſet his *divine Hand* and *Seal* to them by thoſe Supernatural Operations. Whence it follows, that the Teſtimony of *Miracles*, When they

2 are

are above all Suspicion of Fraud, and cannot be question'd but by the blackest Malice, carry with them such a powerful Evidence, as cannot be rejected but by a People given up by God to a reprobate Sense.

This then is the Force of my 5th Observation, to wit, that the Religion planted in *England* by St. *Augustin* and his Followers had the same infallible Mark of Truth stamp'd upon it, as *Christianity* had at it's first Entrance into the World. Because the *Miracles*, by which A. G. was pleased to become a Voucher for the Truth of it, tho' they have not the *divine Authority* of *Scriptural Miracles*, yet are as authentickly attested, as historical Facts can possibly be. And he who will not believe them must throw aside all Ecclesiastical History, but what the *Sacred Penmen* have written.

6*thly*, The Conversion of *England*, to the *Catholick Faith* was entirely *free* and *voluntary*. No Violence was used, no Threats of *Prisons*, *Banishments*, or *Confiscations* were employ'd, no penal Laws enacted to frighten the People into a Compliance: But every Thing was carried on by the Power of *Preaching*, *Miracles*, and *good Example*. By these Methods *England* receiv'd its *first Christianity*: Whereas it is the distinguishing Character of Falshood to establish itself by Violence and Imposture.

7*thly*, The Religion preach'd by St. *Augustin* and his Followers had no sooner got Footing among the *Saxons*, but there appear'd a wonderful Change in their Lives and Manners, which always is the immediate Fruit of a *true* and *solid Conversion*. And there is not perhaps a Nation upon Earth, wherein religious Piety and Devotion flourish'd in a more remarkable Manner for many Years after its Conversion, than in the Island of *Great Britain*.

Mr.

Mr. *Collier* has confirm'd or rather forestall'd my three last Observations in the *Preface* to his *Ecclesiastical History* p. 3. where he writes thus.

" To insist a little upon the last Circumstance [*relating to God's Providence*] we have a remarkable Instance of it, in our own Nation. For the Purpose, when *Augustin* the Monk undertook the Conversion of the *Saxons*, was any Thing humanly speaking, more unlikely to succeed? He had neither *Fleet* nor *Army* to back his Enterprize, and none but a few naked Men to attend him. He had no worldly Motives to recommend him to King *Ethelbert*. He had no powerful Alliances to offer, no new Countries (like *Columbus*) to discover. We do not find him furnish'd with any rich Presents, with any Inventions for the Polishing of Life, with any Curiosities of Art or Nature to make Way for his Design. On the other Side, the Proposals of these holy Men must needs be shocking to a *Pagan* Court. Their Doctrine laid new Restraints upon Pride and Pleasure, and was unfriendly to the Interest of Flesh and Blood. And as for the Happiness they promised, 'twas mostly out of Sight, and not to commence till after Death.

" Nowithstanding these seeming Impossibilities, they were bless'd with surprizing Success: The *Sanctity of their Lives*, and the *Force* of their *Miracles* broke through the Difficulty of the Enterprize. The *Saxons* were quickly prevail'd on to part with their old Idolatry, and resign their *Manners* and *Belief*. The *Practice* of their *Converts* was wonderfully changed, and a glorious Revolution made in the *moral* World. They had now no Delight in Barbarity and Bloodshed. The Ruggedness of their Temper
" was

"was smooth'd, and they grew much more juft
"and benevolent than formerly. Their Purfuits
"were of a different kind, their Affections regu-
"lar and raifed, and every thing brighten'd
"within; as if Nature had been melted down
"and recoin'd. In fhort, the *quatuor noviſſima*,
"Death and Judgment, Heaven and Hell, took
"fuch Hold of their Hopes and Fears, that they
"fometimes ftood off from the more innocent Sa-
"tisfactions of Life, threw up the Advantage of
"their Condition, and removed from Company
"and Bufinefs. The other World fat fo power-
"fully upon their Spirits, that the Entertainments
"of this grew flat and infipid. 'Twas upon thefe
"Thoughts that feveral of our Princes refign'd
"the Government for the *Cloyſter*. And thofe
"who did not conceive themfelves obliged to
"fuch Lengths of Selfdenial, laid out Part of
"their Revenues in the Building and Endow-
"ing of Churches, in Founding Houfes for
"Learning and Education, and for the Benefit of
"Retirement and Devotion."

Thus Mr. *Collier*. And he has but done Juftice to the great Merits of our *Apoſtle* on the one Hand, and to the pious Zeal and Devotion of our *primitive Engliſh Church* on the other.

8thly, When *England* received the *Faith of Chriſt*, all *National* Chriftian Churches both in the *Eaſt* and *Weſt* were united in Communion with the *Apoſtolick See*. For the Rupture of the *Greeks* did not happen till 250 Years after. Either therefore the Church, whereof *England* became a Part by its Converfion, was then the *true Church*, or *Chriſt* had not then a *true Church* upon Earth. If *Proteſtants* grant the firft, they muft own that they ceafed to be a Part of the *true Church*, when they feparated themfelves from the Church of *Rome*.

If

If they choose the latter, it follows that the *Creed* was then false, and continued so for many Ages: And then the *Protestants* of the Church of *England* are bound to renounce their 8th *Article of Religion*, which declares, that *the three Creeds, Nice-Creed, Athanasius's Creed, and that, which is commonly call'd the Apostles-Creed, ought throughly to be received and believed: For they may be proved by most certain Warrants of holy Scripture.*

9*thly* and lastly, I observe that the whole Work of *England*'s Conversion was carried on with the utmost Regularity and Order. The Workmen employ'd in it were qualified according to God's own Appointment. That is, were all of the *Episcopal* and *Priestly* Order. Their Proceedings were according to the establish'd Laws and Canons of the Church. They acted as Ministers of *Jesus Christ*, with a due Subordination to their respective spiritual Superiours, not as Slaves to the arbitrary Will of the *secular Magistrate*. No *Laick* of what Rank soever invaded the *Sanctuary*, or presumed to put his prophane Hands to the *Censer*. Nothing of this Nature was attempted in those early Days of our *English* Church, nor any other Force made Use of, but the prevailing Force of Truth preach'd by Men, that lived up to their sacred Character, were fill'd with the *Spirit of God*, and acted in their proper Sphere.

In a Word, what render'd them like the *primitive Apostles*, powerful both in *Words* and *Works*, was their truly *Apostolical* Method of Life. They had renounced the World with its Riches and Pleasures, to serve God in a State of perpetual Poverty and Penance; and were therefore above the Temptations of Flattery and Avarice, which always have some base Lucre in View. They had neither Wives nor Children to maintain, and So

were

were not folicitous to gain Wealth, but only to gain Souls to God. Their Time was fpent in Prayer and Retirement, as far as their *Apoftolical* Function would permit; and as they walk'd themfelves in the narrow Way of the Gofpel; So they preach'd it boldly to others in Imitation of St. *Paul* without flattering their Inclinations in any Thing contrary to the Law of God.

'Twas thus that *Catholick Religion* now nicknamed *Popery*, was planted in this Ifland by the fame regular and canonical Methods, as had been practifed by the bleffed Apoftles themfelves, in the very Infancy of the Church: That is to fay, not by *Rapine*, *Violence*, and *Bloodfhed*, but by the Power of Preaching only. Nor by the Intrufion of *Lay Perfons* into the *Sanctuary*, but by the Miniftry of *Bifhops* and *Priefts*, eminent for Holinefs of Life, Defpifers of the World; Dead to the ufual Inclinations of Flefh and Blood, and entirely free from the Paffions of *Covetoufnefs and Ambition*, which are the great Corrupters of Men's Hearts, and make them turn Seducers either for the Sake of Lucre, or to domineer and Tyrannize over Men's Faith.

Now do's not the Hand of God appear manifeftly in the whole Management of this Work, but particularly in Relation to the Choice of the Perfons employ'd in it? May we not truly fay they were *according to God's Heart*? For what furer Marks can we have of the *divine Election* of Perfons to the Miniftry of the Gofpel, than when we fee them irreproachable in their Conduct, difinterefted in their Views, free from all Affections to earthly Things, and qualified in all Refpects for their facred Functions? Is this the proper Character of *Mercenaries*, or of *good Shepherds*? of *Intruders* into

the

158 Dial. 2. §. 10. *Some Observations upon the* the *Sheepfold*, or of Guides of *God's own Appointment*? Of *Seducers*, or of Preachers of sound Doctrines?

G. Truly Sir, if Persons of this Character did not preach the true Faith to our Ancestors the *Saxons*, we cannot be sure, that the true Faith of Christ has ever been preach'd to any Nation upon Earth since the Death of the *Apostles*.

P. That's very certain: And I may confidently say, that the whole Collection of Circumstances, upon which I have now made my Observations, both as to the *Means* made Use of in this second Conversion of *England*, and to the *Character* of the Persons employ'd in it, amounts to such a strong Proof of the *Orthodoxy* of the *Faith* and *Religion* preach'd to our Ancestors the *Saxons*, and profess'd to this Day by all *Roman Catholicks*, that a thinking Man cannot regard it otherwise than as a *decisive Mark* plainly shewing in what Communion the *true Church of Christ* is to be found.

But since Opposites, as *Beauty* and *Deformity*, appear in their best and strongest Light, when they are placed near to one another, I must desire you now to turn your Attention from the agreeable Prospect we have had before us of *Regularity* and *Order*, *religious Piety* and *disinterested Zeal*, to a Scene of *Confusion*, *Rapine*, *Bloodshed*, *Desolation*, and every thing that is apt to strike the Heart with Horror. You will there see the Laws of God and Man trampled upon, Religion made a Cloak to cover the blackest Crimes, sacred Places violated, Altars prophaned, the Vessels consecrated to God's Service abused, as in the drunken Feast of *Balshazzer*, the ancient Monuments of Piety destroy'd, the *Ecclesiastical* Authority invaded by *Laicks*, Monasteries plunder'd and laid level with

the

the Ground, the Patrimony of the Church made a Prey to the infatiable Rapacity of *Court-Harpies*, the People forced againſt their Conſcience to a Conformity by the moſt unjuſt and ſanguinary Laws, and Perſons of all States and Degrees dragg'd to Execution like common Felons for Non-compliance with Commands directly contrary to the Law of God.

This, Sir, is a faithful Picture in Miniature of thoſe ſtupendious Changes in Religion, which our modern *Proteſtants* varniſh over with the Name of a *thorough Godly Reformation*. But I leave any Man to judge, whether the *holy Ghoſt* could have any Part in ſuch Counſels: Or whether it be conſiſtent with the infinite *Juſtice* or *Purity* of God to adopt as his *Workmanſhip* a *Reformation*, which forced its Way into the World by the open Violation of his holy Law, was carried on by *Sacrilege* and *Plunder*, cemented with *innocent Blood*, and finally eſtabliſh'd in direct oppoſition to all the *Guides* of God's own *Appointment*!

G. No man will ſurely be ſo extravagant as to ſay that God could approve of ſuch deteſtable Proceedings; Or that a Church, which ows its *Beginning*, *Progreſs*, and *final Eſtabliſhment* to ſuch wicked Means, can be the *true Church of Chriſt*. I have therefore ſome Difficulty to believe, that *Proteſtants* will own the Truth of theſe Facts: Which, if allow'd to be true, utterly diſcredit their Religion; and ſhew the *Reformation* they ſo much boaſt of, to be the Fruit not of *Piety*, or *Zeal* for God's Honour, but of the moſt *criminal Paſſions*, corrupt Nature is capable of.

P. Have but Patience till we meet next, and you ſhall hear every Fact proved from the Teſtimony of unexceptionable *Proteſtant* Writers. But it is

now

150 Dial. 2. §. 10. *Some Observations* &c.

now full Time for us both to rest a while; and the Subject, which remains to be examined, will afford Matter enongh for another Meeting. So I take my Leave of you till to morrow.

G. Sir, I am your humble Servant, and thank you for the Pains you have already taken.

The End of the second Dialogue.

THE
Third DIALOGUE.

CONTAINING,

An historical Collection of Facts relating to the English Reformation *in the Reigns of* Henry *viii.* Edward *vi. and Queen* Elizabeth *examined.*

SECT. I.

Henry *viii. falls in Love with* Anne Bolen. *The Motives of his* Divorce *from Queen* Catharine *examined.*

G. IR, the general Account you gave me, before we parted last, of the *English Reformation*, throws such an Infamy upon the chief Actors in it, and favours so much of a passionate Invective, prompted by a passionate prejudiced Mind, that unless you can produce undeniable historical Facts to support the Truth of it, neither *Protestant* nor *Catholick* will believe you, and you will only prejudice your own Cause by it.

P. I assure you Sir, it has always been my Judgment, that nothing is either more unbecoming the Character of a Christian, or gives a deeper Wound to the Credit and Reputation of any Cause, than to charge Persons either alive or Dead with odious Facts, which cannot be fully and clearly proved against them. But then I take it to be an uncontested Principle, that in Disputes between two Parties an Adversary's own Testimony is always good and legal Evidence against himself: especially if he be of an unexceptionable Character as to the Sincerity of his Affection to the Cause he maintains; Because it is to be supposed that an Historian of this Character will not relate Facts, which reflect upon the Honour of his own Cause, unless the Force of Truth extorts it from him. And therefore it shall be my special Care not to draw any Consequences from, or build upon any Fact, that is dishonourable to the *Protestant Cause*, without producing some *Protestant* Historian, who is known to be sincerely affected to that Cause, and a hearty Enemy to *Popery*, to vouch for the Truth of it.

G. Nothing can be fairer than this. For unless it be an overruled Case, that a Writer is not *compos mentis*, when he cuts the Throat of his own Cause by telling Truth, it is but just at any Time to believe a Man against himself. So pray, Sir, proceed to your historical Account of the *English Reformation*.

P. The first Occasion of the Changes of Religion in *England* (called the *Reformation*) took it's Source from a disorderly Passion entertain'd by

Dial. 3. §. 1. *The Motives of K. Henry's Henry* viii. *for a Court-Lady named Anne Bolen.*

He had lived in Wedlock with his virtuous Queen *Catharine* the Daughter of *Ferdinand* of *Arragon*, and Aunt of *Charles* v. for the Space of about 20 Years, without any Scruple of Conscience concerning the Validity of their Marriage. *Our King* (says the Lord *Herbert* p. 243.) *had now for many Years enjoy'd the virtuous Queen* Catharine, *without that either Scruple of the Validity of the Match, or outward Note of Unkindness had pass'd betwixt them.* But when she grew old, and was past Bearing Children, he began to be disturb'd with most grievous Scruples about it: Nor could his tender Conscience enjoy any Repose, till his Superannuated Wife was removed from his Bed, and the Place made clear for his young intended Bride to take Possession of it.

Dr. *Heylin* tho' a hearty Enemy to the Church of *Rome* has been so sincere as to let the World know, of what Nature King *Henry*'s Scruples were.

" King *Henry* viii. says he, *being violently hurried*
" *with the Transport of some private Affections*, and
" finding the Pope appear'd the greatest Obstacle
" to his Desires, extinguish'd his Authority in
" the Realm of *England*. This open'd *the first*
" *Way* to the *Reformation*, and gave Encourage-
" ment to those, who were inclined to it: To
" which the King afforded no small Encourage-
" ment *for politick Ends.* Pref. p. 2.

Here we have the true Secret of King *Henry's* Scruples (which gave Birth to the *Reformation*) laid open without Disguise: and the plain Truth of the Story is this. He was grown weary of his Wife, and had set his Heart so violently upon Mrs. *Anne Bolen*, that he was resolved to have her, cost what it would. He therefore left no Stone unturn'd to compass his End.

Agents

Agents were sent abroad to tamper with several foreign Universities; many Members whereof were made to *feel* the Justice of K. *Henry*'s Cause in a very sensible Manner, * and both Promises and Threats were employ'd at home to cajole some and frighten others into a Compliance.

But his chief Application was to Pope *Clement* vii. to whom he had been very serviceable in some important Occasions, and therefore despair'd not of Gaining him over to his Side: Which indeed would have given no small Reputation to his Cause, if it could have been effected. But tho' all sorts of Engines were set at Work, and the most importune Solicitations employ'd by the King's Agents at *Rome* to render the Pope pliable to his Desires; tho' they laid before him all that could be said to represent the extreme Violence of King *Henry's* Temper, the pretended Reasonableness and Necessity of a Divorce, and the dangerous Consequences of a Refusal, their Negotiations proved unsuccessful: His Holiness being convinced in Conscience, that it was not in his Power to dissolve a Marriage, which had been authorized, and ratified in the most solemn Manner by his Predecessor *Julius* 2.

However he judg'd it necessary to proceed very warily in a Business of that Importance, and steer his Course with the utmost Caution in a middle Way between two Rocks; so as neither to disoblige the Emperour, who had an Army in the very Heart of *Italy*, or wrong his own Conscience on the one Hand by too great a Condescension, nor exasperate the King by a peremptory Refusal on the other, for Fear of pushing him to the last Extre-

---

* *See the Preface.*

The Motives of K. Henry's Extremities. He therefore made it his Bufinefs to lay hold of all Occafions, or plaufible Pretences of Delays to gain Time, as is the ufual Method in Courts, when they have an odious Caufe before them: Hoping perhaps that Length of Time, or fome favourable Turn of Affairs might either make the King alter his Mind, or at leaft abate in fome Meafure the Violence of his Paffion. In all which there appears nothing of unchriftian Politicks, as *Proteftant* Writers ufually reprefent the Matter; unlefs acting prudently be contrary to Chriftianity.

G. What have you told me, Sir, fuffices indeed to convince me or any rational Man, that King *Henry*'s Scruples were all Grimace, and nothing better than a meer theatrical Farce. For I never heard him reprefented as a Perfon much famed for Tendernefs of Confcience. However were there not fufficient Grounds to give at leaft a plaufible Colour to his Divorce from Queen *Catharine*, who had before been married to Prince *Arthur* his elder Brother?

P. This was the fpecious Pretence laid hold of, by the mercenary Sycophants of the Court, who plainly faw, what the King would be at; and it afforded them an excellent Opportunity to work out their own Ends by humouring him agreeably in a Paffion he was fully refolved to gratify. For this was at that Time a fure Step to Favour and Preferment.

G. But is it not forbidden to marry a Sifter in Law?

P. 'Tis forbidden by the Laws of the *Church*, but not by the Law of *Nature*. On the contrary, God laid a pofitive Command upon the *Jews*, that the younger Brother fhould marry the elder Brother's

Divorce from Q. Catharine examined. 165
ther's Wife, if he died without Issue. *Deut.* 25. v. 5.

G. However I have sometimes heard *Protestants* object, that a Sister in Law being within the Degrees of Affinity prohibited by God himself in *Leviticus*, it could not be justifiable in K. *Henry* to marry his Brother's Wife.

P. Sir, if all the Prohibitions or Commands of God recorded in the Books of *Moses* are to be regarded as Laws, that oblige *Christians*, we are all bound to turn *Jews*, submit to *Circumcision*, and observe the whole *Mosaick Law*: Which being absurd and impious, nothing can be more frivolous, than to object the *Levitical prohibited Degrees*, Unless it can be proved, that the Prohibition was not a meer *ceremonial Law*, but like the *Decalogue*, grounded upon the very Law of Nature. Now if it were against the Law of Nature to marry a Brother's Wife after his Decease, God would not have commanded it, as he did in the abovesaid Case. Because the *Law of Nature* is the *eternal* and *unalterable* Law of God himself; and he cannot command the Violation of his own eternal and unalterable Law.

Hence it follows, that the Unlawfulness of marrying a Brother's Wife has ever since the Abrogation of the *Mosaick Law*, been wholly grounded upon a meer *Ecclesiastical* Precept, like the other *prohibited Degrees*, which may be dispensed with by a lawful Authority: Because the same Authority that makes such Laws, may likewise dispense with them for just Reasons. And this was the Case in Reference to K. *Henry*'s Marriage, which had been dispensed with by *Julius* 2. in the most solemn Manner, and with the general Approbation of the wisest and most learned Men of *England*, *Italy*, and *Spain*. So that it is apparent, that his pretended

166 Dial. 3. §. 1. *The Motives of* K. Henry's
tended Scruples about it, after having acknowledg'd Q. *Catharine* for his lawful Wife, and conversed with her as such for the Space of 20 Years, was all rank Hypocrisy and Dissimulation, and nothing but a Mask to cover his intended Adultery.

G. But let us suppose Queen *Catharine* had never been his *Brother's Wife*, is it probable, he would have entertain'd any Thoughts of procuring a Divorce from her? If not, *Protestants* will say, you bear too hard upon him.

P. Sir, if Actions may be allow'd to be the most faithful Interpreters of Men's Hearts, I dare make bold to say, that tho' Queen *Catharine* had never been married to Prince *Arthur*, King *Henry* would have been *that same King*. Henry, of whom it is writ, that *he never spared Man in his Anger, nor Woman in his Lust*. That is to say, he would have done just as he did: Tho' he would not have had so good a Cloak to cover the shame of it, but been obliged to find other Pretexts for it. This is apparent from his Behaviour afterwards (when no *Levitical prohibited Degrees* could be pretended) towards his 4th Wife, the Lady *Anne of Cleves*; to whom (as the L. *Herbert* tells us 516) he was solemnly married at *Greenwich*. Yet not long after found Means to cast her off, and immediately took the Lady *Catharine Howard* for his 5th. Wife. But to shew the arbitrary Power he had, and to what miserable Servitude he had reduced both his *Parliament* and *Clergy*, let us hear the Relation of it from *Stow*. p. 578.

"After the Death of the Lady *Jane Seymour* the King's third Wife, he married the Lady *Anne of Cleve* in the 30th Year of his Reign. From which Time the King not only continued his *first* misliking of her

[mea-

"[*meaning at their first Interview at* Rochester, *whither the King went to meet her*] but his hatred encreased more and more against her, not only for Want of Beauty, whereof at first he took Exception, but also for sundry other Qualities, whereof he secretly accused her. And being thus so sorely perplex'd and desperate of Redress, he grew wondrous apt and willing to call in Question any Thing, that might tend to the Dissolving of this Marriage. Within 8 Days, the King told his Physicians his farther Cause of Grief, that she was loathsom to him in Bed . . . The King being thus tormented in Body and Mind knew not how to ease himself, until he had procured a speedy Divorce, which was thus effected. Certain Lords came down into the *lower House of Parliament*, expressly declaring the Causes, why this Marriage was not lawful: And in Conclusion the Matter was by the *Convocation* clearly determined, that the King might lawfully marry where he would, and so might she."

This shews plainly, that *conjugal Fidelity*, was none of King Henry's Virtues: And that Queen *Catharine* would in all Probability have been made to drink of the same bitter Cup, tho' she had never been his Brother's Wife: Since the Motives here alledg'd to justify this Divorce are of such a large Extent, that if allow'd of, no conjugal Knot was ever tied fast enough to be secure against a Dissolution. It shews likewise that all the Fences, whether of *human* or *Divine Laws* are too weak to withstand the unbridled Lust of a Prince, when he has a despotick and arbitrary Power in his Hands, as King *Henry* had, to make himself obey'd.

But I have now a curious piece of History to entertain you with; which will make good every Thing I have said concerning the King's *pretended Scruples*, and serve as a Key to let us into the whole Secret of that Mystery of Iniquity. I am indebted for it to my Lord *Herbert*, and you shall have it in his own Words.

"Our King (says he p. 252) thought fit to send
"Sir *Frances Bryan* and *Peter Vannes* to *Rome*. Their
"Instructions in General being sign'd with the
"King's own Hand, were *&c.*"

Here the Author, gives an Account of some Instructions relating to the King's Affairs with the Emperor, and then proceeds thus:

"Furthermore they were required to discover
"in the Name of a third Person, whether if the
"Queen enter'd into a religious Life, the King
"might have the Pope's Dispensation to marry
"again, and the Children be legitimate; and
"what Precedents there were for it. *Secondly*,
"whether if the King for the beter inducing the
"Queen thereunto would promise to enter him-
"self into a religious Life, the Pope might not
"dispense with his Vow, and leave her there.

A most Godly Contrivance! The King was to make a *Vow* to God, which he never intended to keep; and the poor Queen was to be left in the Lurch! If this be not a Mark of Tenderness of Conscience, I know not what is. But listen to what follows.

"*Thirdly*, If this may not be done, whether the
"Pope can dispense with the King to have *two*
"*Wives*, and the Children of both legitimate:
"Since great Reasons and Precedents, especially
"in the old Testament, appear for it. All which
"they were to do with that Secrecy and Circum-
"spection, that the Cause might not be pub-
"lish'd;

"lish'd; propounding therefore the King's Case
"always as another Man's. *Lastly*, as in all other
"Instructions, some *Menaces* were to be ad-
"ded.

G. Here is fine jugling Work indeed for a Pretender to *Scruples*.

P. I shall make a few short Remarks upon it. *First*, I observe how strangely industrious and fruitful of Invention Men are, when they seek to gratify a Passion, which has once taken deep Roots in their Hearts. I observe 2*dly*, that K. *Henry's* seeking partly to *trepan* the Pope by indirect and sinister means, and partly to *frighten* him by Threats into a Compliance with his Desires, is a plain Indication, that he was conscious to himself of the Badness of his Cause. And I observe 3*dly*, that his Shameful Proposal of being dispensed with to have *two Wives at once*, shews no less plainly, that his Conscience would have permitted Queen *Catharine* to continue his Wife, notwithstanding her having been married before to his elder Brother, if Mrs. *Anne Bolen* had but been privileged to share with her in that Honour.

G. But was King *Henry* skilful enough in the Art of Dissimulation to set a serious Countenance upon the Matter, when he pretended a Scruple of Conscience about his first Marriage?

P. No Stage-player ever acted his Part better. You shall have a Specimen of his Skill from the same Author. p. 258.

"This while, says he, the common People,
"who with much Anxiety attended the Success of
"this great Affair, seem'd betwixt Pity to Queen
"*Catharine*, and Envy to *Anne Bolen* now appea-
"ring to be in the King's Favour, to cast out
"some murmuring and seditious Words: Which
"being brought to the King's Ears, he thought
"fit to protest publickly in an Assembly of *Lords*,
"*Judge*

"Judges, &c. call'd to his Palace at *Bridewel*, that
"nothing but a Defire of giving Satisfaction to
"his Confcience, and a Care of Eftablifhing the
"Succeffion to the Crown in a right and undoub-
"ted Line, had firft procured him to controvert
"this Marriage; Being for the reft as happy in
"the Affections and Virtues of his Queen as any
"Prince living.

G. This indeed was acting the Hypocrite to the Life.

P. Nay in this folemn Proteftation he perfonated the *Scrupulous* Man as well in Reference to the *Eftablifhment of the Succeffion in the right and undoubted Line*, as to his *Marriage*. Yet afterwards fettled the Succeffion both on his Daughter *Mary* by Q. *Catharine*, and on his Daughter *Elizabeth* by *Anne Bolen*. Whereas 'tis manifeft both could not be legitimate, nor by Confequence *in the right and undoubted Line of Succeffion* to the Crown. But what Wonder is it, that Men's Actions fhould be incoherent, when their Hearts are double!

SECT. 2.

The Caufe of the Divorce brought before Judges appointed by the Pope.

G. WELL, but what was the final Iffue of this important Affair?

G. The Pope finding himfelf prefs'd fo very hard by the King's Agents at *Rome* to put a fpeedy End to it, that it was not in his Power either to refift or elude their Importunities any longer, gave at length a fpecial Commiffion to Cardinal *Campeius*, a Perfon throughly verfed in the *Canon-Law*, by Virtue whereof he and Cardinal *Woolfey*, who was join'd with him in the fame Commiffion, were

were to act as Judges in the Cause, and had Powers given them to summon the King and Queen before their Tribunal, as they did effectually not long after the Arrival of *Campeius* in *England*. The Place appointed for the Hearing of the Cause was the great Hall in *Black Friars*, to which the King and Queen being cited the last Day of *May* An. 1529 they both appear'd in Person. *Stow* gives this Relation of it. p. 543.

" The Queen according to the Form being
" call'd upon to come to the Court, made no An-
" swer, but rose out of her Chair, and came to
" the King, Kneeling down at his Feet, to whom
" she said.

" Sir, in what have I offended you? Or what
" Occasion of Displeasure have I given you, in-
" tending thus to put me from you? I take God
" to be my Judge, I have been to you a true and
" humble Wife, ever conformable to your Will
" and Pleasure, never contradicting or gainsaying
" you in any Thing: Being always contented with
" all Things, wherein you had any Delight, or
" took any Pleasure, without Grudge or Counte-
" nance of Discontent or Displeasure. I loved
" for your Sake all them whom you loved,
" whether I had Cause or no, whether they
" were my Friends or Enemies. I have been
" your Wife these 20 Years or more, and you
" had by me diverse Children: And when you
" had me first, *I take God to be my Judge that I was a*
" *Maid:* And whether it be true or no, *I put it to*
" *your Conscience.* If there be any just Cause, you
" can alledge against me either of Dishonesty, or
" Matter lawful to put me from you, I am con-
" tent to depart to my Shame and Confusion: and
" if there be none, then I pray you to let me have
" Justice at your Hands. The King your Father
" was in his Time of such an excellent Wit, that

he

"he was accounted amongst all Men for his Wisdom to be a *Second Solomon.* And the King of *Spain* my Father *Ferdinand* was accounted one of the wisest Princes, that had reigned in *Spain* for many Years. It is not therefore to be doubted, but that they gather'd as wise Counsellors unto them of every Realm, as in their Wisdoms they thought meet: And I conceive that there were in those Days as wise and well-learned Men in both Realms, as be now at this Day, who thought the Marriage between you and me, good and lawful. Therefore it is a wonder to me, what new Inventions are now invented against me. And now to put me to stand to the Order and Judgment of this Court seems very unreasonable. For you may condemn me for Want of being able to answer for my self, as having no Counsel but such as you assign'd me, who cannot be indifferent on my Part, since they are your Subjects, and such as you have taken and chosen out of your own Counsel, whereunto they are privy, and dare not disclose your Will and Intent. Therefore I humbly pray you to spare me until I know what Counsel my Friends in *Spain* will advise me to take: And if you will not, then your Pleasure be fulfill'd. And with that she arose and departed. Thus *Stow.*

However My Lord *Herbert* affirms, that she appear'd once more in Person before the Court; but it was only *to protest against the two Cardinals as incompetent Judges: Requiring farther that this her Protestation might be recorded, and so departed presently out of the Court.* p. 263.

After which the Queen being several Times cited, and not appearing was pronounced *contumacious.* And the Court proceeded to the Examination

tion of Witnesses; whose Depositions all center'd in this one Point, to wit, that the Marriage between Prince *Arthur* and Queen *Catharine* had been consummated. The Probability whereof, tho' nothing to the main Purpose, having no other Foundation than bare Guesses grounded upon their having been bedded, and some joculatory Words utter'd by Prince *Arthur*, could not be of sufficient Weight to counterbalance the Queen's *positive Oath* to the contrary, and her *taking God to Witness*, that she came a Maid to *Henry*'s Bed: For the Truth whereof she appeal'd in open Court to the King's own Conscience, who as soon as she was retired, instead of denying it, spoke thus in the Presence of the Commissioners. *I will now in her Absence declare this unto you all, that she has been unto me as true and obedient a Wife, as I could wish or desire. She has all the virtuous Qualities, that ought to be in a Woman of her Dignity, or in any other of mean Condition. She is also surely a Woman nobly born. Her Condition will well declare it.* Stow. p. 543. And now I leave you or any one to judge, whether it be probable that a Person of this Character would publickly forswear herself, and at the same Time have the Confidence to appeal to the King's own Conscience for the Truth of what she said. An abandon'd Creature might do so, but not a Princess of untainted Honour and Virtue.

But, to proceed, the Witnesses against the Queen being thus heard, and their Depositions recorded, the Cardinals adjourned the Court to the *Friday* following, which was *July* 23. An. 1529. When it was expected, they would have proceeded to a definitive Sentence. But to the King's great Surprise and Mortification, they again adjourn'd it from that Day to the first of *October*; pretending that according to the Method of the

Court

Court of *Rome*, , which *Campeius* faid they were bound to follow, no judiciary Caufes could be terminated during the general Vacation of the Harveft and Vintage already begun. However that be, 'tis certain *Campeius* had private Inftructions not to pronounce definitively till farther Orders from the Pope.

During this long Interval the Queen was not idle, but found Means to acquaint the Emperor with all that had pafs'd, intreating him to efpoufe her Caufe, as he did in Effect. For he immediately difpatch'd *Orators* to *Rome* (as my Lord *Herbert* ftiles them) whom the Queen likewife conftituted her *Proctors*, giving them a Commiffion and Inftructions to act in her Name. Who therefore being come to *Rome*, enter'd a Proteftation in her Name againft the two Legates in *England*, intreating the Pope to revoke their Commiffion, and *advocate* the Caufe to himfelf: As likewife to warn the King to defift from his Suit, or at leaft to confent to have it judg'd at *Rome*. The Iffue whereof in fhort was, that the Pope being thus prefs'd by the Emperors Orators, fign'd an *Advocation* of the Caufe to himfelf, forbidding farther Proceedings under great Penalties. This put an End to *Campeius*'s Legantine Power; who foon after took his Leave of the King, and return'd back to *Rome*.

SECT. 3.

Archbifhop Cranmer's *Character. He diffolves the Marriage between K.* Henry *and* Q. Catharine.

KING *Henry* finding himfelf thus difappointed, and that nothing favourable to his Inclinations was to be hoped for from the Pope, resolved to take a shorter Course, which he knew could not fail. For he had taken care to provide himself with an *Archbishop* of *Canterbury* and *Primate* of *England* named *Thomas Cranmer*, whose pliableness he was secure of. And indeed he was a sure Card, and in all Respects fit for his Purpose.

G. I have heard much Talk and great Diversity of Opinions concerning this Archbishop *Cranmer*. But almost all the Discourses I have heard of him were either *Panegyricks* or *Invectives*. I should therefore be glad to have a faithful and impartial Character of the Man.

P. *Panegyricks* and *Invectives* are all but talking in the Air, unless they are supported by unquestionable Facts. For the surest Way of knowing Men is by their Actions, according to this saying of our Saviour, *you shall know them by their Fruits*. However I shall only relate some of his most illustrious Exploits, by which he distinguished himself from all his Predecessors in the See of *Caterbury*: amongst whom (counting from St. *Augustine* downwards) we find so great a number in the Catalogue of Saints, that I believe there is not a Diocess in Christendom can shew the like, except we go back to the very primitive Ages. So that if Archbishop *Cranmer* appears to have been the very Reverse of these, both in *Faith* and *Practice*, I fear his Character will give no great Edification; and the Credit of the *English Reformation* will unavoidably Suffer by having had such a *Reformer* at the Head of it.

First then Bp *Burnet*, his greatest Admirer and profest Encomiast, tells us of him in his History of the *English Reformation* 1. *Part*, p. 92. that he was a *Lutheran* in his Heart, even when he was but a private Fellow in the University of *Cambridge*

176 Dial. 3. § 3. *Archbishop* Cranmer's *bridge*, and 'tis a noted Fact, that he appear'd in all outward Practices a ftanch *Roman Catholick*; and by confequence diffembled his Religion from that Time forwards till the End of King *Henry*'s Reign.

The King was no fooner cold in his Grave, but *Cranmer* threw off the Mask; and, the Duke of *Sommerfet* (who was a rank *Calvinift*, and had likewife diffembled his Religion as long as *Henry* lived) being made Lord *Protector* in the Minority of *Edward* VI. He immediately became the Duke's chief *Ecclefiaftical Inftrument* in pufhing on thofe aftonifhing Changes in the Religion of his Forefathers, which happen'd in that Reign. So that of all the *Bifhops* or *Archbifhops*, that ever were in *Great Britain* from the Converfion of K. *Ethelbert* down to the Reign of *Edward* VI. *Cranmer* was the firft, that openly renounc'd the Religion, which that great fervant of God and Preacher of the Gofpel, St. *Auguftine*, had planted in this Ifland. And therefore if Apoftatizing from the *ancient Faith*, and Broaching *new Doctrines*, be the diftinguifhing Character of a *Heretick*, Archbifhop *Cranmer* has the jufteft Claim to that Title: Since it is an uncontefted Truth, that the Religion he fell from was that which every Chriftian upon Earth, excepting fome Remains of *Hereticks* condemn'd by the Four firft *General Councils*, did profefs when it was brought into *England* by St. *Auguftine*, and his Followers; and that when *Cranmer* abandon'd it, it had not only been publickly profefs'd and taught by the whole *Epifcopal Order* and Body of the *Clergy* in *Great Britain*, but had likewife been fupported by the whole Legiflative Power of the *Englifh Nation*, without any publick Change during the fpace of nine hundred Years and upwards; notwithftanding

ing thofe frequent Revolutions in the State occafion'd by the invafions of the *Danes*, the Conqueft of the *Normans*, the Wars of the *Barons*, and thofe between the Houfes of *Lancafter* and *York*, which divided the Nation in every Thing but *Religion*, wherein all *Parties, Interefts*, and *Factions* continued to the very laft. This then is the firft noble Exploit, whereby Archbifhop *Cranmer* diftinguifh'd himfelf from all the *Archbifhops*, that had gone before him for 900 Years together. 'Tis very Strange indeed, that for the Space of 900 Years there fhould not be a *Bifhop* or *Archbifhop* in the whole *Englifh* Nation either learned enough to See, or zealous enough to oppofe the grofs Errors (if they were really fuch) which *Cranmer* undertook to reform. Yet it either was fo, or *Cranmer*'s Reformation was an Impofture. But it appears much more confonant to Reafon to judge, that this *Reforming Archbifhop* was an impoftor, than that all the *Bifhops* and *Archbifhops* of *England* before him were either *Dunces* or *Prevaricators*.

2*dly*, Archbifhop *Cranmer* diftinguifh'd himfelf in a very particular Manner, by fetting the firft Example of joining *Matrimony* with *Epifcopacy*, contrary to the known Laws and Canons of the univerfal Church, which he had vow'd to obferve at his Admiffion to holy Orders. Nay not content with this, whereas St. *Paul* declares a Perfon unfit for the *Epifcopal* Character, who had been married twice even in his *Lay ftate* 1. Tim. C. 3. v. 2. this good Archbifhop, after the Death of his firft Wife married a Second: And tho' he kept his Wife in a clandeftine Manner as long as King *Henry* lived, for Fear of incurring the Severity of the Law made againft it by that Prince, he lived openly with her in the Reign of *Edward* VI. All which he own'd at his Trial under Queen *Mary*. Burnet 2. Part.

178 Dial. 3. §. 3. *Archbishop* Cranmer's
2. Part. L. 2. p. 332. And it can scarce be questi-on'd but that his Inclination to the married State render'd him so zealous for the *Reformation*, as it did many more of his *Ecclesiastical* Brethren.

3dly. He was the first Archbishop of *Canterbury*, who in Order to obtain his *Bulls*, took the *Oath of Obedience* to the Pope, with a premeditated Design not to keep it. That is, with a full Resolution to separate himself from the *Pope's Communion*, strip him of his *Spiritual Supremacy* in *England*, and bestow it on the King, as he did in Effect soon after his Consecration. Which if it was not down right *Perjury*, I know not what deserves that Name: Tho' Bishop *Burnet*, who could not conceal the Fact, labours hard to gloss it over by saying, that before he took the Oath, *he made a Solemn Protestation, that he did not intend thereby to restrain himself from any Thing, that he was bound to by his Duty to God, the King or his Country; and he renounced every Thing in it, that was contrary to any of these Things* 1 Part L. 2. p. 129. The *true English* whereof is, that he made a *Solemn Protestation* to God, that tho' he was going to take an *Oath of Obedience* to the Pope, his Conscience would not permit him to keep it; and that therefore his real Intention (as his Actions shew'd) was to renounce all Obedience to him. And can any Man doubt after this, but that *Archbishop Cranmer* had a very different sort of Conscience from all his Predecessors, who not only took that Oath from the Time it began to be tender'd, but thought themselves bound to keep it. Tho' indeed I don't find in any History, but that they complied with their Duty to *God*, the *King*, and *their Country*, as fully as if they had forsworn themselves like *Cranmer*.

I only add, that by the Help of such a *Protestation*, whether *Verbal* or *Mental* (if allow'd of) the
Force

Force of any Oath may be eluded; Becaufe the Party to whom it is tender'd, needs but keep this Referve in his Mind, *that he will bind himfelf no further by it, than his Confcience will permit.* And if that will excufe a Man from the guilt of *Perjury*, all Oaths of *Allegiance* or *Abjuration*, or of any other Kind, tho' worded in the Strongeft Terms, may be broke through like Cobwebs, and we muft agree with *Hudibras* that,

Oaths are but Words, and Words but Wind:
Too feeble Implements to bind.

Of which Commodious Doctrine we may fufpect that *Cranmer* had no great Abhorrence.

4*thly*, He was the firft Archbifhop of *Canterbury* that fhew'd his Dexterity in *Tying* firft, and then again *Untying* the Matrimonial Knot: And this he perform'd twice with great fuccefs in Compliance with his Royal Mafter. To explain myfelf, King *Henry* was privately married to *Anne Bolen* in the Prefence of Archbifhop *Cranmer*, (as the Lord *Herbert* relates p. 369) fome Months before the Sentence of the King's Divorce from Queen *Catharine* was pronounced by him. For this was not done, till She appear'd big with Child. Mr. *Collier* adds p. 76. that after *Cranmer* had pronounc'd the Sentence of Divorce, *he held another Court at* Lambeth, *where he confirm'd the King's Marriage with the new Queen* Anne. All which notwithftanding, as foon as this unfortunate Perfon was convicted of Difhonefty, and Sentenced to lofe her Head, the King refolved farther to be divorced from her, that is, to have his Marriage with her declared *Void: Which alfo was perform'd by Archbifhop* Cranmer, fays the fame Lord *Herbert* p. 448.

After that again the King was *folemnly married* to the Lady *Anne* of *Cleves*, with the exprefs Approbation of the fame Archbifhop *Cranmer* fitting

Dial. 3. §. 3. *Archbishop* Cramner's in Council; who Solved all Scruples and Difficulties relating to that Match. p. 516. All which notwithstanding, this complaisant Archbishop, perceiving that the King (who had taken a Liking to the Lady *Catharine Howard* p. 518.) hated his Wife, made no Difficulty to join with others in the Dissolution of this Marriage.

5*thly*, He was the first Archbishop of *Canterbury*, that gave up the *Ecclesiastical* Authority to Secular Hands, betray'd the ancient Immunities of the Church, and Sacrificed her Patrimony to the Lust and Avarice of his Prince; as is attested by all Historians both *Protestants* and *Catholicks*.

6*thly*, And lastly, he distinguish'd himself but a few Days before his Death no less, than he had done in the Course of his Life. For whilst he lay under Sentence of Condemnation, he perjured himself twice in Hopes of the Queen's Pardon. Which Fact is related and very finely dawbed over by Bishop *Burnet*. p. 334. 335 Who compares his Weakness and Fall with St. *Peter's* Denial of Christ, and brings off his *Hero* with flying Colours.

These were the most Distinguishing Actions of the famous *Thomas Cranmer*, the first *Protestant* Archbishop in *Great Britain*. To which high Station King *Henry*, who had taken the true size of his Conscience, prefer'd him; whilst he was yet Negotiating the Business of the *Divorce* in *Germany*; as judging him the fittest Person to put a speedy End to it by a difinitive Sentence; which he readily perform'd, as soon as the King call'd upon him for that Important Piece of Service.

G The Picture, you have here placed before me of Archbishop *Cranmer* must needs be a faithful Copy of the Original, since you have drawn every Feature of it from his own Actions, as related not by his *Enemies* but by his *Friends*. However

since

since Men's Tasts and Fancies differ in most other Things as well as meats, what appears a *Monster* to you and me, may perhaps be a *Beauty* to a true *Protestant* Eye.

P. That may very well be. Nay I am sure he appear'd very beautiful to Bishop *Burnets* Eyes; who, tho' he has furnish'd me with most of the Historical Facts I have mention'd, stiles him a *holy Saint* and *Martyr*, and relates of him that tho' his Body was reduced to Ashes, the Fire spared his Heart. p. 335.

G. That's very Strange. For I presume that *Protestant* Bishop will not allow of *Miracles*.

P. No. For he says expresly, that *if this had happen'd in our Church, we should have made a Miracle of it.* Ibid.

G. I am wholly of his Mind. For such a Thing cannot possibly be ascribed to any Natural Cause.

P. Nay, what completes the Paradox, he himself relates it as a *Testimony* of the Archbishop's *Innocence*. For he concludes from it, that *tho' his* HAND *err'd* (to wit in Subscribing twice before his Death to a formal *Abjuration* of the Errors of *Luther* and *Zuinglius*) *yet his* HEART *had continued true*. Ibid: And was therefore Spared by the Fire.

G. That's both Nonsense and Contradiction with a Vengence. For the *moral Guilt* of outward Actions is in the *Heart*, not in it's outward instrument the *Hand*; which therefore ought rather to have been spared, as being the less guilty of the two. But be that as it will, if the Preservation of the Archbishop's Heart was not *miraculous*, and yet cannot be ascrib'd to any natural Cause (for if it could, it would not be a *Testimony* of *Innocence*) that is, if it was neither *Natural* nor *Supernatural*, I may conclude without Offence, that Bishop *Burnet*'s fine Story,

182   Dial. 3. §. 3.   Cranmer

Story, wherever he has pick'd it up, is a mere Tale of a Tub, and Serves only to render both himself, and his *holy Saint and Martyr* ridiculous. But pray, Sir, proceed to what you have farther to say concerning the Divorce.

P. Archbishop *Cranmer* gave the finishing Stroke to it by a *definitive Sentence* in the Month of *May*. *An.* 1533. Queen *Catharine* being then at *Ampthil* in *Bedfordshire*; whither the King sent some of his Council to lay before her the Reasons of his 2d. Marriage, and exhort her to submit to it. But She persisting to protest against it, the Archbishop cited her to appear at *Dunstable* six Miles off; where he appointed a Court to be held; to which the Queen being cited for Fifteen Days together and not Appearing, he first pronounced her *contumacious*, and then proceeded to give Sentence, whereby (according to the Stile of it) he *pronounced decree'd* and *declared*, that the Marriage between K. *Henry* and the Princess *Catharine* had been *void, null*, and *invali'd*, from the very Beginning; and that it was unlawful for them to Live any more together as Husband and Wife. That therefore he *Separated* and *divorced* them, and in Consequence *pronounced, decree'd*, and *declared* them to be *Separated* and *divorced*. Which Sentence he order'd to be publickly read in our Lady's Chappel in the Priory of *Dunstable*. And then sent to the King to know his farther Pleasure: Who thereupon gave a strict Charge, that *Catharine* should be no more call'd *Queen*, but *Princess Dowager*, and *Widow* of *Prince Arthur*.

Thus ended the Business of the Divorce, which we may justly call the shame and scandal of Christianity. But as it often happens, that the Maintaining of one false step wilfully made by a Man in Power engages him in an endless Train of enormous Crimes; it fell out just so to the unfortunate

nate King *Henry*; the Remainder of whose Reign after the Divorce from Queen *Catharine* was nothing but a continual series of *Rapine, Sacrilege, Bloodshed* and all such Irregularities, as the Passions of *Avarice, Luxury,* and *Revenge* are wont to suggest to Persons deliver'd up by God to a reprobate Sense, and arm'd with Power to gratify their vicious Inclinations in an arbitrary Manner. So that he fully verified the Character given him by Sir *Walter Raleigh*, to wit, that *if all the Patterns of a merciless Prince had been lost in the World, they might have been found in this one King*: Who had struck such a Terror into the *Clergy* as well as *Laity*, and held his *Parliament* as well as *Council* and *Courts* of *Justice*, in such an Awe of him, that very few durst openly oppose his Will. In so much that every Thing, tho' never so unwarrantable, was transacted under the plausible Appearance of *Parliamentary* Proceedings, and the *regular Course of Justice*: And those, who had the Courage to oppose the Torrent, and refuse to *bend their Knees to* Baal, soon felt the smart of the King's Indignation; as I shall shew Immediately.

SECT. 4.

King *Henry* is declared *Supreme Head* of the Church of *England*, in *Spirituals*.

G. SIR as nothing is either more instructive or engaging than History, I desire to know what happen'd upon the Conclusion of the *Divorce*. Because the Decision of a Business of that Importance could not but be attended with extraordinary Consequences.

P. What you say, Sir, is very true. The first Thing therefore King *Henry* did, after his being solemnly excommunicated by *Clement* VII. on the score of his second Marriage, was to throw off all
Obe-

Obedience to the *See Apostolick,* and get himself declared *Supreme Head* of the Church of *England* in *Spirituals :* A most Stupendious Attempt, contrary to the express *Institution* of *Christ,* and unknown to all Antiquity ! However to make every Thing appear with the Authority of the Nation stamp'd upon it, he call'd two *Parliaments,* one in the Beginning, the other towards the End of the Year 1534. In the first amongst other Things it was enacted ; " That Whereas the Clergy had truly
" acknowledg'd, that the Convocation is always
" assembled by the King's Authority, and had
" promised his Majesty, that they would not from
" thenceforth make or alledge any new Constitu-
" tions without his Highness's Assent or Licence :
" And whereas diverse Constitutions *Provincial*
" and *Synodal,* formerly enacted are thought to be
" prejudicial to the King's Prerogative —— and
" the Clergy had therefore humbly beseech'd his
" Majesty, that the said Constitutions and Canons
" might be committed to the Examination of
" thirty two Men named by his Majesty, to wit,
" sixteen of both Houses of Parliament, and six-
" teen of the Clergy, who might annul or confirm
" the same as they found Cause ; it was enacted
" that his Highness should at his Pleasure appoint
" thirty two Men as aforesaid, to Survey the said
" Canons and Constitutions for the Confirmation
" or Abolition of the same.

Here we have a Committee establish'd of thirty two Persons, half *Laymen,* and vested with full power to abolish any *Ecclesiastical Canon* or *Constitution* anciently made by the Authority of a *Provincial* or *national Synod.* So that if the sixteen *Laymen,* who were put upon the Level with the same Number of the *Clergy* in the Regulation of *Ecclesiastical* Affairs, could but gain over to their side any one *Clergyman* of the whole Committee, which was to be entirely model'd and pack'd by the Court, any Thing they pleased was sure to pass by the Plurality of Voices.

G. But how came it, that the *Clergy* was so forward in this Business, as to become Petitioners to the King for the Passing of this Act?

P. Sir, it came thus to pass. The King had some time before trepann'd the *whole Body* of the *Clergy* into a *premunire*, for Acknowledging Cardinal *Wolsey's* legatine Power, tho' he had the King's *broad Seal* for the Exercising of it. Now by this *premunire* their Persons became liable to Imprisonment for Life, and their Estates to Confiscation; so that both the one and the other were entirely at the King's Mercy. But it seems the Generality of them were not fond of Suffering a lingring Martyrdom, and they had but one Way to prevent the Execution of the *premunire*, which was an entire Submission in Matters of Religion to the King; who (says Dr. *Heylin*) *peremptorily required of them, that no Constitution or Ordinance should thenceforth be enacted, promulged, or put in Execution by the Clergy, unless the King's Highness approved of it*; to which they absolutely submitted. Anno. 1532. And so it is no Wonder, that they should be mention'd in the abovesaid Act as Persons running into all the Measures of the Court: Because the same Motive of Fear, which had made them turn *Prevaricators* before, subsisting still, they thought it better and safer to comply with a good Grace, than be dragg'd to it like Bears to the Stake.

Thus you see King *Henry* had brought the *English Clergy* under his *Spiritual Jurisdiction*, and begun to act as *Supreme Head* of the Church of *England*, even before that Title was settled upon him and
his

his *Heirs* and *Succeſſors* in a *Parliamentary* Way: which was not done till the Meeting of the next *Parliament* in the ſame Year 1534. Wherein the following Act paſs'd. *viz.*

"That albeit the King was *Supreme Head* of the Church of *England*, and had been ſo recognized by the *Clergy* of this Realm in their *Convocation*, yet for more Corroboration thereof, as alſo for Extirpating all *Errors, Hereſies*, and *Abuſes* of the ſame, it was enacted that the *King*, his *Heirs* and *Succeſſors,* Kings of *England,* ſhould be accepted and reputed the *Supreme Head* on Earth of the Church of *England,* and have and enjoy united and annex'd to the *Imperial Crown* of this Realm as well the Title and Stile thereof, as all *Honours, Dignities, Preeminences, Juriſdictions, Privileges, Authorities, Immunities, Profits* and *Commodities* to the ſaid Dignity of *Supreme Head* of the ſame Church belonging or appertaining. And that our ſaid Sovereign Lord, his *Heirs* and *Succeſſors,* Kings of this Realm ſhall have *full Power and Authority* from Time to Time to *viſit* and *repreſs, redreſs, reform, order correct, reſtrain,* and *amend* all ſuch *Errors, Hereſies, Abuſes, Offences, Contempts* and *Enormities* whatſoever they be, which by any *Manner of Spiritual Authority or Juriſdiction* ought or may lawfully be *reform'd, repreſs'd, order'd, redreſs'd, corrected, reſtrain'd* or *amended,* moſt to the Pleaſure of A. G. the Encreaſe of Virtue in Chriſt's Religion, and the Conſervation of the Peace, Unity, and Tranquillity of the Realm: Any *Uſage, Cuſtom, foreign Laws, foreign Preſcription,* or any Thing or Things to the Contrary thereof notwithſtanding.

This is that Act, which made the firſt Change in the Religion of our Anceſtors. For tho' ſome Acts had

had pafs'd in former Reigns to put a Stop to some Abuses committed by the Pope's Legates in *England*, as likewise to prevent any unreasonable Encroachments of the *Court of Rome* (because the moſt lawful and beſt eſtabliſh'd Authority may be abuſed) yet the Pope's Title to the *Spiritual Supremacy* over the *Univerſal Church* had always been acknowledg'd by the whole Body of the *Engliſh* Nation, as belonging to him by *divine Right*, and inviolably maintain'd as an Article of the Chriſtian Faith. So far were our Forefathers from Entertaining any Thoughts of placing the *Crown* and *Mitre* upon the ſame Head, or Authorizing the Hand that ſway'd the *Scepter* to Stretch itſelf forth to the *Cenſer*. This on the Contrary was in all former Ages regarded as a Sacrilegious Attempt, and a Violation of Chriſt's own Inſtitution, who never appointed *Kings* but *Biſhops* to Govern his Church in *Spiritual Matters*.

We read indeed of ſome Princes and thoſe none of the beſt, who have endeavour'd to encroach upon the ancient Immunities of the Church. But they were always vigorouſly oppoſed, and their Attempts proved generally unſucceſsful. But to veſt the *Supreme Eccleſiaſtical Juriſdiction* and Authority in the Perſon of a *Layman*, nay and entail it like Farms or Manours upon his *Heirs* and *Succeſſors*, whether *Women* or *Infants*, was a Proceeding not only without Precedent in all the former Ages of Chriſtianity, but has never ſince been follow'd by any other Chriſtian Nation in the World. 'Twas in Effect invading the *Sanctuary* with arm'd Force, and reducing the *Church* into a Province of the *State*. So that I may modeſtly call it one of the moſt Stupendious Actions recorded in Hiſtory: And 'tis ſuch a Stain upon the very *Infancy* of the pretended *Godly Reformation*, as can never be wiped

off

off. Yet 'twas this very Act, that laid the Foundation of it, and the whole Superstructure of the *English Reformation* was built upon this Foundation: It being apparent that all the three reforming Princes, to wit, King *Henry*, *Edward* VI. and Queen *Elizabeth* undertook that Work neither in the *Name*, nor by the Authority of the *Prelatick Order*, but by Virtue of their own *Spiritual Supremacy*: That is, as *Supreme Judges* in Controversies of Religion.

G. But did not the whole Body of the *English Clergy* consent *freely* to it, so as to make it their own Act and Deed?

P. 'Tis certain the *major Part* assented to it, but not *freely*. Because they did not assent to it, till it was altogether unsafe for them to oppose it. For who can deny, but that the imminent Danger of a *Premunire* is a terrible Restraint upon the *Freedom* of *Votes*? And I leave it to the Judgment of any *Protestant*, whether if the *Pope* at the Head of a Council should threaten the Bishops assembled in it with *perpetual Imprisonment* and *Confiscation of Goods*, in Case they should refuse to come into his Measures, whether, I say, that Council would be *free*? Yet this was all the Freedom the *English Clergy* had in Reference to the Act in Question. That is to say, they were perfectly free either to comply with the Court, or rot in Prison.

G. But have not all Sovereign Princes the *Supreme Authority* in their respective Dominions over the *Clergy* as well as *Laity*?

P. I never heard it doubted by any Man in his Senses. For every King as such has the *Supreme Authority* over all his *Subjects*; and *Churchmen* are his *Subjects* no less than *Laymen*. But what is this to the plain Meaning and Intention of the Act we Speak of? For there needed no *Act* of *Parliament*
to

to make King *Henry* the *Supreme Temporal Head* and *Governour* of the whole Body of his People, since no Man upon Earth disputed that Title with him. It therefore bestow'd upon him either more than this, or nothing at all. In a Word, it bestow'd upon him that same *Supreme Spiritual Jurisdiction* and *Authority* of which they had dispossess'd the *Pope*: And that differs as much from the *Temporal Jurisdiction* and *Authority* of Kings, as the *regal* and *Episcopal* Characters differ from one another: Or as the Functions of a *Priest* differ from those of a *civil* or *Military* Officer, who all act in different Capacities, and move in different Spheres.

I insist so particularly upon this because when the Act of *Supremacy* (which was repeal'd in Queen *Mary*'s Reign) was again renew'd in Favour of Queen *Elizabeth*, and great Numbers appear'd grievously Scandaliz'd at it, *the Thing seeming to be abhorrent* (says Dr. *Heylin*) *even to Nature and Policy, that a Woman should be declared Supreme Head on Earth of the Church of* England, I find that to cover the Scandal of it, the Composers of the thirty nine *Articles of Religion* were obliged to gloss it over with this Strain'd Interpretation, *viz. That the Act meant no more than to give that Prerogative to the Queen, which had been given to all Godly Princes in holy Scriptures by God himself; that is to rule all Estates and Degrees committed to their Charge by God, whether they be Ecclesiastical or Temporal, and restrain with the civil Sword the Stubborn and evil Doers.* Art. 37. But who sees not that this was but a Gilding of the Pill to make it go down the better, and meer Trifling instead of a serious Explanation of the Act? But more of this hereafter.

G. But may we not take the *Oath of Supremacy* with this Interpretation tack'd to it?

P. I should be loath to do it: And my Reason is because Oaths are *Sacred Things*, and not to be be trifled with: Nor can any Man warrant me to Swear one Thing, and mean another. As I cannot, for Example, Swear that the King of *Great Britain* is the *Czar of Muscovy*; tho' he that should tender this Oath, should assure me, that nothing more was meant by it, than that the King of *Great Britain* is the *Supreme Head* and *Governour* in his own Dominions, as the *Czar of Muscovy* is in his. Because tho' this Interpretation Imports a real Truth, it differs wholly from the obvious Meaning of the Words of the Oath.

G. However I don't find the above said Act gave King *Henry* any Power either to *preach the Word*, or *Administer* the *Sacraments*. And what then was his *Supreme Headship* any more than an empty Title? And was there any Harm in Making the King and his Heirs the Complement of a Title, that signified Nothing?

P. 'Tis very true, the Act did not give King *Henry* the Power to *preach the Word, or Administer the Sacraments*. For that would have been too gross: But you are under a great Mistake in Imagining, that it bestow'd upon him a meer empty Title. For in the *first* Place it made him *Supreme Judge* in all Controversies of Religion, by giving him full Power to *visit, repress, redress, reform, order, correct, restrain* and *amend* all *Errors, Heresies,* and *Abuses whatsoever*, which by any Manner of *Spiritual Authority* or *Jurisdiction* may lawfully be *reform'd repress'd, redress'd* &c: The plain Meaning whereof is, that he had the same full Power given him to Govern the Church of *England* in all *Spiritual* and *Ecclesiastical* Matters, as the *Pope* in Quality of *Supreme Head* of the *Universal Church*, and the whole Body of *Bishops* in Quality of *Ordinaries* in their several Dioceses ever had before him. Which Power was likewise to descend to his *Heirs* and *Successors* whether *Infants*

fants or *Women*. And was there nothing intended by all this but an *empty Title*?

But 2*dly*, by Impowring him to *visit* with *Supreme Authority*, it united, as I may say, in his Person alone the whole *Episcopal Jurisdiction* of the Nation; which before was divided, as in other National Churches, among the Bishops, to whom alone it belong'd to *visit*, and that only in their own respective Dioceses according to the *Canons*. So that it degraded in a Manner the whole *prelatick Order*: Or at least render'd the Exercise of their Jurisdiction wholly precarious: And they were after that no better than the King's *Vicars* in *Spirituals*; which was giving him a greater Power, than any Pope had ever claim'd by Virtue of his *Spiritual Supremacy*.

3*dly*, It gave the King a power to *revise* and *annul* any *Ecclesiastical Decree* or *Constitution*, tho' enacted by the whole Body of the *English Clergy*, who by that means were divested of their *Divine Right* of *Feeding* and *Guiding* their respective Flocks, and became meer *Executors* of the King's arbitrary Will.

This was the Power King *Henry* obliged the *Parliament* to make him a Present of, and the *Clergy* to truckle to. I say, *obliged*, For their *Voting* was but a Form extorted by Fear; and they gave up the *Rights* of the *Church* with just as much *Freedom* as a Man delivers his Purse, when he has a Pistol presented to his Breast. But I should be glad to know, from which of the *Apostles* King *Henry* descended? And if he could not derive his *Ecclesiastical Pedigree* from any *Apostolical* Family, what Title had he to accept of a *Commission* to govern any Part of the *Church of Christ*, who committed the whole Government of his Church to none but the *Apostles* and their *Successors*? However right or wrong King *Henry* accepted it.

G. I perceive he made no *Scruple* of any Sin, but that of keeping an old Woman for his Wife.

P. Nay he not only accepted it, but soon gave the *English Clergy* an illustrious Specimen of the Authority they had vested him with. For being now made *Supreme Head* of the Church of *England* in Spirituals, he could not well be without a *Vicar General*; or, as my Lord *Herbert* Stiles him, *Viceregent General of the King's Authority in Ecclesiastical Affairs*, which is most certainly an *Ecclesiastical* Dignity. And who do you think was the Person he pitch'd upon for this eminent Station?

G. That's more than I can guess. But according to my weak Apprehension, I conceive it to be most probable, that it was either the Archbishop of *Canterbury*, who is *Primate* of *England*, or at least some other eminent Bishop.

P. Indeed Sir, you are very much out of the Way in your Guess. It was one *Thomas Cromwel*, a *Layman*, and the Son of a *Blacksmith*.

G. I should as soon have guess'd that he had made a *Corn-cutter* his *prime Minister of State*, or his *Coachman high Admiral* of *England*.

P. I believe so: For the one was as repugnant to the establish'd Laws of *Church-government*, as the other would have been to the common Rules of Policy. Yet so it was, and the Fact is thus set down by Sir *Richard Baker*.

"*Thomas Cromwel*, Son to a *Blacksmith* in *Putney*,
" being raised to high Dignities, was lastly
" made *Vical General* under the King in all *Ecclesi-*
" *astical* Affairs: Who sat diverse Times in the
" *Convocation House* amongst the Bishops as *Head*
" over them." p. 408.

This is confirm'd by my Lord *Herbert*, in whose History of King *Henry* p. 468. I find, that in a *Synod* of about twenty *Bishops*, thirty nine *Abbot's*
and

Declared Supreme Head *in* Spirituals &c. 193

and *Priors*, and fifty of the *inferiour Clergy*, being held to Settle some Articles of Religion, they were Subscribed to in the first Place by *Thomas Cromwel*, and after him by *Thomas of Canterbury, John of London*, &c. And I find the same Order of Subscriptions afterwards to a Decree relating to *general Councils*. p. 470. So that altho' this was a Synod held by the *Metropolitan* of *Canterbury*, it was not the Archbishop of that See, but *Thomas Cromwel* that presided in it. This worthy Person was likewise constituted the King's *Visitor* or rather *Plunderer general* of all the *Abbeys, Priories,* and *Monasteries* both of *Men* and *Women* within the Kingdom; a great Number of mercenary Tools of the Court being appointed to Serve under him as their *Master-Workman*: And from this Extent of *Cromwell*'s Commission on this Occasion, we may gather the full Extent of Royal Prerogative in Spirituals. I shall deliver it in Mr. *Collier's* Words 2d. *Part*, 2d. *Book*. *Page* 104. 105.

" *Cromwel*, says he, being authorized by the
" King's *Letters Patents* under the broad Seal to
" constitute Deputies for a Visitation, made
" Choice of *Richard Layton, Thomas Leigh, William*
" *Petre*, Doctors of the Law; Doctor *John London*,
" Dean of *Wallingford* &c. for this Purpose.

" And now the Time for the Visitation drawing
" on, the King issued out Letters of *Inhibition* to
" the Archbishop of *Canterbury*, charging him and
" his *Suffragans* not to visit the *Clergy* or *Religious*,
" till the Royal Visitation was over; Meaning
" that which was to be managed under the Vicar
" general *Cromwel*. And thus all Episcopal Ju-
" risdiction was laid a Sleep, and almost struck
" dead by the *Regale*, during the King's Pleasure.
" The Archbishop of *Canterbury* directed his Man-
" date to the Bp. of *London*, who was to trans-
" mit Copies of the Inhibition to the rest of the
" provincial Bishops.   O   " The

"The next Month *Layton*, *Leigh*, *London* &c: Began their general Visitation under *Cromwel*. They were furnish'd, at least some of those first named, with a Plenitude of Power to Visit all Archbishops, Bishops, and the rest of the inferiour Clergy; and to correct and reform, and exercise all Manner of Discipline, which belong'd to Ecclesiastical Jurisdiction; they had likewise an Authority to confirm or null the Elections of Prelates, to order Instalments, to give Institutions and Inductions, to Sequester the Fruits of Livings, to deprive or suspend Archbishops, Bishops &c. To convene Synods and preside in 'em, and to make such Reformations and Orders, as they shall think expedient. They had likewise an Authority of trying all Ecclesiastical Causes, and Exerting the Censures of the Church upon those, who either refused to appear, or abide by the Sentence. And as to Monasteries, they had, as it were, an unlimited Authority, and were impower'd to allow Pensions to such as were disposed to quit that way of Living."

Such was the exorbitant Commission even of the Sub-delegates, who acted under the King's *Vicar general*. And as to their Visitation of Monasteries 'tis hard to say, whether the *Motives* upon which they acted, or the *Means* they employ'd, or the *Inhumanities* they practised in the Execution of their Commission were more Unchristian.

I shall give you a Relation of it in the very Words of Sir *William Dugdale*, whose Testimony is above all Exception. But if a Reformation set on Foot by such wicked Instruments, as you have already seen the most active in it, and promoted by such unchristian Means and Contrivances, as will now be laid before you, can be look'd upon

by

Declared Supreme Head *in* Spirituals &c. by any sober thinking Man as the *Work of God*, I may boldly say the Enemy of Man never had a Part in any Wickedness committed by Mankind. The Relation is somewhat long, but deserves your most Serious Attention.

SECT. 5.
Sir William Dugdale's *Account of the Dissolution of* Religious Houses *in the Reign of* Henry VIII.

THE Account Sir *William Dugdale* has given us of the Methods and Contrivances used in the Dissolution of *Abbeys* and *Monasteries* is taken out of his celebrated History of *Warwickshire* p. 801. Where Speaking of the Dissolution of a particular Monastery of Nuns call'd *Polesworth*, he takes Occasion to give the following Relation of the Dissolution of all the other Monasteries and Abbeys in the Kingdom.

" I find it left recorded by the Commissioners,
" that were employ'd to take Surrender of the
" Monasteries in this Shire An. 29 *Henry* VIII.
" that after strict Scrutiny not only by the Fame
" of the Country, but by Examination of several
" Persons, *they found these Nuns Virtuous and Religi-*
" *ous Women and of good Conversation*. Neverthe-
" less it was not the strict and regular Lives of
" these devout Ladies, nor any Thing that might
" be said in behalf of the Monasteries, that could
" prevent their Ruine then Approaching. So
" great an Aim had the King to make himself
" thereby Glorious, and many others no less Hopes
" to be enrich'd in a considerable Manner. But
" to the End that such a Change should not over-
" whelm those that might be active therein, in
" Re-

"Regard the People every where had no small
"Esteem of these Houses for their devout and
"daily Exercises in Prayer, Alms-deeds, Hospita-
"lity, and the like, whereby not only the Souls
"of their deceased Ancestors had much Benefit,
"as was then thought, but themselves, the Poor,
"as also Strangers and Pilgrims constant Advan-
"tage; *there wanted not the most subtle Contrivances,*
"*to effect this Stupendious Work, that, I think any Age*
"*has beheld:* whereof it will not be thought
"impertinent I presume, to take here a short
"View."

"In Order therefore to it was that, which
"Cardinal *Wolsey* had done for the Founding his
"Colleges in *Oxford* and *Ipswich*, made a Prece-
"dent; viz: The Dissolving of above thirty
"Religious Houses, most very small ones, by
"the Licence of the King and Pope *Clement* VII.
"And that it might be the better carried on, Mr.
"*Thomas Cromwel*, who had been an old Servant
"to the Cardinal, and not a little active in
"that, was the Chief Person pitch'd upon to
"assist therein. For I look upon this Business as
"not originally design'd by the King, but by
"some principal ambitious Men of that Age,
"*who projected to themselves all worldly Advantages*
"*Imaginable through that Deluge of Wealth, which*
"*was like to flow amongst them by this hideous Storm.*"

"First therefore, having insinuated to the
"King Matter of *Profit* and *Honour*, (viz. *Profit*
"by so vast Enlargement of his Revenue, and
"*Honour* in being able to maintain mighty Ar-
"mies to recover his Right in *France*, as also to
"Strengthen himself against the Pope, whose
"Supremacy he himself abolish'd, and make the
"firmer Alliance with such Princes as had done
"the like) did they procure *Cranmer*'s Advancement

"ment to the See of *Canterbury*, and more of the
"Protestant Clergy to other Bishopricks and
"high Places; to the End that the rest should
"not be able in a full Council to carry any Thing
"against their Design; sending out Preachers to
"persuade the People to stand fast to the King
"without Fear of the Pope's Curse, or his Dis-
"solving their Allegiance.

"Next, that it might be more plausibly carry'd on,
"*Care was taken so to represent the Lives of* Monks,
"Nuns, Canons *&c. to the World, as that the less*
"*Regret might be made at their Ruine.* To which
"Purpose *Tho. Cromwel* being constituted *general*
"*Visitor*, employ'd sundry Persons, who acted
"therein their Parts accordingly: viz. *Rich. Lay-*
"*ton, Tho. Leigh,* and *Wm. Petre* Doctors of Law;
"Dr. *John London* Dean of *Wallingford* and others;
"By which they were to enquire into the Govern-
"ment and Behaviour of the Religious of both
"Sexes: Which Commissioners the better to
"manage their Design, *gave Encouragement to the*
"*Monks, not only to accuse their Governours, but to*
"*inform against each other; compelling them also to*
"*produce the Charters and Evidences of their Lands,*
"*as also their Plate and Money, and to give an Inven-*
"*tory thereof.* And hereunto they added certain
"Injunctions from the King, containing most se-
"vere and strict Rules; by Means whereof divers
"being found obnoxious to their Censure were
"expell'd; and many discerning themselves not
"able to live free from some Exception or Ad-
"vantage that might be taken against them, de-
"sired to leave their Habit."

"Having by these Visitors thus search'd into
"their Lives (which by a *black Book,* containing
"a World of Enormities, were represented in no
"small measure Scandalous) to the End that the

"People might be better satisfied with their Pro-
"ceedings, it was thought convenient to Sug-
"gest, that the lesser Houses for Want of good
"Government were chiefly guilty of these
"Crimes that were laid to their Charge: And
"so they did, as appears by the Preamble of that
"Act for their Dissolution made in the Twenty
"seventh of *Henry* VIII. which Parliament *(consi-
"sting in the most Part of such Members as were
"pack'd for the Purpose through private Interest, as
"is evident by divers original Letters of that Time,
"many of the Nobility for the like Respects also fa-
"vouring the Design)* assented to the Suppressing
"of all such Houses as had been certify'd of
"less Value than 200 Pounds *per Annum*, and gi-
"ving them with their Lands and Revenues to
"the King: Yet so as not only the Religious
"Persons therein should be committed to the
"great and Honourable Monasteries of the
"Realm, where they might be compell'd to live
"religiously for the Reformation of their Lives,
"*wherein Thanks be to God Religion is well kept and
"observed* (they are the Words of the *Act*) but
"that the Possessions belonging to such Houses
"should be converted to better Uses, to the Plea-
"sure of Almighty God, and the Honour and
"Profit of the Realm.

"But how well the Tenor thereof was pursued
"we shall see; these Specious Pretences being
"made Use of for no other Purpose, than by
"*Opening this Gap to make Way for the total Ruin of
"the greater Houses*, wherein it is by the said Act
"acknowledg'd, *that Religion was so well observed*.
"For no sooner were the Monks &c. turn'd out,
"and the Houses demolish'd (that being first
"thought requisite, least some accidental Change
"might conduce to their Restitution) but Care

"was

"was taken to prefer such Persons to the Superiority in Government upon any Vacancy in those greater Houses, as might be Instrumental to their surrender by Tampering with the Convent to that Purpose; whose Activeness was such, that within the Space of two Years several Convents were wrought upon, and Commissioners sent down to take them at their Hands to the King's Use; of which Number I find that besides the before specify'd Doctors of Law, there were 34 Commissioners.

"The Truth is, that there was no Omission of any Endeavours that can well be imagined to accomplish'd these Surrenders: For so subtilly did the Commissioners act their Parts, as that after *earnest Solicitation* with the Abbots, and finding them backward, they first *tempted them with good Pensions during Life*: whereby they found some forward enough to promote the Work, as the Abbot of *Hales* in *Glocestershire* was; who had high Commendation for it from the Commissioners; as their Letters to the *Visitor General* do manifest. So likewise had the Abbot of *Ramsey* and the Prior of *Ely*. Nay some were so obsequious, that after they had wrought the Surrender of their own Houses, they were employ'd as Commissioners to persuade others, as the Prior of *Gisborn* in *Yorkshire* for one. Neither were the Courtiers unactive in Driving on this Work; as may be seen by the Lord Chancellor *Audley*'s employing a special Agent to treat with the Abbot of *Athelney*, and to offer him 100 Marks *per Annum* Pension in Case he would Surrender; which the Abbot refused insisting upon a greater Sum; and the personal Endeavours he used with the Abbot of *S. Osithe* in *Essex*, as by his Letter to the *Visitor General*; wherein

" it is signified, *that he had with great Solicitation*
" *prevail'd with the said Abbot*: But withal insinu-
" ating his Desire, *that his Place of Lord Chancel-*
" *lor being very chargeable, the King might be moved*
" *for an Addition of some more profitable Offices unto*
" *him*. Nay I find that this great Man the Lord
" Chancellor hunting eagerly after the Abbey of
" *Walden* in *Essex* (out of the Ruins whereof af-
" terwards that magnificent Fabrick call'd by the
" Name of *Audley-Inn* was built) as an Argument
" to obtain it, did, besides the Extenuation of
" it's Worth, alledge, *that he had in this World*
" *Sustain'd great Damage and Infamy in serving the*
" *King, which the Grant of that should recompense*.

" Amongst the particular Arguments, which
" were made Use of by those that were averse to
" Surrender, I find that the Abbot of *Feversham*
" alledg'd the Antiquity of their Monastery's
" Foundation, viz: by King *Stephen*, whose Body
" with the Bodies of the Queen and Prince lay
" there interr'd, and for whom were used conti-
" nual Suffrages and Commendations by Prayers.
" Yet it would not avail; for they were resolved
" to effect what they had begun by one Means or
" other: In so much that they procured the Bi-
" shop of *London* to come to the Nuns of *Sion*
" with their Confessor to solicit them thereunto:
" Who after many Persuasions took it upon their
" Consciences that they ought to submit unto
" the King's Pleasure therein by God's Law. But
" what could not be effected by such Argu-
" ments and *fair Promises* (which were not wan-
" ting nor unfulfill'd, as appears by the *large Pen-*
" *sions* that some active *Monks* and *Canons* had in
" Comparison of others even to a fifth or six-
" fold Proportion more than ordinary) was by
" *Terror* and *Severe Dealing* brought to pass. For
" under

"under Pretence of Dilapidation in the Buil-
"dings or negligent Administration of their Of-
"fices, as also for Breaking the King's Injuncti-
"ons they *deprived some Abbots, and then put o-
"thers that were more pliant in their Rooms.*

"From others *they took their Convent Seals*, to the
"End they might not by making Leases or Sale
"of their Jewels raise Money either for Supply
"of their present Wants, or Payment of their
"Debts, and so be necessitated to Surrender. Nay
"to some, as in particular to the Canons of *Lei-
"cester*, the Commissioners threaten'd, *that they
"would charge them with Adultery and Buggery, un-
"less they would Submit.* And Dr. *London* told the
"Nuns of *Godstow*, that *because he found them ob-
"stinate, he would dissolve the House by Virtue of the
"King's Commission in spite of their Teeth.* And
"yet all was so managed that the King was So-
"licited to accept of them; not being willing to
"have it thought they were by Terror Moved
"thereunto, and special Notice was taken of such
"as gave out that their Surrender was by Com-
"pulsion.

"Which Courses (after so many, that through
"under-hand Corruption led the Way) brought
"on others apace; as appears by their Dates, which
"I have observed from the very Instruments
"themselves; in so much that the rest stood a-
"mazed, not knowing which way to turn them-
"selves. Some therefore thought fit to try, whe-
"ther Money might save their Houses from this
"dismal Fate so near at Hand : The Abbot of
"*Peterborough* offering 2500 Marks to the King
"and 300 Pounds to the *Visitor General*. Others
"with great Constancy refused to be thus accesso-
"ry in Violating the Donations of their pious
"Founders. But these, as they were not many,

"so

"so did they tast of no little Severity. For touch-
"ing the Abbot of *Fountaines* in *Yorkshire* I find,
"that being charged by the Commissioners for ta-
"ing into his private Hands some Jewels belong-
"ing to that Monastery, which they call'd *Theft*
"and *Sacriledge*, they pronounced him perjured,
"and so deposing him *extorted a private Resignati-
"on.* And it appears that the Monks of the
"*Charter-House* in the Suburbs of *London* were
"committed to *Newgate*; where with hard and
"barbarous Usage five of them died, and five
"more lay at the Point of Death, as the Com-
"missioners signified, but withall alledg'd, that
"the Suppression of that House, *being of so strict
"a Rule,* would occasion great Scandal to their
"Doings; for as much as it stood in the Face
"of the World, infinite Concourse coming from
"all Parts to that populous City; and therefore
"desired it might be alter'd to some other Use.
"And lastly I find that under the like Pretence
"of Robbing the Church, wherewith the afore-
"said Abbot of *Fountaines* was charged, the Ab-
"bot of *Glastenbury* with two of his Monks being
"condemn'd to Death was drawn from *Wells*
"upon a Hurdle, then hang'd upon the Hill call'd
"the *Tor* near *Glastenbury*, his Head set upon the
"Abbey-gate, and his Quarters disposed of to
"*Wells, Bath, Ilchester* and *Bridgwater*. Nor did
"the Abbots of *Colchester* and *Reading* fare much
"better, as they that will consult the Story of
"that Time may See. And for farther Terror
"to the rest some *Priors* and other *Ecclesiastical*
"Persons, who spoke against the King's *Supre-
"macy*, a Thing then somewhat uncooth, were
"condemn'd as *Traitors* and executed.

" And now when all this was effected, to the
" End it might not be thought that these Things
"were

"were done with a high Hand, the King having
"protested that he would Suppress none without
"the Consent of his *Parliament,* (it being call'd
"*April* 28. 1539. To confirm these Surrenders
"so made,) there wanted not plausible Insinua-
"tions to both Houses for Drawing on their Con-
"sent with all smoothness thereto ; *the Nobility*
"*being promised large shares in the Spoil,* either by
"free Gift from the King, easy Purchases, or most
"advantagious Exchanges, and many of the
"active Gentry *Advancements to Honours with*
"*Encrease of their Estates*: All which we see hap-
"pen'd to them accordingly. And the better to
"satisfy the *Vulgar,* it was represented to them,
"that by this Deluge of Wealth the Kingdom
"should be strengthen'd with an Army of 40000
"Men, and that for the future they should never
"be charg'd with *Subsidies, Fifteenths, Loans,* or
"*common Aids.* By which Means the *Parliament*
"ratifying the above-said Surrenders, the Work
"became compleated : For the more firm Set-
"ling whereof *a Sudden Course was taken to pull*
"*down and destroy the Buildings,* as had been done
"before upon the Dissolution of smaller Houses,
"whereof I have touch'd. Next to distribute a
"great Proportion of their Lands amongst the
"*Nobility* and *Gentry,* as had been projected ; which
"was accordingly done: The *Visitor General* ha-
"ving told the King, *that the more had Interest*
"*in them, the more they would be Irrevocable.*

"And least any Domestick Stirs by Reason of
"this great and strange Alteration should arise,
"Rumours were spread abroad, that Cardinal *Pool*
"labour'd with divers Princes to procure Forces
"against this Realm, and that an Invasion was
"threaten'd ; which seem'd the more credible,
"because the Truce concluded between the *Em-*
peror

"peror and *French King* was generally known, nei-
"ther of them wanting a Pretence to invade
"*England*. And this was also seconded by a
"sudden journey of the King unto the Sea-coasts;
"unto divers parts whereof he had sent sundry of
"the Nobles and expert Persons to visit the
"Ports and places of Danger, who fail'd not for
"their Discharge upon all Events to affirm the
"Peril in each place to be so great, as one
"would have thought every Place needed a For-
"tification. Besides he forthwith caused his
"Navy to be in a Readiness, and Musters to be
"taken over all the Kingdom. All which prepa-
"rations being made against a Danger believed
"imminent, seem'd so to excuse the suppressi-
"on of the Abbeys, as that the People willing to
"save their own Purses, began to suffer it easily;
"especially when they saw Order taken for Build-
"ing such Forts.

"But let us look a little upon the Success,
"wherein I find that the *Visitor General*, the
"grand Actor in this tragical Business, having
"contracted upon himself such an Odium from
"the Nobility by reason of his low Birth (tho'
"not long before made *Knight of the Garter*, *Earl*
"*of* Essex, and *Lord high Chancellor of* England)
"as also from the *Catholicks* for having thus ope-
"rated in the Dissolution of Abbeys, that (be-
"fore the End of the abovesaid Parliament
"wherein that was ratified, which he had with
"so much industry brought to pass) the King
"not having any more Use of him, gave way to
"his Enemy's Accusations. Whereupon being
"arrested by the *Duke of* Norfolk at the Council
"Table, when he least Dreamt of it, and com-
"mitted to the *Tower*, he was condemn'd by the
"same *Parliament* for *Heresy* and *Treason*, unheard
"and

"and little pity'd: and on the 28th of *July*, viz. four Days after the *Parliament* was diſſolv'd had his Head cut off on *Tower-hill*.

"And as for the Fruit which the People reap'd after all their Hopes built upon thoſe ſpecious Pretences, which I have mention'd, it was very little. For 'tis plain that *Subſidies* from the Clergy, and *Fifteenths* of Laymens Goods were ſoon after exacted: and that in *Edward* the VI's time the Commons were conſtrain'd to ſupply the Kings Wants by a new Invention, *viz. Sheep, Cloaths, Goods, Debts,* &c. for three Years: Which Tax grew ſo heavy, that the Year following they pray'd the King for a Mitigation thereof. Nor is it a little obſervable, that *whilſt the Monaſteries ſtood, there was no Act for the relief of the Poor. So amply did thoſe Houſes give Succour to them that were in Want,* whereas in the next Age, *viz.* 39 *Eliz.* no leſs than eleven Bills were brought into the Houſe of Commons for that Purpoſe.

Thus far this learned Knight; who has here diſcover'd ſuch a Complication of the blackeſt Villanies, as ſuffice to ſtrike a Chriſtian's Heart with Horror. However in Confirmation of the Truth of Sir *William Dugdale*'s Relation, I will here add a piece taken from Mr. *Thomas Hearn*'s *Preliminary Obſervations* upon Mr. *Brown Willis*'s *View of the Mitred Abbeys.* This Author, after a ſolemn Profeſſion of his being a ſincere Member of the *Church of* England, writes thus.

"*Popery* (as I take it, *ſays he*) ſignifies no more than the Errors of the *Church of* Rome. Had he (*Henry* VIII) therefore put a ſtop to thoſe Errors, he had acted wiſely, and very much to the Content of all truly Good and Religious Men. But then this would not have ſatisfy'd the *Ends* of himſelf and his *covetous*

"and

"and *ambitious Agents*. They all aim'd at the "*Revenues* and *Riches* of the *Religious Houses*: "For which Reason no *Arts* or *Contrivances* were "to be pass'd by, that might be of use in Ob- "taining these Ends. The *most abominable Crimes* "were to be charg'd upon the Religious, and the "Charge was to be managed with the utmost *In-* "*dustry*, *Boldness* and *Dexterity*. This was a Pow- "erfull Argument to draw an Odium upon them, "and to make them disrespected and ridiculed "by the Generality of Mankind. And yet after "all, *the Proofs were so insufficient*, that from what "I have been able to gather, *I have not found* "*any direct one against even any single Monastery.* "The Sins of one or two particular Persons do "not make a *Sodom*. Neither are *violent* and "*forced* Confessions to be esteem'd as the true "Results of any one's Thoughts. When there- "fore even these Artifices would not do, the "last Expedient was put in Execution, and that "was *Ejection by Force*; and to make these *inno-* "*cent Sufferers* the more content, Pensions were "settled upon many, and such Pensions were "in some measure proportion'd to their *Inno-* "*cence*. Thus by Degrees the Religious Houses, "and the Estates belonging to them being sur- "render'd unto the King, he either sold or gave "them to the Lay-Nobility and Gentry contrary "to what he had at first pretended; and so they "have continu'd ever since, tho' not without "visible effects of God's *Vengeance* and *Displea-* "*sure*, there having been direful *Anathemas* and "*Curses* denounced by the Founders upon such "as should presume to alienate the Lands, or do "any other voluntary Injury to the Religious "Houses. I could myself produce instances of "the strange and unaccountable Decay of some
' Gentlemen

"Gentlemen in my own Time, tho' otherwise
"Perfons of very great Piety and Worth, who
"have been poffefs'd of *Abbey-Lands*: But this
"would be Invidious and Offenfive, and there-
"fore I fhall only refer thofe that are defirous
"of having inftances laid before them to fhew
"the difmal Confequences that have happen'd,
"to Sir *Henry Spelman*'s Hiftory of *Sacrilege*, pub-
"lifh'd in 8*vo.* in the Year 1698.

This agrees in fubftance with Sir *Wm. Dugdale*'s account of the *vile Artifices* made ufe of by the *Vifitors* in compaffing the Diffolution of Monafteries, and overthrows the principal Argument infifted upon by feveral *Proteftant* Writers, fuch as *Fox*, *Burnet*, and others of the fame Kidney; who to palliate the *Infamy* and *Scandal* of thofe unchriftian Proceedings, which they plainly faw would be an everlafting Difhonour to the *Englifh Reformation*, pretend that the *Loofenefs* and *Irregularities* of moft Religious Houfes in thofe Days juftly drew upon them their Deftruction.

But who fees not the Foulnefs of this Calumny; fince we find in Sir *Wm. Dugdale*'s Relation the *Parliament* it felf declaring, that *Thanks be to God Religion was well kept and obferved in the greater Houfes*; which neverthelefs foon follow'd the Fate of the leffer ones; and Mr. *Hearn* fticks not to declare, that after a diligent Enquiry into the Records of thofe Times, *he could not find a direct Proof even againft any one fingle Monaftery* of the Crimes laid to their Charge: tho' as he obferves very juftly the Charge was manag'd againft them with the utmoft *Induftry*, *Boldnefs* and *Dexterity*. Nay *Burnet* himfelf, that unmerciful fcourge of *Papifts*, fpeaking of the Nunnery of *Godftow* in *Oxfordfhire*, after having raked together all the Dirt he could throw at Monafteries, could

not

208 Dial. 3. §. 6. *A farther Account of the*
not but clear the Virtuous Ladies of that House. His Words in his *History of the Reformation* Vol. 3. p. 238. are these: *Tho' the Visitors interceded earnestly for the Nunnery of* Godstow, WHERE THERE WAS GREAT STRICTNESS OF LIFE, *and to which most of the Gentlewomen of the Country were sent to be bred, so that the Gentry of the Country desir'd the King would spare the House*; *yet all was ineffectual.*

'Twas here that Dr. *London* was appointed *Visitor*; whose Behaviour in Executing his Commission was insolent in the highest Degree, and shew'd he was a fit Tool for the Work he was entrusted with. This vile Wretch was afterwards convicted of *Perjury*, and condemn'd to ride with his Face to the Horse's Tail at *Windsor* and *Ockingham* with Papers about his Head declaring his Crime.

SECT. 6.

A farther Account of the Effects of K. *Henry's Reformation.*

G. SIR the Relation you have entertain'd me with is astonishing beyond what I am able to express. For in Reality the the frightful Scene it has set before me, looks more like an *Irruption of Barbarians* Pillaging and Destroying all before them with Fire and Sword, than a *Canonical Visitation* appointed by the *Supreme Ecclesiastical Authority* of a Christian Kingdom.

P. Your Idea, Sir, agrees exactly with that of Sir *Wm. Davenant* in the following elegant Verses.

Who

Who sees these dismal Heaps, but will demand,
What Barbarous Invader *sack'd the Land!*
But when he hears no Goth, *no* Turk *did bring*
This Desolation, but a Christian *King*;
When nothing but the Name *of Zeal appears*
'Twixt our best Actions, and the Worst *of theirs,*
What do's he think our Sacrilege *would Spare,*
Since these th' Effects of our Devotions *are.*

G. And do *Protestants* call this a *Godly Reformation?*

P. Every Thing was carried on under that Religious mask. Plundering the Church, Destroying the Nurseries of Piety and Learning, Demolishing the noble Monuments of the Religious Generosity of their Ancestors, Violating the Wills of the Dead, and Robbing the Living of their lawful Possessions: In a Word, Forcing innumerable Persons of both Sexes, that had consecrated themselves to God by solemn Vows, out of their Solitary Cells to wander up and down in the wide World, and either beg their Bread, or engage themselves in Courses wholly unbecoming their State: All these Unchristian Proceedings have ever since pass'd currently under the Specious Name of Zeal for a *thorough Godly Reformation*, and were the first Fruits of it.

But as there were some at least, whose Conscience would not permit them either to renounce or dissemble their ancient Faith, of which the Belief of the *Pope's Supremacy* in *Spirituals* had always been regarded as a capital Point, these soon soon felt the utmost Rigour of King *Henry's* Law, which made it *high Treason* to refuse the Oath of *Supremacy*, or acknowledge the Bishop of *Rome Supreme Head* of the *universal Church*. So that a large Effusion of Innocent Blood became a necessary Consequence of

210 Dial. 3. §. 6. *A further Account of the*
this *Godly Reformation*, which being built upon the King's *Supremacy* as it's main Foundation, would not have stood upon a firm Bottom, if the Opposers of it had been tolerated to follow the Dictates of their Conscience without Suffering for it.

Dr. *John Fisher* Bishop of *Rochester*, acknowledged by all *Protestants* to have been a learned and holy Prelate, appear'd at the Head of these Champions, who had the Courage to lay down their Lives in Defence of the Ancient Faith. Dr. *Heylin* reckons thirteen *Abbots* and *Priors*, and about Seventy seven *Monks* and other *religious* Persons, besides a great Number of the *Laity*, who all Suffer'd Death as in Cases of *High Treason* for the same Cause. One of these was Sir *Thomas More*, who had been *Chancellor* of *England*, and behaved himself in that high Station with so much Integrity and Disinterestedness, that when by a voluntary Resignation he return'd to a private Life, he had not in the least improved his Fortune. A rare Example! But this great Man had a Heart above this World; the Riches and Honours whereof he despised as much, as they are usually coveted by others.

My Lord *Herbert* relates of him, that finding his Lady and Daughters when they were acquainted, that he had resign'd his Place, in a very great Concern about it by Reason of the Narrowness of their Circumstances, he Spoke thus to them: *We will begin with the slender Diet of the Students of the Law, and if that will not hold out, we will take such Commons as they have at* Oxford: *Which yet if our Purses will not Stretch to maintain, our last Refuge will be to go a Begging, and at every Man's Door sing together a* Salve regina *to get Alms.* p. 372. This tho' a trival Passage in the Life of so eminent a Person, gives us a clearer Idea than the most memorable Actions of the true Character of the Man;

Man; and shews that one, who despised even the ordinary Conveniencies of Life, was above the Temptation of Turning *Trimmer* in *Religion* upon any worldly Considerations, or Damning his Soul to save his Life. And so it is no Wonder, that when he was call'd upon by the King's Officers, he walk'd out of the *Tower*, where he had been kept Prisoner for above a twelve-month, to the Scaffold set up for him, as unconcern'd, nay with as much Chearfulness, as if he had been going to take the Air; and laid down his Head upon the Block with the same Repose of Mind, as he used to lay it down upon his Pillow to take his natural Rest. The same Lord *Herbert* gives the following Account of his Death.

" This great Person going shortly after to the Place of Execution met among many Friends only one Enemy, who openly reviled him for a Sentence heretofore given in *Chancery*; to which he made no Answer, but that if it were to do, he would do it again. And now being resolved to die, he return'd to his wonted Facetiousness. Therefore being to go up the Scaffold, he said to one, *Friend help me up, and when I go down again, let me shift for myself as I can.* Being now mounted, the Executioner, as the Custom is, ask'd him Forgiveness, which he granted, but told him withal, *he would get no Credit in Cutting off his Head, his Neck was so Short.* Then Laying down his Head upon the Block, he bid the Executioner stay till he had laid aside his Beard. *For,* said he, *it never committed Treason.* After which coming to some private Devotions he received his Death. Thus ended Sir *Thomas More*, with so little Consternation, that even Terrors of Death could not take off the Pleasure he had in his conceited and merry Language: which many attributed to his Innocence. p. 422.

212 Dial. 3. §. 6. *A further Account of the*

G. I don't See, how it could possibly be attributed to any other Cause. For a Man must either be wholly *destitute* of all *Sense of Religion*, or have a very *clear Conscience* to look Death in the Face with an intrepid Mind. Now since it is unquestionable that Sir *Thomas More* was the very Reverse of the former, nothing but the inward Testimony of a clear Conscience could render him Proof against the usual Terrors of Death.

P. But *Innocence* and *Virtue*, tho' they took away the Sting of Death, were no Protection against the unbridled Passions of an arbitrary Prince, enraged to see himself openly condemn'd by the resolute Opposition of a Person universally esteem'd both for his Piety and Learning. And in Reality one single Person of Sir *Thomas More*'s, or Bishop *Fisher*'s unspotted Character gives a greater Reputation to a Cause wherein *Conscience* and *Religion* are concern'd, and is a more solid Proof of the Justice of it, than a thousand temporizing mercenary Souls, whose Actions appear manifestly to be the Fruit of their interested *Hopes* and *Fears*.

G. But pray, Sir, after the universal Plunder of *Abbeys* and *Monasteries*, what became of the *Bishopricks?* Did not their rich Lands and Manours stand likewise in need of a *thorough Godly Reformation?*

P. You shall hear what Dr. *Heylin* says of it in his History of the *English Reformation*.

" Most true it is, that it was something of the
" latest before King *Henry* cast his Eye on the
" Lands of Bishopricks; tho' there were some,
" who thought the Time long till they fell upon
" them. Concerning which there go's a Story,
" that after the *Court-harpies* had devour'd the
" greatest Part of the Spoil, which came by the
" Suppression of *Abbeys*, they began to seek some
' other

Effects of King Henry's Reformation. 213

" other Way to Satiate that greedy Appetite,
" which the Division of the former Booty had
" left unsatisfied: and for the Satisfying whereof
" they found not any Thing so necessary as the
" Bishops Lands.

" This to effect Sir *Thomas Seymour* is employ'd
" as the fittest Man, being in Favour with the
" King, and Brother to Q *Jane* his most beloved
" and best Wife: and having Opportunity of
" Access unto him, as being one of his privy Cham-
" ber. And he not having any good Affection to
" Archbishop *Cranmer*, desired that the Experi-
" ment should be tried on him. And therefore
" took his Time to inform the King, that my Lord
" of *Canterbury* did nothing but fell his Woods,
" letting long Leases for great Fines, and making
" Havock of the Royalties of his Archbishoprick
" to raise thereby a Fortune for his Wife and
" Children. Withall he acquainted the King,
" that the Archbishop kept no Hospitality in Res-
" pect of such a large Revenue; and that in the
" Opinion of many wise Men, it were more con-
" venient for the Bishops to have a Sufficient
" yearly Stipend out of the Exchequer, than to
" be so encumber'd with temporal Royalties:
" being so great a Hindrance to their Studies and
" pastoral Charge. And that the Lands and Roy-
" alties being taken to his Majesty's Use would
" afford him besides the said annual Stipends, a
" great yearly Revenue.

' The King considering of it could not think
" fit, that such a plausible Proposition, as taking
" to himself the Lands of the Bishops should
" be made in vain. Only he was resolved to prey
" farther off, and not to fall upon the Spoil too
" near the Court for Fear of having more Par-
" takers in the Booty than might stand with his
" Profit,

214 Dial. 3. §. 7. *The Reformation carried on*

"Profit. And to this End he deals with *Hol-
"gate* prefer'd not long before from *Landaff* to
"the See of *York*: from whom he takes at one
"Time no fewer than Seventy *Manours* and
"*Townships* of good old Rent, giving him in Ex-
"change to the like yearly Value certain Impro-
"priations, Pensions, Tiths and Portions of Tiths;
"but all of an extended Rent, which had ac-
"crued to the Crown by the Fall of Abbeys.

"He dismember'd also by these Arts certain
"Manours from the See of *London*, and others
"in like Manner from the See of *Canterbury*; but
"not without some reasonable Compensation for
"them. And altho' by Reason of his Death,
"which follow'd soon after, there was no farther
"Alienation made in his Time of the Church's
"Patrimony, yet having open'd such a Gap, and
"discover'd this secret, that the *Sacred Patrimony*
"might be alienated with so little Trouble, the
"Courtiers of King *Edward*'s Time would not
"be kept from Breaking violently into it, and
"making up their own Fortunes in the spoil of
"Bishopricks. So impossible a Thing it is for
"the ill Example of Princes not to find Followers
"in all Ages, especially where Profit and Prefer-
"ment may be further'd by it.

SECT 7.

*The Reformation carried on in the Reign
of Edward VI. and the true Motives of
it.*

I Have now done with King *Henry*'s Reign, whom a merry Protestant Writer stiles the *Postilion of the Reformation*. I presume this Author thought
fit

fit to allot him so mean a Post, in Punishment of his not Carrying on the Reformation any Thing considerably farther than the bare *Discarding of the Pope*. For after he had done that useful Piece of Service, and open'd so wide a Gap for a *thorough Godly Reformation*, it was expected by most, that he would have proceeded farther. But he disappointed their Expectation, and continued in most Things a Zealous *Papist*, to the very last. Nay he took Care before his Death to leave his young Successor *Edward* VI. in the Hands of such Persons, as he had Reason to think were cordially affected to the *Six famous Articles* publish'd by him in Defence of the *ancient Faith*, since they had all made publick Profession of them during his Life. But as soon as he was Dead, they wisely remembring the old Proverb, that *a dead Dog cannot bite*, the *terrible Henry*, who a little before had made them all tremble with a Frown, was no more regarded than the meanest of those, he had sent before him to the other World: and his *Will*, which till then had been *arbitrary*, was laid aside like an old Coat worn thread bare.

The Truth of the Matter is, that as long as King *Henry* lived, none could hope for any Share either in his Favour, or the Plunder of Religious Houses without Conforming at least in outward Appearance to the Religion himself profess'd. Nay he was such a Persecutor of *Non-conformists*, that all convicted *Lutherans* or *Zuinglians* were sure to be punish'd with Death. In so much that King *Henry's* last Queen was herself in imminent Danger of Losing her Head upon a bare Suspicion of being addicted to *Lutheranism*. But after his Death there appear'd immediately a new Scene, and a Change of Religion was resolved upon as a necessary Expedient to serve the Ends of those *Court-Harpies*, who were still Gaping after more Booty.

G. It

G. It seems Religion sat as loose upon those Gentlemen as their *Cloaks*, which they could throw off or put on as they found convenient: and served much for the same Use, either to *keep them warm*, or cover them against *foul Whether*. But who were the chief Promoters and Managers of this Affair? And what Part did the young King act in it?

P. As to the King, he was but just of an Age to begin to learn his *Catechism*. So you will easily guess, he had his Lesson taught him. Yet to the shame of the Reformation, he was solemnly declared *Supreme Head* of the Church of *England* in *Spirituals*: that is, *Supreme Judge* of Controversies in Religion, and the *Source* of all *Ecclesiastical Jurisdiction* in the Realm. In so much that in the first Year of his Reign there pass'd an Act entituled; *An Act for the Election of Bishops, and what Seals and Stiles shall be used by Spiritual Persons* &c: Concerning which Act Dr. *Heylin* writes thus p. 51.

"In the composing of this Act, says he, there
"was more danger couch'd than at first appear'd.
"By the last Branch thereof it was plain and Evi-
"dent, that the Intent of the Contrivers was by
"Degrees to weaken the Authority of the *Episco-*
"*pal Order*, by forcing them from their strong
"Hold of *Divine Institution*, and making them no
"other than the King's Ministers only, or his
"*Ecclesiastical Sheriffs* (as a Man might say) to exe-
"cute his will and disperse his Mandates. And of
"this Act such Use was made, that the Bishops of
"those Times were not in a Capacity of *Conferring*
"*Orders*, but as they were thereunto impower'd
"by a *Special Licence*. The Tenor whereof, if
"*Sanders* may be believed, was in these Words.
"To wit, *the King to such or such a Bishop Greeting.*
"*Whereas all and all Manner of Jurisdiction as well*
"*Ecclesiastical as Civil flows from the King as from*
"the

by Edward VI. *and the true Motives of it.* 217

" *the Supreme Head of all the Body* &c: *we there-*
" *fore give and grant to you full Power and Licence (to*
" *continue during our good Pleasure) of Conferring Or-*
" *ders within your Diocess, and Promoting fit Persons*
" *unto holy Orders, even to that of Priesthood.*

A moſt noble Church! wherein Biſhops were obliged to receive their *Powers* or *Faculties* for the Exerciſing of their *Eccleſiaſtical Functions* from a Child! But was it ſo in the Days of Old? was it according to the *Inſtitution* of *Chriſt*? However in Confirmation of this Fact, which indeed appears incredible in itſelf, I ſhall quote a Paſſage from Mr. *Collier* in his 2d. *Part,* 3d. *Book.* p. 169. wherein he rectifies a Miſtake touching this matter of Biſhop *Burnet,* whom he always complements with the Title of *our learned Church-hiſtorian*; I wiſh he could with as much Juſtice have given him the Titles of *true* and *Impartial,* which are as neceſſary Qualifications as *Learning* to make a good Hiſtorian. The Paſſage is ſomewhat long, but very much to the Purpoſe.

" Our learned Church-hiſtorian, *ſays he,* ob-
" ſerves, *this Biſhop* [meaning Biſhop *Bonner,* whom
" he had ſpoke of juſt before] *took a ſtrange Com-*
" *miſſion from the King. Whether the other Biſhops,*
" continues this Author, *took ſuch Commiſſions I know*
" *not, but am certain there is none ſuch in* Cranmer's
" *Regiſter*—— *After* Bonner, *had taken this Com-*
" *miſſion, he might well have been call'd one of the*
" *King's Biſhops*". Theſe are *Burnets* Words quoted by Mr. *Collier*; who go's on thus.

" As this learned Hiſtorian obſerves, the Con-
" tents of *Bonner's* Commiſſion were extraordinary.
" For it begins thus. *That the King is the Fountain*
" *of all Manner of Juriſdiction and Authority, as well*
" *Eccleſiaſtical as Secular: and that thoſe who for-*
" *merly exerciſed this Juriſdiction, did it only in a pre-*
" *carious*

218 Dial. 3. §. 7. *The Reformation carried on*
" *carious Manner, and upon Royal Courtesy, and that*
" *therefore it ought to be return'd, whenever his Ma-*
" *jesty shall please to call for it.* *And that since the*
" *Lord* Cromwell *Knight of the Garter, Viceregent*
" *and Vicar-General to preside, manage, and direct in*
" *all Ecclesiastical Causes, was so far employ'd in Mat-*
" *ters of State, that he was not at Leisure to discharge*
" *the Functions of a Vicegerent, and manage the Eccle-*
" *siastical Jurisdiction wholly delegated to him by the*
" *King,* Supreme Head of the Church of England
" &c.

" Because *Cromwell* was too busy, and could
" not be every where, nor execute the Office of
" an universal Superintendent; *for this Reason* as
" the *Instrument* continues, *the King gives* Bonner *a*
" *Commission to execute all the Branches of the Episco-*
" *pal Authority under his Highness*. For the Purpose,
" he has a *Royal Licence* to ordain within the Dio-
" cese of *London*: to visit the Dean and Chapter of
" St. *Paul*'s, and all other Colleges, Hospitals, Mo-
" nasteries, Clergy and Laity, within his District.
" He has likewise a Power given him to hear
" Causes, and to give Sentence in the Spiritual
" Courts; to exercise Discipline, and inflict Cen-
" sures according to the Directions of the Law,
" and the Degrees of the Criminals Offences:
" And, in short, to execute every Thing belong-
" ing to the Authority and Jurisdiction of a Bi-
" shop.

" And after the King has thus declared himself
" *Patriarch* in his Dominions, claim'd all Manner
" of *Spiritual* Authority, and pronounc'd the Bi-
" shops no more than his *Delegates at Pleasure:* af-
" ter this these Words are thrown into the Com-
" mission to give it the more passable Complexion,
" *besides those Things, which are known from holy Scrip-*
" *tures to belong to you by divine Right.*

" Now,

by Edward VI. *and the true Motives of it.*

"Now, with Submission, this Clause seems to come in too late, and is utterly inconsistent with the former Part of the Commission. For if the King is the *Fountain* of all manner of *Ecclesiastical Jurisdiction*; if his *Lay-vicegerent* might lawfully supply the Room of all the Bishops in *England*, provided he were at Leisure, and able to do it in Person; if the Bishops in the Execution of their Office are only the King's *Representatives*, and *revocable at Pleasure*: If these Affirmations are all defensible, as the Commission sets forth, then without Question the *Hierarchy* can have no Jurisdiction assign'd in the *new Testament*, nor any Authority derived from our Saviour.

"But if the Church is a Distinct and entire Society; if in *pure Spirituals* She is constituted independent on all the Kings on the Earth; if she is furnish'd with Powers Sufficient to answer the Ends of her *Charter*; if these Powers were settled by our Saviour upon the Apostles and their Successors to the World's End; if the *Hierarchy* can make out this Title, then I must crave leave to think, those who Suggested the Draught of this Instrument were no great *Divines*.

"But how extraordinary soever this Commission may seem, it was certainly comply'd with, and that by other Bishops besides *Bonner*. For the Purpose, *Cranmer* took out one of the same Tenor and Form from King *Edward* VI. Now if *Bonner* was so much to blame for Complying to this Latitude, the same Imputation must fall upon *Cranmer*. To which we may add, that this was not the first Commission of this kind taken out by *Cranmer*. For, as our Historian observes, the order of Council made in the Beginning

220 Dial. 3. §. 7. *The Reformation carried on*
" ning of the Reign of King *Edward* VI. *requires*
" *the Bishops to take out new Commissions of the same*
" *Form with those they had taken out in King* Henry's
" *Time: only with this Difference, that there is no*
" *Mention made of a Vicar General in these Commissions,*
" *there being none after* Cromwell *advanced to that*
" *Dignity.* If no such Commission, as this learned
" Gentleman remarks, taken by *Cranmer* from
" King *Henry*, be found in his *Register*, it do's not
" follow he took out no such *Instrument*; for his
" *Register* is imperfect in many Places. To speak
" clearly, he took out such a Commission from K.
" *Henry* some Years before *Bonner*. For from the
" Collections of Dr. *Yale* the learned *Harmer* cites
" a Transcript of this Commission, agreeing ex-
" actly with that of *Bonner* above-mention'd, to
" which this note is Subjoin'd, *tales licentias acce-*
" *perunt Thomas Archiepiscopus Cantuariensis mense*
" *Octobri* 1535. *Edwardus Archiep: Eborac: Johannes*
" *Episc: Lincoln:* 13 *Octob:* 1535. &c: Now this Dr
" *Yale* being an eminent Advocate in *Doctors com-*
" *mons* in *Cranmer's* Time, and afterwards princi-
" pal Registrary, and Vicar general to Archbi-
" shop *Parker*, must be own'd an unexceptionable
" Evidence for this Point. Farther our learned
" Historian has misreported *Bonner*, in saying, he
" was one of the Popish Party at this Time, and
" took out his Commission to serve that Interest.
" For *Fox* has given several Instances to prove,
" that *Bonner* till the Fall of *Cromwell* was a zea-
" lous Promoter of the *Reformation*, which is
" likewise afterwards confess'd by our Historian.

Thus the learned Mr. *Collier*; who has indeed a much juster Claim to that Title, than the Author, he bestows it so liberally upon. Unless numberless gross Mistakes, or, what is worse, wilfull Falshoods are a mark of Learning. But be that

as

as it will, the Piece, I have quoted, justifies the Sharpest Reflections upon *Cranmer's* Memory, that second *Athanasius* as Bishop *Burnet* callshim, who not only had the Meanness to bend his Neck under the most dishonourable Yoke, that ever was laid upon Persons of his Sacred Character, but by his base Flatteries of the worst of Princes, was himself the most busy and active in Preparing it both for himself and his Fellow Bishops.

Now therefore to answer your Question, Who were the chief Promoters of that great Ecclesiastical Revolution, which happen'd in the Reign of *Edward* VI? They were of two different sorts. For the greatest Part of them were but meer Tools set at work like *Day-labourers* by the great Men at Court to do the drudging Part for them: and these, tho' most of them had also their private Views, were never let into the *Secret Mystery* of the *reforming Trade*; left there should have been too many sharers in the Profit of it; which they, who were at the Helm, and had the chief Management and Superintendency of the whole Business, design'd to engross mostly to themselves.

At the Head of these was a no less Man than the Duke of *Sommerset*, the young King's Uncle, declared *Lord Protector* during his Minority; who having thus got the Reins of Government put into his Hands, drove on the *Reformation* with such Violence, that, saving only some Fundamentals, he stop'd not till he had overturn'd the whole Edifice of the ancient Church of *England*, so as scarce to leave one stone upon another of it's former Structure.

G. But I don't well apprehend the Meaning of what you said just now, viz: *that an entire Change of Religion was resolved as a necessary Expedient to serve the Ends of those, who were still Gaping after*

222 Dial. 3. §. 7. *The Reformation carried on more Booty.* For could they not have plunder'd the Church without Disjointing the whole Frame of it's ancient Faith?

P. No, they could not have done it with any plaufible Colour. For if the *ancient Faith* had been kept up, they would not have had the leaft Pretence to lay their Sacrilegious Hands on the rich Spoils, which came in Flowing to them of Courfe upon the Innovations they made in that Faith.

Let us hear Dr. *Heylin* fpeak of the *Motives*, which fpurr'd on their Zeal to thofe aftonifhing Innovations. This Author in the Preface to his *Hiftory of the Reformation*, after a fhort Account of King *Henry*'s Throwing off the Pope's Authority, touches briefly upon what pafs'd in the Reign of his Son *Edward* VI. *Some great Men,* fays he, *about the Court, under Colour of Removing fuch Corruptions as remain'd in the Church, had caft their Eyes upon the* SPOIL OF SHRINES AND IMAGES, AND THE IMPROVING OF THEIR OWN FORTUNES BY THE CHANTERY-LANDS; *all which they moft Sacrilegioufly divided among themfelves.*

Then Speaking of a Propofal ftarted by fome of the *Zuinglian* Party to *pull down Altars*, he go's on thus:

" The Touching on this ftring made excellent
" Mufick to moft of the Grandees of the Court;
" who had before caft many an envious Eye on
" the *coftly Hangings,* that *maffy Plate,* and other *rich*
" and *precious Utenfils,* which adorn'd thofe Altars—— Befides there was no fmall Spoil to be
" made of *Copes:* Some of them being made of
" *Cloth of Tiffue,* of *Cloth of Gold* and *Silver,* or
" *imbroyder'd Velvet.* And might not thefe be
" handfomly converted to private Ufes, to ferve
" as

"as *Carpets* for their Tables, *Coverlets* to their
"Beds, or *Cushions* to their Chairs or Windows?

"Hereupon some rude People are encouraged
"underhand to beat down some Altars; which
"makes way for an Order of the *Council-Table* to
"take down all the rest, and set up *Tables* in their
"Places; follow'd by a Commission to be execu-
"ted in all Parts of the Kingdom for Seizing of
"the Premises for the Use of the King. But as
"the Grandees of the Court intended to defraud
"the King of so great a Booty, and the Commis-
"sioners to put a Cheat upon the Court-Lords,
"who employ'd them in it; so they were both
"prevented in some Places by the Lords and
"Gentry, who thought the *Altar-Cloths* together
"with the *Copes* and *Plate* of several Churches
"to be as necessary for themselves as for others.
"*Pref.*

G. Ay marry, they were in the right to come in for Snacks, if the old Proverb be true, that to *cheat a Cheat is no Fraud*. But what a Deal of Sacrilegious Roguery have we here, and all cover'd with the Religious Mask of a *Godly Reformation!* But did not the Grandees of the Court resent their being thus chowsed by their Inferiours?

P. This Question is answer'd by Dr. *Heylin* upon another Occasion of the like Nature, where he writes thus: *All which Enormities were connived at by the Lords and others, because they could not question those, who had so miserably invaded the Church's Patrimony, without Condemning themselves.* p. 69.

But to return to the Subject we were upon, to wit, the *Motives* for Pushing on the *pretended Reformation*, the same Author writes in the following Manner:

"The *Parliament*, say he, met on the fourth of
"*November*; in which *the Cards were so well pack'd*,
"that

224 Dial. 3. §. 7. *The Reformation carried on*
" that there was no Need of any other Shufling to
" the End of the Game: becaufe they all agree'd
" well enough in one common Principle, which
" was *to ferve the prefent Time*——For tho' a great
" Part of the Nobility, and not a few of the chief
" Gentry in the Houfe of Commons were cordially
" affected to the Church of *Rome*, yet were they
" willing to give Way to all fuch Acts and Sta-
" tutes, as were made againft it, *out of a Fear of*
" *Lofing fuch Church-Lands, as they were poffefs'd of,*
" *if that Religion fhould prevail, and get up again.*
" And for the reft, who either came *to make or im-*
" *prove their Fortunes*, there is no Queftion to be
" made, but they came *to further* SUCH A REFOR-
" MATION, *as fhould moft vifibly conduce to the Ad-*
" *vancement of their feveral Ends*; which appears
" plainly by the ftrange Mixture of the *Acts* and
" *Refults* thereof—— Some tending to the *prefent*
" *Benefit*, and *Enriching of particular Perfons*, and
" fome again being devifed on Purpofe to pre-
" pare a Way *for Expofing the Revenues of the Church*
" *to Spoil and Rapine.* p. 47. 48.

G. I perceive *Religion* was made Ufe of by thefe reforming Gentlemen no otherwife than as a *Stalking-Horfe* to fecure their Game. For tho' fome amongft them differ'd in their Opinions about Religion, they all agreed in one common Principle of GETTING ALL THEY COULD and LOSING NOTHING by it. Even they, who in their Hearts were convinced of the Truth of the *ancient Faith*, gave their Votes in Parliament for *all fuch Acts*, as were againft it. And why fo? For Fear of *Lofing* what they had *already got*, in Cafe *Popery* fhould get the upper Hand again, as it had formerly. But others, it feems were Zealous for SUCH A REFORMATION, as would bring ftill

more

more Grift to their Mills. And who cannot but admire the Religious Purity of their Intentions?

P. One of the Acts that pass'd in this Parliament, was for the Retrieving of a Statute made in the 27th of *Henry* VIII. by which *Chanteries, Colleges, Free Chappels* &c: were granted to the King. But he died before he had taken many of them into his Possession. And the Grandees of the Court not being willing to lose so great a Booty, these together with all *Manours, Lands, Tenements, Rents, Tiths, Pensions, Portions,* and other *Hereditaments,* were again given to the King, his Heirs and Successors for ever: their being ninety *Colleges* within the Compass of that Grant, and no fewer than 2374 *Free-Chappels* and *Chanteries*. Heylin. p. 50. 51.

G. But pray Sir, what were those *Chanteries,* and *Free-Chappels,* which were given to the King?

" P. The *Chanteries,* says Dr. *Heylin.* p. 51,
" consisted of Salaries to one or more Priests, to
" *say Mass daily for the Souls of their deceased Foun-*
" *ders and their Friends :* which not Subsisting of
" themselves were generally incorporated, and uni-
" ted to some *Parochial, Collegiate,* or *Cathedral*
" *Church*. No fewer than forty seven being found-
" ed in St. *Paul's Free-Chappels* ; which tho' or-
" dain'd for the same Intent with others, yet
" were independent, of stronger Constitution,
" and richer Endowment. Tho' therein they fell
" short of the *Colleges,* which exceeded them both
" in the Beauty of their Buildings, the Number
" of their Priests maintain'd by them, and the
" Proportion of Revenue allotted to them.

SECT 8.

The same Subject continued.

WHAT I have hitherto related was all done in the first Year of King *Edward*'s Reign, viz: Anno 1547. In the Year following *Feb.* 11th an Order was sent from the privy Council to all Bishops for Pulling down all Images. *And it may well be thought* (says Dr. *Heylin* p. 56.) *that Covetousness spur'd on this Business more than Zeal; there being none of the Images so poor and mean, the Spoil whereof would not afford some Gold or Silver, if not Jewels also: besides Censers, Candlesticks, and many other rich Utensils appertaining to them.*

" The same Year in the Beginning of *March*
" Commissioners were dispatch'd throughout the
" Realm to take a survey of all *Colleges, Free-Chap-*
" *pels, Chanteries* &c: by which it would be found
" no difficult Matter to know how to parcel out,
" proportion, and divide the Spoil between all
" such, as had in Hopes before devour'd it.

" In the first Place, as lying nearest, came in
" the *Free-Chappel* of St. *Stephen* in *Westminster*, and
" reckon'd for the *Chappel-Royal* of the Court of
" *England*. The whole Foundation consisted of
" no fewer than thirty eight Persons, to wit, a
" *Dean*, twelve *Canons*, fourteen *Vicars*, four *Clerks*,
" six *Choristers*, besides a *Verger*, and one that had
" the Charge of the Chappel —— As for the
" Chappel itself together with the Cloyster of
" curious Workmanship, they are still standing
" as they were: the Chappel having been since
" fitted and employ'd for a *House of Commons* in
" all Times of Parliament.

" At

The same Subject continued. 227

At the same Time also fell the *College* of St.
" *Martin* Situated in the City of *London*, not far
" from *Aldersgate*; first founded for a Dean and
" Secular Canons in the Time of the *Conqueror*.
" This *College* was surrender'd into the Hands of
" *Edward* VI. who gave it to the *Abbey* of *West-*
" *minster*: and they to make the best of the King's
" Donation, order'd that the Body of the Church
" with the *Choir* and *Isles* should be leased out for
" fifty Years; excepting out of the same Grant
" the *Bells*, *Lead*, *Stone*, *Timber*, *Glass*, and *Iron* to
" be sold and disposed of for the Sole Use and
" Benefit of the said *Dean* and *Chapter*. Which
" foul Transaction being made, the Church was
" totally pull'd down, and a Tavern built on the
" *East* Part of it. The rest of the Situation of
" the same Church and College, together with the
" whole Precinct thereof being built upon with
" several Tenements.

" But for this *Sacrilege* the Church of *Westmin-*
" *ster* was call'd immediately to a Sober Recko-
" ning. For the *Lord Protector* cast a longing Eye
" upon the Goodly Patrimony, which belong'd
" unto it: and being unfurnish'd of a Palace, he
" doubted not to find Room enough upon the Dis-
" solution and Destruction of so large a Fabrick
" to raise a Palace equal to his vast Designs. Which
" coming to the Ear of *Benson* the last Abbot and
" first Dean of that Church, he could think of
" no better Means to preserve the whole, than by
" parting for the present with more than half the
" Estate, that belong'd to it. p. 60. 61.

I will now mention a Piece of Sacrilegious Plunder, which indeed was Scandalous in the highest Degree.

The *Protector* having been bought off by *Benson* from his Purpose of Building on the *Deanary* and

228 Dial. 3. §. 8. *The same Subject continued.*

Close of *Westminster*, had cast his Eye, " says Dr.
" *Heylin*, upon a Piece of Ground in the *Strand*;
" on which stood three *Episcopal Houses* and one
" *Parish Church*. The Parish Church was dedicated
" to the *Virgin Mary*, the Houses belong'd to the
" Bishops of *Worcester*, *Litchfield*, and *Landaff*. All
" these he takes into his Hands, the Owners not
" daring to oppose him. Having clear'd the Place,
" but still wanting Materials, he thereupon re-
" solves to take down the Parish-Church of St.
" *Margaret*'s in *Westminster*. But the Workmen had
" no Sooner advanced their Scaffolds, when the
" Parishioners gather'd together in great Multi-
" tudes with Bows and Arrows, Staves and Clubs,
" and other Weapons. Which so terrified the
" Workmen, that they ran away in great Amaze-
" ment, and never could be brought again upon
" that Employment. Upon this he employs
" Workmen to take down the *Cloyster* of St. *Paul*'s
" on the *Northside* of the Church environing a
" large Parcel of Ground call'd *Pardon-church-yard*,
" and beautified with a most curious Piece of
" Workmanship call'd the *Dance of Death*, toge-
" ther with a fair *Charnel-house* and a *Chappel*, and
" leaves the Bones of the dead Bodies to be bu-
" ried in the Fields in unhallow'd Ground. But all
" this not Sufficing to complete the Work, the
" *Steeple* and most part of the Church of St. *John*'s
" of *Jerusalem* not far from *Smithfield*, most beau-
" tifully built, was blown up with Gun-powder,
" and all the Stone employ'd for that Purpose.
" Such was the Ground and such the Materials of
" the Duke's new Palace call'd *Sommerset-house*.
" p. 73.

According to this Beginning, says Dr. *Heylin*, *all the
Year*, viz: 1549 *proceeds*. But this great *Reformer*
and *Plunderer* of the *English* Church did not live
long

long enough to enjoy the Fruits of these enormous Sacrileges, God's Justice pursuing him close at the Heels. For after having put his own Brother to Death, and being thereby deprived of so great a Support, and laid open to the Prosecutions of his Enemies, he lost his Head not long after on a Scaffold. The Palace is yet Standing, and bears his Name to serve as a lasting Monument of the Sacrilegious Rapacity of that capital Reformer of Religion in the Reign of *Edward* VI. But it affords the most melancholly Reflections as to the State of his Soul. For I never read either of any Repentance he ever shew'd, or any Reparation he ever made for the Scandalous Rapines he had both committed himself, and encouraged in others. He was Succeeded in the *Protectorship* by his capital Enemy the Duke of *Northumberland*, who walking in the Footsteps of his Predecessor, and imitating him in all his Crimes, came soon after to the same untimely End. Only with this Difference, that at his Death (for which he had been prepared in Prison by Dr. *Heath* Bishop of *Worcester*) he profess'd himself a *Roman Catholick*, and declared, as Dr. *Heylin* relates, *that being blinded with Ambition, he had been contented to make Wreck of his Conscience by Temporizing: for which he profess'd himself Sincerely repentant, and so accknowledg'd the Justice of his Death.*

Stow relates, that after having made a publick Profession of his Faith upon the Scaffold, he added the following Words. *And here I do protest to you unfeignedly, even from the Bottom of my Heart, that this which I have Spoken is of myself, and not moved thereto by any Man ; nor for any Flattery or Hope of Life. And of this I take to Witness my Lord of* Worcester *my old Friend and Ghostly Father, that he found me in this Mind and Opinion when he came to me.*

Dial. 3. §. 8. *The same Subject continued.*

G. I presume the Substance of the Fact being thus attested can't admit of any reasonable Doubt.

P. I don't know that any Body ever doubted of it. However some *Protestants* have question'd the Duke's Sincerity: and attributed his Profession of the *Catholick Faith* to the Hopes he had of Obtaining thereby Q. *Mary's* Pardon: just as the same Motive induced Archbishop *Cranmer* to renounce *Lutheranism*, whilst he was under Sentence of Condemnation.

G. But since we can only judge by outward Appearances, and all these give Testimony for the Duke's Sincerity, there is no positive Reason to Suspect it. Which renders his Case very different from that of Archbishop *Cranmer*; whom tho' he abjured *Lutheranism* twice before his Death, retracted his double Abjuration, when he was at the Stake. Whereas the Duke of *Northumberland* confirm'd upon the Scaffold the Abjuration, he had made in Prison.

P. Sir, your Reflection is very just. I will now add one Passage more of Dr. *Heylin*, relating to the Rapines committed in the last Year of King *Edward's* Reign; concerning which he writes thus.

"Such was the *Rapacity* of the Times, and
"the Unfortunateness of the King's Condition,
"that his Minority was abused to many Acts of
"*Spoil* and *Rapine*, even to the highest Degree of
"*Sacrilege*, to the Raising of some and Enrich-
"ing of others, without any Manner of Improve-
"ment to his own Estate. For notwithstanding
"the great and almost inestimable Treasures,
"which must needs come in by the Spoil of so
"many *Shrines* and *Images*, the Sale of the Lands
"belonging to *Chanteries, Colleges, Free-Chappels* &c.

"and

" and the Dilapidating of the Patrimony of so
" many *Bishopricks* and *Cathedral Churches*, he was
" nevertheless not only plunged in Debt, but the
" Crown-Lands very much diminish'd and im-
" pair'd since his Coming to it.——— It must there-
" fore be the King's Care and Endeavours of
" those, who plunged him into it, to find the
" Speediest way for his Getting out. In Order
" to which the main Engine at this Time for the
" Advancing of Money, was the Speeding a Com-
" mission into all Parts of the Realm, under Pre-
" tence of Selling such of the Lands and the
" Goods of *Chanteries* &c: as remain'd unsold;
" but in plain Truth it was to seize upon all
" *Hangings*, *Altar-cloths*, *Fronts*, *Parafronts*, *Copes*
" of all Sorts, with all Manner of *Plate*, *Jewels*,
" *Bells* and *Ornaments*, which were to be found in
" any *Cathedral* or *Parochial* Church. To which
" Rapacity the Demolishing of the former Al-
" tars——— gave a very great Hint by rendring all
" such *Furniture*, rich *Plate* and other *costly Utensils*
" in a Manner useless.———

" But notwithstanding this great Care of the
" King on the one side, and the Diligence of his
" Commissioners on the other, the Booty did not
" prove so great as they expected. In all great
" Fairs and Markets there are some Fore-stallers,
" who get the best Penny-worth to themselves,
" and Suffer not the richest and most gainful
" Commodities to be openly Sold. And so it was
" here. For there were some, who were as much
" beforehand with the Commissioners in Embe-
" zelling the said *Plate*, *Jewels*, and other *Furni-*
" *ture*, as the Commissioners did intend to be
" with the King in keeping always most Part of
" it to themselves.——— So that altho' some Profit
" was hereby raised to the King's Exchequer,

"yet the far greatest Part of the Prey came to
"other Hands. In so much that many private
"Men's Parlours were hung with *Altar-Cloths*,
"their Tables and Beds cover'd with *Copes* instead
"of Carpets, and many made *Carowsing-Cups* of
"the Sacred *Chalices* ; as once *Belshazzar* cele-
"brated his drunken Feasts in the *Sanctified Vessels*
"of the Temple.

"It was a Sorry House not worth the Naming,
"which had not something of this Furniture in
"it ; tho' it were only a fair large Cushion
"made of a *Cope* or *Altar-Cloth* to adorn their
"Windows, or to make their Chairs appear to
"have something of a Chair of State. Yet how
"contemptible were these Trappings in Compari-
"son of those vast Sums of Money, which were
"made of *Jewels*, *Plate*, and *Cloth of Tissue*, either
"convey'd beyond Seas, or sold at home, and
"good Land purchased with the Money : no-
"thing more bless'd to the Posterity of them,
"that bought them, for being purchased with the
"consecrated Treasures of so many Churches.
"p. 131. 132. &c.

G. Very fine indeed! The young King is by his Tutors put upon Robbing the Church ; The Commissioners appointed by him defraud the King ; and the Gentlemen of the County get the Start of the Commissioners, and run away with a Part of the Booty. And could any Thing be more *Canonical* and *Regular* than this! But I fear the *Devil* proved too cunning for them all in the Winding up of the Bottom, and was the principal *Gainer* by this Work, as well as *Director* and *Promoter* of it. For I am sure God could have no Hand in it ; unless we can suppose him to be an Abetter of *Sacrilege* and *Rapine* : and you had Reason to tell me, as you did just now, that if God was

the

the Author of *Such a Reformation*, the Enemy of Man never had a Part in any Wickedness committed by Mankind.

P. But pray, Sir, remember, that the Facts I have related, how disadvantageous soever to the *Protestant Cause*, are all faithfully collected from the Writings of a Zealous *Protestant Historian*, who, we may be sure, would not have transmitted them to Posterity, unless the Force of uncontestable Truth had obliged him to it. And indeed I never heard the Truth of the abovesaid Facts question'd by any.

But as the Facts themselves are unquestionable, so they unveil the whole *Secret Mystery* of the *pretended Reformation*, and leave no Room to doubt of the true and real *Motives* of it. For they shew manifestly, that an *insatiable Avarice*, or Desire of *Plundering the Church* was the main Spring, that gave Motion to every Step that was made towards it in the few Years of King *Edward*'s Reign.

As for Instance; the holy *Sacrifice* of the *Mass* had been the publick Worship of the Church of *England* for 900 Years; and of the *British* Church for 1300 Years; because her Conversion to Christianity under Pope *Eleutheris* was 400 Years earlier than that of the *Saxons* under Pope *Gregory*. Now if the Managers of the Reformation had Suffer'd the *Mass* to be kept up, the unavoidable Consequence would have been, that *Altars* (on which the *Sacrifice* of the *Mass* is always offer'd) must likewise have been left Standing. And what a sad Story would this have been to Persons, whose Bowels were Yearning for the *Jewels*, the *rich Plate* and *Furniture*, which they could not possibly lay their Hands on any other Way, than by the Destruction of the *Altars*, to the Service whereof

they

they had been confecrated: nor was there any colourable Pretence for the Deftruction of *Altars*, unlefs the *Mafs* itfelf was firft abolifh'd.

'Tis true, the venerable Antiquity of this holy Sacrifice, which had been offer'd to God for fo many Ages in all the *Chriftian* Kingdoms upon Earth, and in no Place with greater Zeal, than in the Kingdom of *Great Britain* from the very Infancy of it's Converfion, pleaded hard for it's Prefervation: but the *precious Jewels*, the *Maffy Plate*, and *coftly Furniture*, which adorn'd the *Altars* on which it was offer'd, pleaded with a much more powerful Eloquence for it's utter Abolition.

However the People was to be prepared for this monftrous Change of their *ancient Faith* and *Worfhip*. And therefore, as in all Revolutions either of the *Church* or *State*, there never was wanting a fet of mercenary Preachers ready to fell their Souls to the Devil for a valuable Confideration, the choiceft of this Character were difpatch'd by the Court into all Parts of the Kingdom with Inftructions to preach down the *Mafs*, by reprefenting it to the People as an *Idolatrous Worfhip* and contrary to *the Word of God*: becaufe when this Point was once gain'd, the Demolifhing of *Altars*, which were render'd ufelefs by it, as Dr. *Heylin* has obferved, follow'd of Courfe; and then the *Jewels*, *Plate*, and *Ornaments* belonging to them dropp'd of themfelves into the Hands of thofe, who had contrived the whole Bufinefs for that End: And fo 'tis manifeft that their real Motive for *Reforming* the *Mafs* was no other than to have a fair pretence to pull down *Altars*, and by Pulling down Altars to rob the Church of an immenfe Treafure, and fill their own Coffers with it.

It was the fame Godly Motive, that inflamed their Zeal againft the Honour, which the r *Forefathers*

fathers had in all preceding Ages since *England*'s Conversion paid to the *Images* and *Reliques* of Saints. Many of these Reliques were kept in *Silver Shrines* set with *precious Stones*. And as to the *Images* of Christ and his Saints, Dr. *Heylin* has already told us, *that none of them were so poor and mean, the Spoil whereof could not afford some Gold or Silver, if not Jewels also: besides Censers, Candlesticks, and many other rich Utensils appertaining to them.* This doubtless was a very solid Reason to the *Managers* of the Reformation to condemn all Honour paid to *Images* and *Reliques* as an *Idolatrous Worship*. For was not that *Idolatry*, nay *abominable Idolatry*, which if left unreform'd would have spoil'd a considerable Part of their Market, and kept so many worthy Lords and Gentlemen from filling their Coffers with the *Plate* and *Jewels*, they so zealously long'd for? Tho' Dr. *Heylin*, whom I leave to answer for himself, has been pleased to observe, that it may well be thought, *that Covetousness Spurr'd on this Business* (to wit, the Pulling down of Images) *more than Zeal*.

But there remain'd still another Thing to be reform'd which was look'd upon as an intollerable Abuse by the *Directors* of the *reforming Company*, in being an Obstacle to their most pious and laudable Design of Enriching themselves with the Spoils of their *Mother-Church*. I mean the *Doctrine of Purgatory*: on which alone was grounded the old Custom of *Praying for the Dead*. It was indeed a Practice so ancient, that St. *Chrysostom* attributes it to the Apostles themselves. *The Apostles*, says he, *did not in vain command these Things, that in the venerable and dreadful Mysteries* (that is, the *Mass*) *the Dead should be remember'd. For they knew they would derive a considerable Advantage from it.* Hom: 3. *in epist.* ad *Phil*. And S. *Cyril* of *Alexandria*

writes

writes thus: *Lastly we pray for all that die amongst us: thinking it to be the greatest Help that can be to their Souls to have the holy and dreadful Sacrifice of the Altar offer'd in Supplication for them.* Cat: Myſtag: 5. p. 241.

G. I perceive then that it was not *high Treason* either in the Time of those ancient Fathers, or even of the *Apostles* themselves, to *say Mass*. Nay I find they all *pray'd for the Dead* as we do.

P. Very true, Sir. However the *Directors* of the *Reformation*, who were not disposed to see Things with the same Eyes as the *Apostles*, judg'd it an unlawful and pernicious Practice. And well they might. For if it had been suffer'd to continue, the Lands belonging to *Chanteries*, *Colleges*, and *Free-Chapels* (all founded for perpetual Prayers for the Souls of their deceased Benefactors) must have remain'd in the Hands of their former Possessors. And was not that a most *pernicious Doctrine* and *Practice*, which would have hinder'd such a noble Booty from Falling into true *Protestant* Hands unless a Seasonable *Godly Reformation* had put a Stop to it?

G. Sir, the Reflections you have entertain'd me with, are fully justified by Dr. *Heylin*'s saying, as you told me, *that the great Men of the Court* UNDER COLOUR *of Removing such Corruptions, as remain'd in the Church, had cast their Eyes upon the Spoils of Images, and Shrines,* AND THE IMPROVING OF THEIR OWN FORTUNES *by the Chantery-Lands*. And again, *that* SUCH A REFORMATION *was intended, as should most visibly conduce to the Advancement of their several Ends*. For in Reality we must own, the Reformation was perfectly well contrived to answer those Ends: and the Architects of it shew'd themselves to be complete Masters of the Trade.

P. I

The same Subject continued. 237

P. I will here give you some of Mr. *Collier*'s Thoughts upon these Transactions; who, according to his polite and moderate Way of Writing, expresses himself thus:

"It must be confess'd, says he, there were several shocking Circumstances in the Reign of *Henry* VIII. and his Children. For to see Churches pull'd down or rifled, the Plate Swept off the *Altar*, and the holy Furniture converted to common Use, had no great Air of Devotion. To see the *Choir* undress'd, to make the Drawing-Room and Bed-chamber fine, was not very *primitive* at first View. The forced Surrender of Abbeys, the Maining of Bishopricks, and Lopping the best Branches of their Revenues; the Stopping of impropriated Tithes from passing in the ancient Channel: these Things are apt to puzzle a Vulgar Capacity, unless a Man's Understanding is more than ordinarily improved, he'l be at a loss to reconcile these Measures with Christian Maxims, and make them fall in with Conscience and *Reformation*. 2d. Part. 3d. Book. p. 163.

G. But did not the Government meet with any Opposition from the People?

P. Early Care was taken to prevent or disappoint all popular Commotions. For in the first Place, *it was thought fit* (says Dr. *Heylin* in his Relation of the Transactions of the first Year of King *Edward*'s Reign) *to Smooth the Way to the intended Reformation by Setting out some preparatory Injunctions; and this to be done by Sending out Commissioners into all Parts of the Kingdom, arm'd with Instructions to enquire into all Ecclesiastical Concernments; which Commissioners were accompanied with Preachers appointed to instruct the People----All which was done to this Intent, that the People being prepared by little and*

238 Dial. 3. §. 8. *The same Subject continued.*
and little might with more ease and less Opposition admit the total Alteration in the Face of the Church, which was intended in due Time to be introduced.

We may reasonably suppose the *Preachers* here appointed to instruct the People were of the newest Fashion of the Court, grown weary of their *Breviaries*, and the dull Thing call'd *Celibacy*. For it has been observed by many, that *Priests* converted to the *Reformation* have always been Singularly devoted to the State of *Wedlock*: for which they had full Liberty allow'd them by the first Parliament of *Edward* VI. as *Baker* tells us p. 331. However the Number of these Court-Preachers was not so great as might have been expected, considering the Encouragements that were given them by those, who were at the Helm. For the same Author tells us p. 323. that for want of a Sufficient Number of Preachers, *Homilies were appointed to be read in Churches.*

G. What! Were they the Homilies of the *ancient Fathers*?

P. No, No. They were the Homilies of *Father Cranmer*, *Father Latimer*; *Father Ridley*, or such others; much better suited to the Times than those of the *ancient Fathers*, which were grown Stale, and Smelt rank of *Popery*.

G. But was there not some more effectual Course taken to prevent Disturbances, than that of *Preaching* and *Homilizing*?

P. Dr. *Heylin* in the Part of his History above mention'd has answer'd this Question for me.

" The *Lord Protector* and his Party, says he,
" were more experienced in Affairs of State than
" to be told, that all great Counsels tending to
" Innovations in publick Government, especially
" where *Religion* is concern'd, are either to be
" back'd by Arms, or otherwise prove destructive

' to

" to the Undertakers. For this Cauſe he re-
" ſolves to put himſelf at the Head of an Ar-
" my: as well for the Security of his own Perſon,
" and Preſervation of his Party, as for the Car-
" rying on of the Deſign againſt all Opponents.
" And for the Raiſing of an Army, there could
" not be found a fairer Colour, nor a more popu-
" lar Pretence, than a War with *Scotland*: not to
" be made on any new emergent Quarrel (which
" might be apt to breed Suſpicion in the Heads of
" the People) but in Purſuit of the great Project
" of the King deceaſed for Uniting that Realm
" by a Marriage to the Crown of *England*. On
" this Pretence Levies are made in all Parts of
" the Kingdom. He entertain'd alſo certain Re-
" giments of *Walloons* and *Germans*; becauſe
" they were conceived more likely to enforce O-
" dience, if his Deſign ſhould meet with any
" Oppoſition, than the *natural Engliſh*.

Hence it is plain, that this War with *Scotland*, was only a politick Pretence for keeping a *Standing Army* on Foot: but the true Motive of it was to keep the People in Awe, and frighten them into a Conformity by Shewing them the Rod, that was to Scourge them in Caſe they ſhould prove refractory. And for this End the *Protector* was wiſe enough not to put too great a Confidence in the *Engliſh*, who were at that Time too *popiſhly* affected, but to call in *foreign Proteſtant Troops*, who he knew would be ready for any military Execution upon *Papiſts* in Caſe of Need: whereas if nothing but a War with *Scotland* had been intended, the King's own natural Subjects might have ſafely been truſted.

However there were ſome that had the Courage to oppoſe the Torrent, and act according to the Dictates of their Conſcience, which convinced

them,

them, that a new upstart Religion never before heard of in the Nation since it's first Conversion to Christianity, and fabricated only to gratify the *Luxury* of some, and *Avarice* of others, could not be that holy Religion, which the *Apostles* had taught. But the chief of these were made Examples to Strike Terror into others. For no fewer than five of the prelatick Order, to wit, Bishop *Bonner* of *London*, *Gardiner* of *Winchester*, *Tunstal* of *Durham*, *Heath* of *Rochester*, and *Day* of *Chichester*, were deprived of their Bishopricks, and committed to several Prisons, as *Baker* tells us p. 323. And thus we see the politick and violent Means made Use of to establish the *English Reformation* in the Reign of *Edward* VI; The *Scandalous Sacrileges* committed by the most Zealous Promoters of it; and the *vile Motives* that spurr'd them on to it. Which if it Suffices not to convince any Man, that it was not *the Work of God*, it is in vain to argue with him.

SECT. 9.

Of the English *Reformation as establish'd by* Queen *Elizabeth*.

G. WELL, but what is all this to the Reformation as establish'd by Q. *Elizabeth*? From whom alone our modern *Protestants* derive their *reform'd Church*, as it now stands; and glory in having had a *Virgin Queen* for their special Foundress: whom they regard as a Person chosen by God to destroy the Superstitions of *Popery*, and restore Religion to its primitive Purity.

P. As

P. As to her *Virginity*, that is too nice a Point for me to touch upon. However *Gregorio Leti*, a *Protestant* Writer of her Life, tho' he extols her *Wit* and *Beauty*, her *Skill* in Governing, and *Zeal* for the *Protestant Cause*, is not over favourable to her as to that Article; but Disputes it problematically, and leaves it undecided. Nay all Historians agree, that tho' she could never be prevail'd upon to enter into the State of Wedlock, She was not altogether proof against the tender impressions of Love, and had her Weaknesses that Way no less than the meanest of her Subjects.

But, to dimiss this odious Subject (for we are always bound to encline to the most favourable Opinion both of the Living and the Dead, when there are no positive Proofs against them.) This however is most certain, that her Character stands upon Record Sullied with Crimes considerable enough to entertain some Doubts of her *divine Election* to the *Apostleship*. I mean not her having been the Fruit of an adulterous Bed, because that was the Crime of her vicious Parents, not her's: but those of her own free Will. As *first*, her Dissembling her Religion during the whole Reign of her Sister *Mary*. In so much that (as Dr. *Heylin* tells us p. 270.) she appeared not a little dissatisfied in not being able *by her outward Conformity to prevail upon the Queen to believe that she was Catholickly affected.* 2*dly*, her unchristian Politicks in Fomenting and Supporting underhand the furious Rebellion of the *Scots* against their lawful Sovereign, with whom she at that Time entertain'd a friendly Correspondence. How far Tampering with the Subjects of a foreign Prince may be allow'd of in Time of War, I will not pretend to decide: but I cannot think it justifiable in Time of Peace, or consistent with mutual Professions of Friendship. Nay it appears to be directly contrary to an inbred Principle of human Nature, which obliges us to do by others as we would be done by.

Thirdly (besides other Crimes, of which I shall have Occasion to Speak hereafter) her violating the Laws of Nations, nay of God and Nature by the most perfidious and inhuman Treatment of the Queen of *Scots*, is a Stain of Infamy upon her Memory never to be wash'd off. For that unfortunate Princess, after such a barbarous Usage in her own Country, as fill'd all Christendom with Horror, (as a modern *Protestant* Author expresses it) being reduced to a Necessity of seeking her Safety elsewhere, fled for Sanctuary into *England*; to which she had been encouraged by Queen *Elizabeth* herself, who had invited her thither with the most Solemn Promises of Protection and Safety. * But she had no sooner got her into her Power, but she deprived her of her Liberty; refused to see her; and after an Imprisonment of above eighteen Years, imbrued her Hands in her innocent Blood.

Such was the *Virgin-Queen*, in whom our *English Protestants* glory as the Special Foundress of their reform'd Church: and whose *Birth-day* they still keep with an annual Religious Solemnity. So apt are Men, when once engaged in a wrong Cause, to overact their Parts; imagining to conceal it's Defects with the Dust they raise about it. But the more *Protestants* affect to trumpet the Praises of the *Royal Foundress* of their Church, the more they excite Men's Curiosity to enquire into her Life and Conduct; which when, instead of finding it adorn'd with the most beautiful Evangelical Vir-

---

* *See the Preface.*

Virtues of *Humility, Meekness, Sincerity, Justice, Charity* &c, (which are the distinguishing Qualities of Persons chosen by God, to propagate his holy Faith) they find on the contrary stain'd with the blackest Crimes of *Hypocrisy, Duplicity, Injustice, Cruelty, Murder,* and the like, * it makes them apt to reflect, that if the *Reformation*, whereof she was the Author, had been the proper work and Cause of God, his infinite Wisdom would not have chosen a Person for the chief Instrument of it, whose Life and Actions he foresaw would be a Dishonour and Scandal to his holy Cause.

But let us now suppose that Queen *Elizabeth* was Innocence itself; our *English Protestants* ought rather to blush than glory in her as their *Foundress*, and keep a Day of *Humiliation* instead of *Thanksgiving* for the gross Oversight committed by their Forefathers in making a *Woman* the *Head* of their Church. That is, the *Source* of all *Ecclesiastical Jurisdiction*, the *Supreme Judge* of Controversies in Religion, and Governour in *Spirituals*. A Thing unheard of before, and never follow'd since by any *national Church* upon Earth.

I shall here repeat to you a Part of the Speech made by Bishop *Heath* in the House of Lords, when the Subject of the Queen's *Supremacy* was under Debate. That Prelate, after having enlarged in the first Part of his Discourse upon the Inconveniences of a Separation from the *See* of *Rome*, which I omit for Brevity's Sake, proceeds in the following manner.

" Now to the second Deliberation : wherein I
" promised to move your Honours to consider,
" what this *Supremacy* is, which we go about by
" Virtue

---

* *See the Preface.*

"Virtue of this Act to give to the Queen, and "wherein it do's confift, whether in *Spiritual* "Government or *Temporal*. ——— If *Spiri-* "*tual*, as thefe Words of the Act do import, "*Supreme Head of the Church* England *immedi-* "*ately and next under God*, then it fhould be con- "fider'd in what Points this *Spiritual* Government "do's confift; and the Points being well known, "it fhould be confider'd, whether this Houfe has "*Authority* to grant them, and her Highnefs *A-* "*bility* to receive them.

"As concerning the Points, *wherein this Spiri-* "*tual Government* do's confift; I have in Reading "the Gofpel, and the whole Courfe of Divinity "thereupon (as to my Vocation belongeth) ob- "ferved thefe four as chief amongft many others. "The firft is, *the Power to loofe and bind Sins*: "when our Saviour in Ordaining *Peter* the chief "and Head-Governour of his Church, faid unto "him, *to thee will I give the Keys of the King-* "*dom of Heaven*. Now it fhould be confider'd "by your Wifdoms, whether you have Sufficient "Authority to grant unto her Majefty this firft "Part of Spiritual Government, and fay unto "her, *to thee will we give the Keys of the Kingdom* "*of Heaven*. If you fay, yea: then do we re- "quire the fight of Warrant and Commiffion by "Virtue of God's Word; and if you fay, no; then "you may be well affured and perfuade your "felves, that you have not Sufficient Authority "to make her Highnefs *Supreme Head of the* "*Church of Chrift* here in this Realm.

"The Second Point of Spiritual Government "is gather'd out of thefe Words of our Saviour "fpoken to S. *Peter* in the 20th Chapter of *John*. "*Feed my Lambs*; *feed my Sheep*. Now whether "your Honours have Authority by this Court of

Reformation under Queen Elizabeth 245

"of Parliament, to say unto our Soveraign Lady: *feed you the Flock of Christ*, you must shew your Warrant and Commission for it. And farther that her Majesty, being a *Woman* by Birth and nature, is not qualified by God's Word to *feed the Flock of Christ*, appears most plainly from St. *Paul* in this wise: *Let Women be silent in the Church. For it is not permitted unto them to Speak; but to be in Subjection, as the Law saith.* And it followeth in the same Place, *for it is not seemly for a Woman to speak in the Church.* 1 Cor. C. 14. v. 34. 35. And in his 1st. Epistle to *Timothy* he says, *I allow not that a Woman be a Teacher, or be above her Husband, but keep herself in Silence.* Therefore it appears likewise, that as your Honours have not Authority to give her Highness this second Point of Spiritual Government, *to feed the Flock of Christ*, so by St. *Paul*'s Doctrine, her Highness may not intermeddle herself with the same. And therefore she cannot be *Supreme Head* of the Church here of *England*.

"The 3d chief Point of Spiritual Government is gather'd out of these Words of our Saviour Christ to St. *Peter* in the 22d. Chapter of St. *Luke*'s Gospel. *I pray'd for thee, that thy Faith may not fail. Do thou also, when thou art come back, confirm thy Brethren*: that is, ratify them in wholesome Doctrine and Administration of the Sacraments; which are the holy Instruments of God, so instituted and ordain'd for our Sanctification, that without them his Grace is not to be received. But to preach and administer the Sacraments a *Woman* may not be admitted. And therefore she cannot be the *Supreme Head*, of Christ's Church.

"The

"The 4th and laſt chief Point of Spiritual Go-
"vernment, which I promiſed to note unto you,
"do's conſiſt in the Excommunication and Spiri-
"tual Puniſhment of all ſuch as ſhall ſhew them-
"ſelves not to be the obedient Children of
"Chriſt's Church: of which Authority our
"Saviour Chriſt ſpeaks *Mathew* 18. *if thy Brother
"having offended will not hear thy charitable Admo-
"nition, whether Secretly at firſt, or yet before one or
"two Witneſſes; then complain of him to the Church:
"and if he will not hear the Church, let him be unto
"thee as a Heathen or Publican.*

"So the Apoſtle did excommunicate the notori-
"ous Fornicator, that was among the *Corinthians*,
"and this by the Authority of his Apoſtleſhip:
"unto which Apoſtles Chriſt aſcending to Hea-
"ven did leave the whole *Spiritual Government* of
"his Church; as it appeareth by thoſe plain
"Words of St. *Paul* in his Epiſtle to the *Epheſians*
"C. 4. ſaying, *he has given to his Church ſome to be
"Apoſtles, ſome Evangeliſts, ſome Paſtors and Teachers
"for the Conſummation of the Saints, to the Work of the
"Miniſtry, for the building up of the Body of Chriſt.* But
"a *Woman* in the Degrees of the Church is not
"call'd to be an *Apoſtle*, nor *Evangeliſt*, nor to be a
"*Paſtor*, nor a *Teacher*, nor a *Preacher*: therefore
"ſhe cannot be *Supreme Head* of Chriſt's Church,
"nor yet of any Part thereof. For this high Go-
"vernment God has appointed only the *Biſhops*
"and *Paſtors* of his People: as St. *Paul* plainly
"witneſſeth in theſe Words Spoken to the Paſtors
"of the Church of *Epheſus*: *Take heed therefore
"unto yourſelves and to all the Flock, over which the
"holy Ghoſt has made you Overſeers to govern the
"Church of God.* Act. 20. v. 28.

"And thus much I have here ſaid, right honour-
"able and my very good Lords, againſt this
"Act

" Act of *Supremacy*, for the Discharge of my
" poor Conscience, and for the Love and Fear
" and Dread, that I chiefly owe unto God, to my
" Sovereign Lady the Queen's Majesty's High-
" ness, and to your Honours all : whereas other-
" wise without mature Consideration of all these
" Premises, your Honours will never be able
" to shew your Faces before your Enemies in this
" Matter : being so strange a Spectacle and Exam-
" ple in Christ's Church, as in this Realm is only
" to be found, and in no other Christian Realm.

This plain Discourse lays fully open the Absurdity of making a *Woman* the *Supreme Head* of a national Church in *Spirituals*. And indeed the Church of *England* became by it the Subject of Merriment and Laughter in all the Christian Kingdoms upon Earth as it justly deserved. *She abolish'd* (says a modern *Protestant* Writer) *the Supremacy of the Pope, and assumed that Title to herself: which at first seem'd a jest to the rest of the World, by Reason of the Incapacity of her sex for the ministerial Function.* p. 259. *Calvin* himself, tho' a Well-wisher to all sorts of Reformations, could not forbear Making his Satyrical jests upon it : and Dr. *Heylin* had Reason to say, *that the Thing seem'd to be abhorrent even to Nature and Policy, that a Woman should be declared Supreme Head on Earth of the Church of* England.

G. But did you not tell me, that the 37th *Article* of *Religion* declares positively, that the Act of Parliament concerning the Queen's *Supremacy* only gave her *that Prerogative, which has been given to all godly Princes in holy Scriptures by God himself. That is, to rule all Estates and Degrees committed to her Charge by God, whether they be Ecclesiastical or Temporal* ? And do's not this fully justify that Act ?

P. On the contrary, it only shews, that *Protestants* themselves were Scandalized at it, and ought to dawb the Matter over as well as they could by such an ambiguous Interpretation of *it*, as might signify either a *Spiritual* or *temporal Supremacy* only, and should Specify neither. Whereas it is manifest, that the real Intention of the Parliament was, to bestow on Q. *Elizabeth* the very same *Supremacy*, as had before been bestow'd upon her two Predecessors *Henry* VIII. and *Edward* VI. by Virtue whereof they were made *Supreme Heads* of the Church of *England* in *Spirituals*, as has been fully shew'd. Though neither the one nor the other made such an antick Figure either at home or abroad, as a *female Head* set upon the venerable *Mystical Body* of *Christ* : a whole *national Church* built upon the *Foundation* of a *Woman*, and (what was but a jest before) a kind of *Pope-Joan* set up in Sober earnest.

G. But suppose a *Protestant* should insist peremptorily upon the Words of the 37th Article, and maintain from it, that you wrong his Church (which must surely be allow'd to know it's own Meaning best) in Pretending that Queen *Elizabeth* was made *Supreme Head* of it in *Spirituals* ; how would you answer him?

P. With a great Deal of Ease, by shewing *first*, that the precarious Interpretation of a few private Persons cannot invalidate the Force of a *Solemn Act* of *Parliament* with the Royal Sanction to it. But 2*dly*, by shewing, that the Interpretation contain'd in the 37th Article, if meant of the Queen's *Supremacy* over *the Clergy* as well as *Laity* in *Temporals only*, is both *frivolous* and *contradictory* to the plain Meaning of the *Act*. It is *frivolous*, because it renders the Act itself a meer *Mock-Act*, and of no manner of Use. For what Man in his Senses ever doubted, but that a *Soveraign Prince*, acknowledg'd for such, as Queen *Elizabeth* was, has the *Supreme Authority* of Governing

ning all her Subjects both *Clergy* and *Laity* in *temporal* Concerns? Was there any need of a Special Act of Parliament to determine a Point, which no Man had ever disputed? Or is it probable, that if no more had been intended by that Act, it would have met with any Opposition either in the *House of Commons* or *House of Lords*? And yet it was very warmly opposed in both. For in the *House of Lords*, there was not a Bishop, not excepting *Kitchin* of *Landaff* himself, who conform'd afterwards, but voted against it. And in the *House of Commons* (tho' the Duke of *Norfolk* and Earl of *Arundel* in Hopes of Gaining the Queen's Favour, with several others had used their utmost Skill and Industry in Managing the Elections in their several Counties for the Returning of such Persons for Parliament-men, as they conceived most likely to comply with their Intentions for a *Reformation*, as Dr. *Heylin* tells us p. 107.) yet the Struggle was so great, that it was carried in Favour of the *Court-Party* by a very small Majority. I only add, that Bishop *Heath* (who surely understood the true Meaning of that Act, and was a Man of excellent Parts) must be thought to have argued like a Child in the Speech he made against the Queen's *Supremacy*, if nothing more was meant by it than that she had the *Supreme Authority* of Governing all her Subjects both *Clergy* and *Laity* in *Temporal* Concerns, which he fully own'd in the first Part of that Speech.

But this Interpretation of the Act is not only *frivolous*, but over and above inconsistent with the Words both of the *Act*, and the *Oath* annex'd to it. The *Act* is worded thus.

" And that also it may please your Highness,
" that it may be establish'd and enacted by the
" Authority aforesaid, that such *Jurisdictions*,
" *Pri-*

250   Dial. 3. §. 9.   *Of the* English.

"*Privileges Superiorities*, and *Preeminences Spiritual*
"and *Ecclesiastical*, as by any *Spiritual* or *Ecclesiasti-*
"*cal Power* or *Authority* has heretofore been or may
"lawfully be exercised or used for the *Visitation*
"of the *Ecclesiastical* State and Persons, and for
"*Reformation, Order, and Correction* of the same, and
"of all Manner of *Heresies, Errors, Schisms* &c.
"shall for ever by Authority of this present Par-
"liament be united and annex'd to the Imperial
"Crown of this Realm.—— and the *Oath* annex'd
"to the *Act* is as follows.   I. N. N. do utterly
"testify and declare in my Conscience, that the
"Queen's Highness is *the only Supreme Governour* of
"this Realm, and of all other her Highness's Do-
"minions and Countries, as well in all *Spiritual*
"or *Ecclesiastical* THINGS *and* CAUSES as tempo-
"ral.

Now if this *Act* and *Oath* did not fix the *Supreme Ecclesiastical Authority* and *Jurisdiction* in Queen *Elizabeth*; and declare her *Supreme Head* in *Spirituals* of the Church of *England*, then Words must lose their obvious and known Signification.   For I observe,

First, that the Act itself gave the Queen all such *Spiritual* and *Ecclesiastical Jurisdiction* in General, *as by any Spiritual* or *Ecclesiastical Power or Authority had ever been, and can lawfully be exercised*.   And was not this declaring her *Supreme Head* or *Governess*, call'd it by what Name you please, of the Church of *England* in *Spirituals*?   Was it not vesting in her Person all the *Jurisdiction*, which any *Ecclesiastical* Person of what Rank soever had ever exercised in the Dominions of *Great Britain*?

2*dly*, it gave her a special Power or Authority to *visit, reform* or *correct* all manner of *Errors, Heresies, Schisms* &c.   All which are properly Exercises of *Ecclesiastical Jurisdiction*; and tho' in
Bishops

Reformation under Queen Elizabeth. 251
Bishops they are limited to their respective Dioceses, and sometimes restrain'd by particular Exemptions, the full Exercise of this *Ecclesiastical Jurisdiction* was on the Contrary by Virtue of the abovesaid Act granted to Queen *Elizabeth* over all the Dioceses in her Dominions without Restriction or Limitation.

But 3*dly*, the *Oath* annex'd to the said Act of Parliament declares in express Terms the Queen's Highness the *only Supreme Governour as well in all Ecclesiastical or Spiritual* THINGS *or* CAUSES *as temporal.* It do's not say that she had the Supreme Authority of Governing all *Persons*, whether *Ecclesiasticks* or *Laicks*, (for that is implied in every ordinary Oath of Allegiance) but that she was the only Supreme Governour in all *Spiritual* or *Ecclesiastical* THINGS *or* CAUSES; which differs very much from the other, and imports no less than that she was the *Supreme Judge* of all Controversies in Religion, and the *Source* of all *Ecclesiastical* as well as *temporal Jurisdiction* in her Dominions. Because as all *temporal Authority* or *Jurisdiction* in every Government flows from the *Secular Head*, so all *Spiritual Jurisdiction* flows from the *Spiritual Head* as from it's *Source.*

Thus then was laid the Foundation of the *reform'd English* Church, as it now stands. For all former Acts relating to the *Supremacy* having been repeal'd in Queen *Mary's* Reign, the *Reformation* began entirely upon a new Footing in the Year 1558, which was the first of Queen *Elizabeth*'s Reign. And tho' it commonly takes it's Date from the Year wherein King *Henry* assumed the *Spiritual Supremacy*, and thereby open'd the way to the several Reformations, that follow'd afterwards, yet to speak properly, the *reform'd* Church of *England*, as to it's present Establishment and

I   Con-

252 Dial. 3. §. 10. *The Q.* Supremacy

Conſtitution, can trace it's Origine no higher than the Year 1558; when it's Foundation was firſt laid upon Queen *Elizabeth's Spiritual Supremacy* as it's chief Ground-work. And ſo inſtead of being built upon the *Foundation of the Apoſtles*, that is, of having ſome *Succeſſor* of the *Apoſtles* (who, to the beſt of my Knowledge never had any *female Succeſſors*) for it's Founder, it has ſomething very ſingularly different from all national Churches in the World in having been founded and model'd not only by a *Lay* but by a *female Head:* Tho' St. *Paul* would not Suffer a *Woman* even to *Speak in the Church*, that is, to intermeddle with *Eccleſiaſtical* Affairs; as Biſhop *Heath* has very Judiciouſly obſerved.

G. It was indeed ſomewhat aukwardly contrived to conſtitute a Perſon *Supreme Head* and *Governour* of a Church, who by her very Sex was incapacitated even to *Speak in it.* For how can a Church be govern'd by a *Head*, whoſe Tongue is tied up, and not allow'd to Speak?

SECT. 10.

The Queen's Supremacy *eſtabliſh'd without the Concurrence or Conſent of the* Clergy.

P. BUT as the Eſtabliſhment and Conſtitution of the *reform'd* Church of *England*, as it now ſtands, was built upon a wrong Foundation, to wit, the *Spiritual Supremacy* of a Perſon incapable of her very Sex even of the loweſt Degree of *Eccleſiaſtical* Dignity or Function; ſo has it another eſſential Flaw, never to be repair'd: I mean, the *Nullity* of that very Power or Authority by which it was eſtabliſh'd. For it was carried entirely by the

the *Secular Power*, without the Concurrence or Consent of the *Clergy*, nay in direct Opposition to it.

G. But why is that an essential Flaw?

P. Because it is a barefaced Violation of the *Divine Institution*, which no Power upon Earth can alter or reverse.

G. Pray, Sir, explain yourself.

P. I think the matter is self-evident. For as Persons can have no Part in the *civil Government*, unless they be qualified *according to Law*, that is, according to the Laws of the civil Society, whereof they are Members; so neither can they legally exercise any Part in the *Ecclesiastical Government*, unless they be qualified according to the Laws of the Church; but especially those, which Christ himself has establish'd for the Government for it. If therefore they, who disposed of the *Spiritual Supremacy* in Favour of Queen *Elizabeth* and her Successors were wholly unqualified according to the Laws establish'd by Christ, for the Exercise of that *Ecclesiastical Power*; then it follows, that they were as incapable of Bestowing the *Ecclesiastical Supremacy* of the Church of *England* upon her, as she was of Receiving it.

Now 'tis manifest both from the Scriptural Texts quoted by Bishop *Heath*, and from the universal Tradition and Practice of all Ages, that *Christ*, the *divine Founder* and *Lawgiver* of his Church, settled the whole *Spiritual Government* of it immediately upon the *Apostles*, and after them upon the *Bishops* and *Pastors*, that were to be their Successors in the *Apostolical Ministry* as long as his Church should last, that is, to the End of the World. For *he gave to his Church some to be Apostles, and some Evangelists, and some Pastors and Teachers: for the Perfecting of the Saints, for the Work*

254 Dial. 3. § 10. Q. Elizabeth's *Supremacy*

Work of the Ministry, for the Building up of the Body of Christ, till we all meet in the Unity of the Faith, and of the Knowledge of the Son of God. Ephef. 4. v. 11. 12. 13. These therefore alone are the Spiritual Rulers of *God's Appointment*: these alone are qualified according to God's Institution to enact Ecclesiastical Laws, or exercise any Part in the Spiritual Government of his Church. And, by Consequence, if the Bestowing of the *Spiritual Supremacy* on Queen *Elizabeth*, and Entailing it upon her *Heirs* and *Successors* was a meer Gift of the *State*, and wholly Owing to the *Secular Power*, it wanted the *Sanction* of that Authority, which Christ establish'd for the *Spiritual* Government of his Church, and was a manifest Violation of the *Divine Institution*.

Let us then see, what part the *Clergy* had in that Stupendious Act, which is the Ground-work of the *English Reformation*, whereon the whole Fabrick of the present Church of *England*, and it's *reform'd Religion* is built.

In the *first* Place, it is notoriously known, that not one single *Bishop* in the Parliament assented to it. *Against these Statutes* (says *Cambden* p 19.) *nine Bishops in the higher House, which were present that Day, stifly impugn'd. For now there were no more but fourteen left alive.* Dr. *Heylin* says *fifteen*.

G. But since some of the Bishops were absent from the House, we cannot know for certain, whether they would have been for, or against the Bill.

P. Sir, we are sure they were against it after it had pass'd, and express'd their Abhorrence of it in Fact, even with the Loss of their Bishopricks and Liberty over and above. For *Cambden* tells us p. 28. that *all the Bishops* (saving only *Antony Kitchin* of *Landaff*, who had also voted against

it,

it, and whom he calls *the Calamity of his See*) refused the *Oath of Supremacy*; which was tender'd to them soon after the Dissolution of the Parliament, and thereupon were immediately deprived of their Bishopricks, and sent to several Prisons. But let us also see what Dr. *Heylin* writes upon this Subject.

"It was, says he, upon the 8th of *May* that
"the Parliament ended: and on the 24th of
"*June*, that the publick Liturgy was to be offi-
"ciated in all the Churches of the Kingdom. In
"the Performance of which Service the Bishops
"giving no Encouragement, and many of the
"Clergy being backward in it, it was thought fit
"to put them to the final Test, and either to
"bring them to Conformity, or to bestow their
"Places and Preferments on more tractable Per-
"sons. The Bishops at that time were reduced
"to a narrower Number, than at any Time be-
"fore— So that there were no more than *fifteen*
"living of that Sacred Order: and they being
"call'd in the Beginning of *July* by certain Lords
"of the privy Council, were required to take the
"*Oath* of *Supremacy*. *Kitchin* of *Landaff* alone
"takes it: who having formerly submitted to e-
"very Change, resolved to shew himself no
"Changeling. By all the rest it was refused:
"that is by Dr. *Heath* Archbishop of *York*, *Bonner*
"of *London* &c. and they were thereupon depri-
"ved of their Bishopricks.

Here it is manifest, that the Article of the Queen's *Spiritual Supremacy* which not only gave a mortal Wound to the *ancient Faith* of the *Catholick Church*, but was the very Basis, and has ever since been the chief Bulwark of the *English Reformation*, was so far from being countenanced or assented to by those of the prelatick Order, that

256 Dial. 3. §. 10. Q. Elizabeth's *Supremacy*
on the contrary they expres'd their utmost Abhorrence and Detestation of it: and all but *Kitchin*, the Dishonour of his Character, persisted to their very last Breath in their Opposition to it. But let us now see, whether the *Convocation*, which represents the Body of *inferiour Clergy*, or the two Universities were more favourable to it than the Bishops.

Mr. *Fuller* L. 9. writes thus of the *Convocation*, which sat at the same Time with Q. *Elizabeth*'s first Parliament, *'Tis observed in Nature, that when one twin is of an unusual Strength and Bigness, the other born with it is weak and dwindles away. So here Queen Elizabeth's first Parliament being very active in Matters of Religion, the Convocation, younger Brother thereunto, was little employ'd, less regarded.* It seems it was not judg'd Safe at that Time to trust *Churchmen* with *Church-Affairs*. Tho' our Blessed Saviour was of another Mind, and appointed first *Bishops*, and under them *Pastors* and *Teachers* to be the Spiritual Guides and Rulers of his Church unto the End of the World.

However neither the *Convocation* nor *Universities* were wholly Idle, or unconcern'd Spectators of what the Secular Power was busily Carrying on to the Prejudice of the ancient Religion. For, as the same Author tells us L. 9. the Convocation put forth 5 Articles, Subscribed to by both Unisities, as a publick Testimony of their Faith: The three first contain'd a short Exposition of the Catholick Doctrine of the *real Presence*, *Transubstantiation* and the *Mass*. The two last were these, viz. 1. *That the chief Power of Governing the Church of Christ was given to* St. Peter, *and his lawful Successors in the See Apostolick, as to the Vicar of Christ*. and 2dly, *that the Authority of Treating and Defining Matters relating to Faith, Sacraments, and Church-*
Dis-

establish'd wholly by the Secular Power. 257
Discipline has always hitherto belong'd, and ought only to belong to the *Pastors of the Church, whom the holy Ghost has appointed in it for that End, and not to Laymen.*

Thus we plainly See that the Setling of the *Spiritual Supremacy* upon Queen *Elizabeth* and her Successors was carried in direct Opposition to the Judgment of the whole Body of the *English Clergy*.

Whence I infer *first*, that since this was a Matter purely *Spiritual* even of the highest Importance, and therefore belong'd by divine Right to the *Ecclesiastical Tribunal*, it was decided by illegal and incompetent Judges: as being unqualified by God's own Law; who never appointed *Laymen*, but the Successors of the *Apostles* to govern his Church, and decide Ecclesiastical Causes.

I infer 2*dly*, that the *Divine Institution* of *Episcopacy* and *Episcopal Government* was doubly violated in the very Laying of the Foundation of the present *reform'd* Church of *England*. *First*, by Entailing for ever the *Supreme Ecclesiastical Government* of it upon a *Lay-person*, whether *Man, Woman,* or *Child.* 2*dly*, by Setting up this new System of *Church-Government* in utter Contempt of, and Opposition to the whole *national Episcopal Authority* then in Being.

Whence I conclude with this Dilemma, to wit, *Episcopal Government* either is essential to the Constitution of Christ's Church, or not. If it be, the present *reform'd* Church of *England* has an essential Defect in it's very Foundation: I mean, the *Supreme Spiritual Authority* of a *Lay-head*; which also it derives wholly and solely from the *Secular Power* without the least Concurrence or Approbation of the *Episcopal Authority*, as has been fully proved. But if Epifcopal Government be not essential to the Constitution of Christ's Church, and may be either set up, or laid aside like ordinary human Institutions according to the Will and Pleasure of Men, then the *Presbyterians* and other Enemies of *Episcopacy* have as fair a Title to be a Part of Christ's true Church, as the Church of *England* can pretend to. For if *Episcopal Authority* may be laid aside at one Time, I See no Reason why it may not be cast off for good and all. And if the Secular Power may legally new-model the *Hierarchy*, so as to constitute a *Lay-head* over the *Church*, and even that independently of the *Episcopal Authority*, I am not sharp-sighted enough to see any solid Reason, why the same Power may not as legally commit for ever the whole Government of it to such Persons as it thinks fitting: whether they be *Lay-Ministers* made so by *Lay-Ordination*; or of that Rank, whom the Church of *England* calls *Bishops*. Nay I don't See, why the *Secular Power*, when their Hands were in, might not have gone through-stich, and declared Queen *Elizabeth* in express Terms *universal Patriarch*, as well as *Supreme Head* of the Church of *England*. For the one is no more than the other contrary to the express Institution of Christ.

SECT II.

Some Remarks upon the Progress and Motives of Queen Elizabeth's *Reformation.*

G. BUT tho' the *Bishops* and *inferiour Clergy* were against the Act of *Supremacy*, when it pass'd, did they not in Process of Time give their After-Approbation and Sanction to it by Conforming to the Religion establish'd by Law?
For

For I have Heard that but very few, at least of the latter, stood out.

P. As to the *Bishops*, I have already told you, that they persisted to their Deaths in their Opposition to it. And tho' they were violently deprived by the *Lay-Power* both of their *Sees* and *Liberty*, yet like the Apostles in Chains, they did not therefore forfeit that *Spiritual Jurisdiction and Authority*, which belong'd to them by *Divine Right*, and could not be taken from them but in the Case of some Canonical Fault, and by a Canonical Trial, and Judgment pronounced against them.

Whence it follows, that whatever the *inferiour Clergy* did to the Prejudice of the ancient Faith of *England*, whether by a forced or voluntary Compliance with the Times, was of no Manner of Weight, because they acted without Authority, and contrary to the Obedience they had Sworn to those, who were their lawful Superiours in the Sight of God. So that the only Consequence that can be drawn from it is, that there are always great Numbers of unsound and putrid Members in the *visible Church of Christ*, who generally discover themselves either in Time of Persecution and Trial, or when they have a fair Opportunity offer'd them of gratifying some predominant Inclination: which two Circumstances concurring in the Reign of Queen *Elizabeth*, it is no Wonder that great Numbers of the *inferiour Clergy* abandon'd the ancient Religion, as Rats do a House, which is ready to fall, and remove to better Quarters: Some for *Safety*, others for *Ease* or *Profit*; according as their prevailing Passions Sway'd them. And I cannot here forbear Observing, with how much Partiality and little Judgment some *Protestant* Writers glory in the Numbers of these miserable Proselytes: Since 'tis apparent that the *Charms* or *Terrors* of this World had the greatest Influence upon their pretended Conversion.

G. But what Reason have you to say so? For *Protestants* will on the contrary maintain, it was a full Conviction of Conscience, that brought them so readily over to the Reformation.

P. They may pretend what they please: But the very Nature of the Thing Justifies my Observation. For when Punishments are inflicted on the one Hand, and considerable Advantages offer'd on the other: When Non-compliance is attended with bitter Sufferings, and Temporizing encouraged with Rewards, a Sudden Change in Matters of Religion is justly ascribed either to the *Fear* of the one, or *Hope* of the other. And this was the Case from the very Beginning of Queen *Elizabeth*'s Reformation. Great Numbers of the *inferiour Clergy*, who came over to it, were frighten'd into a Compliance, and taught to conform by the Sufferings of others. They saw their Bishops imprison'd, and all those of their own Rank, who had refused the *Oath* of *Supremacy*, turn'd out of their Livings, and reduced to Beggary. So that they had no other Choice left, but either to conform or Starve; having nothing but their Benefices to depend upon for a Livelihood. A terrible Temptation to those, who are not arm'd with Virtue strong enough to undergo a lingring Martyrdom!

But the greatest Part were prevail'd upon by the powerful Charms of *Liberty* and *Ease*. For besides the Liberty they were sure to enjoy of Gratifying their Incontinence, as the Effect soon shew'd, the Queen had by the Plenitude of her *Ecclesiastical Power* contrived such a *commodious*

Reformation for them, that if they would but conform, they should keep their Benefices, and at the same Time be eased of the most painful Part of the Duties annexed to them. This is manifest to the Eyes of all mankind in the remarkable Difference there is between the fatiguing Duties incumbent on the *Pastors* of the *Catholick Church*, and the easy Lives, comparatively, of *Protestant Ministers*.

G. I have heard this Observation made by many, and the Fact is notorious. For *Protestant Ministers* have neither *Mass* nor *Office* to say, nor *Confessions* to hear, nor any Functions to break their Night's Rest: Nor scarce the fifth Part of our *Holy Days* to interrupt their more agreeable Amuzements. So that they are in no Danger of being over-burden'd with *Pastoral Cares*; and a good Living Serves to maintain a female Companion in a very comfortable Way.

P. Compare this easy Way of Serving the Church with the laborious Lives of *Catholick Pastors*, and the Difference will appear as great, as there is between the *broad* and *narrow Way* mention'd in the Gospel. For if we but consider the indispensable Obligation, *Catholick Pastors* are under, of a daily long *Office* besides their *Masses* attended with Prayers before and after, and frequent publick Services for the Dead, we may say without Exaggeration, that taking one Day with another, their daily Task of publick and private Prayers is greater, than a *Protestant Minister* is bound by his Functions to perform in several Days. Add to this the irksome Burden of the *Confessional*, where those especially, who have a numerous Flock under their Charge, are sometimes shut up for several Hours together: and none but they, who have had the Experience of it, it, can be Sensible how heavy a Burden this is. But there flows from it another painful Obligation of being ready at all Hours, and in all Seasons to administer the *Sacraments* of *Penance* and *Extreme Unction*, and the *Viaticum* to the Sick: and it would be highly Scandalous amongst us, if either the Darkness of a rainy and tempestuous Night, or the Rigour of the Season, or finally the Danger of contagious Distempers, tho' never so mortal, should hinder a *Catholick Pastor*, when call'd upon, from Performing this Duty with all Chearfulness even to the meanest of his Flock.

Now since 'tis manifest, that Queen *Elizabeth*'s good-natured Reformation, by Abolishing the *Mass*, together with the *Sacraments* of *Penance* and *Extreme Unction*, and *Prayers* for the *Dead*, and the other commodious Changes made by her, eased all those of the Clergy, that would conform, from the most painful Part of their Functions, I think it is not to be wonder'd (considering Men's natural Proneness to *Liberty* and *Ease*) that great Numbers of them should by this alluring Bait be drawn into a Compliance, which Secured them in the quiet Possession of their *Ecclesiastical Livings*, and at the same Time deliver'd them in a Trice from the *popish Yoke* of those laborious Duties, which till then had been inseparably annex'd to their Livings.

G. Truly if *Protestants* pretend to boast of such Converts as these, we may justly fear, the Enemy of Man's Salvation will come in for a large share in the Glory of their Conquests. For when the Inclinations of *Flesh* and *Blood*, and the Attractives both of *Interest* and *Ease* appear manifestly to favour a Change from one Religion to another, 'tis no rash Judgment to conclude, it is not a *Conviction* but *Want* of Conscience, nor a Love of Truth,

Truth, but the Love of the World, to which such Converſions are Owing.

P. 'Tis a good ſaying of Mr. *Dryden*, that *a Down-hill Reformation rolls apace*. And truly Queen *Elizabeth* took Care to model her Reformation according to this agreeable Platform, by ſuiting it to the natural Inclinations of all Degrees and Conditions of Men. The *Laity*, whether rich or poor, found their Account in it by being deliver'd by it from a great Number of Troubleſome *Faſts* and *popiſh Holy-days*; but above all from the ungrateful Taſk of *Confeſſing their Sins*; which ſubjected them to the importune Remonſtrances and Reprimands of their Ghoſtly Fathers, beſides the Performance of the *Penances* enjoin'd them. The *Clergy*, as you have already ſeen, were over and above eaſed by it of the moſt painful Part of their miniſterial Functions, got Wives into the Bargain, and not only kept their former Livings to maintain them, but lived in Hopes of improving their Fortunes by ſtepping into richer Benefices by the Removal of thoſe, who ſhould refuſe to conform.

The Queen herſelf had the greateſt Intereſt upon Earth to determine her to diſcard the *Pope*: which, as I have already obſerved, was the fundamental Article of the intended Reformation. Let us hear Dr. *Heylin*'s Judgment of the religious Motive that induced her to it. *She knew very well*, ſays he, *that her Legitimacy and the Pope's Supremacy could not ſtand together*. p. 275. Very right. For if ſhe had acknowledg'd the *Pope*'s *Supremacy*, ſhe muſt have ſtood to his Verdict relating to the Invalidity of King *Henry*'s Marriage with her Mother *Anne Bolen*; which would have been to own herſelf a *Baſtard*, and render her Title to the Crown at leaſt doubtful. A Reformation was therefore neceſſary both to ſave her Honour, and ſecure her Title: and theſe were two convincing Proofs, that the *Pope* was no longer *Supreme Head* of the Church of *England,* tho' he had a *Preſcription* of 900 Years to Support his Title to it.

But ſhe had other Motives full as pure and diſintereſted as this to carry on what Godly Work. For tho' the great Harveſt accruing from the *Plunder* of the Church had been reap'd in the two Reigns of *Henry* VIII. and *Edward* VI. yet there were no contemptible Gleanings remaining by the Death of Queen *Mary* to invite her to follow the Footſteps of her two reforming Royal Predeceſſors. Let us hear Dr. *Heylin* ſpeak once more.

"Her firſt Parliament, ſays he, reſtored to the
"Crown the *Tenths* and *firſt Fruits,* firſt ſettled
"thereon in the Time of *Henry* VIII. and after-
"wards given back by Queen *Mary.* They alſo
"paſs'd an Act of Diſſolution of all ſuch *Mona-*
"*ſteries, Convents,* and *religious Orders* as had been
"founded by the Queen deceaſed. By Virtue of
"which Act the Queen was repoſſeſs'd of all
"thoſe Lands, which had been granted by her
"Siſter to the Monks of *Weſtminſter* and *Sheen,*
"the *Knights Hoſpitallers,* the Nuns of *Sion,* with
"the Manſion-houſes re-edified for the *Obſervants*
"of *Greenwich,* and the *Black Friars* in *Smithfield.*
"p. 280.

G. But how could Queen *Elizabeth* hinder the Parliament's generous Liberality towards her? For was it adviſable for her to refuſe the Royal Aſſent to a Bill, they had paſs'd in Favour of her, or diſoblige her Parliament, whilſt it was in ſo good an Humonr?

P. Alas good Lady! Her Caſe was doubtleſs very hard. For it cannot be queſtion'd, but ſhe was forced to use great Violence to her tender Conscience in Condescending to enrich herself with the Spoils of the Church. However She accepted of the Present made her, with a good Grace: nor do's it appear upon Record, that it either broke her Heart or Sleep.

G. I presume at least she kept her Hands clear from Invading any Part of the *Bishops-Lands*. For I have been told she was a Zealous Promoter of *Episcopacy*.

P. If Dr. *Heylin* may be believed (and he relates nothing but plain Fact) she found Ways and Means by the Help of her good Parliament to manage the Revenues of the vacant Bishopricks so discreetly, that her Zeal for *Episcopacy* did not any Ways hinder a very considerable Part of the Church's Patrimony form being safely convey'd into her Coffers.

" It was enacted, says Dr. *Heylin*, by her first
" Parliament, that in the *Vacancy* of any *Arch-*
" *bishoprick* or *Bishoprick*, it should be lawful for
" the Queen to issue out a Commission under the
" great Seal for taking a Survey of all *Castles,*
" *Manours, Lands, Tenements*, and all other *Here-*
" *ditaments* to the said Episcopal Sees belonging
" or appertaining: *and to take into her Hands any*
" *of the said Castles, Manours, Lands, Tenements*
" *Hereditaments* &c, *as to her seem'd good*: giving
" to the said Archbishops and Bishops as much
" annual Rents to be raised upon Impropriati-
" ons, Tiths, and Portions of Tiths, as they did
" amount to. p. 292.

" Of this such Advantages were made, *as most*
" *redounded to the Profit of the Queen and her Cour-*
" *tiers*. Upon which Grounds, as all the Bishops
" *Sees*, were so long kept vacant, before they were
" fill'd, so in the following Times they were kept
" void

"void one after another, *till the best Flowers in the whole Garden of the Church had been cull'd out of it.* p. 292. 293.

"There was another Clause in the said Statute, by which the Patrimony of the Church was as much dilapidated *Sede plena,* as it was by this in Times of Vacancy. For by that Clause all Bishops were restrain'd from making any Grants of their Farms and Manours for more than twenty one Years, or three Lives at the most, *except it were to the Queen, her Heirs and Successors* (and under that Pretence to any of her hungry Courtiers) they might be granted in Fee-farm, or for a Lease of 99 Years, as it pleased the Parties. By which Means *Crediton* was dismember'd from the See of *Exon,* the goodly Manour of *Sherborn* from that of *Salisbury*: And many fair Manours were alienated for ever from the rich Sees of *Winchester, Ely*; and indeed what not? p. 293.

After this the same Author gives a particular Account of the terrible spoil and Wast of the Lands of several other Bishopricks, either by long Vacancies, or other illegal Means. I shall only recite to you what he says of *Oxford.*

"As for *Oxon,* says he, it was kept vacant from the Death of Mr. *King* the first Bishop of it *Dec.* 14. 1557. till the 14 of *Oct.* 1567. at which Time it was conferr'd on Dr. *Curwin* Archbishop of *Dublin*: who having held it but a Year, it was again kept vacant twenty Years together, and then bestow'd on Dr. *Underhil* in *Dec.* 1589. But he dying also shortly after, viz. Anno. 1592. It was once more kept void till the Year 1603. So that this Church was fill'd little more than three Years in forty
six

"fix. The Revenues remaining in the Hands of
"the Earl of *Leicester*, and after his Decease of
"the Earl of *Essex*: by whom the Lands were
"so spoil'd and wasted, that they left nothing
"to the last Bishops but Impropriations. By
"Means of which Havock and Destruction all
"the five Bishopricks erected by *Henry* VIII. were
"so impoverish'd and destroy'd, that the new Bi-
"shops were necessitated to require a Benevo-
"lence of their Clergy to furnish their Episcopal
"Houses p. 328 329.

Thus you see this eminent *Reformer* and *Foundress* of the Church of *England* kept not her Hands so very clear, as you imagined, from being dipp'd in the Plunder of the Church's Patrimony. And as they were not guiltless in this Respect, so were they most deeply imbrued in innocent Blood: especially after the Sanguinary Laws made by her, which during her Life were executed with the utmost Rigour, as may be seen in *Stow*. So that I may say without the least Wrong done to her Character, that (excepting the Vice of Incontinence, with which I cannot charge her) she inherited the very worst of her Father's Qualities. And 'tis remarkable, that the most wicked and profligate Persons of that Age were the most in her Favour: Such as *Leicester*, *Walsingham* and others: of whom the Author of *the short View of the English History* writes, that having *already tasted of the Sweetness of Confiscations, they design'd to make the* English *Roman Catholicks desperate by ill Usage, in Hopes they would rebel, and forfeit their Estates. But when Truth enough could not be found against them,* Walsingham *by counterfeit Letters and Confessions extorted by Pains and Terrors of the Rack, tumultuated the People with chimerical Dangers,*

gers, *only to prepare them for the Murder of the Queen of* Scotland.*

The same Author gives this short general Character of *Leicester.* viz. that *he was one of the worst of Men*: p. 269. *and had all the ill Principles of his Father* Northumberland. p. 273.

But Dr. *Heylin* has left us a fuller Account of him. p. 239, 240. where he tells us that the Queen in her Visit to *Cambridge* Anno. 1564 coming acquainted with Sir *Robert Dudley* made him *Earl of Leicester*, and gave him a great Sway in all Affairs both of Court and Council. And then go's on thus.

" Advanced to this Hight he engross'd to him-
" self the Disposing of all Offices in Court and
" State, and of all Preferments in the Church.
" A Man so unappeasable in his Malice, and in-
" satiable in his Lusts: So Sacrilegious in his
" Rapines, so false in his Promises, and treache-
" rous in Point of Trust: and finally so de-
" structive of the Rights and Properties of par-
" ticular Persons, that his little Finger lay hea-
" vier on the *English* Subjects, than the Loins of
" all the Favourits of the two last Kings.

This was that noble Person, whom Queen *Elizabeth* was so charm'd with, and loaded with so many Favours, that he even conceived no small Hopes of being one day admitted to her Bed, and a Partnership in the Crown. In Order whereunto, *he broke the Neck of his Wife down Stairs* (says the Author of *the short View.* p. 273.) *to make Room in his Bed, when he should have the Happiness to accomplish his Designs on the Queen.* Yet this wicked Wretch, and others as profligate as himself were her
Bosom-

---

* *See the Preface.*

Bosom-Confidents, and chosen Counsellors, whom she advised with, and was directed by in the most weighty Concerns both of *Church* and *State*: In so much that the abovesaid Author sticks not to say, *that she had the most wicked Ministry, that ever was known in any Reign.* p. 273. And what other Consequence can we draw from it, than that she was no Enemy to wicked Counsels and Practices? since instead of Frowning upon those, who were the avow'd Promoters of Wickedness and immorality, she rewarded them with Preferments, and honour'd them with her peculiar Confidence and Friendship. This was a strange Conduct in one, who pretended to so much Zeal for God's Worship; and plainly shews, that Tenderness of Conscience was no distinguishing Part of her Character: which indeed stands upon Record blacken'd with such Stains of Infamy, as cast an irreparable Scandal upon the *Church* and *Reformation*, whereof she was the *Supreme Head* and *Architect*.

G. Truly I cannot but observe, that as they, who willingly herd with Thieves and Pick-pockets, are commonly thought to be no ill-wishers to the Trade; so it can be no rash Judgment to think, that Queen *Elizabeth*, who chose profess'd Libertines for Minions and Counsellors, had not the greatest Hatred possible to wicked Principles and Practices.

P. 'Tis very certain, that if instead of pretending to reform the Church, she had labour'd to reform the Viciousness of her Court and Ministry, she would not only have kept within her proper Sphere, but acted more suitably to the Decorum becoming the Character of a *Virgin Queen*.

But before I take my Leave of Queen *Elizabeth*, I shall make a few Remarks upon that *penal Statute* of her's, whereby *saying Mass* is made *high Treason* and being present at it *Felony*; and accordingly both the one and the other punishable with an infamous Death. Now to the best of my Judgment, *penal Laws* can never change the *Nature* or *Essence* of Things: nor do they make such or such Actions, for the Punishment whereof they are made, become Crimes that were not so before, but they suppose them to be so in their own nature. So that they would be the same enormous Crimes, both in themselves and in the sight of God, tho' there were no human Laws to punish them. Thus *Robberies, Murders, Rebellions* and *Treasons* are justly punish'd with Death, as being in themselves Crimes of such an enormous and pernicious Nature, that Persons guilty of them deserve to be regarded as the publick Enemies of Mankind, and treated with the utmost Rigour.

Hence it follows, that if Queen *Elizabeth's* Law was just, *saying Mass* both is, and has always been a Sin of as black a Die in the sight of God as that of *high Treason*. But how is that credible? Will any one have the Confidence to say, that all the *Bishops* and *Priests of great Britain* for 900 Years together, amongst whom there were a great Number eminent for Holiness of Life and Working of Miracles, lived in the daily Practice of a deadly Sin? Did those great Doctors and Pillars of God's Church St. *Ambrose*, St. *Augustin*, St. *Basil*, St. *Chrysostom* and such others commit as many enormous Crimes, as they said *Masses*? Did St. *Gregory* incur the Guilt of *three mortal Sins* upon every *Christ-mass* Day by saying *three Masses* on that Day, as he himself says, he did?* Finally did St. *Augustin* and his Followers, who converted this Island, begin their holy Mission, with setting a Pattern

to

In his 8th Homily upon the Gospels.

to all to their Succeffors of Committing daily a Crime of fuch a hainous Nature, as deferved to be punifh'd with the moft cruel and Infamous Death? Thefe furely are fuch monftrous Abfurdities as will not enter into the Imagination of any Man in his right Senfes: Yet, if the abovefaid *penal Statute* of Queen *Elizabeth* was juft, all thefe Abfurdities, how monftrous foever, would follow. Becaufe *penal Laws*, that are *Juft*, appoint Punifhments proportion'd to the Enormity of the Crimes, againft which they are made. If therefore the fame infamous and cruel Death, which the Law inflicts upon *Traitors*, was juftly incurr'd for *faying Mafs*, it follows that *faying Mafs* is of its own nature and in the fight of God as black a Crime as that of *high Treafon* againft the State: and, by Confequence, all the eminent Saints I have named, lived in the continual Practice of as great a Sin, as if they had daily committed Treafon againft their Soveraigns. Which, if it be not a Suppofition, which any Man of Senfe and Religion will blufh to own, nothing can be imagined extravagant enough to fhock him. And therefore I cannot but regard that Sanguinary Statute of Queen *Elizabeth*, which during her long Reign was executed with the utmoft Violence and Rigour, as one of the blackeft Stains in her Character.

G. But, Sir, *Proteftants* will fay, that Queen *Elizabeth* regarded the Doctrine of the *Mafs* as an *execrable Herefy*: and when fhe made Laws againft it, and executed thofe Laws, fhe only follow'd the Examples of her Father *Henry* and Sifter *Mary*; who had put feveral Perfons to Death purely on the Score of *Herefy*.

P. Sir, it cannot be queftion'd but that *Herefy* is not only a moft grievous Sin, but many Times of pernicious Confequences to the State: and may therefore in certain Circumftances be Juftly
punifh'd

punish'd with Death. But whether both *Henry* and *Mary* had always a due Regard to those Circumstances, I will not undertake to determine. This however I am sure of, that their Case was very different from that of Queen *Elizabeth*. Because they only punish'd *Heresies*, which had been condemn'd many Ages before by the *universal Church*: whereas, if Queen *Elizabeth* thought fit (as *Supreme Head* of the *English* Church) to regard the Doctrine of the *Mass* as a *Heresy*, it was a Heresy form'd in her own Imagination, never thought nor heard of at least before the *Reformation* in any Christian Nation under the Sun. Nay she herself at her first Coming to the Crown, order'd a solemn *Mass* to be said for the Soul of her Sister *Mary*, and another for *Charles* 5th. But after all Sir, the Priests, that were executed in her Reign, did not suffer for *Heresy* but for *Treason*.

G. But what! were they not found guilty of some Endeavours at least to subvert the Government, or some Designs against the Queen's *Life* or *Crown*?

P. No, no Sir, it was not so much as pretended: and the only treasonable Crimes they suffer'd for were their being *Priests*, and *saying Mass*, or Doing any other Functions of their Sacred Ministry. Their very *blackest Treason* was their Worshipping God by that august and venerable *Sacrifice*, which had been offer'd to him from *East* to *West* in all preceding Ages, and in all the Christian Kingdoms upon Earth. So that Honouring the *Divine Majesty* was regarded by her as a capital Affront upon her own Person, and punish'd accordingly. For I cannot Imagine what other way *saying Mass* could be strain'd into the foul Crime of *high Treason*.

G. This

Q. Elizabeth's *Reformation*. 273

G. This indeed is a moſt flagrant Inſtance of the Cruelty of her Temper. For even *Juſtice* itſelf may be puſh'd too far : and there may be a Degree of Cruelty in Executing Laws, tho' never ſo juſt, and Puniſhing *real Crimes* with too much Rigour. But to make Treaſon of a Thing, that never was ſo before, nor can be ſo in it's own Nature, and then puniſh it with the ſame Rigour, as if it really were ſo, may be call'd Cruelty in the higheſt Degree. But Sir, my Attention has been ſomewhat too long upon the Stretch : So let us if you pleaſe adjourn to another Day.

P. With all my Heart, Sir. For 'tis not good to overcharge your Memory : and one Meeting more will ſuffice to mark out to you the proper Conſequences, that are to be drawn from the *Facts*, have hitherto entertain'd you with.

The End of the third Dialogue.

THE Fourth DIALOGUE.

CONTAINING,

A Comparison *between the most remarkable Circumstances of* England's Conversion *on the one Hand, and it's pretended Reformation on the other.*

SECT. I.

The respective Qualifications of the chief Instruments of England's Conversion *and* Reformation *compared.*

G.  PRESUME Sir, you have now done with the Historical Account you promised me at the Beginning of our second Meeting: and will proceed to give me a Lecture upon the *Use* and *Application*, that is to be made of the Collection of Facts, you have entertain'd me with.

P. 'Tis what I now intend to do. For without this all Knowledge of History is but a meer A-
muze-

muzement, and may serve indeed to entertain a Man's Curiosity, but not to cultivate or improve his Mind. But, tho' the Facts I have mentioned afford Matter for a great Variety of useful Reflections either on the *infinite Mercies* of God, or his *impenetrable Judgments*, in Regard to this Island; or on the *irreparable Consequences* of a Man's giving himself up to the Desires of an irregular Passion; or finally, on the *scandalous Weakness* of some, which may be a Motive of the profoundest Humiliation to us, and the *exemplary Firmness* of others, who made a bold Stand in Defence of the *ancient Faith* of their *Mother-Church*, and the like; I shall wave all Reflections of this Kind, and confine myself wholly to the single Point I have hitherto had in View. I mean, the Judgment we are to form upon *Comparing* together the whole Collection of Circumstances relating to the *Conversion* of *England* on the one Hand, and to its *pretended Reformation* on the other. For since 'tis manifest, that both the one and the other could not have the *Divine Approbation*, nor be properly the *Work of God*, the *Comparison* I propose to make, will of it self lead you to a solid and impartial Determination of this important Question, to wit, Whether the *Conversion* of *England* from *Paganism* to the *Roman Catholick Faith*, or its *Reformation* from that Faith to the Religion now *establish'd by Law* has the *clearest Marks* of being the *proper Work of God*, and having had the *Holy Ghost* for its Author: But before I proceed, I will lay down some general Maxims, which I think are incontestable.

First, That the Conversion of a Kingdom to the true Faith is most certainly the *Work of God*, and that they, who contribute their pious Labours towards it, are the Inftruments of his Mercies.

2*dly*, That tho' A. G. can bring about the Defigns of his Mercies by what Means and Inftruments he pleafes, yet it appears to be the fix'd Order of *Divine Providence* to choofe no other Perfons, than fuch as are of an unfpotted Character and eminent Piety, for Accomplifhing his Defigns of an *extraordinary Mercy:* Infomuch that there is not a fingle Inftance, that any Kingdom was ever converted either from *Idolatry* or *Herefy* to the *true Faith* by Men of fcandalous Lives.

3*dly*, That when a Nation changes from one Religion to another (if either of them be the true one) it is either a *great Bleſſing*, or a *heavy Curſe.* Or, to exprefs my felf in other Words, it is either an *extraordinary Mercy,* or a *dreadful Judgment.* If it changes from *Falſhood* to *Truth,* 'tis an *extraordinary Mercy*; and God, who is the *Father of Mercies,* is properly the Author of it. But if it changes from *Truth* to *Falſhood,* 'tis a *dreadful Judgment*; permitted indeed by God in his Wrath; but the *Devil,* who is the *Father of Lies,* and profefs'd Enemy of Man's Salvation, is the Supreme Director of fuch Counfels.

4*thly*, That the common People and Perfons of no Learning, who have neither Capacity nor Leifure to examine every controverted Point of Religion by itfelf, muft have Recourfe to certain *external Marks* to judge by, in the Cafe of a *national Change* from one Religion to another, whether it be a Change from *Truth* to *Falſhood,* or from *Falſhood* to *Truth*: and, by Confequence, whether *God* or the *Devil* be the principal Author of it.

5*thly*,

5thly, That the *good* or *bad* Characters of the chief Actors in it, the *disinterested* or *interested Motives*, upon which they act, and the *legal* or *illegal Means*, by which they pursue their respective Ends, are *external Marks*, on which a solid Judgment may be grounded, whether it be a Cause, to which God gives his *Approbation*, or which he only permits to prosper, as a just Punishment of the Sins of the People. To this I add,

6thly, That if the *Conversion* of *England* from *Paganism* to the *Roman Catholick Faith* has the external Marks of an *extraordinary Mercy* on its Side, and the *Reformation* of that Faith has on the contrary all those external Marks against it, an unbiass'd Person must necessarily conclude, that the Religion establish'd in *England* by its abovesaid *Conversion* had God for its Author, and the *pretended Reformation* of that Religion had not the *Approbation* of God, but was permitted by him as a *dreadful Judgment* on the Nation.

G. The Truth of these Maxims appears to be self-evident, and the Consequences that flow legally from them, must necessarily be assented to by all, who are not resolved to shut their Eyes against the clearest Light.

P. I have premised them for no other End, than to direct you to form a true and impartial Judgment, whether they who planted in this Island the Religion now nick-named *Popery*, or they, who reform'd that Religion, have the clearest Marks on their Side of having acted under the Direction of the *holy Ghost*? For it is certain, that *Divine Spirit* was not the *Director* or *Guide* of both. Unless we can suppose, that he has been the Author of *Popery* in one Age, and of *Protestancy* in another; that is, of two contradictory Faiths and Religions. Now then let us compare together the Instruments and Means, by which the one and the other were establish'd: and it will be easy to judge, which of the two had the *holy Ghost* for its Author.

G. You have already made your Observations upon the most material Circumstances relating to the *Character*, *Conduct*, and *Canonical Proceedings* of those, who brought the *Roman Catholick Faith* into this Island. And since Opposites placed near to one another appear in the clearest Light, as you told me a while ago, you need but follow the same Method in joining with them your Observations upon the *Character*, *Methods*, and *Conduct* of those, who took upon them to *reform* that Faith.

P. Very right, *Sir*; and 'tis just what I intend to do in Order to convince you, that they are as opposite to one another, as Black is to White.

First then, S. *Augustine* and his Fellow-Missioners, by whom the *Roman Catholick Faith* was planted in this Island, had their *Commission* from the undoubted Successor of Saint *Peter*, who had His immediately from Christ himself. So that the Legality of their *Mission* or *Ministry* was unquestionable, as flowing originally from *Christ* and his *Apostles*: and they were undoubtedly of the Number of those, to whom *Christ* before his *Ascension* promised, that *he would be with them even unto the End of the World*, Matt. 28. v. 20.

But they who took upon them to *reform* this Faith, to wit, a *Layman*, a *Child*, and a *Woman*, being neither of the *Episcopal* nor *priestly Order*, could not derive their *Succession*, nor by Consequence any *Ecclesiastical Commission* from the *Apostles*; who never had either *Female* or *Lay-Successors*

cessors in the *Ecclesiastical Ministry*. Whence it follows again, that they were not of the Number of those, whom Christ promised *to remain with even unto the End of the World*.

G. But *Protestants* will say, that the *Parliament* took away all Defects, by investing them with the *Supreme Ecclesiastical Authority* and *Jurisdiction* in the Realm.

P. Sir, all Power upon Earth, how great soever, has its Bounds, and acts within a limited Sphere. So that altho' the *British Parliament* be as August and powerful an Assembly, as any I know upon Earth, tho' it can make and reverse political Laws at home, and send Fleets abroad to give the Law to foreign Nations, I dare modestly say, it cannot make a *Woman a Man*, nor a *Layman* a *Bishop*, nor invert the Order of *Church Government* establish'd by *Jesus Christ*; who never appointed *Laymen* or *Women* but *Bishops* to govern his Church in *Spiritual* Matters. *Acts* 20. *v.* 28. Nay the *Parliament* may as easily make the River *Thames* flow from a Source in the *West-Indies*, as make a *Layman, Woman*, or *Child* the Source of *Ecclesiastical Authority* or *Jurisdiction* in the Realm.

2*dly*. S. *Augustine* and his Fellow-Missioners, as they receiv'd their *Commission* immediately from S. *Gregory the Great*, so it cannot be doubted, but they profess'd and preach'd the *Faith* of that holy and learned Bishop; with whom every *national orthodox Church* upon Earth was then in Communion. So that his *Faith* was judg'd *catholick* and *orthodox* by the Consent of Nations both in the *East* and *West*. Nor have I ever heard of any Man not utterly void of Shame, so bold as to accuse either of *Idolatry* or *Heresy* that eminent Saint and Pillar of God's Church: And if his Faith was free from all Stains of *Idolatry* or

T 4 *Heresy*

Herefy, that which S. *Auguftine* taught, and *Roman Catholicks* profefs at this Time, muft be fo too.

But was the Religion, which our *pretended Reformers* brought into *England*, fupported by the Credit and Reputation of any fuch illuftrious Prelate? Can it be faid, they were commiffion'd by a Perfon in *Ecclefiaftical Authority*, whofe *Faith* was judg'd *Catholick* and *Orthodox* by the Confent of Nations both in the *Eaft* and *Weft*? Alas! how can that be? Since not only the two great *Patriarchs* of the *pretended Reformation* declared in their publick Writings (and the Fact is unqueftionable) that they had feparated themfelves in Faith and Communion from all the pre-exiftent Churches in the World: but likewife the *Englifh Book of Homilies* recommended by the 35th *Article of Religion*, and ordered to be read in Churches, as containing a *Godly* and *wholefome Doctrine*, has farther declar'd, that *Laity and Clergy, learned and unlearned, all Ages, Sects and Degrees of Men, Women, and Children of* WHOLE CHRISTENDOM *had been at once drown'd in abominable Idolatry: and that* FOR THE SPACE OF 800 YEARS AND MORE. p. 251. 'Tis therefore granted, that for the Space of *eight hundred Years and more* the Religion brought in by our *Englifh Reformers* was fo far from having any eminent Prelate acknowledg'd to be *orthodox* in his Faith by the *Confent of Nations*, that it had not fo much as a fingle *Clergyman* or *Layman*, whether *learned* or *unlearned* in *whole Chriftendom* before the Beginning of the Reformation, to fupport the Credit and Reputation of its Caufe.

G. But Proteftants will perhaps fay, that tho' the Religion of *whole Chriftendom* was againft them for the Space of *eight hundred Years and more*, in which

and Reformation compared. 281

which *Popery* reign'd univerfally, yet it was not fo in the former and purer Ages before Pope *Gregory.*

P. Sir, if any one fhould be either fo ignorant or infincere as to fay fo, I fhould defire him to anfwer the two following Queries; *firſt,* whether it be probable, that the *Engliſh Reformers* at the Diftance of 900 *Years* had a better Knowledge of what was the *publick Faith* and Religion of the *Catholick Church* before the 6th Century, than S. *Gregory* himfelf, who lived in that Century, and all the learned Biſhops of Chriftendom, who were then in Communion with him? 2*dly,* whether it be probable, that if this great Saint, and his contemporary Biſhops had known, that the *Faith* of the *Church* in their Time was not the fame as that of the *primitive Ages,* but had been corrupted by *Hereticks,* they would have perfifted wittingly and knowingly in the Profeffion of it? Efpecially fince it does not appear, that either the Terror of Perfecutions, or any Allurements of worldly Advantages, or the Motives of Liberty and Eafe, could render them capable of fuch an unchriftian Prevarication.

G. I muft needs fay, if thefe Things are probable, we ought not to defpair, but that it may at length become a probable Opinion, that *white* is *black,* or that *Truth* and *Falſhood* are the felffame Things?

P. Well then, the Confequence of all is, that Saint *Gregory*'s Faith and Religion were the Faith and Religion of the *primitive Ages.* And fince it cannot be doubted, but he commiffioned Saint *Auguſtine* and his Fellow-Miffioners to preach the very fame Faith to the *Engliſh Saxons*; and it is no lefs certain, that this Faith was maintain'd inviolably by their Pofterity till the Reign of *Henry* the 8th, it follows, that the

Changes

282 Dial. 4. §. 1.   England's *Converſion*
Changes afterwards made in it, tho' varniſh'd over with the popular Name of a *Godly Reformation*, were in reality a *Corruption* of the *ancient Faith*.

3dly, The Inſtruments of *England*'s *Converſion* to the *Roman Catholick Faith* were Perſons not only of an unſpotted Character, but eminent for the extraordinary Holineſs of their Lives; as is apparent from the Account holy *Bede* gives of them in the firſt Book of his *Eccleſiaſtical Hiſtory*, Ch. 26. where he compares their Religious Comportment, Zeal, and Devotion to that of the primitive Chriſtians, in their aſſiduous Exerciſes of *Prayer*, *Watching*, and *Faſting*; their Entire Contempt of all worldly Things; and finally, their living up to all the Evangelical Rules and Maxims, which they preach'd to others. This is a true and faithful Character in Miniature of thoſe *Apoſtolical Preachers*, who above *eleven hundred Years* ago planted in this Iſland that very Faith, which *Roman Catholicks* profeſs to this Day.

But how different is this Character from that of all the principal Authors and Promoters of the *pretended Reformation?* As *Henry* VIII. *Thomas Cromwell*, Archbiſhop *Cranmer*, the Dukes of *Somerſet* and *Northumberland*, *Walſingham*, *Leiceſter*, &c. whoſe Memories remain upon Record ſtain'd with publick Infamy, and Crimes of the blackeſt Die: Such as *Sacrilege*, *Hypocriſy*, *Rapine*, *Luxury*, *ſhedding of innocent Blood*, and the like! as has been fully ſhewn in my Account of the three *reforming Reigns*, even from the Teſtimony of unexceptionable *Proteſtant* Writers. So that the Characters of theſe *pretended Reformers* of the *Roman Catholick Faith* differ as much from thoſe of the *primitive Planters* of that Faith, as Darkneſs

ness differs from Light, or the Deformity of Vice from the Charms and Beauty of Virtue.

But here, Sir, let us consider, which of these two sorts of Persons have the *clearest Marks* stamp'd upon their Lives and Actions of being *Teachers of Truth, Instruments of God's Mercies*, conducted by the *divine Spirit*, and *chosen by him* to propagate that *holy Faith*, by which Salvation is to be attain'd! Again, which of these two sorts of Persons appear most visibly stigmatiz'd with the Marks of being *Seducers, Ministers of God's Wrath*, actuated by the *Spirit of Lying*, and made his Tools to forward the Perdition of Souls! I think it but conformable to the Dictates of common Sense to judge, that Persons of *irreproachable* and *holy Lives* are in the Rank of those who are chosen by God to be the Instruments of his Mercies to lead Men into the Way of Truth and Salvation: and Persons of *wicked* and *scandalous Lives* are the Agents of Satan to seduce them into the Way of everlasting Perdition: and that, by Consequence, the Planting of the *Roman Catholick Faith* in this Island was the *proper Work of God*; and the *Reformation* of that Faith, if a Judgment may lawfully be form'd from the opposite Characters of the principal as well as immediate Authors of it, was manifestly the Work of the *Spirit of Seduction*.

SECT. 2.

The Methods *and* Means *of* England's *Conversion and Reformation compared.*

4*thly*, THE whole Work of *England's Conversion* was carry'd on with the utmost Regularity and Order. The Workmen employ'd in it were all of the *Epiſcopal* and *Prieſtly* Order according to God's own Appointment. They acted with a due Subordination to their reſpective ſpiritual Superiours, and all their Proceedings were according to the eſtabliſh'd Laws and Canons of the Church. On the contrary the *pretended Reformation* was ſet on Foot, carry'd on, and eſtabliſh'd by the moſt irregular and uncanonical Methods. The chief Managers of it and Actors in it were either *Laymen*, or derived their Juriſdiction from a *Lay-head.* All the three reforming Princes, to wit, *Henry* VIII. *Edward* VI. and Q. *Elizabeth* undertook the Work of the Reformation, not in the Name or by the Authority of the *Clergy*, but entirely by Virtue of their own *Spiritual Supremacy.*

In the firſt reforming Reign a *Layman*, the Son of a *Blackſmith*, was conſtituted *Vicar-General*, or (as the Lord *Herbert* ſtiles him) *Viceregent general of the King's Authority in Eccleſiaſtical Affairs*; had a Commiſſion to *viſit* and *reform* all the Religious Houſes both of Men and Women in the Realm; ſat in a *Synod* at the Head of 20 *Biſhops*, 39 *Abbots* and *Priors*, and ſubſcribed in the firſt Place to the Decrees of it, as *Preſident* of the whole Aſſembly.

The ſame uncanonical Methods were purſued in the following Reign. A *Child* was made *Supreme Spiritual Head* of the Church. And tho' the *Protector* took not upon him the Name or Title of the King's *Vicar general*, he had in Effect, and exerciſed to all Intents and Purpoſes, the whole *Spiritual Authority* and *Juriſdiction*, that *Cromwell* had poſſeſs'd under K. *Henry*. Becauſe tho' all publick Edicts for the Regulating of Eccleſiaſtical Affairs were iſſued out in the King's Name, the whole Regal Power, *Eccleſiaſtical* as well as

temporal

temporal was lodg'd in the Protector as *Regent* of the Kingdom. Infomuch, that (as Dr. *Heylin* has obferved) the *Bifhops* were by an Act of Parliament in the firft Year of *Edward*'s Reign reduced to the mean Condition of *being no better than the King's Minifters, or his Ecclefiaftical Sheriffs, to execute his Will and difperfe his Mandates, fo that they were not in a Capacity even of* CONFERRING ORDERS, *but as they were thereunto impowered by a Special Licence.*

I need not fay much concerning the Meafures taken in the Reign of Q. *Elizabeth.* They were juft as regular and Canonical as in the former Reigns of her Father and Brother. Her *fpiritual Supremacy,* which was no lefs the Jeft than Scandal of Chriftianity, was eftablifh'd by the *Secular Power* alone, in fpite of, and direct Oppofition to the whole Body of the *Clergy*: That is, of all the *Spiritual Guides* and *Rulers* of God's Appointment: as has been fully proved. In this Manner was the whole Frame of *Church-Government,* as inftituted by Chrift, turn'd up-fide down. The fecular Magiftrate invaded the Sanctuary. Perfons unqualified by their State even for the loweft Ecclefiaftical Preferments, were rais'd to the higheft Dignity in the Church; and they whofe Duty it was to obey, according to S. *Paul*'s Injunction, *obey them that have the Rule over you, and fubmit your felves,* Heb. 13. v. 17. were made the fpiritual Directors of their Guides. But I am very fure the *holy Ghoft* had not the fupreme Direction of fuch a Reformation.

5thly, *England*'s Converfion to the *Roman Catholick Faith* was *free* and *voluntary.* No Violence was ufed, no Threats of Prifons, Banifhments, or Confifcations were employ'd to frighten the People into a Compliance: as is particularly taken

ken notice of by S. *Bede*, who tells us, that K. *Ethelbert*, tho' he encourag'd his Subjects to embrace Christianity, as he himself had done, *compell'd none. For he had learn't from his Instructors and Leaders to Salvation, that the Service of Christ ought to be voluntary, not by Compulsion.* L. 1. C. 26. So that the only Force made Use of in the Conversion of *England* to the *Roman Catholick Faith* was the prevailing Force of Truth preach'd by Persons fill'd with the *Spirit of God*, and recommended by the exemplary Holiness of their Lives.

But was the Reformation establish'd by the same Christian Means? Was there no Violence used to drag the People to a Conformity contrary to the Dictates of their Consciences? Or were the *Bishops* and *Clergy* perfectly free either to embrace or reject the Reformation, without Danger of being exposed to grievous Sufferings by it? Were there no Examples of Severity, no Imprisonments, no Forfeitures of Livings, no sanguinary Laws or bloody Executions to convince them of the Necessity of Complying with the Times? The contrary, alas! is so well known, that we may as well deny the Reformation itself, as that it owes its Establishment to the most violent and bloody Means.

G. But what Consequence do you draw from this historical Fact?

P. The Consequence I draw from it is, that a Reformation, which like *Mahometanism* stood in need of being introduced by *Violence*, and cemented with *Blood*, has not the same Marks of God's Approbation, as a Religion, which like the Faith of the primitive Christians came *by Hearing:* That is, by the ordinary Means appointed by God for the Conversion of Souls to the

the *true Faith*; according to S. *Paul.* Rom. 10. v. 17.

If the Apostles had appear'd in the World with Pomp and State, abounding in Wealth, and in a Condition to reward their Proselytes with Places of Honour and Profit: Or if they had come at the Head of arm'd Troops, and encompass'd with Officers ready at their Beck to seize, imprison, condemn and execute all such as should have refused to embrace the Gospel; *Christianity* would have been destitute of one of it's strongest Proofs of being the *proper Work of God*. But their entire Want both of *Riches* to *allure*, and of *Power* to *force* Men to a Compliance, made the Hand of God appear visibly in the wonderful Conversions they wrought. And the same may be said of the Conversion of this Island, undertaken and accomplish'd by a few poor Religious Men, without any Arms but the *holy Cross*, or any other Force than the persuasive Power of their Words and Example. Whereas all the Allurements of temporal Advantages on the one Hand, and all the Terrors of the most dreadful Persecutions on the other, raised by those, who had the supreme Power in their Hands of Making and Executing what Laws they pleased, concurr'd to establish the *Reformation*. So that all the principal Means employ'd to carry on and perfect that Work savour so rank of the very worst of *human Politicks*, that A. G. appears to have had no other Hand in it, than that of suffering Things to take their natural Course; that is, *wicked Instruments* to employ *wicked Means*, and *wicked Means* to produce Effects accordingly. For it has always been so, and will be so to the World's End, that they who have the Power in their Hands of *Rewarding* and *Punishing* as they please, and stick

not

not to employ that Power to compass their Ends, will not fail to have infinite Numbers of Followers to carry on any Cause, though never so wicked in itself. I add, that as no *Pagan* Nation upon Earth was ever converted to the *Roman Catholick Faith* by *Violence* and *Bloodshed*, so no Nation was ever *reform'd* from that Faith, but by such unchristian and terrifying Means. Whence I conclude, in the whole, that *England*'s *Conversion* has on it's side the clearest Marks of *God's Approbation*, and it's *Reformation* is wholly destitute of those Marks.

6thly, The *Faith* or *Religion*, to which *England* was converted by S. *Augustine* and his Followers had the strongest *external Evidence* possible, I mean the Testimony of undoubted *Miracles* to witness, that it was not the Invention of Men, but that God himself was the Author of it. The Reason hereof is plain, because *true Miracles* are God's own *Seal*: and 'tis impossible he should set his Seal to, or give Evidence for the Truth of any Religion, whereof himself is not the Author; since any Religion, but what himself has *reveal'd*, is undoubtedly false, and he cannot bear Witness to a Falsehood.

Now, tho' the Miracles attributed to S. *Augustine*, like those of other Saints in Times subsequent to the Apostles, have not the *Divine Testimony* of *scriptural* Miracles, yet they are as authentickly attested as numberless other historical Facts, which no Man can rationally doubt of. And the same may be said of the Wonders wrought by those other Apostolical Preachers, who gave the finishing Stroke to *England*'s Conversion, so happily begun by that great Saint.

I have already related out of *Bede*, L. 2. C. 2. the celebrated Miracle wrought by S. *Augustine* in Restoring Sight to a blind Man by the Force of his Prayers; the Truth whereof I never heard question'd by any. Nay the Fame of his Miracles was so great, that Pope *Gregory* being inform'd of it, judg'd it expedient to precaution and fortify him against the Temptation of Vanity by a Letter fill'd with Considerations proper to keep him in an humble Opinion of himself. The Letter is recorded in *Bede*'s *Eccl. Hist.* L. 1. C. 31. and ends with these Words. " It remains " therefore, most dear Brother, that amidst these " Things, which by the Working of our Lord " you outwardly perform, you always inwardly " judge yourself with Rigour, and narrowly di- " scern both what you are yourself, and how " much Grace is in that Nation, for the Con- " version whereof you have received the Gift " of working Miracles. And if you remember, " that you have at any Time offended our Crea- " tor either by Word or Deed, that you always " call that to Mind; to the End that the Re- " membrance of your Guilt may crush the Vani- " ty rising in your Heart. And whatsoever you " shall or have received in Relation to Work- " ing Miracles, that you repute the same not as " conferr'd on you, but on those for whose Sal- " vation it has been given.

I add, that *John Fox* himself, who bore S. *Augustine* a mortal Grudge for having taught *Papistical* Doctrines, has attested the Truth of his *Miracles. At length,* says he, *when the King had well consider'd the honest Conversation of their Life, and was moved with the Miracles wrought through God's Hand by them, he heard them more gladly; and lastly, by their wholsom Exhortations and example of Godly Life, he was by them converted, and Christen'd in the Year*
596,

596, *and the* 36*th of his Reign.* Acts and Monu. Col. 2. N. 5. p. 105.

This I think suffices to convince any reasonable Man, that the *Faith* now profess'd by *Roman Catholicks*, tho' blacken'd with the odious Names of *Superstition* and *Idolatry*, was at its first Establishment in this Kingdom confirm'd by *undoubted Miracles*: and had, by Consequence, the very same infallible Mark of *Truth* stamp'd upon it as Christianity had at its first Entrance into the World. If therefore it was the true Faith, when S. *Augustine* preach'd it, I am sure it is so now. Unless Time and Age can change *Truth* into *Falsehood*, and *Divine Faith* be like human Institutions subject to Vicissitudes and Revolutions.

I need not take much Pains to shew, that the *Reformation* is utterly destitute of this Divine Mark or Testimony of Truth, since *Protestants* themselves have saved me the Trouble of doing it by running down all Miracles as pious Frauds, and pretending that the Power of working them has been at least suspended for may Ages. Which, though a mere groundless Assertion, implies at least a plain Confession, that the *Gift of Miracles* never was bestow'd on any of the *reformed Churches*.

G. That's very certain: And *Protestants* pretending that Miracles are ceas'd, looks something like the Fox in the Fable saying that the Grapes were sour, because he could not come at them. However I presume Men may preach *true Doctrine* without *working Miracles*: which being a gratuitous Gift, God may bestow it upon whom, and refuse it to whom he pleases. And how then is it a distinguishing Mark of Truth?

P. Sir, tho' the Want of Miracles be not absolutely Speaking a Proof of Falsehood, yet the Working of Miracles, especially when join'd with other

other Circumstances, is an infallible Mark of Truth, and it has always been regarded as such. So that in the Concurrence of two contradictory Doctrines, if one of them has the *Evidence of Miracles* on its side, the other is manifestly convicted of Falsehood. Not precisely because it is not confirm'd by Miracles, but because it is the contradictory to that Doctrine, to which God himself has set his Seal, and given Testimony by the most authentick and solemn Approbation. Which makes a very material Difference between the Doctrine which *England* received at its *Conversion*, and that which was introduced nine hundred Years after by the *pretended Reformation*.

However I answer 2*dly*, that there are certain Cases, in which the Proof of Miracles may justly be demanded; because in such Cases they never are refused by God. This was the Case of *Moses* when he was sent by God to demand of *Pharaoh* the Deliverance of the *Israelites* from the *Egyptian* Bondage. For what Regard would *Pharaoh* have had to the Demand of a private Man, unless he had proved his Commission from God by the Testimony of Miracles? This was likewise the Case of the *Apostles*, when they were sent by Christ to preach the Gospel to all Nations. For unless he had sent them arm'd with the Power of *working Miracles*, no *Idolatrous* Nation would ever have been converted to the Faith. Lastly, it was the Case of S. *Augustine* and his Fellow-Missioners, when they undertook the Conversion of the *Idolatrous Saxons*: and God bestow'd upon them the Power of *working Miracles*, to shew that it was *his Cause* they had undertaken. Now I dare boldly say, there scarce ever was a *Religious Cause*, that stood more in need of *Miracles* to prove, that it was *the Cause of God*, than that of the *pretended Reformation*.

G. Sir, I don't well apprehend the Reason of this your positive Assertion.

P. My Reason for it is plain and convincing. Because the *first Reformers* at home as well as abroad pretended to nothing less than to introduce a Doctrine contrary to that of the *universal visible Church* then in Being: to revoke the Decrees of ancient Councils, and declare such Doctrines *Orthodox*, as had been condemn'd by the *whole Ecclesiastical Authority* upon Earth, and all the *Guides of God's Appointment* in former Ages. They pretended, by Consequence, to *new Revelations*, without which it can't be doubted but that *new Doctrines* in Matters of Faith are meer Forgeries, and the Inventions of Man's Brain. They set up a *new Ministry*, not flowing from the *Successors* of the *Apostles*, but from the *Secular Power*. They retrench'd *five* of the *seven Sacraments*, and abolish'd the *venerable Sacrifice*, which had been offered in all the Kingdoms both of the *East* and *West*, from the Time of their first Conversion to Christianity. In a Word, they accused the *whole visible Church* upon Earth of *Superstition* and *Idolatry*.

Now if there was no Need of *Miracles* to warrant the Legality of these extraordinary Proceedings, and convince the World that they were approved by God, it will be impossible to shew that there was any Need of *Miracles* for the first Establishment of *Christianity*. For if the Church of *Rome*, (which in all preceding Ages had been regarded as the Bulwark of Christianity by all Churches, but those which Protestants themselves disown) was effectually fallen into the *abominable Idolatry*, it is accused of even to this Day; and

if

if the *Protestant Doctrine*, as far as it is opposite to *Popery*, be a *reveal'd Doctrine* (for otherwise God has no Share in it) the first Teachers of it, to whom we must suppose it was *reveal'd*, were bound to prove the *Revelation* of it by the Testimony of uncontested Miracles; as the Apostles proved the Revelation of their Sacred Doctrine, and as their true Successors have done since, in most Nations of the Universe. Yet to the everlasting Dishonour of the *pretended Reformation*, not any one of the *reforming Apostles* ever had the Confidence to hazard the Reputation of his Cause upon this infallible Test: but on the contrary, they all judg'd very wisely, that it was much easier to ridicule than work Miracles.

G. I commend them for it. For *Laughing* is a very easy Way of *Proving*. And it is found by Experience, that a pleasant Jest is many Times as succesful as a Demonstration. But, pray Sir, go on with your Comparison.

SECT. 3.

The Motives *of* England's *Conversion and Reformation compared.*

P. 7ly. ST. *Augustine* and his Fellow-Missioners undertook the Conversion of this Island with a Zeal entirely free from all interested Views, as is attested by holy *Bede*. And indeed what other Interest than that of Eternity could possibly have induced them to quit for ever their native Country, Friends and Relations, which all Men are more or less link'd to by a natural Affection, and undertake a painful Journey to a barbarous and infidel Nation, where, tho' they had been even secured before-hand of Succefs, they could hope for nothing in Prefent, but the Fatigues and Hardfhips of a moft laborious Miffion among a People drowned in *Ignorance*, *Idolatry*, and *Vice*; and in a Word, a Courfe of Life diametrically oppofite to all the natural Inclinations of Flefh and Blood. So that nothing could be more pure and difinterefted than the *Motives*, upon which thefe holy Miffioners engaged themfelves in fo difficult and laborious an Undertaking. And I infift fo particularly upon this Circumftance, becaufe when there is nothing to be got, and a great deal to be fuffer'd in this World by an Enterprize; as there can be no Temptation, fo there can be no Sufpicion of Hypocrify or Fraud: And therefore an entire Difintereftednefs in a *religious Caufe* may be regarded as a fure Mark of an interiour Conviction of Confcience in the Parties concern'd, that the Caufe they efpoufe is acceptable to God, and that their Labours in Promoting it will be rewarded by him in the Life to come.

But did there appear any Marks of this *Purity of Intention* and *difinterefted Zeal* in the chief Promoters and Managers of the *pretended Reformation?* On the contrary, they made not any one confiderable Step towards it, but what favour'd rank of being guided either by fome criminal Paffion, or fome private Ends, or Intereft of State.

K. *Henry* VIII. is known by all the World to have been in his Heart and Judgment as ftanch a *Roman Catholick* as any Chriftian Prince upon Earth. Nay in the Book he wrote againft *Martin Luther* he carried the Prerogatives of the *Apoftolick See* to fuch a Hight, that even Bifhop *Fifher*, who had the Revifing of it before it was prefented to the Pope, advifed him, tho' in vain, to make fome Alterations

tions in it upon that Article. Yet this very Man but a few Years after gave the firſt fatal Blow to the *Catholick Faith*, and laid the Ground-work of the enſuing Reformation, by withdrawing his whole Kingdom from its former Obedience to the *See Apoſtolick*, and aſſuming the *Spiritual Supremacy* to himſelf.

But was it pure Zeal for Religion, which wrought this ſudden Change in him? Did he conſult purely God's Honour and the Good of his Church in making himſelf *Supreme Head* of it? Dr. *Heylin* has anſwer'd theſe Queſtions for me by telling us, *that* Henry *being violently hurried with the Tranſport of ſome private Affections, and finding the Pope the greateſt Obſtacle to his Deſires, extinguiſh'd his Authority in the Realm of* England: *and that this open'd the Way to the Reformation, to which the King afforded no ſmall Encouragement for politick Ends*. Pref. p. 2. Whence it is plain, that the two Paſſions of *Luxury* and *Revenge*, of which I am ſure God was not the Author, gave Birth to the Reformation: That the Violence of King *Henry*'s Paſſion for *Anne Bolen* was the true and only *Motive* of his Purſuing with that indefatigable Earneſtneſs the ſhameful Buſineſs of the *Divorce*; and his Deſire to be reveng'd of the Pope, who was *the greateſt Obſtacle to it*, put him upon the extravagant Expedient of Breaking thro' the *Divine Inſtitution*, by ſtripping him of the Authority which had been acknowledg'd by his Predeceſſors for many Ages, and by himſelf for many Years. Such were the *Religious Motives* upon which the firſt *Royal Reformer* ſet the *Engliſh Reformation* on Foot!

As to K. *Edward*, he knew ſo little of Religion, when he came to the Crown, that if his Governor had been a *Mahometan* as he was a *Zuinglian*,

Zuinglian, that Prince might have been made as true a *Musselman* as he was a *Protestant*. In short, the whole Management of Religious Matters as well as State Affairs was in the Hands of the Duke of *Sommerset*, his Governor and *Lord-Protector of England*: whose Sacrileges in Rifling Churches, Prophaning the Sacred Vessels, Pulling down Altars, and Converting the Plate, Jewels, and other precious Ornaments belonging to them, to private Uses, are so well known, that there is no Room left to doubt, but that the Desire of Satisfying the Avarice of that Prime Minister and other Court-Harpies under him, was the true and real Motive that spurr'd on those stupendious Innovations, which were made in the ancient Faith and Worship of this Kingdom during the short Reign of *Edward* VI. And it may be as reasonably maintain'd, that a *Religious Zeal* moved *Antiochus* to sack the City and Temple of *Jerusalem*, as that the Duke of *Sommerset* and his Accomplices committed all the Sacrilegious Robberies and Depredations, that *Turks* and *Infidels* are capable of, upon a pure and disinterested Motive of Religion.

Nay there was not one Change made in the Religion, which S. *Augustine* and his Followers had establish'd in so edifying a Manner, but what tended directly to the Enriching of the chief Instruments and Managers of this blessed Reformation with the Spoils of their *Mother-Church*. As for Instance, by Abolishing the *Mass*, which render'd *Altars* with all the massy Plate, Jewels, costly Furniture and priestly Ornaments wholly useless, a Deluge of Wealth came flowing into their Coffers. Again, by suppressing *Prayers for the Dead*, all the Lands belonging to *Free-Chappels* and *Chanteries*, founded for the Perpetuating of those
Prayers,

Prayers, fell of Course into their Sacriligeous Hands. 3*dly*. By forbidding all *Religious Honour* to be paid to *Images* and *Pictures*, even those of *Jesus Christ*, a Licence was given to a general Plunder of all the *Cathedrals*, *Parish-Churches* and *Chappels* in the Kingdom, which were all stripp'd as naked as a *Quakers Meeting-House*, so that nothing but the bare Walls were left standing. 4*thly* and *lastly*, By Running down the Veneration of *Reliques*, a Devotion as antient as Christianity, all the rich *Shrines* and *Reliquaries*, many of which were of inestimable Value, became a Prey to the insatiable Rapacity of the pretended Reformers of those Days. A strange Way of Reforming Religion, by Gratifying the most hateful Passions of corrupt Nature!

G. But, Sir, *Protestants* will say, that the *Lands* belonging to *Free-Chappels*, *Colleges*, and *Chanteries*, as likewise the *Plate*, *Jewels*, and other *Ornaments* of any Value, were all seized for the King's Use: and that, by Consequence, the Changes in Religion made by the Lord *Protector*, and others under him, cannot justly be attributed to their *Avarice*, but may be regarded as the Fruit of a disinterested Zeal.

P. Sir, *Protestants*, who know nothing of the History of the *Reformation*, may perhaps say so. But the learned Dr. *Heylin*, who cannot be suspected of Partiality, has told another Story. I shall repeat some Part of his Words, which justify every Thing I have said upon this Head. *Some great Men*, says he, *about the Court, under Colour of Removing such Corruptions as remained in the Church, had cast their Eyes upon the Spoil of* Shrines *and* Images, *and the improving of their own Fortunes by the* Chantery-Lands. *All which they most sacrilegiously divided among themselves.* And again concerning

cerning the Order of the privy Council sent to the Bishops for pulling down *Images*, he writes thus : *It may very well be thought, that* COVETOUSNESS *spurr'd on this Business more than* ZEAL. *There being none of the Images so poor and mean, the Spoil whereof would not afford some Gold or Silver, if not Jewels also, besides Censers, Candlesticks, and many other Utensils appertaining to them.* And lastly, concerning the Proposal made for Demolishing *Altars*, he writes thus: *The touching on this String made excellent Musick to most of the Grandees of the Court, who had before cast many an envious Eye on the costly Hangings, that massy Plate, and other rich and precious Utensils, which adorn'd those Altars.*

Here then we plainly see the true Motive of all the Changes I have mention'd ; which *under Colour of Reforming Abuses* had no other End in View, than the Enriching of the Contrivers and Managers of this pretended Reformation. Nay and the same Author has let us know, how shamefully the King was imposed upon and defrauded by these Zealous Reformers.

" Such was the Rapacity of the Times, says
" he, and Unfortunateness of the King's Condi-
" tion, that his Miniority was abused to many
" Acts of Spoil and Rapine, even to the highest
" Degree of *Sacrilege* ; to the Raising of some
" and Enriching of others, without any Manner
" of Improvement of his own Estate. For not-
" withstanding the great and almost inestimable
" Treasures, which must needs come in by the
" Spoil of so many *Shrines* and *Images*, and the
" Sale of Lands belonging to the Chanteries,
" Colleges, Free-Chappels, &c. he was never-
" theless not only plunged in Debt, but the
" Crown-Lands were very much diminish'd and
" impair'd since his Coming to it.

Now

Now 'tis very obvious to think, that if there had been the leaſt Grain of *Religious Zeal* in the Seizure of theſe ineſtimable Treaſures belonging to the Church, they would at leaſt have been employ'd in ſome pious or charitable Uſes: As the Founding of Alms-Houſes for the Poor, Hoſpitals for the Sick, Schools for the Education of Children or Improvement of Learning, and the like. But nothing of all this anſwerable to the immenſe Value of the Spoil appears upon Record. On the contrary, *the Grandees of the Court*, ſays Dr. *Heylin, intended to defraud the King, and the Commiſſioners to put a Cheat upon the Court-Lords; and both the one and the other were prevented by many of the Gentlemen in the Country*, who were reſolved to have their Share in the Booty. In this pious and religious Manner were the *Lands, Plate, Jewels*, and *coſtly Ornaments* belonging to the Church diſpoſed of.

G. I confeſs it is impoſſible not to judge that there was a great Deal of Knavery, and nothing of Religion in theſe Proceedings.

P. You will be more fully convinced of it, if you but call to mind, what Dr. *Heylin* has told us concerning K. *Edward*'s Parliament, which ſets the whole Matter in the cleareſt Light.

"The *Parliament*, ſays he, met on the 4*th*
" of *November*, in which *the Cards were ſo well*
" *pack'd*, that there was no Need of any other
" Shuffling to the End of the Game: Becauſe
" they all agreed well enough in one common
" Principle, which was *to ſerve the preſent Time*.
" ―― For tho' a great Part of the Nobility,
" and not a few of the chief Gentry in the Houſe
" of Commons were cordially affected to the
" Church of *Rome*, yet were they willing to give
" Way to all ſuch Acts and Statutes, as were
" made

"made against it, *out of fear of losing such Church-Lands, as they were possess'd of, if that Religion should prevail, and get up again.* And for the rest, who either came *to make or improve their Fortunes,* there is no Question to be made, but they came *to further* SUCH A REFORMATION, *as should most visibly conduce to the Advancement of their several Ends.*

Nothing more can be said to give us a true Idea of the *English Reformation,* and convince the most prepossess'd in Favour of it, that it cannot be regarded as the Workmanship of God. For we have here a pack'd Parliament, and so well pack'd for the *Protector*'s Purpose, that all the Members of it agreed in *one common Principle.* But what was that *Principle?* Was it to act like Men of Honour and Religion, and vote according to the Dictates of Conscience? Nothing less: it was *to serve the present Time.* And in this they all agreed so well, that even those both of the Nobility and Gentry, who were cordially affected to the Church of *Rome,* that is, were convinced in their Hearts that it was the *true Church,* yet voted for all the Bills that were brought in against it. And why so? *Out of a Fear of losing such Church-Lands, as they were possess'd of,* if the *Roman Catholick Religion* should get the upper Hand. So that the only Motive these mercenary Souls had of Desiring and Forwarding the pretended Reformation, was to save their Bacon; and they would have voted as readily for *Quakerism* as they did for the *Protestant Religion,* if it had been necessary to secure them in their Possessions.

G. 'Tis very certain, that they, who voted against their Conscience, could not have a *Religious Motive* in so Doing. But alas, to those, who lay Conscience aside, and only consult Interest,

that

that Religion is beſt, by which moſt is to be got.

P. But beſides theſe Members of Parliament, who were only ſolicitous to ſecure what they had already got, Dr. *Heylin* mentions another Set of Gentlemen, who *came to make or improve their Fortunes*; and to be ſure theſe were very religiouſly zealous for a Reformation. But what Sort of Reformation did they come to make? My Author tells us, *that there is no Queſtion to be made, but they came to further* SUCH A REFORMATION, *as ſhould moſt viſibly conduce to their ſeveral Ends*. Well then, there I leave them buſily Reforming; ſome to *ſecure*, and others *to make or improve their Fortunes*. And I muſt do them the Juſtice to own, that the Reformation they made fully anſwer'd all their pious Ends, as has been already ſhewn. But I cannot believe that *Chriſt* was *in the midſt of them*: or that they could ſay with the *Apoſtles* at the Council of *Jeruſalem*, *it has ſeemed Good to the holy Ghoſt and to us*, &c. Acts 15. v. 28. For I dare poſitively aver, it never *ſeem'd good to the holy Ghoſt*, to make a Child *Supreme Head* of a *National Church*; to deſtroy Altars, rob Churches, and invade the Property of Perſons conſecrated to God's Service. Neither could it *ſeem good to the holy Ghoſt*, that Men ſhould become inſtrumental to the Ruin of a Religion, which they believed in their Hearts to be the true one; or aſſemble together to *further* SUCH A REFORMATION, *as ſhould moſt viſibly conduce to the Advancement of their ſeveral Ends*. In ſhort, the *holy Ghoſt*, who had no private Ends to advance, could have no Part in a Reformation ſet on Foot for no other Motive, than to ſerve ſuch Ends.

G. But what do you think of Q. *Elizabeth's* Reformation?

P. I think

P. I think it was but K. *Edward*'s Reformation twice sodden, with some Variety in the Cooking and Dressing of it to fit it for Q. *Elizabeth*'s nice Palate. But as to the *Purity* and *Disinterestedness* of her Intentions, I fear they will not be found to hold Weight in the Balance of the Sanctuary, any more than those of her reforming Predecessors. Bishop *Burnet* acquaints us in his *History of the Reformation*, that Q. *Elizabeth* scrupled at first very much to accept the *Supremacy*. And well she might. For she could not but know herself unqualified by her very Sex, even for the lowest Degree of any *Ecclesiastical* Dignity or Function. Yet she accepted it, and discarded the Pope as her Father had done before her, tho' upon a different Motive. For *Henry* did it to be reveng'd of the Pope; but Q. *Elizabeth*'s Motive was, *because she knew very well*, says Dr. *Heylin*, *that her Legitimacy, and the Pope's Supremacy could not stand together*. So that, altho' her Motive was not quite so bad as her Father's, it was meer *Policy* and *Interest of State*, that determined her to this capital Article of her Reformation; and the Considerations of *Religion* had no part in it.

Nay there appear'd as little true Zeal for Religion in all her other Proceedings: As for Instance, her *Depriving* and *Imprisoning* no fewer than fourteen Bishops, who were the undoubted *Guides* of *God's Appointment* in Matters appertaining to Religion; Her Appropriating to the Crown the *Tenths* and *First Fruits* which her Sister *Mary* had restored to the Church; Her Pillaging and Dissolving all such *Monasteries, Convents*, and *Religious Houses*, as her said Predecessor had re-established; Her Dilapidating the Patrimony of the Church by *long Vacancies* of Bishopricks, and *Taking into her Hands all Castles, Manours, Lands, Tenements,*

nements, and other *Hereditaments* to the said *Episcopal Sees* belonging, *as seem'd good to her*; and finally, her Choosing the most wicked Men in the Nation for her Ministry, and Entrusting them with the most weighty Concerns both of *Church* and *State*: Unless such scandalous Actions as these be the Marks of a *true Zeal* for Religion in the Person that commits them, it must be own'd, that Q. *Elizabeth*'s Reformation was not the Fruit of such a Zeal, nor directed by God's *holy Spirit*, but by the most worldly and interested Views.

G. But, pray Sir, may not a *good Cause* be undertaken and forwarded upon bad Motives? If so, as it cannot be question'd but it may, why may not the *Reformation* be perfectly good and justifiable in itself, tho' it was set on Foot and managed by Persons of corrupt Morals, and upon interested Views?

P. Sir, I don't pretend, that espousing a Cause upon interested or wicked Motives either supposes it to be bad, or renders it so. Because the very best Cause may possibly be espoused with the most corrupt Intentions, and by Persons void in Reality of all true Sense of *Religion*. But I think we ought to be very circumspect and wary in Trusting such corrupt and mercenary Wretches in *Matters of Religion*, let them profess as much Zeal for it as they please. For since we cannot reasonably suppose, that they love their Neighbour better than themselves, we may justly suspect them to be as ready to sell their Neighbours Souls as their own to the Devil for a valuable Consideration. 'Tis very certain, that all those were in this pious Disposition, who voted against their Conscience in both Houses of Parliament, as Dr. *Heylin* has told us. Whence I infer, that the *Religion* preach'd by the good Monk *Augustine* and

his

his Companions ought in Prudence to be embrac'd preferably to a *Reformation* begun, carried on, and finally eftablifhed by a Set of the moft wicked and interefted Perfons in the Nation. Becaufe the former could have no mercenary Views, no Paffions of *Luxury, Revenge,* or *Avarice* to gratify, nor the leaft Profpect of Getting any Thing in Prefent but their Labour for their Pains ; and were therefore out of the Reach of all Temptations to turn *Cheats* or *Impoftors.* Whereas the latter, who had the moft vifible Intereft in Forwarding their *pretended Reformation,* and were guided by their feveral Paffions in all the Meafures they took, Thefe, I fay, were under the ftrongeft Temptation poffible of making the popular Pretence of Religion a meer Cloak to cover their feveral private Ends : And may therefore be juftly fufpected of *defigned Fraud* and *Seduction* in all the Changes they made in the ancient Faith and Worfhip of their *Mother-Church.*

G. Sir, I muft own it appears plainly from this Branch of your Comparifon, that *Proteftants* have the ftrongeft Prefumptions againft them ; and that the Security of Salvation, as far as it depends upon Profeffing the *true Faith,* is entirely on the *Catholick* Side.

P. There remain but two Parts more of my intended Comparifon, with which I will end.

SECT. 4.

The Unity of Faith *on the one Side compared with the* Difagreements *on the other.*

8*thly,* THerefore, tho' the feveral petty Kingdoms of the *Saxons,* as likewife the Kingdoms of *Scotland* and *Ireland* were converted by different Miſſioners, and at different Times, they all received the ſame *Faith* and Form of *Worſhip*. The Doctrine, which S. *Auguſtine* with his Fellow-Preachers had taught, was taught by all that came after him upon the ſame religious Deſign. No contradictory Schemes of Faith or Worſhip were found amongſt them: nor did one Preacher pull down, what another had built up before him, or *reform* the Articles his Predeceſſor had eſtabliſh'd: but with the moſt perfect Harmony of Hearts and Tongues, all preach'd *one Lord, one Faith, one Baptiſm.* And as they were all but *one Body* under *one Head*, they were all *of one Accord, and one Mind.* Phil. 2. v. 2. *and all ſpoke the ſame Thing,* according to St. *Paul*'s Direction, 1 Cor. 1. v. 10.

But was there the ſame harmonious Agreement in *Faith* and *Doctrine* among the Preachers of the Reformation either at home or abroad? The contrary is notoriouſly known to all Mankind. *Martin Luther*, its firſt Patriarch and Architect, had ſcarce laid the Foundation of it by Renouncing the Pope's *Supremacy*, but ſome of the chief Labourers under him began to quarrel with their Maſter, and, like the Builders of *Babel*, fell into the utmoſt Confuſion and Variance about the Superſtructure. Two of his Principal Diſciples, to wit, *Carolſtadius* Archdeacon of *Wittenberg*, and *Oecolampadius* a *Brigitine* Monk, tho' they agreed very well with *Luther* in caſting off the Pope, and taking each of them a Wife, were of too generous Spirits to work long under him as meer Journey-Men, but in a ſhort Time ſet up for themſelves, and commenced *Reformers* of their Maſter's Reformation. *Zuinglius* a Canon of *Conſtance* join'd himſelf with theſe, and not long after became the Head of that Party. But *John Calvin* appearing soon after upon the Stage undertook to reform them all by a Reformation of a newer Invention, commonly call'd the *Geneva-Platform*. So that within a few Years there were three Head-Reformations set up: One in *Saxony* by *Luther*, another in *Switzerland* by *Zuinglius*, and a third at *Geneva* by *Calvin*; and all three had soon after their Sub-divisions, and became as fruitful in new Sects, as a Dunghil is in Breeding Vermin.

Nor was there any better Agreement among our Reformers at home. For even before the End of K. *Henry*'s Reign, which of all the three Reforming Reigns produced the fewest Changes in Religion, the Nation by having separated itself from the *Center of Unity* was become like a Ship broke loose from its Anchor, and reduced to a strange floating Condition: Or, to express myself in S. *Paul*'s Words, was *tossed to and fro, and carried about with every Blast of Doctrine*: as may be seen in Sir *Richard Baker*, who writes thus, p. 408.

" And now, says he, was the State of Religion come to a strange Pass; because always in Passing, and had no Consistence. For at first the Authority of the Pope was excluded in some Cases only, a while after in all. Yet his Doctrine was wholly received. Afterwards his Doctrine came to be impugn'd; but yet in some few Points only: a while after in many. So that the Fable of *Proteus* was no longer a Fable, when the Religion of *England* was it's true Moral. The Confusion was so great in these Times, that in Parliament one call'd the other *Heretick* and *Anabaptist*, and he again call'd him *Papist* and *Hypocrite*. And this not only amongst the Temporality, but even the *Clergymen* themselves preach'd and inveigh'd against one another. So that the Frame of Religion was ex-
" tremely

" tremely disjointed: the Clergy that should set
" it in Frame being out of Frame themselves;
" the Minds of the People extremely distracted,
" and the Nobility, that should have cemented
" them, scarce holding themselves together."

This was the State of Religion in *England* in the latter Years even of K. *Henry*'s Reign. But after his Death, as if the Nation were not already sufficiently distracted with its domestick Divisions, foreign Supplies of *new Gospellers* composed of *Lutherans, Zuinglians,* and *Anabaptists,* were invited over by the Lord *Protector,* and his trusty Friend *Archbishop Cranmer*; the former being himself a *Zuinglian* in Principles, and the other a *Lutheran*. But all was Fish that came into their Nets, provided they were but Enemies to the ancient Faith, and hated the Pope heartily.

At the Head of these outlandish Adventurers (who, like the *Saxons* and *Danes* in former Ages came for Plunder, and to settle in a better Climate) were *John Alasco,* a *Pole,* and profess'd *Anabaptist*; *Peter Martyr* and *Martin Bucer,* two apostate Priests. *John Alasco* soon after his Arrival, obtain'd the Privilege of a Church for himself and his *Poles*. *Peter Martyr,* a rank *Zuinglian,* was made the King's Professor of Divinity in *Oxford*; and *Martin Bucer,* partly a *Zuinglian* and partly a *Lutheran,* had a Chair at *Cambridge* bestow'd upon him. But as they all brought over with them different Systems of Faith, it is easy to imagine what Confusion their Lectures and Sermons, supported by publick Authority, occasion'd in the *English* Church; and into how many Pieces Christ's *seamless Garment* was torn by the Diversity and Incoherence of their Opinions. This however is certain, that these *Polish* and *German* Divines, and those who brought their Principles from *Geneva,* left behind them in this Island the Spawn of that Multiplicity of Sects, which have since like *Egyptian Locusts* overspread the Kingdom, and devour'd the very Vitals of Christian Religion. Insomuch that it is at length become a serious Question, especially amongst Men of Figure, whether there be any such Thing as a *reveal'd religion* upon Earth.

The Church of *England* itself, tho' establish'd *by Law*, and supported by it, can scarce keep upon it's Legs, but is reduced to the State of a Body in a deep Consumption, dwindling away still more and more, and always complaining of its *being in Danger* from the formidable Power and Number of the *Dissenters*, such as *Presbyterians, Puritans, Fanaticks, Independents, Anabaptists, Quakers, Socinians, occasional Conformists, Anti-trinitarians, Free-Thinkers*, and other of less Note; who are all but younger Broods of the *Reformation*, and have claim'd a Right to reform the Church of *England* upon the very same Principle, as she took upon her to reform the Church of *Rome*. And 'tis remarkable, that *England* was as free from these pernicious Insects as from *Wolves*, 'till the first *English Reformers* broke down the strong Fences of *Church-Authority* by Prostituting the *Scriptures* to the Arbitrary Interpretation of every *private Judgment*. But when the Way was once laid open in this Manner, the whole Rifraff both of foreign and domestick Sects came pouring in at the very Breach, they themselves had made; and set up their Standard of *Separation* from their *elder Reformers*, as they had separated themselves from their *old Mother-Church*.

G. But if it be no Blemish to the Church of *Rome*, that the *reform'd* Churches have separated themselves from her Communion, why should it be a Blemish to the *reform'd* Church of *England*, that

that the *Dissenters* have separated themselves from her?

P. Sir, I perceive you don't apprehend me right. For I don't pretend that the Separation of one or many Sects from any Church can justly cast a Blemish upon it, unless their Separation flows naturally from a Principle avow'd and maintain'd by that very Church, from which they separate themselves.

Now this is the very Case between our *English Dissenters* and the *Church of England as established by Law*: Because it is a fundamental Principle of this Church, that every Man's only *Rule of Faith* is the *written Word of God*, not as interpreted by the Church, but as understood by himself. Nay, the whole Fabrick of the Reformation is built upon this Principle in such a Manner, that they must stand or fall together. But the Church of *Rome* detests it as the very Bane of that *Unity of Faith*, which is essential to the Church of *Christ*. For where will Schisms and Divisions stop, if every Man be privileg'd to interpret *Scriptures* by his *private Judgment*, and make that the Rule and Standard of his Faith? Will it not naturally follow, that since Mens Judgments are as various as their Tempers and Complexions, this Principle instead of Uniting them in one and the same Faith, will divide them into an endless Variety of contradictory Schemes of Religion? Yet it was upon this pernicious Principle the *first Reformers* at home, as well as abroad, presumed themselves sufficiently authorized to reform their *Mother-Church*. For they all pretended *plain Scripture* for their jarring Doctrines. *Luther* found his Doctrine plainly in Scripture, and so did *Calvin* his, and *John Alasco* his, and *Thomas Cranmer*, *Ridley*, *Latimer*, and *Hooper* theirs, and so did all the Ringleaders of the

Reformation, both Foreign and Domestick; nay no one found his Doctrine and Religion more clearly in *Scripture* than honest *James Nailor*, as his whole Crew of *Quakers* do to this very Day. But they all took Care it should be Scripture interpreted by themselves, and contrary to the Judgment of that Church, which was the only *visible Catholick Church* upon Earth before the Reformation. And is it then a Wonder the *Dissenters* from the Church of *England* should challenge the same Privilege to themselves, and follow the Rule, they had receiv'd as a *sacred Trust* from the very Apostles of the Reformation? The Thing could not naturally be otherwise; and it is but consonant to Reason that it should be so, according to the celebrated Saying of *Tertullian*, that *what was warrantable in* Valentine *and* Marcion, *was likewise warrantable in the* Valentinians *and* Marcionites *to hammer out a new Faith out of their own Brains.* L. de Præscrip. C.42. For in like Manner, what was maintain'd as lawful by the Heads of the Reformation both at home and abroad, who by their Practice as well as Doctrine set up the proud Idol of *private Judgment* against the whole *Ecclesiastical Authority* then in Being, cannot be justly blamed in those who only walk'd in their Footsteps, and guided themselves by the very Rule and Principle they had taught them.

Let us suppose a *Doctor* of the Church of *England* should tell a *Dissenting Minister*, that he ought to submit himself to the Judgment and Authority of the Church *established by Law*. The Minister would readily answer him, that this was sapping the very Foundations of all the reform'd Churches in *Europe*, and even Cutting the Throat of his own Church. For if there were an Obligation of submitting a Man's *private Judgment* to a-

ny

ny *human Authority*, the Church of *England* became manifeſtly guilty of *Schiſm* in not ſubmitting to the Church of *Rome*, which was the greateſt viſible Authority upon Earth, when ſhe ſeparated herſelf from it. If the *Doctor* ſhould reply, that his Church had the Warrant of *Scriptures* for what ſhe did, that is, the *written Word of God*, which is above all *human Authority*: The *Miniſter* would readily ſtop his Mouth by ſaying, that the *Diſſenters* were always ready to have the Cauſe of their Church tried by the *written Word of God*; provided they were but allow'd to be themſelves the Interpreters of it. That this Condition could not be refuſed them with any Colour of Reaſon, ſince it was a fundamental Principle of the Reformation, *that the Word of God interpreted according to every Man's private Conſcience is the only Rule of his Faith*; and the *Doctor's* own Church had arrogated this Privilege to itſelf, when it broke off from the Church of *Rome*: and that he might modeſtly ſuppoſe there were Perſons amongſt the *Diſſenters* of as *ſound Judgments*, as *tender Conſciences*, and as completely qualified to interpret *Scriptures*, as in the *Doctor's* own Church.

This would undoubtedly be the Subſtance of the *diſſenting Miniſter's* Defence, if attack'd by a Member of the Church of *England*. Nay there is not an *Anabaptiſt*, *Quaker*, *Socinian*, or *Free-Thinker* in the World, but will maintain his Ground againſt that Church, or any reform'd Church whatſoever, whilſt he is thus ſtrongly entrench'd behind the *Letter of the Scripture* interpreted by his own *private Judgment*.

G. But what do you conclude from all this?

P. I conclude from it, that a Reformation, which by its very Principles has been the fruitful Mother of endleſs Diviſions, was not the Work of the *holy Ghost*. And then it is easy to guess what *Spirit* presided in all its Counsels. It could not be that *Spirit of Truth* whom Christ promised to send to his holy Church as a Guide to *abide with her, and lead her into all Truth, even unto the End of the World*. For the *Spirit of Truth* is essentially the Spirit of *Unity* and Concord. And therefore as he cannot contradict himself, so he cannot be the Author of Contradictions in those, who are guided by him. Christ pray'd for them, that were to be the Members of his *Mystical Body*, that *they might all be made perfectly one*, John 17. v. 23. And conformably to this Prayer of our B. Redeemer, who never pray'd in vain, S. *Paul* exhorts the Faithful *to be of one Accord and one Mind*. 1 Phil. 2. v. 2. That *they may be one Body and one Spirit*. Eph. 4. v. 4. That *they may all speak the same Thing: that there may be no Divisions amongst them, but that they may be perfectly joined together in the same Mind, and in the same Judgment*, 1 Cor. 1. v. 10. And hence it is, that *Unity* in Faith and Communion is express'd in the *Nicene Creed* as an essential Attribute of the *Church of Christ*; which therefore is described in holy Writ to be *one Fold under one Shepherd*, Joh. 10. v 16. to be *one Body and one Spirit*, Eph. 4. v. 4. to have *one Lord, one Faith and one Baptism*, v. 5. and to be *under one Head, from which all the Body being by Joints and Bands supplied and compacted together, receives the Encrease of God*. Col. 2. v. 19.

Pray tell me, Sir, could the *holy Ghost* be the Inspirer of *Lutheranism* in *Saxony*, of *Zuinglianism* in *Switzerland*, of *Calvinism* at *Geneva*, of *Fanaticism* in *Scotland*, and of a Religion different from them all in *England*? What other Spirit therefore but the Spirit of Lying and Seduction can have been the Author of a Reformation built upon a
Principle

and Reformation compared. 313

Principle, which has been an inexhauſtible Source of Diviſions in every Nation, where it got Footing?

G. 'Tis very plain, that all theſe jarring Sects could not be *of God.* And ſince they all flow from the ſame poiſonous Source, 'tis impoſſible they ſhould be any Thing better than tainted Streams, and void of that Purity of *ſaving Faith,* which is the ſpecial Bleſſing and Gift of the *holy Ghoſt.*

P. We may as well ſeek for Figs upon Thorns, or Grapes upon a Crab-Tree, as *true Faith* amongſt Men, who abandoning the *Unity* of the *Catholick Church,* which Chriſt has eſtabliſh'd to be our Guide, and S. *Paul* calls *the Pillar and Support of the Truth,* make their own *private Judgments* the Rule and Standard of what is to be believed, and what not. So that the only Difference between the ſeveral Sects I have mentioned is, that ſome went ſooner ſome later out of the Pale, and ſome choſe one Way ſome another to go aſtray in, according as their ſeveral private Judgments lead them.

Here then is a plain diſtinguiſhing Mark to judge by, whether the Religion planted in *England* and other *Pagan* Nations, by their firſt Converſion from *Idolatry* to *Chriſtianity,* or the *pretended Reformation* of that Religion is to be attributed to God as to its principal Author. On the one Side there appears nothing but *Harmony* and *Unity of Faith*; on the other nothing but Diſagreement, and a meer *Babel* of Confuſion in Hearts and Tongues. Is the *Holy Ghoſt* the God of Unity and Peace, or the Spirit of Diſcord and Contention? The Kingdoms of *England, Scotland* and *Ireland,* and all the foreign Countries, where the pretended Reformation is now eſtabliſh'd, tho' all converted at different Times, and by different Preachers, were all gather'd into the *ſame Sheepfold*

fold under the *same Shepherd*, and continued in the Unity of the same Faith for several Ages, as all the World knows. On the contrary, the pretended Reformation was no sooner set on Foot in the foremention'd Countries, but they were all divided into disagreeing Schemes of Faith and Worship, and united in nothing but their common Hatred to their *Mother-Church*. The *Lutherans*, who led up the Dance, were reform'd by the *Zuinglians*, and they by the *Calvinists*, and all three by the *Anabaptists*. And at home K. *Henry*'s Reformation was reform'd by K. *Edward*, and his by Q. *Elizabeth*, and her's has since been reform'd by the *Presbyterians, Independents, Fanaticks, Quakers*, and the Lord knows how many more. If therefore the *holy Ghost* be not the Spirit of *Discord* and *Contention*, he could not be the Author of a Reformation, which by its Principles gave Birth to such scandalous Divisions. I leave you to judge on what Side the Truth appears to be.

G. The *Unity* you speak of is most certainly a Mark of Truth. For Truth is essentially one, but the Errors opposite to it are infinite. So that it is altogether unconceivable, that if the Faith, which was received by so many *different Nations*, at *different Times*, and by the Ministry of so many *different Preachers*, were not the *true one*, nor directed by an *unerring Hand*, nor guided by an *unerring Rule*, it should nevertheless happen to be every where one and the same. But that Men swerving from the *Unity* of *Truth*, should run astray into an endless Diversity of Errors, is naturally speaking unavoidable. And if they be united in Opposing their *Mother-Church*, it is no more than what their common Interest, and the Support of a *Party-Cause* obliges them to: For at the same Time they hate one another, as I have been

been told, as heartily, as the several *Jew*-ctions did in the Siege of *Jerusalem*, who were continually cutting one anothers Throats, except when *Interest* and a more prevalent Hatred united them to oppose their Common Enemy, the *Romans*.

P. Your Comparison is very just, and the first Part of your Observation exactly agrees with *Tertullian*, in his Treatise of *Prescriptions &c.* where speaking of *Catholick Unity* he argues thus: *Is it likely that in so large a Body all should err into one Faith? An Agreement of so many does not happen by Chance: Differences would have sprung from the Church's Errors. Where so many agree, it is not an Error, but a Doctrine handed down by Tradition. And let any one dare to say, that they err'd, who transmitted it down to us.* I shall now come to the last Branch of my Comparison.

SECT. 5.

The general external Marks of the true Church on the one Side compared with the entire Want of them on the other.

9*thly*, THerefore *England converted* was at the same Time, like other converted Nations, incorporated with the great Body of the *Catholick* or *Universal Church*. That is, it became not a separate Society, or new-raised Communion, subsisting by itself, but it was made a Part of that *Mystical Body*, whereof Christ is Head, and by Consequence entituled to a Partnership in all the spiritual Advantages and Prerogatives belonging to that Body. So that the Words of S. *Paul* to the *Ephesians* were truly applicable to the converted *Saxons*. *Now therefore you are no more Strangers and Aliens,*

Allens, but *Fellow-Citizens of the Saints, and the Domesticks of God; built upon the Foundation of the Apostles and Prophets, Jesus Christ himself being the chief Corner Stone.* Eph. 2. v. 19, 20. In a Word, *England* by it's *Conversion* became a Part of that Society of Christians, which alone can glory in having all those *external Marks* of the *true Church of Christ*, which are so essential to her, that they cannot be attributed to any other Society upon Earth.

I have already spoken of *Unity*, which is the first essential Mark of the *true Church* mention'd in the *Nicene Creed*. *Perpetual Visibility* and *Catholicity* or *Universality* are two other external Marks inseparable from the *true Church of Christ*, and incommunicable to a new-raised Communion.

As to *perpetual Visibility*, it is clearly mark'd out both in the *Old* and *Testament*. The Prophet *Isaiah* foretells, C. 59. v. 21. that the Gospel shall be preach'd to the End of the World. And it is very plain, that a *perpetual preaching Ministry* must be perpetually both *audible* and *visible*. He also describes Christ's future Church by comparing it to a House situated on the Top of a high Mountain. *The Mountain of the Lord's House*, says he, *shall be established on the Top of the Mountains. It shall be exalted above the Hills, and all Nations shall flow to it.* Isa. 11. 2. This surely is not the Character of an *invisible Church*. Our B. Saviour insinuates the same Comparison, and draws the same Inference from it, *Matt.* 5. v. 14. where he speaks thus to his Apostles, *You are the Light of the World. A City that stands on a Mountain cannot be hidden.* And again in the 18*th* Chapter, v. 17. of the same Evangelist he sends us to his Church, and commands us to *hear* it. Now I cannot well conceive how any one can be bound to hear an *invisible Church*; or how

how we can have Recourse to it for Instruction unless it be *visible*.

But nothing is more express upon this Point, than St. *Paul*'s Words to the *Ephesians*, C. 4. v. 11, 12. &c. where he tells them, that God has placed in his Church not only *Apostles*, *Prophets*, and *Evangelists*, but also *Pastors and Teachers, for the Perfecting of the Saints, for the Work of the Ministry, and for the Building up of the Body of Christ, till we all meet in the Unity of Faith*: Whence it follows, that the *Church*, which is *Christ's Mystical Body*, is, according to the Divine Establishment, a Society compos'd of *Pastors* and *People*: or what amounts to the same, a Congregation consisting of believing Persons, whereof some are *Shepherds*, that feed and govern; others are the *Flock*, that are fed and govern'd by them: And that this is to continue, *till all meet in the Unity of Faith*; that is, as long as the World shall last. Now if such a Body or Congregation of Christians, can ever be *invisible*, I am yet to learn what Nonsense is.

I add, that *Invisibility* is repugnant to the very End, for which Christ has establish'd *Pastors* and *Teachers* in his Church; to wit, that they should be the *Stewards* or Administrators *of the Mysteries of God*, 1 Cor. c. 4 v. 1. that they should feed us with the Bread of Life, and be our Guides to Heaven. But I have never heard of any one, that could receive the holy Mysteries from an *invisible Steward*, or be fed by an *invisible Hand*, or conducted by an *invisible Guide*. In a Word, all the Arguments, which prove that Christ has always had, and always will have a *true Church* upon Earth, prove likewise that *Visibility* is an essential Propriety of that Church.

As to the Church's *Catholicity* or *Universality* both in Regard of *Time* and *Place*, besides that it

318 Dial. 4. §. 5. England's *Converſion*
is explicitly profeſs'd as an Article of Faith both in the *Apoſtolical* and *Nicene Creed*, it has the cleareſt Warrant of Scripture to prove it. Her *Univerſality* of *Time* is mark'd out by Chriſt promiſing his Apoſtles, *that the Gates of Hell ſhall not prevail againſt it.* For if his Church ſhould ever ceaſe to have a Being, it would be manifeſtly true to ſay, that *the Gates of Hell had prevail'd againſt it.* And again, by his Promiſe of being with the Apoſtles *always, even unto the End of the World.* Becauſe if the *Apoſtolical Succeſſion* of *Biſhops* and *Paſtors* in *one* and the *ſame Communion* ſhould be at any Time entirely extinct, it could not be ſaid, that Chriſt has remain'd with the Apoſtles *to the End of the World.*

Her *Univerſality* of *Place* is likewiſe mark'd out *firſt* by God's Promiſe to *Abraham*, that *all Nations of the Earth ſhall be bleſſed in his Seed*, Gen. 22. v. 18. 2*dly*, by the Pſalmiſt. *Ask of me, and I will give thee Nations for thy Inheritance, and the Bounds of the Earth for thy Poſſeſſion.* Pſ. 2. v. 8. And again, *He ſhall govern from Sea to Sea, and from the River to the Bounds of the Earth —— all Kings ſhall fall down before him, all Nations ſhall ſerve him.* Pſ. 71. v. 8, 11. 3*dly*, by *Eſaiah* deſcribing the future Glory and Splendor of the Church of Chriſt, by the Multitudes of *People* and *Nations* flocking to her. *Eſa.* 60. And *laſtly*, by Chriſt himſelf commiſſioning his Apoſtles and their Succeſſors *to go and teach all Nations.* Matt. 28. v. 19.

G. Sir, I ſee very plainly, that *perpetual Viſibility* and *Catholicity* are external Marks inſeparable from the true Church of Chriſt. But I don't ſo very well ſee, what Connection this has with the Subject we have before us.

P. Sir, the Subject we have before us is the laſt Branch of my Compariſon between the *Converſion of* of *England* and its *Reformation*: by which I pretend to shew, that as *England* was by its *Conversion* made a Part of that Society of Christians, to which those Marks of the *true Church* most undoubtedly belong'd, so was it by its *Reformation* cut off from that Society; and forfeited, by Consequence, the Title it had before to a Share in those Marks.

As to the Mark of *Visibility*, *England* was by its Conversion incorporated with the Church of *Rome*: that is to say with the whole Body of Christians then in Communion with the *See* of *Rome*. Now the Pastors of this Church had *in their own Communion* an uninterrupted *visible Succession* of Bishops from the *Apostles* down to the Time wherein *England* was converted. It therefore became a Part of that Church, which had the Mark of its being the *true Church* demonstrable in its *perpetual Visibility*. When therefore by its pretended Reformation it separated itself from the *Communion* of the Church of *Rome*, and so became a *new raised Communion*, it ceased to be a Part of the *true Church*.

G. 'Tis very plain indeed, that it ceased to be a Part of the Church of *Rome*. But your Inference, that therefore it was no longer a Part of the *true Church* will not be so easily allow'd of.

P. Sir, if *England*, when it separated itself from the Church of *Rome*, did not at the same Time separate itself from the *true Church*, the Advocates for the Church of *England* are bound to mark out to us, in what other *visible Society* of Christians the true Church subsisted before the Reformation. Nay over and above they must shew, that at the Time of its Separation from the Church of *Rome* it became a Part of, and was incorporated with that other *pre-existent visible Church*. But since it is impossible for the reform'd Church of *England*, or indeed for any other reform'd Church to perform this Task, the Consequence is undeniable, that when it ceased to be a Part of the Church in Communion with the See of *Rome*, it ceased likewise to be a Part of the *true Church*.

Here then I shall repeat once more my *Dilemma* against all the *reform'd Churches* in the World, which I think is unanswerable. For when they separated themselves from the Church of *Rome*, it either was the *true Church of Christ*, or it was not. If they say it was not, they must either shew us another *visible Society* of Christians upon Earth, in which the *true Church of Christ* was preserved before the Reformation, and this is impossible for them to do; or they must say, that Christ had no *true Church* upon Earth before that Time; and that by Consequence the *Creed* was false for many Ages; which is downright Blasphemy. But if they own, that the Church of *Rome* was the *true Church of Christ* before the Reformation, then they must own of Course, that they separated themselves from the *true Church of Christ*, and continue separated from it to this Day: which is pronouncing their own Condemnation. Unhappy Reformation! which cannot answer for itself without either Renouncing the *Creed*, or Confessing itself guilty of *Schism*.

G. I must needs say the reform'd Churches are so closely shut up betwixt the Horns of this *Dilemma*, that I see no Hole for them to creep out at. For let them turn themselves to what Side they please, it gives them a mortal Wound.

P. Sir, it was the Force of this Argument, that obliged several *Protestant* Writers, especially in the Beginning of the Reformation to have Recourse to the wretched *Chimera* of an *invisible Church*, as the best Expedient they could then

think

think of to maintain the Antiquity of their Doctrine, and Succession of their Pastors. I call it a *Chimera*, because an *invisible Church* is in Reality a Church and no Church: For it is inconsistent not only with the Character of the Church as describ'd in holy Writ, but with the very Essence of its Constitution, and principal End of its Establishment, as has been fully shewn. So that Persons reduced to this miserable Shift give up the Cause of Religion as effectually, as if they fairly own'd themselves non-plus'd. I add, that a *Quaker* or *Muggletonian* needs not be in any Pain to trace the Antiquity of his Church and Doctrine even to *Noah* or *Adam*, if he pleases, so he be but allow'd to have Recourse to an *invisible Church* to make good his Pretensions.

When therefore they were driven out of this defenceless Entrenchment by the forcible Arguments of their Adversaries, many of them, as the *Calvinists* in *France*, call'd to their Aid all the broken and shatter'd Troops of old condemn'd *Hereticks* to patch up a kind of ridiculous Succession, with as many different Sects as there are Shreds or Colours in a *Harlequin*'s Dress. These were the old *Iconoclasts*, the *Berengarians*, the *Albigeoise* a Spawn of the *Manicheans*, the *Hussites* and *Vaudois*, or *poor Men of* Lions, the *Bohemian Brethren*, and such others. A strange Sort of *Apostolical Succession!* which began not 'till many Ages after the *Apostles*, was interrupted with Gaps of several hundred Years, and composed of Sects, all differing as well from one another, as from the *Calvinists* themselves in their Systems of Religion. But they all agreed in hating the *Pope*; and that sufficed to render them worthy of being adopted into the *Apostolical Family*, and regarded by them as their true Predecessors and *Forefathers in God*,

Y   who

who in their Persons had preserved the *Church's Visibility*, and continued the *Succession* of her Pastors in the right Line. But in Reality it shews only, what inextricable Difficulties, and extravagant Absurdities Men are reduced to, when they Apostatize from the ancient Faith, and set up a *new Communion* in Opposition to the *Catholick Church*.

As to the *Protestants* of the Church of *England*, I know not what Way they pretend to derive their *Ecclesiastical Succession* from the *Apostles*. Only this I am sure of, that *Thomas Cranmer* was the first *Protestant Bishop* and *Primate* of *England*. He had not therefore any Predecessors of the *Protestant Communion*. And by Consequence, tho' he sat in the *Archiepiscopal Chair*, which S. *Augustine* and others had possess'd before him, he could not justly pretend to derive his Succession from the *Apostles*, after he had separated himself from the *Communion* of those, who were the *true* and *undoubted Successors* of the *Apostles*. For surely the Apostles will never own any for their true and lawful Successors, but *Bishops* and *Pastors* of *their own Communion*, and Members of that Church, which they founded.

To clear this Matter by a Fact, that is unquestionable, if *Thomas Cranmer* by being Archbishop of the *See of Canterbury* was entituled to a Place in the *Apostolical Family*, all the *Arian*, *Novatian*, and *Donatist Bishops* were likewise entituled to the same Prerogative. Because they were all *true Bishops*, and possess'd the *Episcopal Sees*, which had been founded by the *true Successors* of the *Apostles*. But this has not hinder'd, but that they have been always regarded as a *spurious Race*, unworthy to be counted among the true Successors of the Apostles. And why so? Because by teaching Doctrines

&ctrines unknown to the Bishops that went before them; they broke off, or were spew'd out of the Communion of those, who were the true and undoubted Successors of the Apostles. So that we may put the Questions to Archbishop *Cranmer*, wherewith *Tertullian* puzzled the Hereticks of his Time. *Qui estis vos, quando & unde venistis*? Who are you, *Thomas Cranmer*? When and whence did you come? Who gave you a Commission to enslave the *Hierarchy* to the *Secular Power*? or to make a *Layman* and a *Child* supreme Judges of Controversies in Religion, and the Fountains of *Ecclesiastical Jurisdiction*? Whence had you your *Powers* to turn upside down the Frame of the Church committed to your Charge, to change the Faith and Worship, which S. *Augustine* had established, and introduce Doctrines, to which the Bishops your Predecessors had been utter Strangers for nine hundred Years together?

Now whoever will pretend to answer these Questions for *Cranmer*, I defy him to shew, that his Condition was any Thing better, than that of the ancient *Arian, Novatian*, or *Donatist Bishops*: or that the Case of his *reform'd Church* was not exactly Parallel with that of all the *Heretical* or *Schismatical* Churches that ever were before it.

G. But can this be apply'd to Qu. *Elizabeth*'s Bishops, or the *reform'd Church* establish'd by her?

P. I see no Difference, but what makes rather to their Disadvantage. Because the Validity of *Cranmer*'s Ordination never was disputed by any. Whereas that of Queen *Elizabeth*'s Bishops has never been allow'd of by the Church of *Rome*; and her Authority is of no small Weight. But supposing even that it were unquestionably valid: it would avail them nothing in the Main. For in that Supposition they would at the best be but

324 Dial. 4. §. 5.   England's *Conversion*
upon the Level with *Cranmer*, and under the same
Incapacity of Proving their *Apostolical Pedigree* by
a Succession of Bishops in their *own Communion* ;
because there was no *visible Protestant Communion*
before the *Protestant Reformation*. And this alone
suffices to degrade all the reform'd Churches from
being a Part of the true *Apostolical Church* of Christ,
which has always had, and will always have a
visible Being in an uninterrupted Succession of Bishops and Pastors in the *same Communion*, as long
as the Sun and Moon shall endure ; as has been
fully proved.

Thus it is plain, that as *England* by its *Conversion* became a Part of that Church, which has the
external Mark of a *perpetual Visibility* on its Side ;
so by its *pretended Reformation* it ceased to be a
Part of that Church : and by Consequence of the
true Church of Christ, whereof *perpetual Visibility* is
an essential and incommunicable Propriety.

It remains now only to speak a Word of the o-
ther *external Mark* call'd *Catholicity*, which never
was denied to the Church in Communion with the
See of *Rome*, even by its profess'd Enemies. Nay in
all *Protestant* Countries, where there is a Mixture
of various Religions, we are as well distinguish'd
by the bare Name of *Catholicks*, as a Native of
England, for Example, is known by the Name of
an *Englishman*. Therefore, as *England* by its *Conversion* became a Part of the Church in Communion with the *See* of *Rome*, so it became by Consequence a Part of the *Catholick* or *Universal*
Church. That is to say, of that Church, which
we profess to believe in the 9th Article both of
the *Nicene* and *Apostles Creed* : both which *Creeds*
(says the *Church of England, Art. 8th.*) *ought throughly
to be received and believed : because they may be
proved by most certain Warrants of holy Scripture.* In
a Word

a Word, it became a Part of that Church, which has *Univerſality* both of *Time* and *Place*. Of *Time*, by having had an *uninterrupted viſible Being* from the Time of the *Apoſtles* to this Day: And of *Place*, by having not only extended her Faith to the moſt remote and barbarous Nations in the World, tho' now apoſtatized from it, but by having likewiſe been in full Poſſeſſion of all thoſe Nations of *Europe*, where the reform'd Churches are now eſtabliſh'd. Nay ſhe has at this very Time Biſhops and Paſtors Propagating the Goſpel among the Infidels both of the *Eaſt* and *Weſt Indies*. Therefore *Univerſality of Place*, which St. *Auguſtine* calls *the Conſent of People and Nations*, cannot be denied her. Nor can it conſequently be denied, but that *England* by its *Converſion* had the Advantage of being made Partaker of the illuſtrious Title of *Catholick* in the full Extent of its Signification.

But did its Separation from the *Communion* of the Church of *Rome* procure it any Advantage equivalent to this? Was there beſides the *Roman Catholick Church* another *Catholick Church* of a different Communion, to which *England* was aſſociated by its Reformation? That's giving the Lie to the *Creed*, by which we are taught, that there is but ONE, *Holy, Catholick* and *Apoſtolick Church*. Or was there no *Catholick Church* before the Reformation? if ſo, whoever then ſaid the *Creed*, profeſs'd that he believ'd a *Falſhood:* Nay and a Falſhood *which may be proved by moſt certain Warrants of holy Scripture*. Art. 8*th*. Or was the *Catholick Church inviſible* before the Reformation? That is very ſtrange! For how can a Church of all *Times* and *Nations*, and conſiſting of *Paſtors* and *People* be *inviſible* for many Ages? Or finally, did *England* itſelf become the *Catholick Church* by its Separation from the Church of *Rome*? That is

ſtill

still stranger and stranger! and indeed the same stupendious Wonder, as if a little Finger cut off from the Body should become the *whole Body*.

I need not ask any more Questions: For the Impossibility of answering these, without falling into some Absurdity, is a Demonstration that *England* by its *Reformation*, that is, by its Separation in Doctrine and Communion from the Church of *Rome*, was cut off from that *One, Holy, Catholick* and *Apostolick Church*, which we profess to believe in the *Creed:* and that, by Consequence, it has never since been a Part of the *true Church of Christ*.

However, as it is much easier to confute than silence certain People; there are some who pretend to answer all by Owning, that the Church of *Rome* both is, and was a *true Church* before the Reformation: because it always believed and taught all the *Essentials* of *Christianity*. And so Christ always had a visible true Church upon Earth, and the *Creed* never was false. Which they think is a full and direct Answer to my *Dilemma*.

G. But how then do they justify their Separation from the Church of *Rome*, if it both is, and was a true Church before the Reformation?

P. By saying, that besides *Essentials* it imposes many Articles as *Terms of Communion*, which at the best are doubtful, and not necessary to be believed. For which Reason they compare it to a *human Body* disfigured with *Wens* and other *Blemishes*, tho' it has all the *noble* and *essential Parts* of a *true Body*.

G. Very fine indeed! The Thought is quaint and new.

P. I know not whether it be Old or New: But I am sure it will not answer any other End,

than

and Reformation compared. 327

than to throw Duſt before the Eyes of ignorant People. For in the *firſt* Place, their charging the Church of *Rome* with Impoſing Articles as *Terms of Communion, which are not neceſſary to be believed,* is a meer precarious Aſſertion, which never was, nor ever can be proved. On the Contrary, it has been demonſtrated a thouſand Times, that their pretended *Wens* and *Blemiſhes* are found *Apoſtolical* Doctrines, as ancient as *Chriſtianity* itſelf, taught in the very primitive Ages, and handed down as *Terms* of *Catholick Communion* from Age to Age to this very Time.

But 2*dly.* from their Owning, that the Church of *Rome* both is, and was a *true Church* before the Reformation, it will follow, that *Chriſt,* in their Opinion, has ever ſince the Reformation had more than *one true Church* upon Earth. For ſince they are ſo generous as to allow the Church of *Rome* to be one, I preſume they have no worſe Opinion either of their *own,* or other *reform'd Churches.* So that theſe, tho' all contradicting one another in many important Points, are nevertheleſs all *true Churches.* Which I think is Nonſenſe with a Witneſs. Nor will the Matter be much mended by their Saying, that they are all but *one Church* to *Chriſt,* in as much as they all believe in *Chriſt.* For if this large Notion of *Unity* be allow'd of, the *Myſtical Body of Chriſt,* inſtead of being compoſed of uniform Parts, will rather reſemble the *Monſter* deſcribed by *Horace,* with a *Man's Head* join'd to a *Horſe's Neck, &c.* And his *Garment* inſtead of being *ſeamleſs,* will be ſtitch'd up together with as many different Pieces, as there are Patches in a Beggar's Coat. But is it not ſomewhat ſurprizing, that all the *reform'd Churches* and the *Church of Rome,* that Church ſo hated and rail'd at not only by the *firſt Reformers,* but by their

Succeſſors

Succeffors to this Day, fhould at length be found to be but *one* and the *fame Church*? Or that fo many Churches of *different Communions* and *Religions* fhould be that *One*, *Holy*, *Catholick*, and *Apoftolick Church*, which we profefs in the *Creed*?

3*dly*. From their Owning, that the Church of *Rome* believes and teaches all the *Effentials* of *Chriftianity*, it follows by a neceffary Confequence, that if they judge coherently, they muft regard the very beft of their *Writers* and *Preachers* as a Pack of the vileft Calumniators upon Earth, in continually charging the Church of *Rome* with abominable *Idolatry*. For I cannot poffibly conceive, how *Idolatry* can be reconciled with the *Effentials* of *Chriftianity*.

Laftly, their Owning, that the Church of *Rome* was A *true Church* before the Reformation, is a meer Put off, and does not anfwer either Part of my *Dilemma* directly. For my Queftion is not, whether the Church of *Rome* was A *true Church* before the Reformation? For that imports no more than Asking whether it was *a Part* of the *true Church of Chrift*? But my Queftion or *Dilemma*, to which I demand a direct Anfwer, is precifely this: *viz*. Whether before the Reformation the Church of *Rome* with all the Churches in Communion with that *See*, was that *One*, *Holy*, *Catholick and Apoftolick Church*, the Belief whereof we profefs in the *Nicene Creed*, or not? If they fay *not*: then the *Creed* was falfe before the Reformation. Becaufe they cannot fhew any other Society of Chriftians, which was that Church. But if they anfwer in the Affirmative, then the *Church of Rome*, with all *the Churches in Communion with that See*, was not only A *true Church*, but THE SOLE *and only true Church of Chrift upon Earth*. And, by Confequence, *England* was by its pretended

tended Reformation cut off from *the sole and only true Church of Christ upon Earth*. And there I leave it. For I have now done; and fear I have exceeded in Length. But since I have been instrumental to your Education in the *Roman Catholick Faith*, I thought it my Duty to convince you so fully of the Truth of that Faith, that you may have no Reason to reproach me hereafter.

G. Sir, you have acted the Part of a true Friend, and satisfied me so fully, that I can now safely say, it is not *Education*, but a full Conviction of Conscience, that determines me in my Choice of the Religion, wherein I am resolved with the Help of God's Grace to live and die. And indeed I should be guilty of shutting my Eyes against the clearest Light, if I should not prefer the *Roman Catholick Faith* before that of any of the *reform'd Churches*.

'Tis true indeed I have not yet Capacity enough to examine every Branch of Controversy by itself. But I thank God I am sufficiently capable of Discerning *Black* from *White*, and *Light* from *Darkness*. And indeed, as you have handled the Matter, no more than this is requisite to form a fix'd and determinate Judgment, whether the *Conversion* of *England*, or its *Reformation* was the *proper Work of God*: and, by Consequence, whether the Religion establish'd in *England* by its *Conversion*, or that, which was introduced nine hundred Years after by its *pretended Reformation* is to be preferr'd. Nay an ignorant Tradesman may, by the Lights you have given, resolve this Question, if he be but sincere at Heart, as solidly as the ablest Scholar; since nothing can be more manifest even to common Sense, than that all the Marks of Truth appear on the *Roman Catholick* Side,

Side, and not one can be produced, that is any Thing favourable to the *Reformation*.

P. Sir, 'tis no small Joy to me to find you in so good a Disposition: And I heartily pray God to strengthen you so powerfully with his holy Grace, that no worldly Allurements may ever prevail upon you, or Terrors force you to change the Christian Resolution you have taken.

G. I hope, Sir, my eternal Salvation will be always dearer to me, than the short Advantages and Satisfactions of this Life.

FINIS.

THE CONTENTS.

The First DIALOGUE.

Containing the General Grounds of the Catholick Faith.

SECT. 1.

THE *Obligation of submitting our private Judgment does not exclude Examination.* Page 1

SECT. 2

Faith is not against Reason. p. 8

SECT. 3.

Faith depends in a different Manner on the Testimony of God, and the Testimony of Men. p. 16

SECT. 4.

The Church of Christ consider'd as infallible. p. 21

SECT.

The CONTENTS.

SECT. 5.
The Church's perpetual Indefectibility and Infallibility proved from the 9th Article of the Creed.   p. 30

SECT. 6.
The Rule of Faith.   p. 39

SECT. 7.
Of Scriptures and Church Authority.   p. 49

SECT. 8.
A Recapitulation of the foregoing Sections.   p. 58

The Second DIALOGUE.

Containing a brief historical Account of the Conversion of the Britons *and* Saxons, *with Proofs of their Agreement in Faith, and some Remarks upon Circumstances relating to the Conversion of the* Saxons.

SECT. 1.
The Importance of Enquiring into the Marks of the true Church, in which alone Salvation is proved to be possible.   p. 66

SECT. 2.
Neither Education nor Interest are to be consulted in the Choice of our Religion.   p. 72

SECT.

The CONTENTS.

SECT. 3.

Of the first Entrance of Christianity into Britain; and its Progress and Establishment there in the Reign of K. Lucius. p. 79

SECT. 4.

Of the Conversion of the English Saxons from Paganism to Christianity. p. 88

SECT. 5.

A Relation of St. Augustine's Conference with the British Bishops. p. 97

SECT. 6.

St. Augustine vindicated. p. 102

SECT. 7.

Roman Catholicks profess to this Day the Faith, which St. Augustine preached. p. 114

SECT. 8.

The same Faith was preach'd to the Saxons, as had been preach'd four hundred Years before to the Britons. p. 128

SECT. 9.

The same Subject continued. p. 138

SECT. 10.

Some Observations upon the Conversion of the English Saxons. p. 148

The CONTENTS.

The Third DIALOGUE.

Containing an historical Collection of Facts relating to the English Reformation *in the three Reigns of* Henry VIII. Edward VI. *and* Q. Elizabeth.

SECT. 1.

Henry VIII. *falls in Love with* Anne Bolen. *The Motives of his Divorce from* Q. Catharine *examined.* p. 160

SECT. 2.

The Cause of the Divorce brought before Judges appointed by the Pope. p. 170

SECT. 3.

Archbishop Cranmer's *Character. He dissolves the Marriage between* K. Henry *and* Q. Catharine. p. 174

SECT. 4.

Henry *is declared* Supreme Head *of the Church of* England *in* Spirituals. 183

SECT. 5.

Sir William Dugdale's *Account of the Dissolution of religious Houses in the Reign of* Henry VIII. p. 195

SECT. 6.

A farther Account of the Effects of K. Henry's *Reformation.* p. 208

SECT. 7.

The Reformation carried on in the Reign of Edward VI. *and the true Motivves of it.* p. 214

SECT.

The CONTENTS.

SECT. 8.
The same Subject continued. p. 226

SECT. 9.
Of the English *Reformation as established by Queen* Elizabeth. p. 240

SECT. 10.
The Queen's Supremacy *established without the Concurrence or Consent of the Clergy.* p. 252

SECT. 11.
Some Remarks upon the Progress and Motives of Queen Elizabeth's *Reformation.* p. 258

The Fourth DIALOGUE.

Containing a Comparison between the most remarkable Circumstances of England's *Conversion on the one Hand, and its pretended* Reformation *on the other.*

SECT. 1.
The respective Qualifications of the chief Instruments of England's Conversion *and* Reformation *compared.* p. 274

SECT. 2.
The Methods and Means of England's Conversion *and* Reformation *compared.* p. 283

SECT.

The CONTENTS.

SECT. 3.

The Motives of England's Conversion *and* Reformation *compared.* p. 293

SECT. 4.

The Unity of Faith *on the one Side compared with the* Disagreements *on the other.* p. 304

SECT. 5.

The general external Marks *of the* true Church *on the one Side, compared with an entire Want of them on the other.* p. 315

The Reader is desired to correct the following Mistakes of the Press with his Pen.

PAG. 36. l. 2. *for* inconfistent *r.* inconfiftent.
Pag. 38. *last Line but one, for* with *r.* without.
Pag. 93. l. 19. *blot out* fhould.
96. l. 30. *for* Fuuctions *r.* Functions.
144. l. 5. *for* tohfe *r.* thofe. *and* l. 6. *after* refufing *add* to.
160. *which is wrong printed* 150. l. 14. *in the general Title of the Third Dialogue, blot out* examin'd. *and at the Bottom, for* paffionate *r.* prejudiced.
193. l. 16. *for* this *r.* the. *and* l. 18. *for* of Royal. *r.* of the Royal.
225. *for* their *r.* there.
252. l. 29. *for* of her *r.* by her.
265. l. 17. *for* form *r.* from.
271. l. 1. *after* to all *blot out* to.
308. l. 17. *for* other *r.* others.
216. l. 1. *for* Allens *r.* Aliens.

END

Milton Keynes UK
Ingram Content Group UK Ltd.
UKHW011844050324
438776UK00017B/1088